Political Violence in Context

Time, Space and Milieu

Edited by

Lorenzo Bosi, Niall Ó Dochartaigh
and Daniela Pisoiu

ecpr PRESS

First published by the ECPR Press in 2015

The ECPR Press is the publishing imprint of the European Consortium for Political Research (ECPR), a scholarly association, which supports and encourages the training, research and cross-national co-operation of political scientists in institutions throughout Europe and beyond.

ECPR Press
Harbour House
Hythe Quay
Colchester
CO2 8JF
United Kingdom

Typeset by Lapiz Digital Services

Printed and bound by Lightning Source

British Library Cataloguing in Publication Data

A catalogue record for this book is available from the British Library

HARDBACK ISBN: 978-1-785521-44-7
PAPERBACK ISBN: 978-1-785522-37-6
PDF ISBN: 978-1-785521-70-6
EPUB ISBN: 978-1785521-71-3
KINDLE ISBN: 978-1-785521-72-0

www.ecpr.eu/ecprpress

You may also be interested in

Spreading Protest: Social Movements in Times of Crisis
Edited by Donatella della Porta and Alice Mattoni
ISBN 9781785521638
Which elements do the Arab Spring, the *Indignados* and Occupy Wall Street have
in common? How do they differ? What do they share with social movements of
the past? This book discusses the recent wave of global mobilisations from an
unusual angle, explaining what aspects of protests spread from one country to
another, how this happened, and why diffusion occurred in certain contexts but
not in others. In doing this, the book casts light on the more general mechanisms
of protest diffusion in contemporary societies, explaining how mobilisations
travel from one country to another and, also, from past to present times. Bridging
different fields of the social sciences, and covering a broad range of empirical
cases, this book develops new theoretical perspectives.

Causes of War: The Struggle for Recognition
Thomas Lindemann
ISBN 9781907301018
Theories on the origins of war are often based on the premise that the rational
actor is in pursuit of material satisfaction, such as the quest for power or for
wealth. These perspectives disregard the need for *homo symbolicus* – the
preservation of a positive self-image for both emotional and instrumental reasons.
A good reputation ensures authority and material resources. Non-recognition can
be as much as an explanation of war as that of other explicative 'variables'. Two
empirical studies examining the role of non-recognition in great power conflicts
and in international crises demonstrate the value of this symbolic approach.

**Please visit www.ecpr.eu/ecprpress for up-to-date information about new
and forthcoming publications.**

Table of Contents

List of Figures and Tables

Contributors

LORENZO BOSI is Assistant Professor at the Scuola Normale Superiore (SNS). He holds a BA (2000) from the Faculty of Political Science at the Università degli Studi di Bologna and a PhD (2005) from the School of Politics and International Relations at Queen's University, Belfast. His academic work earned him three very prestigious successive international postdoctoral fellowships in social science and sociology departments, one at the University of Kent (ESRC) and two at the European University Institute (Jean Monnet and Marie Curie). His main research interests are in political sociology and historical sociology. His academic work deals primarily with qualitative research of social movements and political violence.

AURÉLIE CAMPANA is Associate Professor of Political Science at Laval University. Since 2007 she holds the Canada Research Chair on Conflicts and Terrorism. She is also deputy director of the Peace and Security Program (Institut des Hautes Etudes Internationales, University of Laval), member of the Executive Committee of the Canadian Research Network on Terrorism, Security and Society, and member of the Centre International de Criminologie Comparée. Her recent research has focused on terrorism in internal conflicts, the diffusion of violence across movements and borders, and discourses on terrorism and counterterrorism. Her research has appeared in numerous journals, including *Civil Wars*; *Studies in Conflict and Terrorism*; *Terrorism and Political Violence*; *Critical Studies on Terrorism*; *La Revue Française de Science Politique*, and *Études Internationales*.

JOVANA CARAPIC has recently defended her doctorate at the Graduate Institute of International and Development Studies in Geneva, Switzerland. Her research focuses on the conceptualisations of 'authority' with respect to various types of armed groups and what this means for how they interact with the state. She is also interested in issues of urbanisation and urban violence, and was part of the research team for the Urban Tipping Point project, run from the University of Manchester and funded by an award from the ESRC/DFID Joint Scheme for Research on International Development (Poverty Alleviation).

LUIS DE LA CALLE is Professor and researcher at the Centro de Investigación y Docencia Económicas (CIDE). Before taking up this position, he was a postdoctoral fellow at the Juan March Institute. He wrote his dissertation at the European University Institute, Florence. His work focuses on the study of the dynamics of violence of terrorist groups and on insurgencies more generally. His research has appeared in journals such as *Journal of Conflict Resolution*; *Politics and Society*; *International Studies Quarterly*; *European Journal of Political Research*, and *The Annual Review of Political Science*.

DONAGH DAVIS is a PhD candidate at the Department of Political and Social Sciences (SPS) at the European University Institute, Florence. His interests include historical sociology, the sociology of revolutions, and contentious politics. His doctoral research is a case study of the early twentieth-century Irish independence struggle. The dissertation considers the episode in relation to different levels of causation, and their interaction – from long-term structural factors, to medium-term conjunctural circumstance, and short-term contingency and volition. His most recent publication is 'Revolution' which appeared in Gregory Claeys (ed.) *Encyclopedia of Modern Political Thought* Vol. II (2013), Thousand Oaks, CA: CQ Press, pp. 694–700.

JÉRÔME DREVON is a PhD Candidate at Durham University and a Junior Research Fellow of the Swiss National Science Foundation (SNSF). He studies the evolution of the Egyptian militant groups *al-jama'a al-islamiya* (the Islamic Group) and *jama'a al-jihad* (the Jihad Group). He has interviewed many of their leaders and senior members in Egypt, as well as dozens of militants and sympathisers. He has published a forthcoming article in *Digest of Middle East Studies* and submitted two additional articles on the emergence of ex-*jihadi* political parties in Egypt and on *salafi jihadi* socialisation among *salafi* youths in Egypt. In addition to this he has written for Carnegie Endowment for International Peace and presented his research at several international conferences in Europe and North America.

LUCA FALCIOLA is a Research Fellow in History of Political Institutions at the Catholic University of Milan. He received his PhD in History from Sciences Po, Paris, in 2011 and in 2012–13 he was a Postdoctoral Fellow at Yale's Program on Order, Conflict, and Violence. His research interests embrace the logic of political violence, the relationship between state and protest movements, and the history of leftist revolutionary groups. He has written various papers about Italian, US, and Romanian history that have been published in academic journals such as *Contemporanea* and *Ricerche di storia politica*.

JAKE LOMAX is a doctoral researcher at the University of East Anglia School of International Development. His work focuses on the micro dynamics of civil wars, especially the nature of wartime threats, displacement decisions and other civilian protection strategies, and rationales for wartime violence against civilians. Prior to his PhD, Jake spent five years working for local and international NGOs in London, Kenya and the occupied Palestinian territory, and he now works primarily on West African conflicts.

STEFAN MALTHANER is Assistant Professor at Aarhus University. Before coming to Aarhus, he spent three years as Marie Curie Fellow and Max Weber Fellow at the EUI, worked as a researcher at the Institute for Interdisciplinary Research on Conflict and Violence (IKG) at University of Bielefeld, Germany, and was a member of the Micropolitics of Armed Groups research group at Humboldt University, Berlin. His research focuses on political violence and social (especially Islamist) movements, from a comparative perspective. He is the author of *Mobilizing the Faithful: Militant Islamist Groups and their Constituencies* (Campus, 2011), and co-editor of *Control of Violence* (Springer U.S., 2011), *Radikale Milieus* (Campus, 2012), and *Dynamics of Political Violence* (Ashgate 2014). Among the large-scale academic events he has organised or co-organised were the conferences Radicalization and De-Radicalization (ZiF, Bielefeld, 2001), Radical Milieus (University of Bielefeld, 2011), and Micropolitics of Armed Groups (Humboldt University, Berlin, 2007).

NIALL Ó DOCHARTAIGH is Senior Lecturer in the School of Political Science and Sociology at the National University of Ireland, Galway. He previously worked as a research officer at the International Conflict Research Institute of the University of Ulster and the United Nations University. A range of journals have published his work on conflict, negotiation, territory and new technologies and he is also the author of two books: *From Civil Rights to Armalites: Derry and the Birth of the Irish Troubles* (1997; 2005) and *Internet Research Skills* (2002; 2007; 2012). He is convener of the Specialist Group on Peace and Conflict of the Political Studies Association of Ireland and a founding convener of the ECPR Standing Group on Political Violence. Further information is available at https://niallodoc.wordpress.com.

DANIELA PISOIU is a Researcher at the Institute for Peace Research and Security Policy (IFSH) at the University of Hamburg. She is the author of *Islamist Radicalisation in Europe: An Occupational Change Process* (2011) and editor of the forthcoming book *Arguing Counterterrorism: New Perspectives* (2014). She currently researches subcultural aspects of radicalisation and political violence in a comparative perspective and is more broadly interested in social movement theory, terrorism and political violence, critical terrorism studies, political extremism and EU and US security policies.

JOSEPH RUANE was Professor at the School of Sociology and Philosophy, University College Cork, until 2010. During 2011–2016 he is Visiting Professor of Sociology at University College Dublin. His research interests include theorising social and historical change; sociology of state- and nation-building; comparative colonial, ethnic, religious and centre–periphery relationships, and sociology of contemporary transition. Among his most important publications are *The Dynamics of Conflict in Northern Ireland* (1996) and *Ethnicity and Religion: Intersections and Comparisons* (2010).

PATRICIA STEINHOFF is Professor of Sociology at the University of Hawaii. She studies social movements in Japan. Her research has been published in *Mobilization*; *Contemporary Japan*, *Journal of the German Institute for Japanese*

Studies in Tokyo; *Militantisme et Répression*; *Social Psychology Quarterly*; *Qualitative Sociology*, as well as in numerous edited volumes. She recently edited the book *Going to Court to Change Japan: Social Movements and the Law* (2014).

JENNIFER TODD is Professor at the School of Politics and International Relations, University College Dublin. She holds a BA from the University of Kent, and an MA and PhD from the University of Boston. Todd is a member of the Royal Irish Academy and Director of the Institute for British Irish Studies at UCD. Her research interests include ethnicity, ethnic conflict, collective identity, and Northern Ireland. Among her most important publications are *The Dynamics of Conflict in Northern Ireland* (1996) and *Ethnicity and Religion: Intersections and Comparisons* (2010).

LORENZO ZAMPONI is a PhD candidate in Political and Social Sciences at the European University Institute, working on a research project on the relationship between collective memories and social movements. His research interests include public memory, contentious politics, student movements, anti-austerity activism and media analysis. Among his most recent publications are '"Why don't Italians Occupy?" Hypotheses on a Failed Mobilisation', *Social Movement Studies*, 11(3–4), 2012, and 'Protest and policing on October 15th, global day of action: The Italian case', *Policing and Society*, 23(1), 2013 (with D. della Porta).

GILDA ZWERMAN is Professor of Sociology at SUNY, Old Westbury. She studies social movements with a specialisation in radicalisation and political violence. Her research has been published in the journals *Qualitative Sociology, Social Justice, Feminist Review* and *Mobilization* as well as in co-edited volumes on political repression, left-wing protest, and protest cultures.

Acknowledgements

The idea for this book originated at the ECPR General Conference at Sciences Po, Bordeaux, September 4–7 2013, where Lorenzo Bosi and Niall Ó Dochartaigh, as convenors of the Standing Group on Political Violence (http://www.polviolence. net), organised the section on 'Political Violence in Time and Space'. This event brought together distinguished scholars and younger scientists from various disciplines, including political science, sociology, history, international relations, and area studies. We thank all the colleagues who participated at that event. We thank all authors represented in this volume, the external reviewers, and the editors and staff at ECPR Press, in particular Alexandra Segerberg and Laura Pugh.

Lorenzo Bosi, Niall Ó Dochartaigh and Daniela Pisoiu
October 2015

Chapter One

Contextualising Political Violence

Lorenzo Bosi, Niall Ó Dochartaigh and Daniela Pisoiu

Political violence involves a heterogeneous repertoire of actions aimed at inflicting physical, psychological and symbolic damage on individuals and/or property with the intention of influencing various audiences in order to effect or resist political, social, and/or cultural change. This edited volume aligns itself with the recent shift in political science towards contextualisation of political phenomena (Goodin and Tilly 2006; Lawson 2008), with particular consideration of some of the concerns raised by critical terrorism studies (Jackson *et al.* 2011) and social movement scholars (Bosi and Malthaner forthcoming), and focusing on the crucial importance of the contexts within which political violence by non-state actors occurs. Despite recent developments, as pressures for decontextualised explanations persist both from the broader society and from within academia itself, this is not necessarily a straightforward task. Furthermore, efforts to conceptualise and empirically analyse the various facets and dimensions of context are still in an initial phase of development.

Political science approaches that are directed towards identifying law-like regularities in political conduct are ill-equipped to explain periods of protracted transformation associated with the emergence of political violence, and the dynamics that political violence sets in motion across time and space. Political violence is particularly resistant to this type of explanation not just because of the exceptional importance of contingency – imagine how different current global patterns of political violence would be if the 9/11 attacks had been disrupted at the planning stage – but also because many of the most important features of violent political conflicts are endogenous to those conflicts. Moreover, the political structures that social scientists often treat as though they were stable frameworks for interaction and decision making – institutions, boundaries, power configurations, and the rules of the game – are frequently the targets that armed actors seek to eliminate or, at least, change. Much of the literature on political violence still focuses on explanatory approaches that resort to macro-level examination of initial conditions or root causes. Frequently, explanations are discussed in terms of the international system, material deprivation and economic grievances, processes of modernisation – or interruptions thereof – and political culture, such as the cultural acceptance of violence (for an overview see Franks 2006). With the exception of emergent psychological and social movement research on individual pathways emphasising 'soft' rationality and the intentionality of involvement (Horgan 2005; Wiktorowicz 2005; Pisoiu 2011; Bosi and della Porta 2012), a similar focus on root causes is also evident in work conducted at the micro level, on dependency, circular reactions, and identity-seeking personalities (Victoroff 2005 provides a review). However, these supposed root causes seem to provide neither necessary nor sufficient conditions for explaining the phenomenon of political violence. Political violence has occurred in wealthy and poor regions alike, in modern industrialised countries as well as in less developed ones. Furthermore, as Tore Bjørgo's points out, a 'limitation of the "root cause" approach is that it may give the impression that insurgents or terrorists are merely passive objects of social, economic and psychological forces: puppets obeying what these causes compel them to do' (2005: 3), thus depriving armed activist behaviour of meaning, agency and legitimacy. Because root causes imply general and prior causal factors, these are ill-suited to explain nuances and variations in the processes by which political violence emerges, persists, and declines. One of the responses to these elements of contingency and endogeneity has been to treat individual conflicts and pathways as unique. However, to analyse individuals, groups or conflicts as though they were *sui generis* limits our capacity to understand political violence as a phenomenon and it carries the danger of impoverishing our analysis and understanding, leading to what Rose and Mackenzie have called a 'false particularisation' (1991: 450). Furthermore, a fixation on case idiosyncrasies, while certainly allowing for richness of detail, can hinder the development of theory, which is an important aim of social science research.

Goodin and Tilly's *Handbook of Contextual Political Analysis* (2006) articulates the paradigmatic gist of positivist and empiricist approaches:

> Some observers speak of choices between positivism and constructivism, between covering laws and hermeneutics, between general and local knowledge, or between reductionism and holism. Regardless of the terminology, at one end of the range we find claims for universal principles that cut across particular social contexts, at the other claims that attempt to describe and explain political phenomena that have no means of escaping particular social contexts. (Tilly and Goodin 2006: 9)

In the specific area that is political violence, and in contrast to the dominant paradigm of identifying law-like relationships between political violence and various macro and meso-level variables, Martha Crenshaw's seminal edited volume *Terrorism in Context* (1995) emphasised already twenty years ago how vital context is to understanding and explaining political violence. Also central to her approach is the relationship between structure and agency, in that

> [b]oth the phenomenon of terrorism and our conceptions of it depend on historical context – political, social and economic – and on how the groups and individuals who participate in or respond to the actions we call terrorism relate to the world in which they act. (Crenshaw 1995: 3)

More recently, Bosi, Demetriou and Malthaner (2014) have taken a closer look at the immediate context of political violence, inscribing it in the broader context of political contention. Here the emphasis on the contextualisation of political violence allows us to avoid the deterministic, essentialist, and reifying readings that characterise much of the literature. It helps us to understand this phenomenon, instead, 'as one of several forms of confrontation within a wider repertoire of actions and strategies'; to appreciate 'that militant groups are embedded within the broader field of actors involved in the conflict'; and to 'recognize that violent interactions are embedded in the wider processes of political contention' (Bosi, Demetriou and Malthaner 2014: 2). Analysing political violence in context allows us to examine questions about how and when, rather than why, a group or an individual would engage in violence, persist in using this repertoire of action, and eventually disengage from it. It locates the choice for that particular tactic in the context of its strategic aims and other tactical choices.

Context has, in much of the work on political violence, been understood to refer to the specificities of particular historical, political, social and economic situations. Going beyond this empirical level of analysis, this volume aims to lay the foundations for uncovering new territory in the effort to contextualise political violence. In doing so it introduces and elaborates on specific dimensions of context that shape political violence and that – although taken into consideration – has been neither fully conceptualised nor theorised in the literature. Accordingly, it relocates political violence within the contexts of time, space, and milieu. This is not done with an aim – as Koopmans puts it – to treat the latter 'as dimensions on which to sample "cases", but as variables that are an intrinsic and central part of the analysis of contention' (2004: 32). This volume is divided into three thematic sections addressing these contexts, and each section is preceded by a brief introduction. In the remainder of this introduction we illustrate the value of focusing on these three contextual dimensions by looking at four crucial themes in the analysis of political violence. In each case we outline the importance of our three contextual dimensions for understanding these key themes.

Political violence and contentious politics

The distinctively unpredictable, endogenous and intense features of political violence have been cited in recent scholarship in support of the argument that it is necessary to study violence as a distinctive phenomenon in its own right, separately from the broader category of conflict or contentious politics (Brubaker and Laitin 1998: 427; Kalyvas 2006). Scholars particularly emphasise the sharp changes in patterns of individual decision making that occur upon the introduction of the prospect of terminal violence. While we accept that, for individuals, violence creates a very different kind of context for decision making, focusing on the broader political context of the outbreak and the persistence of violence is vital to understanding the processes through which violence escalates, and through which it eventually ends (della Porta 2013; Alimi et al. 2015). The issues around which a conflict begins may be altered in the course of that conflict, but they nonetheless often remain a vital source of motivation, as well as a key point of orientation for attempts to end the conflict (O'Connor and Oikonomakis, forthcoming). For example, during the Italian 1968–9 period, the early emergence of armed left-wing groups was related to right-wing violence and indiscriminate police repression of the mass upsurge of students and workers. As soon as this broader cycle of contention moved towards a conclusion – partly as a result of the violent actions of armed left-wing groups – the violent conflict began to progressively decline (Alimi *et al.* 2015).

Social movement scholars, in locating political violence in a continuum of contentious politics, have never argued that violent and non-violent repertoires are equivalent. Rather than developing a separate perspective particular to violence, the aim has been to provide an integrated perspective capable of contextualising violence within broader processes of contention of which it forms a part (Bosi and Malthaner 2015). This process of contention provides much of the explanation for the emergence of violence, while the temporal, spatial, and milieu contexts of the broader mobilisation that precedes violence are essential to understanding the pattern that violence subsequently follows. Beissinger (2002), for example, shows how nationalist violence in the former Soviet Union was strongly correlated with levels of popular mobilisation at the earlier stages of the cycle of contention. Violence was intensely clustered in time and played essentially the same role in several distinct cycles of – largely peaceful – nationalist contention throughout the Soviet Union. He shows how violence intensified at a crucial moment of decision concerning state boundaries. In this example, a historically specific struggle over territorial boundaries in a time of transition was central to an episode of contention in which political violence was integrated with other forms of contention. In most cases, the violence abated as the issues at the centre of contention were settled. Its spatial contours, and its timing, progress, and termination were all shaped by the temporal, spatial and milieu contexts of the broader mobilisation of which it formed a part. The temporal context of a long phase of contention; the spatial context of clusters of local mobilisation, and a struggle oriented around boundaries, and the context of nationalist milieus are all essential to understanding how this violence emerged from a broader episode of contention, and how its termination was directly connected to issues central to the broader episode of contention.

The work on political violence also emphasises that certain individuals become specialists in violence, and that this is a very distinctive kind of expertise, of quite a different order than the kind of expertise involved in non-violent contention (Collins 2009). Specialists in violence are, in certain ways, fundamentally different kinds of actors from those involved in non-violent contention. But as Collins and other scholars of the micro-sociology of violence have shown, individuals become specialists in violence in specific temporal and spatial contexts and in specific milieus. For many, this path to specialisation begins during early episodes of non-violent contention and street protests that are deeply embedded in specific social contexts and shaped by relational dynamics. The contention on the streets of Kiev in 2014 – characterised by interrelated incidences of street protest, rioting, and gun battles – provides a powerful recent example of the direct relationship between non-violent contention and the emergence of specialists in the use of violence on the political scene. Similar stories can be traced with micro-mobilisation paths in the Provisional IRA (Bosi 2012); in ETA (Reinares 2001); in left-wing clandestine groups in Western countries (della Porta 1992, 1995; Zwerman, Steinhoff and della Porta 2000); or in the FMLN (Viterna 2013). Furthermore, only a small minority of armed activists are involved in violent activities throughout all of their lives. Most of these people disengage at some stage during the cycle of violence or when an armed group calls for an end to violence (Bjørgo and Horgan 2009). As with social movement activists, individuals involved in political violence experience post-activism consequences, often keeping them socially and politically active throughout their lives (Viterna 2013; Bosi 2014).

The way in which violence is deployed changes over time, in the targets that are chosen, the repertoire deployed, and in the intensity of the violence. Sometimes actors shift back and forth between violent and non-violent forms of action and in many cases violence does not mark a new and separate phase of contention but proceeds in parallel with non-violent mobilisation, with street protests, marches, boycotts, and strikes. And violence is deployed in territorially and spatially distinctive ways that are related to the broader contention of which it forms a part. In many cases certain forms of violence are seen as appropriate and legitimate only at certain times (Rucht 2003), in certain kinds of spaces (Ron 2003), and within specific milieus (Malthaner and Waldmann 2014). This contextual shaping of patterns of violence is connected to the broader episodes of contention from which the violence emerges. Patterns of violence are shaped by the wider political culture of these movements, a political culture that is formed through the experience of peaceful mobilisation as well as through violence. Tilly (2006) points out that the repertoires of contention deployed – including forms of violence – 'draw heavily on historically accumulated and shared understandings with regard to meanings, claims, legitimate claimants, and proper objects of claims' (426). That is, violence is shaped by meanings and understandings formed during earlier phases of the cycle of contention.

Rationality and mobilisation

In its classical formulation, rational choice theory provides one of the most important law-seeking analytical traditions within political science, focusing on identifying trans-historical and context-free laws of decision making with predictive power. In the case of political violence, however, such economic rationality is hardly suitable for explaining organisational and individual involvement in violence, given the free-rider dilemma and the high costs involved. One way in which the literature has attempted to resolve this is by proposing different types of rationality, namely political-strategic for organisations, and selective incentives for individuals. A series of authors analyse insurgent and terrorist organisations as rational decision makers (Crenshaw 2000; della Porta 1995: Ch. 5), which implies a methodological approach to political violence as a strategic choice (see Garrison 2003, 2004; Kalyvas 1999; Westine 2007). Others, drawing on criminological rational choice and social movement resource mobilisation approaches, have argued that not material but, rather, immaterial – including emotional – benefits are decisive for the explanation of individual involvement (Horgan 2005; Wiktorowicz 2005).

Furthermore, the type of rationality considered here is not an economic one, but rather an 'everyday' type of rationality, whereby individuals act against the background of an expectation of gain. Clearly, the concrete manifestations of strategic choice and individual incentives are not the same every time, so that the working of both types of rationalities depends on different types of context. In the case of the use of suicide attacks, their instrumental rationality can be observed once the political context in which armed groups are acting has been taken into account (Bloom 2005: 75–6; Bloom 2006; Elster 2005; Gambetta 2005). Among the specific circumstances leading a group to use extreme forms of political violence, such as suicide tactics, is the existence of an imbalance of power, that is, an asymmetry in terms of resources and combatants between groups and their enemy (Boyns and Ballard 2004: 10; Pape 2005: Ch. 3), but also specific dynamics of competition among various groups for popular support (Bloom 2004). Another element of context that shapes the manifestations of individual choices towards involvement in armed groups in general and politically violent acts in particular concerns the frames of the broader cultural and discursive context (Wiktorowicz 2005; Pisoiu 2011): elements of context that shape the criteria according to which particular rewards function as such or not.

Apart from the political and cultural discursive context, time, space, and milieu can also usefully complement rationalist analyses of political violence. Patterns of mobilisation for violence tend to be jaggedly uneven in both temporal and spatial terms. Sharply uneven increases or declines in recruitment over time and unusually intense levels of recruitment within certain localised areas can certainly be profitably examined in terms of reasoning and choice, but these sharp variations are clear evidence of the decisive shaping importance of temporal and spatial contexts in such mobilisation (Viterna 2013; Bosi and della Porta 2012). Given that we frequently find exceptional levels of mobilisation for violence to be concentrated in certain residential areas at very specific historical junctures, the key questions to ask concern those contextual factors that shape the kind of choices that are open to people in these contexts, and the range of responses that people consider reasonable, appropriate, or morally compelling in these specific contexts (Ó Dochartaigh 2012). Zukerman Daly's (2012) recent work on organisational legacies of violence in Colombia provides strong evidence that the context of particular milieus – in this case strong and intensely localised social networks and networks of solidarity established during previous phases of contention – are also essential to understanding patterns of mobilisation in subsequent phases of violent contention. Similarly, authors working on jihadi terrorism have attested to the important role of social networks and milieus in the initial phases of individual radicalisation (Sageman 2004; Malthaner 2014).

Organisations and political culture

Roger Gould's (1995) comparative study of two phases of contention in nineteenth century Paris provides a clear outline of the way in which changes to the built environment of the city promoted changes in the demographic mix of neighbourhoods. This, in turn, changed the kinds of milieus in which political debate and mobilisation were generated and organised. Gould shows how this chain of transformations of contexts for mobilisation changed what he refers to as 'insurgent identities', consequently enuring that the mobilisation of 1871 and the establishment of the Paris Commune took quite a different form to the earlier rebellion of 1848. Contexts shape both the organisational forms that mobilisation for violence assume, as well as the political cultures that are so important for sustaining those organisations. And these organisational milieus, in turn, provide a context that is central to understanding patterns of violence. The importance of spatial contexts for organisation and development of oppositional cultures was clearly identified by Marx and Engels (1998 [1848]) who placed the end of peasant isolation at the centre of their political analysis. They emphasised that the concentration of the new industrial working class in conditions of co-presence, allowing for intense contact, coordination, and organisation was decisive for the mobilisation and development of class consciousness. That is, the emergence of certain kinds of spatial contexts for action at a particular historical juncture contributes to the emergence of novel milieus that both facilitate and shape mobilisation. A focus on context also helps us to understand how organisations and political culture develop. Wolford's (2003; 2004) study of the MST movement in Brazil, for example, illustrates how the same organisation, working with similarly poor and exploited rural workers in two different local contexts, experienced two very different outcomes. Locally distinctive patterns of land tenure, and sedimented local political cultures associated with such differences, ensured that this uneven contextual effect then served to reinforce the organisation's spatially uneven identification with specific regions. A consequence was that the political culture of the organisation became heavily inflected by its association with specific regions.

The social and organisational context of oppositional milieus is central to sustaining violent rebellion despite the high costs and suffering involved. As Wood (2003: 225) shows in her study of support for left-wing rebels in El Salvador in the 1980s, 'an emergent insurgent political culture was key to generating and sustaining the insurgency despite its high costs'. As Guichaoua (2011) notes, oppositional and insurgent milieus provide a context that is important to personal transformation as well as to the development of political interpretations and commitment. Rather than having fully-formed rational actors joining an organisation and becoming part of a milieu in order to advance their preferences, the milieu-context is itself crucial in influencing and shaping those preferences and providing motivation, most importantly through the development of small-group solidarity of the kind necessary for violent actors, whether they be national armies or poorly-equipped rebels. New norms develop through interaction over time, new skills are learned, views are formed, and interpretations shaped. The new organisations also have a transformative impact on other contexts, often displacing and disrupting existing networks of patronage and clientelistic relations, as well as the networks that link people to the state apparatus (Wood 2003). They thus contribute to the creation of new contexts for action.

Ideology and interpretation

Ideology has been a hotly debated topic, with conflicting arguments regarding whether or not it has an impact on political violence and, if so, what kind of impact. Some assessments hold ideology to be a primary cause of mobilisation, while – at the other extreme – recent econometric analyses have tended to marginalise ideology. These analyses focus instead on interests, to the extent that, in the latest iteration of the 'greed and grievance' argument, motivation – and thus ideology – has almost entirely disappeared, with mobilisation into violence explained in terms of opportunity alone: where rebellion is feasible, it will occur (Collier *et al.* 2009). Without delving too much into these debates, it would be safe to assume, first, that opportunity cannot explain everything, since many rebellions break out despite the fact that they are not 'feasible', in the sense that many are quickly crushed, or else fail after an immense and fruitless expenditure of life and effort. Second, while ideology may not *determine* political violence, it certainly shapes its form and justifies its means. However, the existence and widespread popularity of radical ideologies is not a necessary or sufficient condition for political violence.

Violent conflict may no longer be as deeply informed by the ideological struggles between left and right as it was during the Cold War, but it is important to keep in mind how central master narratives of class, nation, and religion are to contentious politics in many violent conflicts. Even where actors and organisations are not oriented towards these dominant master narratives, ideology and interpretation remain essential to understanding the patterns of violence, and the processes of escalation and demobilisation. Ideas and ideology are important both in motivating and interpreting action, and context is in both cases inextricably bound up with ideas.

Understandings and ideology have always been shaped by context. This was so even during the most rigidly ideologically defined phase of contention in human history, namely, the great confrontations between fascism, liberal democracy and communism, and – subsequently – between communism and capitalism that structured global political discourse and competition from the 1920s until the 1990s (Mazower 1998). The importance of national contexts to shaping versions of Marxism was clearly evident from the 1950s onwards, after the split between Moscow and Beijing. The war, in the 1970s, between communist Vietnam and communist China, and the distinctively ethnonationalist programme of the Khmer Rouge in Cambodia, all reinforced the point that Marxist ideology and practice was deeply shaped by national contexts, by ethnonational milieus, and by changes occurring over time. Ideology remained important, but in a complex interaction with the contexts in which it was appropriated.

The importance of ideology is most clear in providing standards and benchmarks for justice, equity, and fairness, whose perceived violation is an important mobilising factor. It is these – often highly localised – norms of justice and fairness, and interpretations of the actions of other actors, that help to explain spatially uneven patterns of mobilisation. Those who experience direct ongoing violent oppression from one set of actors are much more likely to be open to interpretive frames that identify current systems as unjust, and violent resistance as morally justified – even where direct involvement may be seen as too dangerous. These understandings and ideas help to create a particular ideational context for action.

For Wood (2003) 'moral outrage' and a sense of injustice is crucial in motivating support for, and mobilisation into, guerilla organisations. Such interpretations involve an implicit ideological frame for analysis, and actors make such judgements based on locally contextualised sets of ideas with regional or international circulation.

Context is important, too, for conveying meaning. The temporal and spatial contexts of an act of violence or aggression influence its interpretation and the extent to which it provides a motivation for subsequent action. In his analysis of interethnic relations in the Romanian city of Cluj, where Hungarians form a large minority, Brubaker (2007) notes that incidents whose ethnic dimension might be emphasised at times of tension or in a certain location, will, in other periods and in other parts of town, be characterised as interpersonal. Context provides meaning and shapes interpretation.

Conclusion

Our undertaking, in this volume, is aligned with political science's recent shift towards the contextualisation of political phenomena and, more broadly, the relationship between structure and agency, which we read as varying across time, space and types of milieu. Contextualising political violence does not mean that we prioritise macro-structural explanations over meso and micro-agential ones. Armed groups are constrained in their actions because they are embedded in complex webs of relations with other actors. Their strategic choices are conditioned by their interpretation of the actions of others, with whom they continue to interact. They are not outside of time, space, and milieu. Jessop (1996) and Hay (2002) have outlined a strategic-relational approach to understanding the relationship between structure and agency, emphasising the importance of context and, in particular, the 'interaction of strategic actors and the strategic context in which they find themselves' (Hay 2002: 129). We suggest, then, that to better explain political violence we should locate the choice for a particular tactic within the context of strategic ambitions and the other tactical choices made from that repertoire. To select the dependent variable, and to focus exclusively on violent actors while excluding other actors that form the same context, risks treating armed groups as unique, exceptional, or even pathological actors. Contextualising political violence in time, space, and milieu allows us to, instead, explain the large co-evolving contexts that facilitate and constrain the characteristics and actions of any actor in relation to the characteristics and actions of all others in the environment.

References

Alimi, E., Demetriou, C. and Bosi, L. (2015) *The Dynamics of Radicalization: A Relational and Comparative Perspective*, NY: OUP.

Beissinger, M. R. (2002) *Nationalist Mobilization and the Collapse of the Soviet State*, Cambridge: Cambridge University Press.

Bjørgo, T (2005) *Root Causes of Terrorism: Myths, Reality and Ways Forward*, London: Routledge.

Bjørgo, T. and Horgan, J. (2009) *Leaving Terrorism Behind: Individual and Collective Disengagement*, London: Routledge.

Bloom, M. (2004) 'Palestinian suicide bombing: Public support, market share and outbidding', *Political Science Quarterly*, 119(1): 61–88.

— (2005) *Dying to Kill: The Allure of Suicide Terror*, NY: Columbia University Press.

— (2006) 'Dying to kill: Motivations for suicide terrorism', in A. Pedahzur (ed.) *Root Causes of Suicide Terrorism: The Globalization of Martyrdom*, Abingdon: Routledge.

Bosi, L. (2012) 'Explaining pathways to armed activism in the Provisional IRA, 1969–1972', *Social Science History*, 36(3): 347–90.

— (2014) 'Contextualizing the biographical outcomes of Provisional IRA former activists: A structure–agency dynamic', paper presented at the conference Activists Forever? The Long-term Impacts of Political Actvisim in Various Contexts, Rennes, May 2014.

Bosi, L. and della Porta, D. (2012) 'Micro-mobilization into armed groups: Ideological, instrumental and solidaristic paths', *Qualitative Sociology*, 35(4): 361–83.

Bosi, L., Demetriou, C. and Malthaner, S. (eds) (2014) *Dynamics of Political Violence: A Process-Oriented Perspective on Radicalization and the Escalation of Political Conflict*, Farnham/London: Ashgate.

Bosi, L. and Malthaner, S. (forthcoming) 'Political violence', in D. della Porta and M. Diani (eds) *Oxford Handbook of Social Movements*, Oxford: OUP.

Boyns, D. and Ballard, J. D. (2004) 'Developing a sociological theory for the empirical understanding of terrorism', *The American Sociologist*, 35(2): 5–25.

Brubaker, R. (2007) *Nationalist Politics and Everyday Ethnicity in a Transylvanian Town*, Princeton: Princeton University Press.

Brubaker, R. and Laitin, D. D. (1998) 'Ethnic and nationalist violence', *Annual Review of Sociology*, 24(1): 423–52.

Collier, P. and Hoeffler, A. (2004) 'Greed and grievance in civil war', *Oxford Economic Papers*, 56(4): 563–59.

Collier, P., Hoeffler, A., and Rohner, D. (2009) 'Beyond greed and grievance: Feasibility and civil war', *Oxford Economic Papers*, 61(1): 1–27.

Collins, R. (2009) *Violence: A Micro-Sociological Theory*, Princeton: Princeton University Press.

Crenshaw, M. (1995) 'Thoughts on relating terrorism to historical contexts' in M. Crenshaw (ed.) *Terrorism in Context*, Pennsylvania: Pennsylvania State University Press.

—   (2000) 'The psychology of terrorism: An agenda for the 21st century', *Political Psychology* 21(2): 405–420.

Della Porta, D. (1992) 'On individual motivations in underground political organizations', in D. della Porta (ed.) *Social Movements and Violence: Participation in Underground Organizations: International Social Movement Research* Vol. 4, Greenwich, CT: JAI-Press, pp. 3–28.

—   (1995) *Social Movements, Political Violence and the State*, NY: CUP.

—   (2013) *Clandestine Political Violence*, Cambridge: CUP.

Elster, J. (2005) 'Motivations and beliefs in suicide missions', in D. Gambetta (ed.) *Making Sense of Suicide Missions*, Oxford: Oxford University Press, pp. 233–58.

Franks, J. (2006) *Rethinking the Roots of Terrorism*, Basingstoke: Palgrave Macmillan.

Gambetta, D. (ed.) (2005) *Making Sense of Suicide Missions*, Oxford: Oxford University Press.

Garrison, A. (2003) 'Terrorism: The nature of its history' in *Criminal Justice Studies: A Critical Journal of Crime, Law and Society*, 16 (1): 39–52.

—   (2004) 'Defining terrorism: philosophy of the bomb, propaganda by deed and change through fear and violence' in *Criminal Justice Studies: A Critical Journal of Crime, Law and Society*, 17 (3): 259–279.

Goodin, R. E., and Tilly, C. (eds) (2006) *The Oxford Handbook of Contextual Political Analysis*, Oxford: Oxford University Press.

Gould, R. V. (1995) *Insurgent Identities: Class, Community, and Protest in Paris from 1848 to the Commune,* Chicago: University of Chicago Press.

Guichaoua, Y. (ed.) (2011) *Understanding Collective Political Violence*, Basingstoke: Palgrave.

Hay, C. (2002) *Political Analysis: A Critical Introduction*, Basingstoke: Palgrave.

Horgan, J. (2005) *The Psychology of Terrorism*, London/New York: Routledge.

Jackson, R., Jarvis, L., Gunning, J. and Breen Smyth, M. (2011) *Terrorism: A Critical Introduction*, New York: Palgrave Macmillan.

Jessop, B. (1996) 'Interpretive sociology and the dialectic of structure and agency', *Theory, Culture & Society*, 13(1): 119–128.

Kalyvas, S. N. (2006) *The Logic of Violence in Civil War*, Cambridge: Cambridge University Press.

Koopmans, R. (2004) 'Protest in time and space: The evolution of waves of contention', in D. Snow, S. Soule and H. Kriesi (eds) *The Blackwell Companion to Social Movements*, Oxford: Blackwell Publishing, pp. 19–46.

Lawson, S. (2008) 'Political studies and the contextual turn: A methodological/ normative critique', *Political Studies*, 56(3): 584–603.

Malthaner, S. (2014) 'Contextualizing radicalization: The emergence of the "Sauerland-Group" from radical networks and the *salafist* movement', *Studies in Conflict and Terrorism*, 37(8): 638–653.

Malthaner, S. and Waldmann, P. (2014) 'The radical milieu: Conceptualizing the supportive social environment of terrorist groups', *Studies in Conflict & Terrorism,* 37(12): 979–98.

Marx, K. and Engels, F. (1998 [1848]) *The Communist Manifesto*, London: Verso.

Mazower, M. (1998) *Dark Continent: Europe's 20th Century*, London: Penguin.

McAdam, D., Tarrow, S. and Tilly, C. (2001) *Dynamics of Contention*, Cambridge: Cambridge University Press.

O'Connor, F. and Oikonomakis, L. (forthcoming) 'Pre-conflict mobilization strategies and urban-rural transition: The cases of the PKK and the FLN/EZLN', *Mobilization*.

Ó Dochartaigh, N. (2012) 'Nation and neighborhood: Nationalist mobilization and local solidarities in the North of Ireland', in A. Guelke (ed.) *The Challenges of Ethnonationalism*, Basingstoke: Palgrave, pp. 161–76.

Pape, R. (2005) *Dying to Win: The Logic of Suicide Terrorism*, New York: Random House.

Pisoiu, D. (2011) *Islamist Radicalisation in Europe: An Occupational Change Process*, London: Routledge.

Reinares, F. (2001) *Patriotas de la Muerte: Quiénes han militado en ETA y por qué*, Madrid: Taurus.

Ron, J. (2003) *Frontiers and Ghettos: State Violence in Serbia and Israel*, Berkeley: University of California Press.

Rose, R. and Mackenzie, W. (1991) 'Comparing forms of comparative analysis', *Political Studies* 39(3):446–62.

Rucht, D. (2003) 'Violence and new social movements', in W. Heitmeyer and J. Hagan (eds) *International Handbook of Violence Research*, Dordrecht/Boston/London: Kluwer Academic Publishers, pp. 369–83.

Sageman, M. (2004) *Understanding Terror Networks*, Philadelphia: University of Pennsylvania Press.

Tilly, C. and Tarrow, S. (2006) *Contentious Politics*, Oxford: Oxford University Press.

Victoroff, J. (2005) 'The mind of terrorists: A review and critique of psychological approaches', *Journal of Conflict Resolution*, 49(1): 3–42.

Viterna, J. (2013) *Women in War: The Micro-processes of Mobilization in El Salvador*, Oxford: Oxford University Press.

Weinstein, J. (2007) *Inside Rebellion: The Politics of Insurgent Violence*, Cambridge: Cambridge University Press.

Wiktorowicz, Q. (2005) *Radical Islam Rising: Muslim Extremism in the West*, Lanham, MD: Rowman & Littlefield.

Wolford, W. (2003) 'Families, fields, and fighting for land: The spatial dynamics of contention in rural Brazil', *Mobilization*, 8(2): 157–72.

— (2004) 'This land is ours now: Spatial imaginaries and the struggle for land in Brazil', *Annals of the Association of American Geographers*, 94(2): 409–24.

Wood, E. J. (2003) *Insurgent Collective Action and Civil War in El Salvador*, New York: Cambridge University Press.

Zukerman Daly, S. (2012) 'Organizational legacies of violence conditions favoring insurgency onset in Colombia, 1964–1984', *Journal of Peace Research*, 49(3): 473–91.

Zwerman, G., Steinhoff, P. G. and della Porta, D. (2000) 'Disappearing social movements: Clandestinity in the cycle of New Left protest in the US, Japan, Germany and Italy', *Mobilization* 5(1): 83–100.

PART ONE

TIME

Chapter Two

Political Violence in Time

Lorenzo Bosi

This volume – and this section in particular – gives us good reason to think that the contextualisation of political violence can hardly move forward without explanations sensitive to the element of time. The everyday life of armed groups is marked with references to correct timing: when to start an armed campaign; when to end it; carrying out attacks on certain recurrent dates, and avoiding others; whether to use the shocking, unexpected suddenness of bomb explosions, or the long, drawn-out and gruelling timing of kidnappings and hostage-taking; when to release a communiqué; when to declare ceasefire; when to recruit new members, and so on. All of these considerations refer to timing – a topic heavily discussed within armed groups. Armed activists themselves, whether socio-revolutionaries, religious fundamentalists or ethnonationalists, are said to 'have in mind alternative visions of history and alternative experiences of time' (Verhoeven 2010: 254). Refusing the 'laws of history', that is, teleological temporalities, armed activists justify violent repertoires of action on the basis that these accelerate or temporarily block the subjective and intersubjective dimensions associated with people's experience of time (Verhoeven, forthcoming). Meanwhile, we should recognise that counterterrorism laws also use explicit articulations of time when rendering a counter-terrorist measure necessary, legitimate, coherent, and meaningful, as seen in the context of the global War on Terror (Jarvis 2009; Fisher 2013). It is, then, important to point out that armed groups and states not only compete over particular spaces and/or constituency support, but also to control the unfolding of time.

Mainstream political violence research is pervaded by implicit notions of time, often following 'teleological' or 'experimental' temporalities, these being central to frameworks that aim to explain political violence. Collective behaviour interpretations, treating violence as spontaneous, abnormal or deviant, refer to noticeable episodes of disruption to an otherwise orderly balance of power relations. Such episodes of disruption motivate individuals and groups to mobilise towards political violence (for an overview see Franks 2006). This is, for example, the case with modernisation, which is said to involve a logic of irreversible social development – politically violent phenomena being just one manifestation of this. Other scholars have referred to certain types of initial conditions, such as the stored historical specificities distinguishing different regions. These are said to explain why violence emerges, develops and is tolerated – thus also explaining, for example, the history of violence of a given region (Townshend 1995). Such interpretations tend to suggest that violence is a quality intrinsic to some actors or specific conflicts, rather than the result of the interactive context within which political violence takes place. The life cycle of the approach of an armed group builds, instead, on the assumption of sequential stages of development in a forward direction: from emergence towards decline. These studies scarcely recognise the possibility of reversals, as if the development of an armed group always moves in a prescribed order, with similar episodes of intense rapid change. However, other scholars have focused on the simultaneity of specific types of political violence, pointing to the occurrence of particular waves of violence through certain historical periods (Rapoport 2004). Each wave of political violence has been said to be quantitatively and qualitatively more violent and less legitimised than the previous ones.

The dimension of time, often treated as self-evident, has not been systematically examined or theorised in mainstream studies of political violence, despite a growing interest, in the social sciences, in how and why time matters (Mahoney 2000; Abbott 2001; Tilly 2001; Pierson 2004; Sewell 2005). The same goes for the key concepts needed to bolster analysis of temporal processes, such as 'periodisation'; 'transformative events'; 'generations'; 'historical experience'; 'duration'; 'process'; 'path dependence'; 'cycles'; 'trajectories'; 'timing'; 'cultural epochs', and 'sequences', these having seemingly gone largely unnoticed by most scholars interested in explaining political violence. Perhaps the main reason for the atemporality and tenselessness in conceptions of time in this field of research is that many of its scholars have been mainly interested in answering questions concerning the security of the public and/or the state. Because the ultimate aim is often to produce policy-oriented knowledge for the sake of predicting violent political phenomena, the focus is on the 'snapshot' that exemplifies past and future as objective forms of chronological time, thus working to make sense merely of the ongoing present.

Such dominant linear conceptualisations of time, which aim to discover the law-like regularities – the general causal laws – that essentially rule the whole, interpret change as progressing through a series of sequential stages, entangling past, present and future. From this determinist cause–effect logic political violence goes through a number of prescribed and contextualised stages, from emergence, through development, to decline: all of which are implicitly or explicitly assumed to be independent of the temporal context in which they occur. Pierson's critique of contemporary social science seems to apply very well also to mainstream political violence research:

[B]oth in what we seek to explain and in our search for explanations, we focus on the immediate—we look for causes and outcomes that are both temporally contiguous and rapidly unfolding. In the process, we miss a lot. There are important things that we do not see at all, and what we do see we often misunderstand (2004: 79).

The chapters in this section suggest, instead, that political violence is an inherently contingent, discontinuous, and open-ended phenomenon. In recognition of the importance of different temporalities we should aim to explain the complex social dynamics that stand behind and enforce political violence. This volume – and this section in particular – provides chapters that extend beyond the existing research on temporalities of political violence at the empirical, methodological and analytical levels. The chapters in this book show that political violence can emerge out of certain sequences of events and/or as an outcome of a particular transformative event (*see* Ó Dochartaigh, Chapter 7). It can develop over time, last for short periods (*see* Lomax, Chapter 10), or endure for long ones. It can involve long-term interaction patterns and processes of violent escalation (*see* Drevon, Chapter 13 and Malthaner, Chapter 16) and de-escalation (*see* Falciola, Chapter 15) between an armed group and its own constituency. It can be shaped by state repression over time (*see* Campana, Chapter 9). It can follow a similar trajectory across spaces, and it can involve the settlement of violent conflict as the result of short-term strategies or the resolution of deep-set problems of legitimation, depending on the type of conflict (*see* Ruane and Todd, Chapter 4). But political violence does not only happen *in* time and is not only constrained *by* time: it also shapes time itself. It can, for example, help promote transformative events (*see* Davis, Chapter 3). It can reinforce narrative accounts, or violate those continuities on which most accounts depend (*see* Zamponi, Chapter 6).

In this section, Donagh Davis's chapter seeks to demonstrate the explanatory power of the transformative event concept through an empirical case study drawn from early twentieth-century Irish history: that of the 1916 Easter Rising. Rarely considered by social scientists, this case provides a convenient testing ground for ideas about the relation between structural and conjunctural circumstance on the one hand, and contingency and volition on the other. It is also an example of how unpredictable short-term events can significantly shape history in the medium to long term. This chapter considers the 1916 Easter Rising as a highly contingent event that changed the course of Irish history, foreclosing opportunities for a peaceful settlement, and forcing an escalation of violence. It identifies 'reversal of expectations' and a 'provocation-repression-backlash' dynamic as the causal mechanisms that made this event so transformative – feeding the episode into a wider process of 'regime delegitimisation'.

Comparing ethnic conflicts in Northern Ireland, the Basque Country, and Macedonia, Joseph Ruane and Jennifer Todd argue for the importance of the multi-temporal constitution of the development, decline, and final settlement of violent conflict, and the dangers that remain when it ends. This chapter shows how an approach that interlinks short, medium, and long-term processes has not only theoretical and comparative power, but provides a better empirical explanation of the success or failure of settlement initiatives than do the wider and flatter generalisations of synchronic approaches. It shows why superficially similar settlement initiatives lead to very different outcomes at different stages of the same conflict, and why it is important to take the particularities of each case into account. Ruane and Todd suggest that, more so than short-term strategies, solving deep-set problems of legitimation is fundamental to the settlement of violent ethnic conflicts.

Patricia Steinhoff and Gilda Zwerman, relying on a sample of nearly 150 individual cases from twelve different New Left groups prosecuted in the United States and Japan between 1970 and 2010, examine temporal factors in the judicial processes and outcomes for persons prosecuted for participation in political violence. They ask whether there are clear patterns of variation in the outcomes, and whether there is any temporal logic to these variations. Their comparative analysis focuses on the sequential stages of the criminal justice process: arrest; interrogation; construction of charges; trials; sentencing structure; patterns of incarceration, and the possibilities for release offered by each country. The actual calendar period – or 'clock time' – for underground political violence and its adjudication through the criminal justice system follows different temporal patterns in the two countries (it is much longer in Japan), although they proceed through a parallel sequence of stages, with similar timing at the outset. When it comes to the severity of punishment for acts of political violence, the temporal trajectory is quite different in the two countries, and so requires employment of different explanatory concepts of temporality: 'cycles'; 'transformative events'; 'sequences', and 'cultural epochs'. Steinhoff and Zwerman thus challenge the progressive, linear, interpretation of temporality as the arrow of time.

Concluding the section on time, Lorenzo Zamponi's chapter looks at how the memory of events of both active and passive violence has an impact on collective action, and how these change over time to correspond with changes in the social and cultural environment. Zamponi identifies different specific mnemonic processes related to the contentious remembrance of episodes of political violence, namely as 'identity-shaping device'; 'proscription device', and 'depoliticisation'. The chapter draws on a critical discourse analysis of media material, as well as forty interviews with contemporary activists in Italy and Spain. Increasing the variety of episodes taken into account throughout history, this chapter places particular focus on four cases of remembered political violence from the Italian and Spanish student movements of the 1960s and 1970s: the Battle of Valle Giulia, in Rome, 1968; the Chase of Lama, in Rome, 1977; the Angelo Azzurro fire in Turin, 1977, and the death of Enrique Ruano in Madrid 1969.

In calling for a more time-sensitive investigation, we are not suggesting that we simply add another dimension to the search for data as a dependent variable (quantitative temporality), nor are we suggesting an increase of thick descriptions. In the interest of aiding analytical explanations of the unfolding of social processes and generate usable knowledge, time should, rather, be considered a 'constitutive social phenomenon' (Giddens 1984). As Paul Pierson suggests '[r]eal social processes have distinctly temporal dimensions' (2004: 5). Paying attention to issues of temporality emphasises features of political violent phenomena that are basically invisible from an atemporal point of view. Each chapter in this section introduces significant themes, which will be further developed in future research. The aim of this section is to encourage a research approach that makes the temporal context more explicit in the analysis of political violence phenomena. I conclude this short introduction with some suggestions for the productive development of future research on the temporality of political violence.

Following McAdam, Tarrow and Tilly's (2001) path-breaking work in social movement research we should seek to identify a number of robust temporal sequences of connected events – mechanisms and processes – that transcend single social settings in our research on how political violence emerges, develops and declines (Alimi, Bosi and Demetriou 2012; della Porta 2013). A process-tracing research strategy takes a middle path between that of social scientists seeking to find those conditions that favour, for example, the emergence of political violence, and the path taken by historians who are not, for the most part, interested in these kinds of causal linkages. Mechanisms are, here, the recurrent social dynamics over a variety of situations that concatenate over time to drive the process of emergency of political violence (Tilly 2001).

Instead of methods such as 'event counts' – large-N data – or 'events in history' – shifting patterns – Marshall Sahlins (1985) and William Sewell (2005) have recommended that greater attention be paid to singular transformative events capable of transforming political power configurations. Transformative events promote less determinist and non-linear explanations of contentious politics (McAdam and Sewell 2001). Armed groups, for example, can plan important transformative events, such as the September 11 attacks in the USA. They can also emerge or develop out of particular transformative events of state repression, such as Bloody Sunday in Derry, in 1972. External transformative events, such as natural disasters, can also favour decline in political violence. While recognising the importance of transformative events, we must not forget other temporalities. The same studies should also prioritise multiple temporalities, that is short-term sequences, medium-term conjunctures and long-term processes à la Braudel (1996).

Time is clearly a dimension central to explanations of the large co-evolving context in which political violence emerges, develops and declines. If unpacked, it can help refine and revise approaches to political violence. There is a need for promotion of explicit notions of time, not only in the design of empirical studies, but also for theoretical explanations.

References

Abbott, A. (2001) *Time Matters: On Theory and Method*, Chicago: University of Chicago Press.

Alimi, E., Bosi, L. and Demetriou, C. (2012) 'Relational dynamics and processes of radicalization: A comparative framework', *Mobilization*, 17(1): 7–26.

Braudel, F. (1996) *The Mediterranean and the Mediterranean World in the Age of Philip II*, Berkeley: University of California Press.

della Porta, D. (2013) *Clandestine Political Violence*, Cambridge: Cambridge University Press.

Fisher, K. M. (2013) 'Exploring the temporality in/of British counterterrorism law and law making', *Critical Studies on Terrorism*, 6(1): 50–72.

Franks, J. (2006) *Rethinking the Roots of Terrorism*, Basingstoke: Palgrave Macmillan.

Giddens, A. (1984) *The Constitution of Society*, Glasgow: University of California Press.

Lorentz, C. and Bevernage, B. (2013) *Breaking Up Time: Negotiating the Borders between Present, Past and Future*, Gottingen: Vandenhoeck & Ruprecht GmbH & Co.

Jarvis, L. (2009) *Times of Terror: Discourse, Temporality and the War on Terror*, Basingstoke: Palgrave Macmillan.

Mahoney, J. (2000) 'Path dependence in historical sociology', *Theory and Society*, 29(4): 507–48.

McAdam, D. and Sewell, W. H. (2001) 'It's about temporality: In the study of social movements and revolutions', in R. Aminzade, J. Goldstone, D. McAdam, E. Perry, W. Sewell, S. Tarrow and C. Tilly (eds) *Silence and Voice in the Study of Contentious Politics*, Cambridge: Cambridge University Press, pp. 89–125.

McAdam, D., Tarrow, S. and Tilly, C. (2001) *Dynamics of Contention*, Cambridge: Cambridge University Press.

Pierson, P. (2004) *Politics in Time: History, Institutions, and Social Analysis*, Princeton: Princeton University Press.

Rapoport, D. (2004) 'Modern terror: The four waves', in A. Cronin and J. Ludes (eds) *Attacking Terrorism: Elements of a Grand Strategy*, Washington, D.C.: Georgetown University Press, pp. 46–73.

Sahlins, M. (1985) *Islands of History*, Chicago: University of Chicago Press.

Sewell, W. H. (2005) *Logics of History: Social Theory and Social Transformation*, Chicago: University of Chicago Press.

Tilly, C. (2001) 'Historical analysis of political processes', in J. H. Turner (ed.) *Handbook of Sociological Theory*, New York: Kluwer/Plenum, pp. 567–88.

Townshend, C. (1995) 'The culture of paramilitarism in Ireland', in M. Crenshaw (ed.) *Terrorism in Context*, University Park: Pennsylvania State University Press, pp. 311–51.

Verhoeven, C. (2010) 'Time of terror, terror of time: On the impatience of Russian revolutionary terrorism', *Jahrbücher für die Geschichte Osteuropas*, Special Issue: *Terrorism in Imperial Russia: New Perspectives* LVIII(2): 254–73.

—— (Forthcoming) 'Time bombs: Terrorism, modernism, and temporality in Europe and Russia during the long nineteenth century', in C. Dietze and C. Verhoeven (eds) *The Oxford Handbook of the History of Terrorism*, Oxford: Oxford University Press.

Chapter Three

What's so Transformative about Transformative Events? Violence and Temporality in Ireland's 1916 Rising

Donagh Davis

The subject of temporality has received little systematic attention in the study of political violence, leaving certain important issues unaddressed. In cognate fields of study – in historical sociology, for example, and particularly in the literature on 'contentious politics' broadly defined, taking in social movements, revolutions, and other forms of non-institutional politics – scholars have wrestled with questions of temporality somewhat more often (Abbott 1990, 1992, 2001; Abrams 1983; Aminzade 1992; Beissinger 2002; Goldstone 1990, 1998; Griffin 1992; Mahoney 2000; Sahlins 1985, 1981; Sewell 1996, 2005; Sewell and McAdam 2001). Questions of temporality include questions such as: Why do episodes of social change or political contention occur when they do? When they do occur, are they to be explained on the basis of big, slow, and long-term social processes – the *longue durée* spoken of by Fernand Braudel (1995)? Or can they sometimes be explained as much more contingent happenings, much more sensitive to the twists and turns of short-term happenstance? How are these episodes affected by sequence, pace and duration? Is their unfolding path dependent, or determined by initial conditions?

Similar puzzles ought to apply to the specialist study of political violence, but are rarely confronted head-on. How can the timing of political violence be explained? In what proportion is political violence determined by long, medium and short-term factors? How do social tensions smouldering away in the long term beget paroxysms of violence in the short term, as well as more medium-term cycles of violence? The approaches of contentious politics scholars to temporal puzzles provide important reference points for temporally minded students of political violence. But translating these approaches to the study of political violence may require some fine-tuning.

This chapter attempts to build on one such approach, namely the 'eventful' approach, which focuses on the critical role of certain 'transformative events' in the transition from long-term processes to short- and medium-term developments (Sewell 1996, 2005; Sewell and McAdam 2001). While this approach has not been used extensively within political violence studies per se, it has gained a foothold elsewhere within the study of contentious politics. In that context it has been used notably – albeit not exclusively – to explain the significance of violent episodes such as the outbreak of revolutionary processes (Sewell 1996), making it readily adaptable to the field of political violence studies.

Nonetheless, this chapter 'tweaks' the eventful approach while applying it to a historical case study of political violence. The chapter argues that, while the transformative power of events has often been identified with their capacity to open up new possibilities, in reality episodes of political violence sometimes draw their transformative power from their capacity to *foreclose* on certain possibilities for peaceful settlement, and to impel actors down a road of violent escalation in newly dangerous circumstances that the events have themselves created or exacerbated. In turn, the chapter argues that the specific mechanisms by which events become transformative have often been left implicit or obscure, and that explicating these ought to facilitate stronger causal accounts of just how events can become transformative.

The case study the chapter turns to is that of the Easter Rising in 1916 Dublin. This insurrection by Irish rebels against British rule lasted less than a week, and was militarily crushed, but it lit the fuse for the struggle for Irish independence seen in the ensuing years, and thus ranks as one of the great transformative events of Irish history. The chapter will attempt to explain why it was transformative, arguing that the actions taken by rebels and state forces in 1916 had the cumulative effect of killing off lingering hopes of a peaceful settlement to 'the Irish question', that is, the question of how Ireland was to be governed, and whether it would attain some kind of autonomy from Britain. The chapter argues that this effect can be attributed to specific causal mechanisms unfolding in 1916, and that the transformative event of the Easter Rising can be understood as the concatenation of those causal mechanisms, which themselves hinged on the popular backlash to the state's indiscriminately brutal suppression of the Rising.

This case analysis is based on a larger doctoral research project. As a study of political violence via the methodology of qualitative historical sociology (Amenta 2009; Mahoney and Rueschemeyer 2003; Ritter, forthcoming; Rueschemeyer 2003; Sewell 2005) it draws on both primary and secondary sources in its analysis, with the former including personal testimonies of contemporaries of the Easter fighting, from eyewitnesses to participants to policymakers. The chapter's case selection comes down to two main considerations. First, while the 1916 Rising easily fits the bill of a 'transformative event', it has rarely been studied in any theoretically-minded way, making it 'fresh meat' in social science terms. Second, the chapter argues that the Rising shows there can be more to explanations of transformative events than creative interpretation of new possibilities, thus, as it were, opening the transformative events approach to creative interpretation and new possibilities.

Before considering the events of 1916 directly, the chapter will establish the theoretical basis for understanding the Easter Rising as a transformative event. After providing an overview of 'eventful' approaches to contentious politics, the idea of transformative events as conjunctures of key causal mechanisms will be outlined. After empirically applying this approach to the case of the Rising in the following section, some conclusions will be considered.

Analytical approach

Social scientists were long happy to leave 'events' to historians, preferring to study 'structure' (Sewell 2005: 197–9). It has taken the efforts of scholars such as Abbott (1990, 1992, 2001), Abrams (1983), Staggenborg (1993), Sahlins (1985, 1991), and – perhaps most importantly – Sewell (1996, 2005; McAdam and Sewell 2001) to seriously put events on the agenda of social science theory.

McAdam and Sewell (2001) call for greater attention to the temporal rhythms of the short term, and of the transformative event within the study of contentious politics, arguing that traditional overemphasis on the long and medium terms can lead to a crude structural determinism, if the implicit logical conclusion to an emphasis on long-term change processes and medium-term cycles of contention is that the latter inevitably spring from the former. McAdam and Sewell suggest that when new cycles of contention emerge, they can be far from inevitable, and in fact highly contingent upon unpredictable, short-term events.

The transformative events approach has already provided an important corrective to structurally determinist and 'temporally challenged' traditions in the study of contentious politics, but as it becomes a more established tool, it becomes time to consider possible gaps in the approach, and to consider how it might be further developed. As stated above, the focus of this chapter is to consider how the approach might be refined for the particular purpose of studying violent political events. One problem is that if the meaning of 'transformative events' is not sufficiently specified, the concept could become nebulous, and – indeed – certain recent 'eventful' writings have stretched the concept to breaking point, branding relatively quotidian political 'events' as being somehow 'transformative'. The eventful approach emerged in response to a perceived gap in causal explanations, because – as its pioneers pointed out – saying that 'long-term change processes cause cycles of contention' is not very revealing in social scientific terms. However, saying 'transformative events cause cycles of contention' is not necessarily much better. Indeed, it could be worse: at least long-term change processes demonstrate the unfolding of certain objective conditions, the tensions around which explode in new cycles of contention, even if a detailed explanation of how exactly that happens is not always forthcoming. If poorly executed, an explanation for a cycle of contention based on a transformative event might tell us still less.

Since transformative events are not magic wands, we need to specify the ways that they can be transformative. In the best work carried out on transformative events so far, some of these have been uncovered (Beissinger 2002; della Porta 2011; Ramos 2008; Sewell 1996; Staggenborg 1993). However, it is likely that more remain.

In the works of Sewell and other event-focused scholars, considerable emphasis has been placed on the capacity of events to disturb prevailing assumptions about the stability of the status quo, and to broadcast new possibilities. Scholars of the event routinely stress the role of interpretation – particularly retrospective interpretation – in this process, and emphasise the creativity and agency involved in such interpretive acts. McAdam and Sewell state that

> ... the key feature of transformative events is that they come to be interpreted as *significantly disrupting, altering, or violating taken-for-granted assumptions governing routine political and social relations*. In so doing, they serve to dramatically ratchet up (or down in the case of demobilising events...) the shared sense of uncertainty (with its partisan variants, "threat" and "opportunity") on which all broad episodes of contention depend. (2001: 110)

In this analysis, events only really become 'events' after the fact. For instance, in Sewell's seminal eventful analysis of the early stages of the French Revolution, it takes some time for the Storming of the Bastille to become the transformative event that it ultimately does. Sewell points out that while representatives of the Third Estate had initially been aghast at what happened at the Bastille, a number of contingent factors led them to retrospectively reframe the event in a radically different way. The repressive backlash they had expected from royal forces failed to happen (Sewell 1996: 854), and the conquest of the fortress seemed to infuse the streets of Paris with an air of euphoria. But when copycat acts of violence began breaking out (Sewell 1996: 856–60), certain National Assembly members hit on the rhetorical conceit of lauding the Storming of the Bastille as a legitimate act of 'revolution' (giving new meaning to an old term), while condemning subsequent violent acts as perversions of the righteous anger expressed at the Bastille (Sewell 1996: 857–9). This collective scramble over the meaning of what had happened at the Bastille led to its retrospective construction as a transformative, epoch-defining moment.

This account of eventful transformation hinges on creative interpretation, meaning making, and the evocation of new possibilities. However, this does not exhaust the ways that events can be transformative. We may be able to demystify events by identifying more explicitly the particular mechanisms through which they effect change. This could be aided by drawing upon studies of causal mechanisms lying beyond the consciously 'eventful' literature. The most famous example within the field of contentious politics is that of McAdam, Tarrow and Tilly (2001) who, in turn, drew on authors outside this field such as Merton (1968), Elster (1989) and Stinchcombe (1991). Such a turn towards mechanisms might allow us to open up the study of events to different possibilities as to how they effect change. Indeed, this chapter will argue that mechanisms are as capable of closing down certain possibilities as opening up others, and that this can be an important source of events' power to upset social life.

One way to look at events could be as crux moments when certain critical causal mechanisms conjoin. This does not mean that the category of the event is superfluous, or that events are just 'normal' causal mechanisms by another name.

Rather, it is to suggest that events may comprise particularly dense concentrations of such mechanisms, unfolding in particularly rapid succession, and that this can be what makes them such exceptional happenings. Beissinger (2002) has referred to periods when the pace of events seems to speed up as 'thickened history'. Following this logic, we might say that transformative events are the thickest coagulations within this.

Mechanisms and events

Identifying causal mechanisms is one of the many techniques in the social scientists' toolbox. Mechanisms are the observable cause–effect relationships between particular occurrences and their consequences, and identifying them allows social scientists 'to fill in the void (the 'black box') left when general effects are imputed to general causes' (della Porta and Keating 2008: 13). Though attention to causal mechanisms is not new, the approach has seen something of a resurgence in recent years, arising from the complaint that other types of causal explanation in the social sciences often fail to truly 'causally explain' very much, veering wildly from 'thick description' of micro-level phenomena – often poorly connected to the macro-level – to broad gestures at explanation of macro-level phenomena that identify correlations between variables, while often failing to find what joins these variables up. As an explanatory mode of the middle range, between the micro and the macro, the search for causal mechanisms steps into this gap.

In studies explicitly concerned with causal mechanisms, the salience of events is often left implicit, or taken for granted. But when it is made explicit, it becomes clear that causal mechanisms are inseparable from events, with the latter initiating, reflecting, and (sometimes) stopping and reversing particular causal mechanisms in their tracks. McAdam *et al.* (2001: 24), in the most sustained book-length study of mechanisms in contentious politics, identify mechanisms as 'a delimited class of events that alter relations among specified sets of elements in identical or closely similar ways over a variety of situations'. This is a rather different vision of events from that of Sewell. For while Sewell emphasises the subtle and contingent acts of (often ex post facto) interpretation that give events their meaning, McAdam *et al.* suggest that events are connected to powerful and dynamic cause–effect relationships that can be found recurring in similar ways from one context to another.

That is not to say that, following McAdam *et al.*'s line of thought, events cannot involve contingency or interpretation. But it is to give contingency and interpretation a different accent. For Sewell, action is contingent, and so are the interpretations and/or repercussions of that action. If we focus on mechanisms, however, we could see action as contingent, but its effects as *sometimes predictable*, or at least as pointing towards a handful of potential paths that are roughly identifiable in advance.

For instance, if the peasants of the kingdom come to the king's palace with a petition of their grievances, and the king responds by slaughtering half the peasants, two possible outcomes spring to mind: the remaining peasants may be so terrorised that they turn their backs on any form of dissent indefinitely; or they may feel that they have no option but to engage in open rebellion, and to try to kill the king. Which path is taken depends on many factors but the important point is that if the peasants respond with rebellion, then attributing this to their creative retrospective interpretation of the king's slaughter of their peers would be a weak explanation indeed. Much better would be to see the peasants' response as reflecting one of a number of familiar mechanisms seen repeatedly in contentious politics – namely a response to severe repression that backfires by driving actors over the edge and into outright rebellion (Goodwin 2001).

The scenario of the above thought experiment is highly schematic, and reality tends to be more complicated. But in however complicated ways, such mechanisms do play important roles in social life, and are seen again and again. These mechanisms can be sparked by individual, short-term, contingent events. And while the word 'event' is thoroughly ambiguous, we might say that the difference between an 'event', and a 'great transformative event' is simply that the latter is a conjuncture of particularly consequential causal mechanisms, unfolding in rapid succession.

Identifying mechanisms

There is no scholarly consensus as to a finite list of causal mechanisms to be found in social life, and hence no definitive 'periodic table' of relevant mechanisms to draw upon. While many different mechanisms can potentially be read into the story of Ireland's 1916 Rising and subsequent independence struggle, this chapter focuses on two key mechanisms. Suggesting that it was the interaction of these mechanisms that drove the cycle of contention seen in the Irish independence struggle, this chapter shows that these mechanisms were catalysed by the contingent event of the 1916 Rising.

One of those had already been swinging into motion prior to the Rising. This mechanism can be called 'reversal of expectations', and entails the widespread sense of betrayal and breach of trust experienced by the nationalist majority in Ireland as they came to the conclusion that their hopes and expectations of limited Irish autonomy within the UK ('Home Rule') were being skewered by the bad faith of the British government.

This was the direct result of British policy decisions made from 1914 on (Jackson 1997; Lustick 1991; Wilson 1985), and for some Irish nationalists, this sense had already started to set in before the 1916 Rising. But that event – along with another particular causal mechanism it set in motion – was key in crystallising this breakdown of hopes, expectations, and trust for the majority.

The Rising also set in motion the single most central mechanism of the Irish independence struggle, here referred to as the mechanism of 'provocation–repression–backlash'. The armed insurrection of the 1916 rebels was calculated as the most provocative action possible to take against the British state, and the British state responded by terminating the Rising 'with extreme prejudice'. Through its harsh response to the Rising – executing rebel leaders, interning thousands, and exacting heavy collateral damage on the city and its inhabitants – the British state cast itself in the role of brutal oppressor in the eyes of the Irish nationalist majority watching the devastation of Easter 1916 unfold. The Home Rule project – already on life support by 1916 – now looked moribund, and its sponsors, the moderate constitutional politicians of the Irish Parliamentary Party (IPP), suddenly looked irrelevant. The rebels, meanwhile, looked like rash but brave upstarts in a David and Goliath struggle against the might of the British Empire and, given the now superfluous appearance of the IPP in a newly militarised situation, the rebels also looked like the only show in town.

These mechanisms were related, but distinct. To be more precise: while one of them, that of 'reversal of expectations', was already incubating prior to the 1916 Rising, that contingent event – along with the further mechanism of 'provocation–repression–backlash' that it unleashed – accentuated the former mechanism exponentially. Thus, the two mechanisms intwined and catalysed one another, with explosive effect. As suggested above, this is what made the Easter Rising a transformative event: the conjuncture of a number of particularly powerful causal mechanisms reacting upon one another with force.

McAdam *et al.* suggest that groups of mechanisms can combine to form larger processes – phenomena that are simply too 'big' to be usefully conceptualised as individual mechanisms (McAdam *et al.* 2001: 27). From the perspective of this chapter, the mechanisms of 'reversal of expectations' and 'provocation–repression–backlash' would go on to feed into a wider process of 'regime delegitimization' that would – along with certain other mechanisms – be of decisive importance for the duration of the independence struggle, and these mechanisms would continue to be reproduced and accentuated during the following years. However, the focus of this chapter is on the 1916 event that started this sequence, leaving the discussion of what followed for another occasion.

Ireland 1916

In Irish historiography and popular understanding alike, the 'Easter Rising' of 1916 has traditionally been understood as what might be called a 'transformative event without the theory'. The reasons it has implicitly been understood in this way are clear enough, for while British colonialism in Ireland had been fuelling political and social conflict for centuries (Canny 2001; Cleary 2007; Lenihan 2008), and a self-consciously nationalist movement had been calling for greater Irish autonomy since the late 1700s (Whelan 1996), it was only after the Easter Rising that British rule in Ireland would for the first time be seriously challenged. The event marked a decisive break between an era of lukewarm Irish nationalism led by the IPP in their pursuit of Home Rule, and the era when leadership of Irish nationalism passed to a much more militant and separatist cadre. Arising from relative obscurity in the milieu of radical nationalism – and in particular in the secret society within that known as the Irish Republican Brotherhood (IRB) or 'Fenians' (Garvin 1987; Kee 1976) – this cadre was able to marshal the support of a critical mass of the Irish populace for an armed struggle against British rule that would lead to the partition of Ireland in 1920, and the foundation of a new Irish state by as soon as 1922: a remarkable turnaround in the affairs of Ireland and Britain, even if the new state encompassed only five sixths of the island of Ireland, the rest (Northern Ireland) remaining within the UK.

These developments were scarcely imaginable before the 1916 Rising. Thus, the Rising marked the fateful moment when long-term processes met with certain political tensions that had been brewing in the medium term, and when the resultant political conjuncture was catalysed by the contingent, short-term action of the 1916 rebels, launching a new cycle of violent contention.

The long-term processes in the background of the political conjuncture of 1916 had to do with the struggles between different social blocs in the deeply divided society of Ireland under British rule. On the surface, the major cleavage in Irish society was religious, but more importantly, 'Catholic' overwhelmingly denoted people of roughly indigenous or 'mestizo' origins, while 'Protestant' overwhelmingly reflected colonial settler roots (Cleary 2007; Crotty 1986). Catholics were more numerous, but subordinate. However, thanks to profound changes in the demographic and socio-economic structures of Ireland since the upheaval of the 1840s famine, Catholics – and most importantly the Catholic middle classes – were growing in clout and assertiveness by the late nineteenth century (Cullen 1976; Whelan 1999). Seeking political recognition, Catholics en masse backed the Home Rule project of the IPP from the late 1800s on.

By the pre-World War I years, the Liberal government of the UK looked set to grant Home Rule. But deep problems arose when it became clear that Protestants in Ulster – the northern part of the island, where Protestants outnumbered Catholics – were determined to resist Home Rule by any means, seeing in it a reversal of their traditional domination of Catholics. Sensing trouble, the British government considered imposing Home Rule on the Ulster Protestants by force, but balked at the last minute (Lustick 1991: 308–12). When World War I broke out in 1914, the government used it as an excuse to suspend the implementation of Home Rule, already on the statute books but now on ice, ostensibly until the conclusion of the war.

The IPP leadership gambled on the British government acting in good faith, and supported the war effort, even urging their supporters to show their loyalty to Britain by enlisting to fight. Many did, and it was over the next year and a half, as both Irish nationalists and Ulster unionists fought and died in Europe, that the political conjuncture that would incubate the 1916 Easter Rising took shape. As the war dragged on longer than expected, it became increasingly unpopular in nationalist Ireland. The longer it continued, the further away seemed Home Rule. The mood in Catholic and nationalist Ireland became volatile and ambivalent, but the challengers to the hegemony of the IPP still looked weak. All that was certain was that the conjuncture of long-term structural processes and medium-term political manoeuvring made for what Charles Tilly (1978) might have called a political 'traffic jam': a three-way standoff between the Irish nationalists, the Ulster unionists, and the British government, from which there was no obvious or easy way out. This tense impasse was only shattered by a dramatic contingent event, when a small and politically marginal group of separatists launched a surprise insurrection in Dublin at Easter 1916.

Members of the IRB had infiltrated the Irish Volunteers, a nationalist militia founded in 1913 as a counterweight to the armed mobilisation of unionists in Ulster, and one of the very few mass nationalist groupings beyond the control of the IPP. On Easter Monday, under cover of Volunteer manoeuvres, and in spite of the attempts of other Volunteer leaders to stop them, IRB men among the Volunteer officer corps ordered their men into action. By afternoon, up to 1,600 Volunteers and other militants had occupied several landmark Dublin buildings and other prominent positions around the capital (McGarry 2010: 120), chief among them being the General Post Office, where the rebels set up their headquarters. It was outside the GPO that the rebels read out to bemused passers-by the Proclamation of the Irish Republic, with the rebel leaders being named its Provisional Government.

Amazingly, despite numerous telltale signs that trouble of some sort was brewing – not least the interception of a German arms ship destined for the rebels in the previous days – the authorities had apparently made no preparations to contain a possible revolt. Thus, the rebels took their objectives with relatively little force, and only a handful of casualties. Even Dublin Castle, the seat of British government in Ireland, was all but defenceless, and was almost captured by a small group of rebels in an ultimately botched attack (Townshend 2005: 100).

The authorities might have been caught unprepared by the Rising, but their response, when it came, was robust. Martial law was declared, and British Army recruits on their way from Britain to France were redirected to Ireland. Soon Dublin was flooded with about 16,000 troops (Townshend 2005: 191). Intense firefights raged in parts of the city, while the Army deployed heavy artillery, and even a gunboat, to shell the main rebel positions. Rebels in well-chosen positions were able to inflict painful losses on British troops. But under heavy bombardment, the Rising could only last so long.

Remarkably, the rebels held out under the Army's superior firepower for the better part of a week. On Saturday, after several hundred deaths, with much of the city centre now in ruins, and with the main rebel garrison fallen, rebel leader Pearse issued orders to surrender, citing the Provisional Government's intention to 'prevent the further slaughter of Dublin citizens' (Kiberd 1998: xii). More than 3,000 people were initially arrested, and about 1,500 sent to prisons and camps in Britain under emergency powers, some of them uninvolved in the fighting. Fifteen were executed in the weeks (and in once case months) following the Rising, including all of the main ringleaders.

Dublin had been quite literally transformed by the Rising: beforehand, Ireland was still relatively peaceful, relatively far removed from the ravages of World War I. Afterwards, the centre of her capital was a bombed-out warzone. However, the real changes effected by the Rising would take some time to become visible. Though initial popular reactions to the Rising were famously mixed – and at times downright hostile – within months it had become clear that an overwhelming wave of sympathy for the rebels had swept nationalist

Ireland (Hart 2011), along with rage at the heavy-handed response of the British forces. This sympathy was expressed politically, and at the expense of the IPP, which quickly saw its near-monopoly on Irish nationalist politics crumble. In the UK general election of December 1910, the IPP had taken seventy-three Irish seats, and other moderate nationalists ten, with the rest (twenty) going to unionists, and a single Liberal. Separatists were not represented. In the 1918 general election, the IPP collapsed, its Irish seats dropping to six, while *Sinn Féin* – the party now squarely associated with the 1916 Rising – took seventy-three, many of them going to 1916 veterans (Mair 1987).

But there was more to the post-Easter Rising transformation than electoral upsets, and *Sinn Féin* did more than win seats: a 'dual power' situation emerged, as *Sinn Féin's* elected representatives shunned Westminster, swearing allegiance to the Irish Republic declared in 1916, and founding their own parliament and elements of a shadow state. Meanwhile, the remnants of the Volunteers gradually cohered into the 'Army of the Republic', or 'Irish Republican Army'. It was this military wing of the separatist movement that would fight the 1919–21 guerrilla war that would lead to partial Irish independence. Thus, the 1916 Rising was the event that decisively brought an end to business as usual in Irish politics, and that set in motion the sequence that would lead to Irish partition, and to the founding of the Irish Free State.

Violence and transformation

How can this transformation – one hinging on a seismic shift in popular sentiment – be explained? This has been the subject of considerable debate among historians and other commentators. But the parameters of the debate are limited. It is widely taken for granted that the unpopular post-Rising executions were a key factor in shifting the public mood, and the 'common wisdom' explanation of the change effected by the Rising could be summed up – not too uncharitably – as 'the decision to slowly and callously execute the fifteen rebels moved the public from opposition to sympathy for the rebels'.

While it is universally acknowledged that the executions were significant for the change in the public mood, what historians have tended to debate is the extent of that change: whether it was really as stark as has often been portrayed, or whether it was more of a 'crystallisation' than a true transformation, as the historian Joseph Lee (1989: 36) famously put it.

This discussion is remarkable for what it leaves out. Remarkably little attention is paid to the fact that the number of executed rebels pales in comparison to the civilian death toll of the Rising. At least 254 civilians were killed – the vast majority almost certainly by British forces – dwarfing the sixty-four rebels and 132 soldiers and police killed in action during the Rising (Foy and Barton 2011: 271). Partly because of inattention from historians, and partly because they were never properly investigated – or were covered up – the details of the circumstances of many of these killings remain obscure. But some key facts can be pieced together.

Although the rebels apparently assumed that British forces would not use artillery against them (Townshend 2005: 98), seeing it as unthinkable in a major UK population centre, in fact the army lost little time in despatching field guns and even a gunboat to Dublin. Soon the centre of the city was in ruins and – inevitably – rebel positions were not the only ones hit, with at least 179 buildings being destroyed (Foy and Barton 2011: 270).

The decision to use artillery in an urban population centre showed a wilful disregard for civilian life, with heavy collateral damage being an inevitable result of these tactics. But such disregard did not stop there. The street-fighting of Easter Week represented a type of combat little known to the officers and men of the British Army, trained – in many cases only barely – for the trenches and battlefields of France. Orders were given to troops not to advance beyond any building from which they came under fire, until its occupants had been 'destroyed' (McGarry 2010: 168). British troops paid dearly for this policy, as at Mount Street Bridge, where a handful of well-placed rebel snipers killed or wounded more than 200 soldiers under orders to take the bridge 'at all costs' (McGarry 2010: 172–3). But civilians paid a still heavier price. The concentration of artillery, armoured cars and machine guns on city streets left civilians highly vulnerable (Foy and Barton 2011: 248). During savage house-to-house fighting in residential North King Street, at least thirteen civilians were killed in their homes under highly suspicious circumstances. Some of the bodies were hastily buried at the scene, with some evidence pointing to execution-style reprisal killings carried out by British troops after they had secured the area (McGarry 2010: 187).

Many other civilians were simply cut down in crossfire, shot at their windows by troops scouring for rebel snipers, or killed by trigger-happy soldiers confused by orders not to take prisoners, and by warnings that rebels might be dressed as civilians. Evidence of the circumstances of these killings is fragmentary but the various eyewitness accounts that do survive are suggestive of the kind of chaotic and deadly environment in which a civilian death toll in the hundreds becomes not just possible, but highly likely. A British officer recalled one of his sentries killing two young ladies because he had been told the rebels were 'dressed in all classes of clothes' (Foy and Barton 2011: 245). A Dubliner described seeing an old lady shot dead for failing to stop at a checkpoint: 'Afterwards a girl who had known her told my sister that the old woman had been stone deaf for many years' (Foy and Barton 2011: 243). And the death toll was also boosted by the behaviour of some Dublin citizens drawn towards the fighting for both entertainment and looting. Many of these died in the crossfire (Foy and Barton 2011: 254–6). More notoriously, an apparently mentally ill Anglo-Irish army officer arrested and executed several civilians entirely unconnected to the Rising (McGarry 2010: 186).

And yet perhaps the most damning indictment of the British handling of the Rising comes not from these fragmentary pieces of evidence, but from the utterances of senior British officials themselves. General Maxwell, sent to Dublin during the Rising to take over as British commander-in-chief, bridled soon afterwards at criticisms of the army's conduct at North King Street and elsewhere, making candidly clear in his report to Cabinet on 26 May what he thought about the question of collateral damage:

> No doubt in districts where the fighting was fiercest, parties of men under the great provocation of being shot at from front and rear, seeing their comrades fall from the fire of snipers, burst into suspected houses and killed such male members as were found. (Townshend 2005: 293)

Maxwell suggested that it was 'perfectly possible' that this had led to civilian deaths, but that 'the number of such incidents that have been brought to notice is happily few' (*Ibid.*). In the confidence of his wife he struck a somewhat less strident note, admitting to being 'bothered to death with these cases where soldiers are accused of having murdered innocent civilians in cold blood. I fear there have been some cases of this' (Foy and Barton 2011: 249). But his comments to British Army icon Lord Kitchener made it clear that, the inherent unpleasantness of such killing aside, civilian casualties of the order seen in Dublin – or even greater – were to his mind simply par for the course:

> It must be borne in mind in these cases that there was a lot of house-to-house fighting going on, wild rumours in circulation and owing to darkness, conflagrations, etc., apparently a good deal of 'jumpiness'. With young soldiers and under the circumstances I wonder there was not more. (*Ibid.*)

Lord French, Commander-in-Chief of British Home Forces, backed Maxwell up on this point, counselling that '"regrettable incidents" such as those you refer to are absolutely unavoidable in such a business as this'. French echoed Maxwell's view that 'the only wonder is there have been so few of them'. Referring to disquiet at Westminster over British heavy-handedness in Dublin – disquiet largely stoked by Irish nationalist MPs – French advised Maxwell that 'You must not think too much about what goes on in Parliament... We soldiers have always to put up with that.' (Townshend 2005: 293).

But try as they may to absolve themselves of responsibility, invariably laying all blame on the rebels for creating the chaos in Dublin, the high civilian death toll clearly did flow largely from specific British decisions. The decision to use heavy artillery and raze central Dublin – something they would presumably not have done had there been an armed uprising around the same time in England (not so unimaginable given the social unrest experienced in Britain a few years later, which saw troops and armour deployed to Glasgow in 1919) – was an obviously fateful British policy choice. But it was not the only one. While Maxwell might dismiss killings like those at North King Street as what happened when troops, under great pressure, 'saw red' (Foy and Barton 2011: 249), the government's expert advisor on the matter, the permanent secretary at the Home Office Sir Edward Troup, saw things differently. Reporting directly to Prime Minister Asquith on the military's handling of the Rising, he suggested that abuses had not occurred because troops were 'exasperated or reckless', but that 'the root of the mischief' lay elsewhere, in the orders of Brigadier-General William Lowe, who had been in charge of British forces until Maxwell's mid-week arrival. Troup pointed out that, based on Lowe's free interpretation of his powers under martial law, his soldiers were given 'orders not to take any prisoners, which they took to mean that they were to shoot anyone whom they believed to be an active rebel'. Troup pointed out that 'it should have been made clear that it did not mean that an unarmed rebel might be shot after he had been taken prisoner: still less did it mean that a person taken on mere suspicion could be shot without trial.' Appreciating the highly charged atmosphere in the wake of these events, Troup advised Asquith against revealing in public any more evidence of what had happened in Dublin, suggesting that 'there are many points that could be used for the purpose of hostile propaganda, and I have no doubt its publication would be followed by a strong demand for a further inquiry' from which 'nothing but harm' would arise (Townshend 2005: 294).

Troup's comments pointed to a growing unease within ruling circles about a brooding anger in Ireland at the British response to the Rising. Stories such as those of North King Street and Portobello Barracks, along with the whiff of cover-up, fed lurid rumours worthy of the Great Fear of 1789, alluding to hushed up mass killings. In the House of Commons the independent Irish nationalist MP Laurence Ginnell alleged there had been seventy-three summary executions at Richmond Barracks, with even John Dillon, deputy leader of the IPP, suggesting there was 'very considerable foundation' to the story (McGarry 2010: 280).

Discussion and conclusions

While the names of the executed fifteen were etched into the annals of Irish history, the names of the more than 250 dead civilians slipped into obscurity. However, the indifference to human life shown by British forces in pulverising the city centre could hardly have gone unnoticed in a relatively small and tight-knit city like Dublin. The smouldering shell of the city centre would be a potent reminder of the events of Easter week for some time to come. Neither would the incarceration of up to 1,500 men and women – many of them untried, others unconnected to the Rising altogether – help people in Ireland to quickly forget what had happened.

Though good data is hard to come by on how ordinary Irish people subjectively experienced all of this, the bare facts speak to a number of important themes animating many studies of insurgent movements and state violence. As in the thought experiment presented above concerning the hypothetical king's decision to slaughter large numbers of peasants when given a list of their grievances, we are familiar with the idea that harsh repression, collective punishment, and indiscriminate killing on the part of the state can be a double-edged sword. These practices can have the desired effect. Frequently, though, they do precisely the opposite: burning bridges and sowing a popular sense of injustice and resentment, to the extent that it is hard for a given state to win the people back. If hegemony rests on 'the combination of force and consent, which balance each other reciprocally' (Gramsci 1971: 80), then this is the point at which consent, such as it is, can crumble, leaving only coercion in its place – a precarious position for any ruler to be in. The dynamics surrounding repression and its sometimes unintended consequences have animated many studies of contentious politics and political violence (Earl 2006; Hess and Martin 2006; Johnston 2006; Rasler 1996; Sørensen and Martin 2014), notably forming an important plank of Goodwin's (2001) argument that revolutions tend to happen primarily when states leave their inhabitants with little choice but to fight back against the institutions that they perceive as threatening their survival. It is impossible to go into this literature in any depth here, but a handful of points are worth noting.

In their attempt to inventory the recurring components of political contention, McAdam *et al.* (2001) list repression as an important mechanism of escalation for social movements and revolutionary situations. They focus on repression in its narrowest sense, in terms of repression's effects on political actors subjected to it. McAdam *et al.* (2001: 69) define repression as *'efforts to suppress either contentious acts or groups and organizations responsible for them* [original emphasis]'. They see it as:

> ... a predictable response to contention, with relatively predictable effects – generally stiffening resistance on the part of threatened communities, encouraging evasion of surveillance and shifts of tactics by well organized actors, and discouraging mobilization or action by other parties. (*Ibid.*)

We should bear in mind – as hinted by McAdam *et al.* – that repression does not just impact on the political actors that make up its 'prime targets', and that civilians and non-combatants can get caught in the crossfire – often literally, as in the case of the Easter Rising. This is when repression blurs into collective punishment and indiscriminate state killing:

> Repression may be selective, in which case it isolates more militant groups and closes off to them prescribed or tolerated means of contention. Or it can be generalized, in which case it throws moderates into the arms of the extremists. (*Ibid.*)

But if repression can go either way, why would it have gone this way this time? While there are many roads to repression, and repression can often be a brutal response to peaceful protest, in this case it was very much provoked by the violent initiative of the rebels. Goodwin points out that when this is the case – when rebels 'start it' – the dynamic of violence can backfire on them as much as on the state:

> ... some [revolutionaries] employ violence purposely to incite or provoke the [indiscriminate] state repression that will presumably expand their ranks. But this can easily become a self-defeating strategy since the targets of such violence are likely to blame the revolutionaries as much as the state for their travails. Indiscriminate counterstate violence can produce a popular backlash as easily as state violence. (Goodwin 2001: 48–9)

Regardless of whether or not the 1916 rebels intended to provoke the state in this way, the question remains: Why did violence backfire on the state this time round, and not the rebels? McAdam *et al.* point out that while the purpose of studying mechanisms is to chart how particular phenomena recur from one case to another, this does not mean they are entirely predictable, as if bound by 'iron laws' of history; and indeed, the direction mechanisms take is often determined by other mechanisms, or more precisely, by the particular conjuncture of mechanisms found in a given scenario. Mechanisms rarely occur in exactly the same combination or sequence, guaranteeing a degree of contingency and unpredictability, depending on the mix that occurs: '... much of the contingency unfolding in our narratives results from the concatenation of different mechanisms... similar mechanisms can yield very different outcomes when they combine with other mechanisms' (McAdam *et al.* 2001: 224).

Nowhere was this truer than in 1916 Ireland. This chapter has argued that the traditional explanation for the change in popular feeling following the Rising – that hinging on the fifteen executions – is a weak one. It is not dynamic, and it treats the instance of change as a 'magic wand' moment: the executions changed public opinion simply 'because'. Instead, this chapter has suggested that a wider focus on the more general repression and state violence experienced in 1916 makes for a much more powerful explanation. However, even this cannot tell the whole story of why public opinion changed in the way that it did in 1916. For the state violence of Easter 1916 only took on the meaning it did in the context of other mechanisms working themselves out at the time, which were, in turn, acted upon by the mechanism involving backfiring repression and state violence, referred to in this chapter as 'provocation–repression–backfire'.

The intersection of these mechanisms was the meeting point between *longue durée* processes spanning decades and centuries, a medium-term political conjuncture of several years, and the catalytic injection of short-term contingency via certain critical decisions made by the rebels and their opponents on the side of the state.

Long-term developments meant that by the years leading up to 1916, some kind of confrontation between unionists and nationalists over Ireland's political fate was inevitable. In the medium term, in turn, the British government's decision to dilute its commitment to Home Rule and favour the unionists meant that in this increasingly zero-sum game, an expression of nationalist consternation was inevitable sooner or later. But it was in the short term that the highly contingent courses of action taken by the 1916 rebels, and by the British state in suppressing them, set the coordinates for low-intensity war, for Irish partition, and for the creation of the Irish Free State – developments that had been in no way inevitable prior to the 1916 Rising.

Thus, the Rising did two things in particular: by militarising the Irish question, it made the constitutional wranglings of the IPP over Home Rule – a prospect already withering on the vine – suddenly seem utterly irrelevant. And it made it dramatically harder for a critical mass of people in Ireland to dispel the feeling that they were *not* living in a state whose government, as neutral and benevolent arbiter, was honestly trying to find a solution to their problems but, rather, that they were living in a brutally oppressive and indifferent state, whose government would respond to the threat posed by marginal subversives by blowing up a major population centre, and shooting its citizens on the streets. The British response to the Rising had, as it were, been all gunboat and no diplomacy.

Part of the importance often attributed to transformative events is their capacity to open up possibilities, but the Easter Rising was as much about foreclosing on possibilities: when the centre of Dublin went up in flames, with it went what was left of the IPP's Home Rule project. Home Rule was supposed to provide a way out of long-term, intractable Irish problems. Without it, or a plausible constitutional alternative, stakeholders of the Irish question were left with little option but to fight. This was so striking that even the IPP leadership – those with the most to lose from the latest turn of events – could not publicly ignore the shifting of the ground beneath their feet. In parliament, John Dillon – an arch-nemesis of the separatists – incensed his House of Commons colleagues by charging the government with unleashing 'a sea of blood... a river of blood, that is washing away our whole life's work' (Townshend 2005: 282). Dillon pointed out that thousands of people in Dublin 'who ten days ago were bitterly opposed to the whole Sinn Fein [sic] movement and the rebellion, are now becoming infuriated against the government' (Townshend 2005: 281). The brutal British response to the Rising, then, militarised the Irish question, marginalised the moderates of the IPP, and suddenly – albeit somewhat paradoxically – gave ordinary people a reason to look upon the erstwhile marginal separatists with both sympathy and respect. Long-term and medium-term developments had placed Ireland at a crossroads. In the short term, the contingent event of the Rising sent the country hurtling down a road to rupture, partition, and civil war.

References

Abbott, A. (1990) 'Conceptions of time and events in social science methods: Causal and narrative approaches', *Historical Methods,* 23(4): 140–50.

— (1992) 'From causes to events: Notes on narrative positivism', *Sociological Methods and Research,* 20(24): 428–55.

— (2001) *Time Matters: On Theory and Method,* Chicago: University of Chicago Press.

Abrams, P. (1983) *Historical Sociology,* Ithaca: Cornell University Press.

Amenta, E. (2009) 'Making the most of an historical case study: Configuration, sequencing, and casing, and the U.S. old-age pension movement', in D. Byrne and C. C. Ragin (eds) *The SAGE Handbook of Case-Based Methods*, Thousand Oaks, CA: Sage, pp. 351–66.

Aminzade, R. (1992) 'Historical sociology and time', *Sociological Methods and Research,* 20(24): 456–80.

Bartlett, T. (1991) 'The rise and fall of the Protestant nation, 1690–1800', *Éire-Ireland,* 26(2): 7–18.

Beissinger, M. (2002) *Nationalist Mobilization and the Collapse of the Soviet State,* Cambridge: Cambridge University Press.

Braudel, F. (1995) *The Mediterranean and the Mediterranean World in the Age of Philip II*, Berkeley: University of California Press, 2 vols.

Canny, N. (2001) *Making Ireland British, 1580–1650,* Oxford: OUP.

Cleary, J. (2007) *Outrageous Fortune: Capital and Culture in Modern Ireland,* Dublin: Field Day Publications.

Crotty, R. (1986) *Ireland in Crisis: A Study in Capitalist Colonial Undevelopment,* Dingle, Co. Kerry and Wolfeboro, New Hampshire: Brandon Book Publishers.

Cullen, L. M. (1976) *An Economic History of Ireland Since 1660,* London: Batsford.

della Porta, D. (2011) 'Eventful protest, global conflicts: Social mechanisms in the reproduction of protest', in J. Goodwin and J. M. Jasper (eds) *Contention in Context: Political Opportunities and the Emergence of Protest,* Stanford: Stanford University Press, pp. 256–76.

della Porta, D. and Keating, M. (eds) (2008) *Approaches and Methodologies in the Social Sciences: A Pluralist Perspective,* Cambridge: CUP.

Earl, J. (2006) 'Introduction: Repression and the social control of protest', *Mobilization,* 11(2): 129–43.

Elster, J. (1989) *Nuts and Bolts for the Social Sciences,* Cambridge: CUP.

Foy, M. and Barton, B. (2011) *The Easter Rising,* Stroud, Gloucestershire: The History Press.

Garvin, T. (1987) *Nationalist Revolutionaries in Ireland, 1858–1927,* Oxford: Oxford University Press.

Goldstone, J. A. (1990) 'Sociology and history: Producing comparative history', in H. J. Gans (ed.) *Sociology in America,* Newbury Park, CA: Sage, pp. 275–92.

—— (1998) 'Initial conditions, general laws, path dependence, and explanation in historical sociology', *American Journal of Sociology*, 104(3): 829–45.

Goodwin, J. (2001) *No Other Way Out: States and Revolutionary Movements, 1945–1991*, Cambridge: Cambridge University Press.

Gramsci, A. (1971) *Selections from the Prison Notebooks*, New York: International Publishers.

Griffin, L. J. (1992) 'Temporality, events, and explanation in historical sociology: An introduction', *Sociological Methods and Research*, 20(24): 403–27.

Hart, P. (2011) 'What did the Easter Rising really change?', in T. E. Hachey (ed.) *Turning Points in Twentieth-Century Irish History*, Dublin: Irish Academic Press, pp. 7–20.

Hess, D. and Martin, B. (2006) 'Repression, backfire, and the theory of transformative events', *Mobilization*, 11(2): 249–67.

Jackson, A. (1997) 'British Ireland: What if home rule had been enacted in 1912?', in N. Ferguson (ed.) *Virtual History*, New York: Basic Books, pp. 175–227.

Johnston, H. (2006) '"Let's get small": The dynamics of (small) contention in repressive states', *Mobilization*, 11(2): 195–212.

Kee, R. (1976) *The Bold Fenian Men (The Green Flag, Volume II)*, London: Quartet.

Kiberd, D. (1998) *1916 Rebellion Handbook*, Boulder CO: Mourne River Press/ Roberts Rinehart.

Lee, J. J. (1989) *Ireland, 1912–1985: Politics and Society*, Cambridge: CUP.

Lenihan, P. (2008) *Consolidating Conquest: Ireland, 1603–1727*, London: Pearson Longman.

Lustick, I. S. (1991) *Unsettled States, Disputed Lands: Britain and Ireland, France and Algeria, Israel and the West Bank-Gaza*, Ithaca: Cornell University Press.

Mahoney, J. (2000) 'Path dependence in historical sociology', *Theory and Society*, 29(4): 507–48.

Mahoney, J. and Rueschemeyer, D. (eds) (2003) *Comparative Historical Analysis in the Social Sciences*, Cambridge: Cambridge University Press.

Mair, P. (1987) *The Changing Irish Party System: Organisation, Ideology and Electoral Competition*, London: Francis Pinter.

McAdam, D., Tarrow, S. and Tilly, C. (2001) *Dynamics of Contention*, Cambridge: Cambridge University Press.

McAdam, D. and Sewell, W. H., Jr. (2001) 'It's about time: Temporality in the study of social movements and revolutions', in S. Tarrow, R. Aminzade, D. McAdam, W.H. Sewell, Jr., J. Goldstone, E.J. Perry and C. Tilly (eds) *Silence and Voice in the Study of Contentious Politics*, Cambridge: Cambridge University Press, pp. 89–125.

McGarry, F. (2010) *The Rising: Ireland: Easter 1916*, Oxford: Oxford University Press.

Merton, R. K. (1968) 'The self-fulfilling prophecy', in *Social Theory and Social Structure*, New York: The Free Press.

Moore, A. (2011) 'The eventfulness of social reproduction', *Sociological Theory*, 29(4): 294–314.

Ramos, H. (2008) 'Opportunity for whom?: Political opportunity and critical events in Canadian Aboriginal mobilization, 1951–2000', *Social Forces*, 87(2): 795–823.

Rasler, K. (1996) 'Concessions, repression, and political protest in the Iranian Revolution', *American Sociological Review*, 61(1): 132–52.

Ritter, D. P. (Forthcoming) 'Comparative historical analysis', in D. della Porta (ed.) *Methodological Practices in Social Movement Research*, Oxford: Oxford University Press, pp. 97–116.

Rueschemeyer, D. (2003) 'Can one or a few cases yield theoretical gains?', in J. Mahoney and D. Rueschemeyer (eds) *Comparative Historical Analysis in the Social Sciences*, Cambridge: CUP, pp. 305–66.

Sahlins, M. (1985) *Islands of History*, Chicago: University of Chicago Press.

—   (1991) 'The return of the event, again: With reflections on the beginnings of the Great Fijian War of 1843 to 1855 between the kingdoms of Bau and Rewa', in A. Biersack (ed.) *Clio in Oceania: Toward a Historical Anthropology*, Washington, DC: Smithsonian Institution Press, pp. 37–100.

Sewell, W. H., Jr. (1992) 'A theory of structure: Duality, agency, and transformation', *The American Journal of Sociology*, 98(1): 1–29.

—   (1996) 'Historical events as transformations of structures: Inventing revolution at the Bastille', *Theory and Society*, 25(6): 841–81.

—   (2005) *Logics of History*, Chicago: University of Chicago Press.

—   (2008) 'The temporalities of capitalism', *Socio-Economic Review*, 6(3): 517–37.

Sørensen, M. J. and Martin, B. (2014) 'The dilemma action: Analysis of an activist technique', *Peace & Change*, 39(1): 73–100.

Staggenborg, S. (1993) 'Critical events and the mobilization of the pro-choice movement', *Research in Political Sociology*, 6: 319–45.

Stinchcombe, A. L. (1991) 'The conditions of fruitfulness of theorizing about mechanisms in social science', *Philosophy of the Social Sciences*, 21(3): 367–88.

Tilly, C. (1978) *From Mobilization to Revolution*, New York: Random House.

Townshend, C. (2005) *Easter 1916: The Irish Rebellion*, London: Penguin.

Whelan, K. (1999) 'Economic geography and the long-run effects of the Great Irish Famine', *The Economic and Social Review*, 30(1): 1–20.

—   (1996) *The Tree of Liberty: Radicalism, Catholicism and the Construction of Irish Identity*, Cork: Cork University Press.

Wilson, R. (1985) 'Imperialism in crisis: The Irish dimension', in M. Langan and B. Schwarz (eds), *Crises in the British State, 1880–1930*, Birmingham: Hutchinson University Library/Centre for Contemporary Cultural Studies, pp. 151–78.

Chapter Four

Multiple Temporalities in Violent Conflicts: Northern Ireland, the Basque Country and Macedonia[1]

Joseph Ruane and Jennifer Todd

Ethnic conflicts are multi-layered and multi-temporal in their causality.[2] To understand the meaning, function and consequences of violence in these conflicts we are required to place them in their historical, as well as spatial and relational, contexts. In this chapter we compare three conflicts: the Northern Irish, the Macedonian, and the conflict in the Basque Country.[3] We show how in each case longer-term structures and processes defined the shape of the conflict, constrained the options of its parties, informed the meanings of violence, shaped the conditions under which agreed settlement became possible as well as the dangers that remain even after agreement is reached.

After an initial clarification of concepts and claims we examine each case, showing the multi-temporal constitution of violent conflict, its course and ending, and the significance of the agreed settlement. This provides the basis for an analytical comparison of the role of violence in each case. It shows that the course of violent anti-state conflict is not determined simply by military logic and resources. In these cases, its capacity to produce socio-political change was directly dependent on the existence of historically deep cleavages and embedded patterns of governance that gave it a wider legitimation and, for a period, effectiveness. In each case, violence was marginalised only by costly interventions at these levels.

Multiple temporalities in conflict processes

Violence within ethnic conflicts typically emerges in response to contingent short-term opportunities and threats, although it may then assume a logic of its

1. Acknowledgements to the Irish Research Council for the Humanities and Social Sciences and the Irish Department of Foreign Affairs for funding the Patterns of Conflict Resolution project 2010–11, and to co-participants, in particular to Lidija Georgieva, Ardit Memeti, Ali Musliu and Pascal Pragnere, and more recently to Roland Gjoni. We thank the editors of this volume for comments on an earlier draft.
2. We use the term 'ethnic conflict' in a broad sense to mean any intra-state conflict with a social basis in a culturally differentiated population.
3. The Republic of Macedonia is a recently formed independent state with a population of about two million. The autonomous community of the Basque Country is a self-governing region within Spain, with a population of 2.2 million. Northern Ireland is a devolved region of the United Kingdom with a population of 1.8 million.

own (Laitin 2007; Kalyvas 2006). Much of the effort in conflict resolution goes into stopping cycles of violence and counter-violence (Zartman 1989; Hartzell and Hoddie 2007; Mattes and Savun 2010). These cycles, however, arise out of longer-term processes. For example, processes of nation state consolidation with a build-up of coercive capacity and practices of territorial governance that are implicitly or explicitly biased against one or another group, give incentive to violence, which is taken up when the opportunity arises (Wimmer 2002, 2013; Malesevic 2013). These processes are, in turn, shaped by slowly changing patterns of demography and economy, spatial relations, and identity (Flora 1999).

An adequate explanation of the course of any particular conflict, including its violent episodes, requires contextualisation at each of its constitutive levels (Bosi *et al.* Chapter One in this volume). It also requires identification of the interrelations of these levels. Most generally, longer-term structures set limits for shorter-term processes, embedding horizontal inequalities between populations, defining constraints on reform and compromise, and thus providing more or less strong incentives for conflict and violence. For example, whether or not a march turns violent, a social movement becomes radicalised, or a single episode of violence escalates into a society-wide one is largely determined by middle range social institutions and longer-term social structures.[4] Contextualising action and choice in embedded structural contexts of different temporal depth reveals how different layers of the past shape the present and do so not just through 'mythical' perceptions and ideologies but also through real social processes and structural relations that limit available choices and define likely outcomes.

While slow moving, these long-term structures are themselves in a process of change, with their own moments of transition – what Katznelson (2003) calls critical junctures – when more radical possibilities for change and settlement open up. At this point, intervention can have a radical impact, sometimes determining the form of an emerging path. In the case studies that follow we show the varying effects of actions and interventions – be they violent episodes or settlement initiatives – on the slower moving patterns that converged to make conflict likely.

Violence is typically conceived in terms of insurgent or military action, but it is also a characteristic of coercive institutions and the cultural and structural relations they uphold. As action, violence has lasting social consequences when it embeds itself at these deeper levels, for example by creating spatial, social or cultural inequalities that are then stabilised by coercive power. In specific circumstances, violent action may help undo such structures of coercion, thus opening up the possibility of constructing relationships of a less contentious kind.

---

4. For example, both Wright (1987) and della Porta (2013) show comparatively that state structures and embedded practices affect whether or not protest movements become violent. Brass (1998) shows the role of embedded habits of policing and politics and Varshney (2002) the role of cross-community institutions in rioting and the spread of violence. Stewart (2014) shows the impact of horizontal inequalities on the likelihood of violent conflict.

Through the case studies we ask how far and when violence shifted a society from the path it was already on, and whether it impacted upon long-term as well as short-term processes.

This approach has implications for the ending of violence and the achievement of political agreements. Common explanations of the end of violence focus on short-term factors such as military defeat of terrorism (Bew *et al.* 2009) or military stalemate (Zartman 1989). Political settlement is typically explained in terms of short-term strategies such as confidence building, or particular institutional innovations such as power-sharing (Hartzell and Hoddie 2007). Yet if longer-term relations, inequalities, and structural processes underlie conflict, intervention in these helps to achieve settlement. There is evidence that in protracted conflicts the actors themselves – including the militants – judge the significance of short-term setbacks or opportunities in light of longer-term trends (see, for example, Tonge *et al.* 2011). In the case studies that follow we show that intervention in long-term processes helps in achieving settlement.

European temporalities

We have chosen to compare three conflicts – in Northern Ireland, the Basque Country and Macedonia – that differ in their geo-political and geo-historical context; in the historical depth and extent of violence; in the social and political processes that produced it, and in the form of settlement reached. At the same time, they are sufficiently similar to permit meaningful comparison. By using each to throw light on the others, our aim is to develop general insights into the role of longer-term processes in violent conflicts.

The cases we are concerned with emerged from long-term processes of state, empire, and nation-building, and later contraction and/or dissolution. In schematising this, we draw on Stein Rokkan's theoretical approach to Europe's historical development (Flora 1999: 95–273) adapting and elaborating this to distinguish three phases of post-medieval development particularly relevant to our case studies:[5]

First, the early modern period was one of state and empire formation; emergent agricultural and merchant capitalism; religious reformation and confessional division; the opening up of global trade routes, and emergence of a system of sovereign states throughout Europe and interlocking with the Ottoman Empire. Each of our cases was located at a distinctive point within three different state-empires (British, Spanish and Ottoman).

Second, the modern period saw the birth of the bureaucratic, liberal democratic nation state; industrialisation and urbanisation on a large scale; major advances in transportation and mass communication; the spread of literacy; the birth of nationalism and the emergence of bounded national societies, and differential

---

5.   For the need for both adaptation – to include states beyond Western Europe and highlight the imperial contribution – and elaboration – to the current phase of globalisation – see Ruane 2003.

processes of imperial expansion and contraction. Each of our cases was defined by the timing and manner of transformation of the state(s) to which it was subject, and the expansion and contraction in the larger state-empires to which it belonged.

Third, and finally, the contemporary period is characterised by intensifying globalisation of trade, financial flows and popular culture; the replacement of a two-bloc world by a multipolar one, and a weakening of the boundaries, autonomy and status of national societies.

We also take from Rokkan his view of modern societies as layered phenomena. Successive epochs do not create social structures and divisions anew, but draw on and incorporate the structures and institutions of the period that preceded them. Whether and to what extent these elements are changed in their functioning in the new epoch, or instead shape its development, is a matter for empirical analysis in each case.

Northern Ireland

A sustained period of violence began in Northern Ireland in 1969 and lasted until the late 1990s, resulting in over 3,500 deaths.[6] Explanations for the conflict tend to be framed in terms of short-term processes: communal mobilisation and counter-mobilisation around civil rights in the late 1960s leading to a cycle of state repression and paramilitary violence that came to a close only when the evidence of stalemate – or, on some interpretations, defeat – became overwhelming in the mid-1990s. This leaves much unexplained: why reform was not offered earlier; why the Northern Ireland regime collapsed so quickly; why the British state was for so long unable either to bring violence to an end or to broker a viable settlement amongst the Northern Ireland political parties, and why this changed in the 1990s. To answer these questions requires attention to multiple layers of structure and temporality.[7]

Multi-temporality in the constitution and reconstitution of the Northern Ireland conflict

English state building began in the medieval period and the late medieval English state was one of the most centralised in Europe. A new phase of state building began in the 1520s and was this time extended to Wales, Scotland and Ireland (Pocock 2005: 24–103). Wales was annexed during the 1530s. Scotland entered a union of Crowns in 1603 and of parliaments in 1707. Ireland, though a lordship of the English Crown from the end of the twelfth century, proved much more difficult to integrate, and was secured only by the dispossession of the vast majority of the island's native Catholic landowners and their replacement with

---

6. Both the dating of 'the conflict' and the death count are contentious, see McKittrick *et al.* 2004: 13–21.

7. The analysis below is a development of Ruane and Todd, 1996, 2007, 2014. See also Wright 1987.

Protestant settlers from England and Scotland. In Ulster in particular the process of displacement and replacement took place at all levels (Canny 2001). Political stability depended thereafter on the continued economic containment and political exclusion of the Catholic majority population, achieved by the concentration of power in British and Protestant hands.[8] This system of rule was inherently conflictual, but Catholics had, from the end of the seventeenth century, lost the capacity to challenge it, and for the British to reconstitute or reform it risked general destabilisation.

In 1798, rebellion was crushed, but potential French involvement highlighted the dangers to British security. The British government pushed through an Act of Union (1800) with the object of strengthening its control and allowing Catholic grievances to be addressed without provoking a Protestant response. However, Catholic emancipation was delayed until 1829 and was then achieved only by mass Catholic mobilisation. As the century progressed, an economic cleavage was added to the political and religious ones: the Protestant north-east prospered under the Union, developing a local version of British industrialism, while the predominantly Catholic rest of the country experienced economic dislocation, a massive famine at mid-century, and de-industrialisation. What chance there had been to persuade Catholics to accept the legitimacy of the British state had been lost: by the end of the century they had become nationalist and were demanding Home Rule as a matter of right. By contrast, the overwhelmingly Protestant Ulster unionists opposed Home Rule and mobilised militarily against any attempt to impose it on Ulster.

Home Rule was legislated for in August 1914 but its implementation was suspended for the duration of the war. Ulster unionists won (temporary) exclusion of six counties. Two years later, taking advantage of the war, radical nationalists staged a rising. It was rapidly put down, but it began a process of wider politicisation and radicalisation. Using a combination of political agitation and – after 1919 – a campaign of violence, radical nationalists made British rule unworkable. They succeeded in getting a higher degree of independence sooner than would have been achieved by parliamentary means alone. But the price was partition, with the location of the border determined by balance of forces on the island. Unionists secured their own (devolved) parliament within the United Kingdom.

The formation of Northern Ireland (1920–1) reconstituted the historic system of Catholic disadvantage with Protestant power and privilege backed by the British state. During the decades that followed, Northern Ireland achieved stability through a coercive, discriminatory and clientelist mode of government. It reproduced sectarian division and Catholic weakness, undermining any possibility of the state achieving legitimacy among Catholics. New opportunities opened up with the development of a nationally cohesive and socially egalitarian

---

8. There were crosscutting divisions within the Protestant population, so that significant democratisation in Protestant access to the means of violence coexisted with class and denominational differentiation in control of property and politics.

post-war Britain. Radicals, nationalists of different hues, and liberals in the Civil Rights Movement of the late 1960s, put the constitutional issue to one side and campaigned for reform in Northern Ireland. The movement alarmed sections of unionists who responded by counter-mobilisation, repressive policing, and loyalist attacks on civil rights marchers and Catholic neighbourhoods. The Irish Republican Army (IRA) re-emerged, first as community defenders and later as insurgents against the state. The British state supported the unionist government militarily and politically, while backing (most of) the civil rights demands. When this failed to win stability, it instituted Direct Rule from London (March 1972) thus ending unionists' political rule, but remaining reliant on them in the security forces, the civil service, and the higher reaches of the economy. Violence intensified in the years immediately following Direct Rule and continued for another quarter century.

So profound a political crisis and so rapid a descent into violence requires a multi-levelled explanation. Viewed at the local level and over the very long term, it was yet another episode in a local struggle over power, property and security that began with the period of the plantations. Viewed geo-politically, it was a manifestation of a long and uneven Catholic, political, and economic recovery that began throughout the island in the eighteenth century, continued after 1921, and in the 1960s made possible a serious challenge to the political structures of unionist dominance.

Other processes of different time-depths also helped shape the context out of which conflict had emerged: the chronic long-term failure of British institutions in Ireland to secure general legitimacy which made violence an option for all sides; the decline of the nineteenth century industrial economy of the Irish north-east and Northern Ireland's growing economic dependence on the British state; the contradictions that Catholics encountered in dealing with a state that simultaneously showed a benign (educational, welfare), discriminatory (public sector employment) and repressive (security) face; the as yet incomplete – at least in Ireland – British transition from quasi-imperial habits of indirect rule and harsh response to revolt to a state based on equal rights for all (Ruane and Todd 1996). These processes continued as the United Kingdom transformed itself from a post-imperial national society in the 1960s to a highly diversified and multi-cultural polity in the 1990s.

The significance of settlement

With Direct Rule in 1972, the British government's aims were to restore stability, this time by creating a devolved settlement that would have the support of both unionist and nationalist communities. The 'Sunningdale' experiment, agreed in December 1973 involved power sharing between moderate nationalists and moderate unionists, and an 'Irish dimension' to give formal recognition to the Irish identity of nationalists. In less than five months, the new power-sharing executive was brought down by a mass loyalist (Protestant) workers strike. It took a further quarter century for another cross-community agreement to be reached – the Good

Friday Agreement (GFA) of 1998 – this time paralleled by an end to violence and including the extremes as well as the moderates in a power-sharing executive with an Irish dimension.

Why did it take so long? How has the GFA survived when Sunningdale so quickly failed? We have argued elsewhere that the difference lies in a change in the longer-term conditions of conflict: in the repositioning of the British government in respect of the communities, and in a substantive equalisation of the communities in every field (Ruane and Todd 2007, 2014). This began with an Irish government role in policy making (the Anglo-Irish Agreement of 1985) and progressed through a strong and effective Fair Employment Policy (1989), projected reforms of security and cultural institutions (after 1998), and new channels of cross-border institution building. An internationally ratified British-Irish agreement guaranteed to enact the will of a majority in respect to constitutional (British or Irish) preference, and to respect the rights of all to be, and to be recognised as, British or Irish or both. This was a new political configuration. It meant that for the first time the structural relations of Catholic inequality and Protestant power, established by plantation, reconstituted in an urban industrial setting in the nineteenth century, and actively maintained by the British state, was being dismantled by the British government and that this was guaranteed internationally.

Violence played a role in provoking these changes. It was not, as some unionists claimed, that these were concessions to the IRA, nor were they 'figleaves' to cover the IRA's failure to achieve a united Ireland. Nor was it – as some republicans latterly claimed – that the struggle had been for 'equality' all the time. Rather, increasing public support for republicanism stimulated the Irish government to propose a new track of British-Irish policy (Todd 2014) and – in the complex processes by which the British and Irish governments planned, negotiated, and finally brokered an agreed settlement – the balance of coercive power was one element in the wider power balance that they took into account. The latter had changed such that nationalists could no longer be marginalised, nor – as an increasing 40 per cent of the population and of the voters – treated as a 'minority' whose identity and aspirations were of lesser importance than those of the 'majority'. But it remained unthinkable to force or even to try to persuade unionists to Irish unity: the destabilising potential of armed and determined loyalists remained too strong. The settlement was legitimated by a set of egalitarian and human rights principles, and a new and more open concept of sovereignty (Meehan 2014). That these finally prevailed – pushed hard by the two governments and the US in an effective negotiation process – was in part because nothing else could cope with a situation of relatively equal power balance of the two blocs, with uncertainty whether and when the demographic and political balance would shift in the future.

The historic significance of the GFA was that for the first time the British government had disengaged from its dependence on and privileged support for the Protestant community and was creating a political system open to all sections of the population and open to further change. Is this an undoing of the longer-term conditions of conflict? With a loyalist flags protest (2012), loyalist mobilisation (2013) and near political breakdown (2014), it is clear that conflict remains

(Nolan 2014). While significant structural and institutional change has taken place, cultural change – both in the everyday embeddedness of cultural division and in the public place of British and Protestant symbolism – is slow and deeply contested. The battle is over the trajectory of the society. Is the implementation process now complete and British rule here to stay? Or are the principles of the GFA iterative, requiring ongoing changes in institutions and public culture long before constitutional change becomes possible? While this continues to divide unionists and nationalists, the historic conflict is far from undone (Ruane 2014).

The Basque Country

The militant separatist group ETA began a campaign of violence against the Spanish state in 1968 with the goal of an independent and united Basque Country. The campaign ended only in 2011. This, however, is but one strand of a much broader Basque nationalist movement that has challenged the Spanish centre since the late nineteenth century. A political settlement has been in place since the Basque Statute of Autonomy was accepted by a narrow majority in 1979. There is, however, widespread dissatisfaction that this has not led to further autonomy. To understand the dynamics of nationalism in the Basque country and its internal dynamic, we have to situate it within the multi-layered processes that shaped it.

Multi-temporal processes and the constitution of conflict

As in the case of Britain, Spanish state and nation-building enjoyed uneven success.[9] It began as the expansion southwards of the northern kingdoms into territories recovered from the Moors and was completed with the conquest of Granada in 1492. The final stage was achieved by the union of the crowns of Castile and Leon. This was in principle a union of equals, but Castile was the larger and stronger partner and became the political centre into which the regions would be integrated. Resistance came mainly from Catalonia with its orientation to the Mediterranean and historic ties to France. Two rebellions ended in defeat, and the second one, in 1714, saw Catalonia stripped of its fueros (regional institutions and rights). By contrast, the Basques kept their fueros for another century and a half. Although the Basque Country also bordered France, their relationship was more fractious and they benefitted from their strategic importance in the chain of trade linking Castile with Northern Europe and the North Atlantic (Medrano 1995: 21–8).

Basque autonomy would become an issue in the nineteenth century as Spain adjusted to the loss of its empire and began its long and difficult transition to economic and political modernity. The strong and absolutist Spanish state of the eighteenth century became a battleground between rival economic interests and

---

9.   For analytical overviews, see Linz 1973; Smith and Mar-Molinero 1996: 1–30; Medrano 1995; Mees 2003.

conflicting political and religious ideologies, further complicated by political factionalism and dynastic rivalry. At issue was the degree to which the state should be centralised and the autonomy of the regions reduced; the position of the traditional elites and the question of popular political access; the burden of taxation; the wealth and power of the Church and the role of religion in Spanish society; the uneven progress of agricultural and industrial capitalism and contrasting views about how to speed it up; the conditions of national progress, and the reasons for Spanish decline (Junto and Schubert 2000; Medrano 1995: 56–68). Much of the conflict was confined to the elites, but it had broader ramifications and open conflict could trigger popular revolt.

The divisions twice converged in wars of dynastic succession (the Carlist Wars of 1833–9 and 1872–6), with rival claimants supported by the traditionalist Carlists on the one hand and by centralising liberals on the other. On each occasion the Basques sided with the Carlists for religious and economic reasons, and also – crucially – as a way of retaining their fueros. The final defeat of Carlism in 1876 resulted in the abolition of the Basque fueros, and nurtured a deep sense of Basque grievance. But also other factors contributed to the emergence of a separatist Basque nationalism. The new political and economic order opened up the Basque region to rapid industrialisation and exposed it to new class, urban-rural and cultural divisions and to an inflow of immigrants from other parts of Spain. Separatist nationalism was a reaction to this. It was conceived in a quasi-racist, ruralist, anti-centralist, and anti-capitalist form with a marked 'nostalgic' aspect and had limited appeal (Muro 2005; Conversi 1997; Mees 2004). There was, however, substantial support for Basque autonomy.

The issues that had divided Spain in the nineteenth century continued to do so in the twentieth century, given new forms and further depth by the crisis of 1898, the extension of the franchise, and the advance of industrialisation, socialism and anti-clericalism. Basque nationalists continued to press for autonomy and in the 1920s they, along with the Catalans, espoused federalism, briefly securing autonomous status in the Second Republic. By this stage the multiple lines of tension had converged into a single political opposition – for or against the Republic – and the Franco-led rebellion produced civil war, with Basques and Catalans siding with the Republic.

Franco's regime was not simply violently imposed, it was violently maintained, for reasons that were partly punitive and vindictive, and partly a response to continued conspiracy, challenge and subversion. But there was also symbolic violence in the attempt to impose a single model of Spanishness – Catholic, Castilian, traditional and imperial – on the whole of Spain (Grugel and Rees 1997). While superficially successful, in that it further diluted the regional cultures and languages, it produced a reaction that undermined any possibility of eventual success.

That reaction was the context in which ETA began its campaign of violence. The national goals that ETA set for itself came directly from the more radical versions of nineteenth century Basque nationalism, purged of its racist assumptions. It also modelled itself on Third World liberation movements. Its intention was to decolonise the Basque region, and violence was to be used to provoke the state to counter violence that would, in turn, provoke a wider Basque mobilisation. The strategy had a degree of success in the early period, and ETA played a significant role in the Spanish transition to democracy by killing Franco's designated successor Carrero Blanco and by foregrounding the urgency of the regional question. On the other hand, even a democratised Spanish centre was not willing to entertain ETA's goal of Basque independence.

Spain's 1978 Constitution was intended as a compromise that would reconcile democrats, monarchists and military, regionalists and centrists, in a democratic, unitary state and it represented the by far most radical regionalisation of any European state at the time. The regions would enjoy a high measure of autonomy that could be expanded over time, while remaining within the framework of a unitary Spanish state (Wilson and Keating 2009; Comas 2003). The Constitutional referendum of 1978 failed to secure a majority in the Basque Country but the 1979 Statute of Autonomy was supported by a narrow majority. Unlike the Constitution, it recognised the fueros, and included the right of the Basque Country to raise its own taxation before transmitting a segment to the central government. For ETA, however, this was a defeat and it continued its campaign.

The 1980s and 1990s were decades of economic and social transformation in the newly democratic Spain. The regional question was, however, far from settled and the centre resisted granting further autonomy to the strong regions, as in the 'coffee for all' decrees of the 1980s and 1990s (Comas 2003: 49–50). In the Basque Country, the PNV – usually the major party in the Autonomous Community (AC) government – enacted policies that ensured both greater economic development and greater social equality than in the rest of Spain (Goikoetxea 2013). The PNV were too weak in the central parliament to leverage concessions on further autonomy (Idoiaga 2006; Comas 2003) and even moderates remained unhappy with the autonomy achieved.

ETA violence was met by exceptional security responses from the Spanish state (Heiberg 2007: 42–3; Conversi 2010). There were also attempts to broker an end to violence, all of which failed, as much from governmental refusal to give concessions as from ETA intransigence (Idoiaga 2006; Pragnere 2011; Keating and Bray 2007; Wilson and Keating 2009). Increasing public anger with the campaign, overt opposition, falling sympathy and improved security measures, set in the context of international mediation, eventually convinced ETA to end the campaign (Heiberg 2007; Pragnere 2011). Although formally undefeated, and without concessions by the state, it declared a ceasefire in 2011 and an end to its campaign in 2012.

The significance of settlement

The search for a political settlement to the Basque conflict began with the death of Franco and was – by comparison with Northern Ireland – quickly achieved. Agreement was reached on the Statute of Autonomy in 1979. It can be seen as a compromise between two existential imperatives, with the terms of the compromise set by the balance of power between them. The Spanish state would not entertain the possibility of secession by either the Basque country or Catalonia. If by the late twentieth century the British state could declare that it had 'no selfish strategic or economic interest' in holding onto Northern Ireland,[10] in the 1970s and later, the Spanish state had both. It had a clear economic interest in retaining its two most advanced and wealthy regions, and a strategic interest in stopping a process of state contraction that had begun with the end of empire and if it continued would relegate Spain to one of Europe's small and backward states.

Basque nationalism was divided between independentists and autonomists. Its maximal goal was a unified Basque-speaking homeland. This, however, was from a weak basis: it was a region divided by an international frontier in which – even on the Spanish side – not all citizens were Basque, not all Basques were nationalist, and not all nationalists wanted independence. In the early 1980s in the Basque AC, still almost half of the population felt more Spanish than Basque, the Basque language was spoken by only a fifth of the population, and only a quarter wanted full independence (Keating 2001: 80–1; Conversi 1997: 163). Autonomy was as much as could be achieved politically.

ETA continued its campaign. But while violence became self-sustaining, it achieved little: it weakened Basque nationalism by dividing it. Meanwhile, autonomy was showing some results. Nearly half of Basques, and a full 75 per cent of young Basques, now speak Basque (Bray 2012); a distinctive Basque society and economy has been created (Goikoetxea 2013); an increasing majority identify as Basque and an increasing percentage – if still a minority – want independence.[11] Significantly, once violence ended, radical nationalism rebounded in popular support, winning over a quarter of the Basque vote in the 2011 regional elections, at the expense of the socialists, with the moderate PNV taking a similar proportion.

The end to ETA's campaign does not, therefore, mean the end of radical Basque nationalism. On the contrary, it may be strengthening at a time when the centre has been seriously damaged by the economic crisis of 2008. That crisis resurrected the perennial question of Spain's difficulty with modernisation and strengthened the Basque (and Catalan) desire for independence. The core Basque demand now is not for independence but for the right to exercise a choice about it. This is not a right that the Spanish state is currently willing to concede. If it were granted, it would introduce a new element of uncertainty. While it is not, it represents a continuing source of grievance.

---

10. Downing Street Declaration (1993), https://www.dfa.ie/media/dfa/alldfawebsitemedia/ ourrolesandpolicies/northernireland/peace-process--joint-declaration-1993-1.pdf §4, (accessed 12 November 2014).

11. Only 10 per cent feel more Spanish than Basque. Euskobarometer poll, May 2013, http://www. ehu.es/documents/1457190/1525260/EUSBAR+MAY13.pdf (accessed 31 October 2014).

Macedonia

The Macedonian-Albanian conflict is the most recent of the three conflicts and began in its present form with the breakup of Yugoslavia and the formation of the Republic of Macedonia in 1991. In 2001, after a decade of simmering conflict, an influx of refugees and fighters from neighbouring Kosovo triggered violence that lasted seven months and led to over 100 deaths. It alarmed the international powers in the region (EU, NATO and UN) and they quickly negotiated a peace settlement that remains in place. This may give the appearance of a conflict of minor proportions produced by short-term conjunctural processes and addressed by quick and effective external intervention. A longer-term view shows that while the conflict is recent, longer-term processes exacerbated it, prevented the stabilisation of settlement, and could, if not addressed, make this conflict much more serious.

Multitemporal processes and the constitution of conflict

Today's Republic of Macedonia is based on the region of Vardar Macedonia, the north-western portion of the historic region of Macedonia. The latter was a geographical rather than a cultural or political entity but it had strategic significance as a trade route from the Aegean to the Danube, and from the Black Sea to the Adriatic, which remains in place despite tensions and recent (May 2015) violence. It was already a complex weave of religions, languages and ethnicities when, in the fourteenth century it came under Ottoman rule, and the Ottomans were added to the mix (Agnew 2007). Ottoman rule was based on religion rather than ethnicity: identities were local, ethnicity was often fluid and indeterminate and frequently followed religion rather than language. Where ethnic conflict existed it was also, on occasion, outweighed by other cleavages (Braude 2013; Balalovska 2002). The decline of Ottoman power in Europe in the nineteenth century created a new situation. Greater Macedonia became a zone of interlocking great power and small state rivalry, and its historically varied ethno-religious landscape was subjected to the logic of modern competitive state and nation-building.

Greece gained independence in 1830 with French and British help. Serbia achieved autonomy in 1817 largely by its own efforts, progressing to full independence with great power support. Bulgaria secured autonomy in 1878, following the Russian defeat of the Ottomans in the war of 1876–7. All three countries were expansionary and had designs on different parts of Greater Macedonia, basing their claims on their version of its history and ethnic composition. For the Bulgarians, the fact that the peasants of Vardar Macedonia spoke a dialect of Bulgarian made them part of the Bulgarian nation; Serbians claimed it as historically part of Serbia. Greece wanted as much of Aegean Macedonia as it could Hellenise. The three states cooperated to defeat the Ottomans in the war of 1912, after which Serbia secured most of Vardar Macedonia, Greece got a large part of Aegean Macedonia, including Thessaloniki, and Bulgaria secured Pirin Macedonia, by far the smallest portion.

Bulgarian dissatisfaction led to a second Balkan War in 1913. Bulgaria attacked the combined forces of Serbia and Greece, but in doing so it triggered Romanian and Ottoman invasions to recover territory lost to Bulgaria. The outcome confirmed the earlier division, led to a further extension of Greek territory and the emergence of Albanian statehood.

As a province of Serbia, Vardar Macedonia was, after 1919, part of Yugoslavia, a period marked by both Macedonian and Albanian grievances against the Serbs (Balavovska 2002). As Yugoslavia disintegrated under German invasion, Bulgaria reasserted its claims on Vardar Macedonia and occupied most of it, with some remaining with Serbia – now under German control – or going to Albania, now under Italian control. The re-establishment of Yugoslavia in 1945 gave Macedonia national status as the Socialist Republic of Macedonia, reframing historical tensions between Slavs, Serbs and Albanians within a narrower Macedonian-Albanian compass, although also diffusing them by means of Albanian cultural rights and mobility within Yugoslavia.

In 1991, as Yugoslavia began to break up, the parliament of the Socialist Republic of Macedonia declared the right of its citizens to determine their future. Independence was overwhelmingly supported by referendum in September 1991, and parliament approved the constitution of the new sovereign Republic of Macedonia in Novemeber. It faced external as well as internal challenges. Greece recognised its claims to statehood but objected to its name, preventing its admission to the UN under that title (Risteska and Daskalovski 2011; Vancovska 2013). By 1994 it was subjecting Macedonia to a trade blockade. Bulgaria recognised the new state, but by refusing to regard its language as separate from Bulgarian it implicitly questioned the Macedonian status as a separate nation. Serbia raised similar doubts about the Macedonian claim to nationhood and delayed recognition until 1995. Albania recognised it but objected to its relegation of Albanian citizens to secondary status (Engström 2002).

The challenge from within came from the Albanian population who refused to participate in the census of 1991, contested the results, and boycotted the referendum on independence in protest against the secondary status they were being accorded within the new state (Risteaka and Daskalovski 2011). That status was most evident in the preamble to the new constitution, which declared the state to be the 'national state of the Macedonian people', with Albanians – along with Turks, Vlachs and others – given the lesser status of 'nationalities'. But it was also in provisions that declared Macedonian to be the official language and gave official status to the Macedonian Orthodox Church (Georgieva et al. 2011; Daskalovski 2002). In January 1992 Albanians held their own referendum – declared illegal by the government – in which a large majority voted for territorial autonomy within the Macedonian state.

In the period that followed, Macedonians made some attempt to reconcile Albanians to the new state, granting them formal political rights and seats in cabinet, and addressing their underrepresentation in state positions. This was partly in response to international pressure (Ahrens 2007: 401–12; Ackerman 1999: 102–5) and partly from a desire to build a model, plural, and peaceful

Balkan state. However, the pace of reform was slow and Albanian political representatives were easily outvoted (Ackerman 1999: 88–94; Hislope 2003: 132–3). The constitution remained a serious bone of contention, for it lessened the rights Albanians had enjoyed in Yugoslavia – both formally and substantively – to access Albanian language education (Agnew 2007: 404). Restrictions on language rights threatened the linguistic reproduction of the community and – by default – made Macedonian the language of higher position in the state (Koneska 2012: 36–40).

The Macedonian-Albanian conflict was fed by a number of streams. One was the historical grievances carried over from the immediate and more distant pasts (Balalovska 2002). Another was social (Sofos 2001). Albanians had a lower socio-economic status in a state where poverty and unemployment were generally high (Georgieva *et al*. 2011). Religious and linguistic differences made for greater social distance between the two groups than was typical of the Western Balkans (Bieber 2011). Albanians were more likely to be rural and there was a concentration of Albanians in the western and northern border areas (Neofotistos 2004). Most of all, internal and external challenges intersected: Macedonians feared that anything less than a unitary Macedonian national state could create the conditions for its breakup (Engström 2002).

In the 1990s Albanian discontent expressed itself in low-scale confrontation and occasional local violence. In 2001, the influx of some 360,000 Kosovan refugees, including armed rebels, triggered seven months of more extensive and serious violence (Georgieva *et al*. 2011). This did not just put an enormous strain on local resources, it also destabilised existing interethnic relations and provided unemployed Albanian youth with the resources and repertoires of violent conflict (Gleditsch 2007). The National Liberation Army (NLA) emerged as a spin-off from the KLA, seeking equal rights for Albanians within a federated Macedonia (Vankovska 2013; Ackerman 1999). Armed clashes in so volatile a region brought immediate international attention, with offers of mediation and pressure to reach an agreed settlement: the Ohrid Framework Agreement (OFA) of 2001 remedied the immediate problems and remains in place.

The significance of settlement

The OFA promised a substantial improvement in the position of Albanians. First and foremost, it provided for constitutional amendments that no longer privileged the nationality of Macedonians, while retaining a unitary inclusive Macedonian Republic (for details, see Georgieva *et al*. 2011). Albanians were no longer defined as a 'minority' or 'nationality' but as one of the constituent communities in the state. The OFA also provided for increased inclusion at all political levels, with proportionality in state employment, including in the military and police. The conflict over Albanian education was addressed with new state-funded Albanian language universities (for details, see Koneska 2012) and new language rights. A strong level of local territorial autonomy was instituted, which would permit greater Albanian self government in areas where they were a majority (Lyon 2011, 2012), thus creating local areas where Albanian language and education were not only official but also predominant.

Macedonians were also promised benefits. Macedonia would remain a unitary state and would be offered EU and NATO membership conditional on its fulfilment of the OFA obligations. This promised economic opportunities and support in a state where unemployment averaged 30 per cent – stimulating massive outmigration (Georgieva *et al.* 2011) – and it would give the Albanian population an economic incentive to remain in Macedonia. Just as important, it would guarantee Macedonian statehood and borders. Meanwhile, immediate and future financial and other support was made conditional on Macedonian agreement and implementation of the OFA (Koksidis 2013: 295).

Implementation has taken place, although unevenly and under pressure. Benchmarks on policing reform and, later, on civil service reform, have been implemented (Vasilev 2011: 55, 57). However, some benchmarks are met by the dominant Macedonian and Albanian parties distributing state positions – some fictive – to party supporters, rather than by a sharing participation and power. Greece has blocked Macedonian accession to the EU and to NATO, and many Macedonians no longer see the conditional promises of membership as credible (Ilievski and Taleski 2009). There is also continuing Albanian demographic advance: there are now at least 700,000 Albanians in a population that, due to economic emigration, has shrunk to below two million.

Frustration at this progress and concern regarding the weakening of their position has spurred Macedonian nationalist resentment, favouring the election of the more extreme nationalist party VMRO-DPMNE (International Crisis Group 2011). The result has been stronger affirmation of Macedonian nationalism at the level of the state, including nationalist symbolism and architecture.[12] Albanians, on their side, have been supporting the more extreme Albanian nationalist party. Increasing tensions have led to a series of local clashes and, more generally, a symbolic contest between the two dominant parties that paves the way for more serious confrontation (Gjoni and DioGuardi 2014).

The Macedonian case exemplifies the way that wider regional processes from the end of the nineteenth century have limited the options available to Macedonians and Albanians. While historic repertoires of resentment and conflict were available to each group, the formation of a Macedonian nation state in 1991 resulted in these elements being forged into a conflict configuration. The Kosovo War triggered a period of violence: the importance of this was that it tapped into horizontal inequalities and cultural hierarchies surrounding the Macedonian-Albanian distinction and brought them sharply onto the political agenda. In so doing, it also highlighted the long-term regional dynamics that made Macedonian statehood insecure. While the OFA addressed these problems

---

12. Macedonian symbolism is pervasive in the capital, Skopje, with a giant statue in the main square, enormous Macedonian flags, the renovation of the fort, and the building of state offices on the Albanian side of the city.

in principle, other long-term patterns have prevented its effective implementation: low state capacity, deep poverty and unevenness of economic development, a historic fluidity of state boundaries, and – in the short term – indecision from the EU and NATO.

Analytic comparison

The three cases show differences in social, political and historical contexts as well as similarities in the mechanisms by which political violence functions within ethnic conflicts and the paths by which it may be overcome.

The geopolitics of each case are very different. Northern Ireland is a small part of the strong and – since the Scottish referendum 2014 – stable United Kingdom, and is financially entirely dependent on it. The Irish Republic aspires to Irish reunification in the long term, but its short to medium-term concern is political stability and it engages with the British government in consensual conflict-management. The US government maintains an interest in helping resolve the conflict and both the Irish and British states have been amenable to its influence. The Basque Country AC is a small but relatively wealthy part of the fissiparous Spanish state that faces another separatist movement in Catalonia. France has small, potentially irredentist, Basque and Catalan minorities and – like the EU – an interest in Spain surviving in its present form. Macedonia is a small and impoverished state surrounded by larger states, two of which claimed its territory in the past and would, in the event of Macedonia's breakup, reassert those claims, while both Albania and Kosovo would be open to including the Albanians of Macedonia in their state. For the moment, a still fragile stability is buttressed by the presence of NATO, the UN and the EU in the region. Despite these differences, there is a notable similarity: support for the insurgents came from sympathetic co-nationals on the other side of the international border (with the Irish Republic, France, and Kosovo, respectively).

In all three cases, ethno-national relations are characterised by 'horizontal inequalities' (Stewart 2014), but these differ markedly in extent and type and in the state's capacity to tackle them. Catholics and nationalists in Northern Ireland, like Albanians in Macedonia, have long experienced deep and systemic disadvantage across a wide range of political, economic and cultural fields. The British government never lacked the resources to address this inequality but, until recently, they prioritised unionist concerns over nationalist ones. The economically weak Macedonian state has a limited capacity to address Albanian inequality, while also – until the 2001 crisis – lacking the will to do so. The Basque Country is economically more developed and has higher levels of income than most of Spain. Until at least 1979, however, it was seriously disadvantaged in cultural and national status and in political influence. The Spanish state's dilemma, in contrast to that of the British and Macedonian states, is how to secure redistribution of a portion of Basque wealth across the country while recognising Basque distinctiveness and without adding to the region's separatist tendencies.

Each case shares a very similar dynamic of legitimation. In all three examples, the political system is what Jung *et al.* (2005) have called an 'imperfect' democracy.[13] For our purposes, the central feature of an imperfect democracy is that the legitimacy of the state is differentially accepted. This legitimation deficit coincides with the ethnic distinction and is often articulated by militants in terms of nationalist ideology. However it is not a function of ethnic identity or nationalist ideology alone, but rather of the structural positioning of the population. The colonial manner in which the British state established itself in Ireland in the sixteenth and seventeenth centuries left it with a chronic legitimation deficit for Catholics long before they became nationalist. But a state that lacks foundational legitimacy can still attain a high level of practical legitimacy by adhering to democratic norms of fairness and justice and by good governance. Northern Ireland lacked foundational legitimacy for nationalists, but it was only the breach of the latter norms, in and after the Civil Rights Movement, that completed delegitimation (see Ó Dochartaigh and Bosi 2010). In the Macedonian case, the Macedonian parties created a new legitimation deficit by defining the state as 'their' state, and by failing to do much to ameliorate this on the practical level. In the Basque Country there was interplay between nationalist resistance to accepting the legitimacy of Spanish rule, and practical acceptance of the legitimacy of the post-1978 order, not for its national but for its functional benefits and its wider democratic values. The latter predominated among the Basque public after 1979, even while Basque national identification and desire for greater autonomy grew.

The imperfect democracy of each state was central to the mechanisms by which violence functioned, drew support, and had effect. On the one hand, the insurgent groups emphasised and highlighted the imperfections: the 'colonial' rule of the British or the Spanish; the marginalisation of minorities by the power of majorities. Many of these imperfections were addressed in the agreed settlements – the constitutionally guaranteed autonomy accorded to the Basque Country in 1979, the consociationalism and constitutional guarantees of the GFA of 1998, and the OFA of 2001, although for some militants – and in particular for ETA – they were radically insufficient in guaranteeing popular and national rights.

In each of the cases, violent insurgency was sustained by a legitimacy deficit, permitting popular understanding and tolerance of violence even among those who did not support it. ETA emerged from the long years of Francoist oppression and this assured a significant degree of sympathy through the 1970s. In Northern Ireland the IRA emerged from the violence directed at the civil rights marchers and the wider Catholic community by security forces, loyalists and, later, by the British army. While the mass Catholic public rejected IRA violence they also rejected that of the state security forces. Violence in Macedonia was initially

---

13. They see imperfect democracies as central to processes of negotiation. We see them as central to processes of conflict and the role of violence within it.

an overspill of the Kosovan crisis. Its support base, however, lay in Albanian public alienation from the procedures, policies, and even the very existence of the Macedonian state.

Once violence began and became embedded, it produced a level of political polarisation that enabled it to continue. In both the Basque and Northern Irish cases, it began to take on an autonomous logic and to nurture a self-contained culture of violence – what Bar-Tal (2013) calls an institutionalised 'conflict ethos' – on which it then drew. But the role of wider public tolerance remained important: where it was lacking – as it increasingly was for ETA in the 1990s and 2000s – the security options available to the state were much enhanced and the resources of insurgents reduced.

A limited amount of political violence can make a major impact in democracies, and still more in imperfect democracies. Liberal democracies have a limited range of responses they can make to political violence without incurring domestic and international costs. They offer a range of easy targets, and are vulnerable in respect of foreign investment and international reputation. Protracted violence and emergency anti-terrorist measures tend to corrupt democratic principles and practices and to damage public culture. A public legitimacy deficit makes state responses more difficult and dangerous. In each of our case studies, the central state intervened to repair the legitimation deficit. It did so with considerable effort and to considerable effect in the Basque Country in 1979, in Northern Ireland in the 1990s, and – with strong international help and pressure – in Macedonia in 2001.

Is anti-state violence effective in achieving its goals? States resist the claim, not least because they have a strong interest in retaining their authority, monopoly on violence, international and domestic reputation, and in deterring future insurgencies. In the cases discussed here, the insurgents did not achieve their explicit goals. Plausibly, however, violence did have an effect, if different from the intended one. In each case, it incentivised the state and the international community to act decisively to repair the wider democratic deficit. This was most evident in Macedonia, where the onset of violence focussed the attention and resources of the international community and led to the brokering of a comprehensive agreement. Here, a decisive response in the early phase of crisis stopped further destabilisation and the embedding of a culture of violence. In Northern Ireland, the opportunity for such an early decisive response was not taken, the process of reform was much slower and much more indirect, with parallel security and political paths (see Todd 2014; Ruane and Todd 2014). In the Basque Country, the legitimation deficit was substantially addressed in the democratisation and autonomisation process, and the state's responses were thereafter primarily in the realm of security.

The cases also show important features of settlement. In these cases, it was not simply – as Jung et al. (2005) have argued – a matter of ensuring legitimacy for the negotiations and agreements. This also required intervention in longer-term structural processes. In Macedonia, the OFA addressed two sets of historically deep problems: the role of regional instability and insecurity, and the horizontal inequality of the Albanian population. In Northern Ireland, the GFA changed the state's relation to the communities, and addressed the long-term inequality of Catholics. It did not resolve the national question, but it removed one of the reasons for Catholics to become nationalist. It did so with considerable effort and to considerable effect in the Basque Country in 1979 and in Northern Ireland in the 1990s. With strong international help and pressure, this also occurred in Macedonia, although continuing elite political corruption has limited its effects (Gjoni and DioGuardi 2014).

Conclusion

The three cases discussed in this chapter are not representative of the wide diversity of ethnic conflicts, not least because each takes place within a European democracy. In each case, the conflict is fought not simply by paramilitary groups but also by political parties, supported by large sections of the populations. Each involves popular as well as elite divisions. In each case, violence has been limited, and both a political agreement and an end to violence have been secured. But these are also the reasons that the cases are significant. They show factors – the interaction of changing political strategies and change in embedded slow-moving structures – that may be missed when large powers take the opportunity to carve up territories, or when conflicting armies hold sway over them, and the interest of the powerful prevails.

In these cases, violence did not follow an autonomous logic, determined by the aims of military success independent of political aims and public norms. Nor was it simply an expression of cultural divisions, myths and ideologies. Rather, it was intimately if also indirectly linked to social structure and to deeply rooted patterns of governance. For this reason, violence could be marginalised only by directly addressing these issues. This suggests the need to reconsider some of the common wisdoms of peacemaking and to bring in a longer temporal perspective. Our analysis suggests that the factors that are correlated with settlement stability – for example confidence building measures (Hartzell and Hoddie 2007) and costly gestures (Glassmyer and Sambanis 2008) – succeed in building confidence because they tackle deep-set problems of legitimation and are costly because this typically involves a difficult and costly process of restructuration. In each case, as we have traced, implementation has been uneven.

In conclusion, political violence must be placed in its temporal context if we are to understand its causes, course, and the dangers that remain when it ends. Doing so reveals causal processes that are missed by wider and flatter generalisations, namely the social relations and structural processes of long provenance that increase the propensity to violence and determine the success or failure of settlement initiatives. Long-term structures can be changed, and small changes in them may make a big difference to the outcome. The actors most able to change them are powerful states and international actors. This is a difficult and costly task and they may be tempted to stop when political agreement is reached. We have argued that much more is needed.

References

Ackerman, A. (1999) *Making Peace Prevail: Preventing Violent Conflict in Macedonia*, Syracuse: Syracuse University Press.

Agnew, J. (2007) 'No borders, no nations: Making Greece in Macedonia', *Annals of the Association of American Geographers*, 97(2): 398–422.

Ahrens, G. H. (2007) *Diplomacy on the Edge: Containment of Ethnic Conflict and the Minorities Working Group of the Conferences on Yugoslavia*, Washington D.C.: Woodrow Wilson Center Press and Baltimore: Johns Hopkins University Press.

Balalovska, K. (2002) 'A historical background to the Macedonian-Albanian inter-ethnic conflict', *New Balkan Politics*, 3(4) http://www.newbalkanpolitics. org.mk/item/A-Historical-Background-to-the-Macedonian-Albanian-Inter-Ethnic-Conflict#.VDzSXRZS6R8 (accessed 16 October 2014).

Bar-Tal, D. (2013) *Intractable Conflicts: Socio-Psychological Foundations and Dynamics*, Cambridge: Cambridge University Press.

Bew, J., Frampton, M. and Gurruchaga, I. (2009) *Talking to Terrorists: Making Peace in Northern Ireland and the Basque Country*, London: Hurst and Co.

Bieber, F. (2011) 'Introduction: Assessing the Ohrid Framework Agreement', in M. Risteska and Z. Daskalovsk (eds) *One Decade after the Ohrid Framework Agreement: Lessons (to be) Learned from the Macedonian Experience*, Friedrich Ebert Stiftung and Center for Research and Policy Making Skopje 2011 http://www.crpm.org.mk/wp-content/uploads/AboutUS/OneDecade.pdf (accessed 18 February 2014), pp. 12–24.

Braude, B. (2013) 'The success of religion as a source for compromise in divided empires', in J. McEvoy and B. O'Leary (eds) *Power-Sharing in Deeply Divided Places*, Philadelphia: University of Pennsylvania Press, pp. 176–97.

Bray, Z. (2012) 'Basque nationalism at a political crossroads', *World Politics Review*, Feature Report on 'People without borders: Kurdish, Basque and Tuareg nationalism' May 9, pp. 9–13.

Canny, N. (2001) *Making Ireland British 1580–1650,* Oxford: Oxford University Press.

Comas, J.-M. (2003) 'Spain: The 1978 Constitution and centre-periphery tensions' in J. Ruane, J. Todd and A. Mandeville (eds) *Europe's Old States in the New World Order: The Politics of Transition in Britain, France and Spain*, Dublin: UCD Press, pp. 38–61.

Conversi, D. (1997) *The Basques, the Catalans and Spain: Alternative Routes to Nationalist Mobilisation*, London: Hurst and Co.

— (2010) 'Building bridges on the road to peace: Centralism, resistance and the Basque revival', *Political Geography*, 29(8): 463–5.

Daskalovski, Z. (2002) 'Language and identity: The Ohrid Framework Agreement and liberal notions of citizenship and nationality in Macedonia', *Journal on Ethnopolitics and Minority Issues in Europe*, 1: 2–32.

della Porta, D. (2013) *Clandestine Political Violence*, Cambridge: Cambridge University Press.

Engström, J. (2002) 'The power of perception: The impact of the Macedonian question on inter-ethnic relations in the Republic of Macedonia', *The Global Review of Ethnopolitics* 1(3): 3–17.

Flora, P. (ed.) (1999) *State Formation Nation Building and Mass Politics in Europe: The Theory of Stein Rokkan*, Oxford: Oxford University Press.

Georgieva, L., Memeti, A., and Musliu, A. (2011) 'Patterns of conflict resolution in Macedonia', IBIS discussion papers, no. 8, http://www.ucd.ie/ibis/publications (accessed 17 October 2014).

Gibbons, J. (1999) *Spanish Politics Today*, Manchester: Manchester University Press.

Gjoni, R. and DioGuardi, S. C. (2014) 'Brewing crisis in Macedonia', Open Security: Conflict and Peace Building, September 23, https://www.opendemocracy.net/opensecurity/roland-gjoni-shirley-cloyes-dioguardi/crisis-brewing-in-macedonia (accessed 19 October 2014).

Glassmyer, K. and Sambanis, N. (2008) 'Rebel military integration and civil war termination', *Journal of Peace Research,* 45(3): 365–84.

Gleditsch, K. S. (2007) 'Transnational dimensions of civil war', *Journal of Peace Research*, 44(3): 293–309.

Goikoetxea, J. (2013) 'Nationalism and democracy in the Basque Country (1979–2012)', *Ethnopolitics*, 12(3): 268–89.

Grugel, J. and Rees, T. (1997) *Franco's Spain*, London: Arnold.

Hartzell, C. and Hoddie, M. (2007) *Crafting Peace: Power-Sharing Institutions and the Negotiated Settlement of Civil Wars*, University Park: The Pennsylvania State University Press.

Heiberg, M. (2007) 'ETA: Euskadi 'ta Askatasuna' in M. Heiberg, B. O'Leary and J. Tirman (eds) *Terror Insurgency and the State: Ending Protracted Conflicts*, Philadelphia: University of Pennsylvania Press, pp 19–50.

Hislope, R. (2003) 'Between a bad peace and a good war: Insights and lessons from the almost-war in Macedonia', *Ethnic and Racial Studies*, 26(1): 129–51.

Idoiaga, G. E. (2006) 'The Basque conflict: New ideas and prospects for peace', USIP Special Report, http://www.usip.org/sites/default/files/sr161.pdf (accessed 17 October 2014).

Ilievski, Z. and Taleski, D. (2009) 'Was the EU's role in conflict management in Macedonia a success?', *Ethnopolitics*, 8(5–6): 355–67.

International Crisis Group (2011) 'Macedonia: Ten years after the conflict', Europe Report no. 212, 11 August, http://www.crisisgroup.org/~/media/Files/europe/balkans/macedonia/212%20Macedonia%20---%20Ten%20Years%20after%20the%20Conflict (accessed 17 October 2014).

Jung, C., E. Lust-Okar, E. and Shapiro, I. (2005) 'Problems and prospects for democratic settlements: South Africa as a model for the Middle East and Northern Ireland?', *Politics and Society*, 33(2): 277–326.

Junto, J. A. and Schubert, A. (2000) *Spanish History Since 1808*, London: Arnold.

Kalyvas, S. (2006) *The Logic of Violence in Civil War,* Cambridge: Cambridge University Press.

Katznelson, I. (2003) 'Periodization and preferences: Reflections on purposive action in comparative historical science', in J. Mahoney and D. Rueschemeyer (eds) *Comparative Historical Analysis in the Social Sciences*, Cambridge: Cambridge University Press, pp. 270–301.

Keating, M. (2001) *Plurinational Democracy: Stateless Nations in a Post-sovereignty Era*, Oxford: Oxford University Press.

Keating, M and Bray, Z. (2007) 'Renegotiating sovereignty: Basque nationalism and the rise and fall of the Ibarretxe plan', *Ethnopolitics*, 5(4): 347–64.

Koksidis, P. I. (2013) 'Nipping an insurgency in the bud – Part II: The success and limits of non-military coercion in FYRMacedonia', *Ethnopolitics,* 12(3): 290–306.

Koneska, C. (2012) 'Vetoes, ethnic bidding, decentralisation: Post-conflict education in Macedonia', *Journal on Ethnopolitics and Minority Issues in Europe*, 11(4): 28–50.

Laitin, D. D. (2007) *Nations, States and Violence,* Oxford: Oxford University Press.

Linz, J. (1973) 'Opposition to and under an authoritarian regime: The case of Spain', in R. Dahl (ed.) *Regimes and Opposition*, New Haven: Yale University Press, pp. 171–259.

Lyon, A. (2012) 'Between the integration and accommodation of ethnic difference: Decentralization in the Republic of Macedonia', *Journal on Ethnopolitics and Minority Issues in Europe,* 11(5): 80–103.

— (2011) 'Municipal decentralisation: Between the integration and accommodation of ethnic difference in the Republic of Macedonia', in M. Risteska and Z. Daskalovski (eds) *One Decade after the Ohrid Framework Agreement: Lessons (to be) Learned from the Macedonian Experience*, Friedrich Ebert Stiftung and Center for Research and Policy Making Skopje 2011, http://www.crpm.org.mk/wp-content/uploads/AboutUS/OneDecade.pdf, pp. 86–105 (accessed 18 February 2014).

Malesevic, S. (2013) *Nation-States and Nationalisms,* Cambridge: Polity Press.

Mattes, M. and Savun, B. (2010) 'Information, agreement design, and the durability of civil war settlements', *American Journal of Political Science*, 54(2): 511–24.

McKittrick, D., Kelters, S., Feeney, B., Thornton, C. and McVea, D. (2004) *Lost Lives: The Stories of the Men, Women and Children who Died as a Result of the Northern Ireland Troubles*, London: Mainstream Publishing (revised edition).

Medrano, J. D. (1995) *Divided Nations: Class, Politics and Nationalism in the Basque Country and Catalonia*, London: Cornell University Press.

Meehan, E. (2014) 'The changing British-Irish relationship: The sovereignty dimension', *Irish Political Studies*, 29(1): 58–75.

Mees, L. (2003) *Nationalism, Violence and Democracy: the Basque Clash of Identities*, New York: Palgrave Macmillan.

—— (2004) 'Politics, economy or culture? The rise and development of Basque nationalism in the light of social movement theory', *Theory and Society*, 33(3/4): 311–31.

Muro, D. (2005) 'Nationalism and nostalgia: The case of radical Basque nationalism', *Nations and Nationalism*, 11(4): 571–89.

Neofotistos, V. P. (2004) 'Beyond stereotypes: Violence and the porousness of ethnic boundaries in the Republic of Macedonia', *History and Anthropology*, 15(1): 47–67.

Nolan, P. (2014) *Northern Ireland Peace Monitoring Report. Number Three*, Belfast: Northern Ireland Community Relations Council.

Ó Dochartaigh, N. and Bosi, L. (2010) 'Territoriality and mobilisation: The civil rights campaign in Northern Ireland', *Mobilization: An International Journal*, 15(4): 405–24.

Pocock, J. G. A. (2005) *The Discovery of Islands: Essays in British History*, Cambridge: Cambridge University Press.

Pragnere, P (2011) 'Protracted violence in democratic Western Europe: The case of the Basque Country', IBIS Discussion Papers, *Patterns of Conflict Resolution*, No. 12, University College Dublin: IBIS.

Risteska, M. and Daskalovski, Z. (2011) 'One decade after the Ohrid Framework Agreement: Lessons (to be) learned from the Macedonian experience', Friedrich Ebert Stiftung and Center for Research and Policy Making Skopje 2011, http://www.crpm.org.mk/wp-content/uploads/AboutUS/OneDecade.pdf (accessed 18 February 2014).

Ruane, J. (2003) 'Theorising the transition: *Longue durée* and current conjuncture in centre–periphery relations in Britain, France and Spain', in J. Ruane, J. Todd and A. Mandeville (eds) *Old States in a New World Order*, Dublin: UCD Press, pp. 115–32.

—— (2014) 'Conflict and reconciliation in Northern Ireland', in T. Inglis (ed.) *Are the Irish Different?*, Manchester: Manchester University Press.

Ruane, J. and Todd, J. (1996) *Dynamics of Conflict in Northern Ireland: Power, Conflict and Emancipation*, Cambridge: Cambridge University Press.

—— (2007) 'Path dependence in settlement processes: Explaining settlement in Northern Ireland', *Political Studies*, 55(2): 442–58.

—— (2014) 'History structure and action in the settlement of complex conflicts: The Northern Ireland case', *Irish Political Studies*, 29(1): 15–34.

Smith, C. and Mar-Molinero, A. (eds) (1996) *Nationalism and the Nation in the Iberian Peninsula*, Oxford: Berg.

Sofos, S. (2001) 'Macedonia at the crossroads', *Journal of Balkan and Near Eastern Studies*, 3(2): 145–51.

Stewart, F. (2014) 'Why horizontal inequalities are important for a shared society', *Development*, 57(1): 46–54.

Todd, J. (2011) 'Institutional change and conflict regulation: The Anglo-Irish agreement of 1985 and the mechanisms of change in Northern Ireland', *West European Politics*, 34 (4): 838–58.

—— 2014) 'Thresholds of state change: Changing British state institutions and practices in Northern Ireland after direct rule', *Political Studies*, 62(3): 522–38.

Tonge, J., Shirlow, P. and J. McAuley (2011) 'So why did the guns fall silent? How interplay, not stalemate, explains the Northern Ireland peace process', *Irish Political Studies*, 26(1): 1–18.

Vankovska, B. (2013) 'Constitutional engineering and institution-building in the Republic of Macedonia 1991–2011', in S. P. Ramet, O. Listhaug and A. Simkus (eds) *Civic and Uncivic Values in Macedonia*, Basingstoke: Palgrave Macmillan, 87–108.

Varshney, A. (2002) *Ethnic Conflict and Civic Life: Hindus and Muslims in India*, New Haven Ct: Yale University Press.

Vasilev, G. (2011) 'EU conditionality and ethnic coexistence in the Balkans: Macedonia and Bosnia in a comparative perspective', *Ethnopolitics*, 10(1): 51–76.

Wilson, A. and Keating, M. (2009) 'Renegotiating the state of autonomies: Statute reform and multi-level politics in Spain', *West European Politics*, 23(3): 536–58.

Wimmer, A. (2002) *Nationalist Exclusion and Ethnic Conflict: Shadows of Modernity*, Cambridge: Cambridge University Press.

—— (2013) *Waves of War: Nationalism, State Formation and Ethnic Exclusion in the Modern World*, Cambridge: Cambridge University Press.

Wright, F. (1987) *Northern Ireland: A Comparative Analysis*, Dublin: Gill and Macmillan.

Zartman, I. W. (1989) *Ripe for Resolution: Conflict and Intervention in Africa* (Second Edition), Oxford: Oxford University Press.

Chapter Five

Temporal Factors in Prosecutions for Political Violence: The New Left in Japan and the United States

Patricia Steinhoff and Gilda Zwerman

This chapter examines temporal factors in the judicial process and outcomes for persons who were prosecuted for their participation in political violence in Japan and the United States. Through close analysis of a sample of nearly 150 individual cases from twelve different New Left groups that were prosecuted between 1970 and 2010, we examine patterns of variation in outcome in order to ascertain whether there is any temporal logic to the variations.

Based on data collected separately we have previously examined the process of involvement in political violence at the macro and meso levels as an outcome of interaction between forces of social control and the actions of participants. Our studies show that severe repression at the peak of the New Left protest cycle in the late 1960s was a primary factor in causing segments of these groups to go underground or into exile and, ultimately, to engage in political violence (Zwerman, Steinhoff, and della Porta 2000). The infusion of a younger second generation of participants who entered the movement at the peak of the protest cycle, when conflict between dissidents and the state was most intense, helped first-generation participants to survive the pressures of underground life and sustain a limited offensive campaign of violent actions (Zwerman and Steinhoff 2005). Throughout the 1970s and 1980s, as activists associated with armed underground groups were apprehended and imprisoned, most continued to assert their movement identity. Forty years later, a retrospective look at our cases found that, in the context of movement decline and long-term incarceration, the above-ground legal support networks that were integral to sustaining arrested protesters in the 1960s and 1970s continued to play a critical role in sustaining our subjects' movement identity in the courts, jails and prisons (Zwerman and Steinhoff 2012).

The analyses offered in these related studies were built on standard narratives of space and time in the New Left protest cycle (McAdam and Sewell 2001). Our approach throughout has been to compare what Abbott (2001) terms 'narrative sequences' in our respective samples, essentially applying the method of paired comparisons in order to analyse similarities in the protest cycles in Japan and the United States (Tarrow 2010). We viewed the experiences of individual violent actors as part of the inclusive, nested temporalities affecting individuals, organisations, and organisational networks. First, we found that, in contrast to studies of the New Left that have focused almost exclusively on public non-violent social movement organisations, our research on violent groups led us to identify submerged sites of movement activity – including small insurgency groups, clandestine organisations, exiles, legal support networks, and the criminal justice system itself – that were integrally linked to the broader protest cycle. Second, activists occupying these spaces had the effect of prolonging the cycle: as they maintained strong ties to activists in the public sphere they developed new strategies for resisting intense state repression, sustaining a movement identity for many years – even decades – and long after the collapse of public organisations and the decline of mass protests.

We now examine the outcomes of the legal process for those individuals in our sample who were prosecuted for their participation in underground political violence. Our analysis focuses on the sequential stages of the criminal justice process. The key stages include arrest, interrogation, construction of charges, trials, sentencing structure, patterns (length and conditions) of incarceration, and the possibilities for release that each country offers. Taking into consideration the actions of state authorities and the organisation of the criminal justice system, as well as the defendants and the legal support network, we examine the range of outcomes within our sample and explore the logic underlying the variations between nations. In contrast to the strong similarities found in our previous organisational-level comparisons, this time we found significant temporal differences in the patterns of Japan and the United States. We have analysed this using contemporary social science discussions of temporality (Abbott 1995a, 1995b, 2001; McAdam and Sewell 2001).

Some of these parallel the forms of temporality that have been outlined by McAdam and Sewell (2001), such as protest cycle effects, transformative events, and even cultural epochs. Others derive from our comparative analysis of the temporal sequence (Abbott 1995a, 2001) of the criminal justice process, which follows Abbott's logic but for which his specific sequential analysis procedure was not appropriate. Due to the complexity of presenting comparative qualitative information about each case, we have organised the main body of the paper as a systematic comparison of each sequential step in the criminal justice process, noting similarities and differences between nations. In the final section we examine these steps in terms of theoretical types of temporality and how they interact with spatial and milieu factors.

Clandestine political violence and the criminal justice system

In both the United States and Japan, we have found it helpful to examine the process of radicalisation and the emergence of clandestine political violence within the New Left protest cycle in terms of similar dynamics, including social movement decline, state-dissident interactions, and multiple activist generations. Once groups went underground and began to engage in clandestine political violence, both countries adjudicated cases by modifying and enhancing investigative, prosecutorial, and correctional tools that already existed within the criminal justice system, as opposed to creating a separate set of new political laws. The governments of both countries drew on existing laws concerning overtly political acts, and on criminal laws, especially those intended to increase the severity of punishment.

In the case of Japan, activists were brought into a uniform, highly bureaucratic national criminal justice system that became incrementally more restrictive and punitive over time, partly in response to the defiant stance of the defendants. The treatment of activists in the United States varied widely depending on the priorities and political orientation of the national administration at the time of arrest. That is to say, the severity of charges and the possibilities for negotiating with the prosecutor shifted with each change of administration. Moreover, the American system is complicated by a major spatial factor: there are jurisdictional differences between individual states, and criminals are tried for offences occurring within their geographic borders according to criminal laws that vary from state to state, while there is also an overarching federal system that deals with criminal offences that cross state borders. These political cases were adjudicated in both the state and federal courts, and in some cases defendants faced both state and federal charges in relation to the same action.

Despite these structural differences, Japan and the United States held similar goals concerning the outcomes of cases involving armed militants from the 1960s and 1970s. Both aimed to (1) detach the individuals and groups involved in the cases from their histories in the broader cycle of public protest; (2) ensure that individuals perceived as leaders and militant members of the groups received the longest possible sentences under the most restrictive conditions; (3) pressure and obstruct the support structures that connected defendants to the New Left cycle of protest, and (4) use policies and practices concerning the adjudication of these cases to increase the authority and resources of social control agencies in law enforcement, courts, and prisons. At the same time, there are clear temporal differences in sentencing patterns between the two sets of cases, which reflect structural differences in the two criminal justice systems as well as differences in the sociological composition of defendant populations.

Background

In both countries there was, from 1967 until the early 1970s, an initial wave of clandestine political violence that was closely connected to above-ground insurgency groups active in the New Left protest cycle. Clandestine activity was a direct result of the sudden, forceful repression of protest in response to escalating violence. There was then a second wave of clandestine political violence in the mid-1970s, undertaken by activists who differed from the first wave in terms of age, time spent in public protest organisations, political socialisation, and goals. In the United States, the second wave included some holdovers from the first wave, recently politicised prisoners, and ethno-nationalist activists (Puerto Rican, African-American, etc.), that formed later in the protest cycle. They were active from the late 1970s through the early 1980s and carried out bank robberies and the robbery of an armoured car. In Japan, one group from the first wave was in exile in North Korea from 1970, after the hijacking of a domestic airplane. The second wave consisted of first and second-generation Japanese activists who had quietly gone into exile and conducted international attacks from their base in the Middle East. Through 'free the guerrilla' guerrilla attacks in 1975 and 1977, they obtained the release of a dozen people from the Japanese criminal justice system, who then joined them in the Middle East. Among the released were their own members who had been deported back to Japan and arrested, people in custody for several domestic clandestine political violence cases, plus two prison activists. The 1970s was their main period of active clandestine political violence, but they remained at large outside Japan for one to two more decades, along with those exiled in North Korea (*see* Figure 5.1 for a diagram of both sets of groups).

Government officials in both countries pursued strategies aimed at dismantling these underground organisations, a goal that extended well beyond using the criminal justice system to punish individuals for their involvement in specific criminal offences. To accomplish this, they used harsh detention measures before and during trial in order to separate defendants from their organisations and outside support networks, and they imposed long, harsh sentences that would remove the offenders from society for as long as possible. These broader intentions are expressed in documents from individual cases, such as trial and hearing transcripts; prosecutors' arguments for continued detention in the case of Japan, or preventive detention in the case of the United States; written judicial decisions, and in policy documents related to specific cases involving 'terrorists'. As part of a broader turn towards more punitive measures in both countries over time, governments were not merely processing existing cases, but they were trying to use the cases as deterrents to prevent future generations of young people from engaging in similar forms of political activity.

In Japan, where the same conservative political party remained in power from 1955 until 2010 and where the criminal justice system was administered by elite career bureaucrats, there was a gradual shift from a rehabilitation-oriented criminal justice system towards a more severely punitive one, with relatively little formal change in the system until the late 1990s. However, a transformative event known as the United Red Army incident appears to have produced a sudden shift towards more severe charges and sentences both for pending and subsequent cases. In February 1972, police had finally, after a string of robberies, caught up with the remnants of two underground groups that had merged to form the United Red Army. They had retreated into the mountains for the winter, harbouring most of the people on Japan's top ten police wanted list. After several members were arrested, the remaining five armed activists remained holed up in a mountain lodge with a hostage and engaged in a ten-day standoff with 3,000 riot police. Finally, police demolished the front of the building and brought out the hostage and all the militants unharmed. The entire incident was aired live on national television. Subsequent interrogation revealed that the participants had engaged in a deadly internal purge in which, during the winter of 1971–2, twelve members were tortured and killed. This case had a profound effect on Japanese society and is generally cited as the end point of the New Left protest cycle. It led to a highly negative retrospective evaluation of the entire protest cycle and to a widespread avoidance of street demonstrations and similar forms of protest activity for the next two decades (Gonoi 2012; Steinhoff 1992, 2013).

Figure 5.1: The origins of armed clandestine groups in the repression of New Left organisations

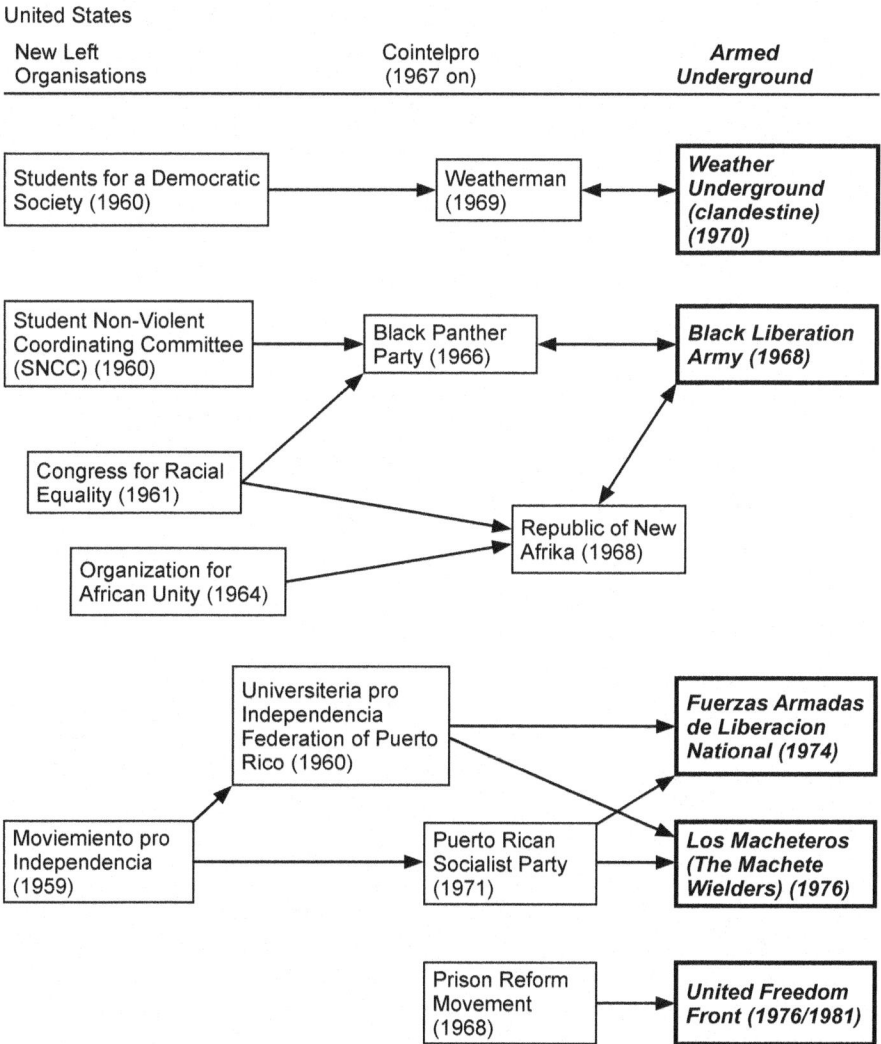

United States

| New Left Organisations | Cointelpro (1967 on) | *Armed Underground* |

Students for a Democratic Society (1960) → Weatherman (1969) ⇄ *Weather Underground (clandestine) (1970)*

Student Non-Violent Coordinating Committee (SNCC) (1960) → Black Panther Party (1966) ⇄ *Black Liberation Army (1968)*

Congress for Racial Equality (1961)

Organization for African Unity (1964) → Republic of New Afrika (1968)

Universiteria pro Independencia Federation of Puerto Rico (1960) → *Fuerzas Armadas de Liberacion National (1974)*

Moviemiento pro Independencia (1959)

Puerto Rican Socialist Party (1971) → *Los Macheteros (The Machete Wielders) (1976)*

Prison Reform Movement (1968) → *United Freedom Front (1976/1981)*

Figure 5.1 cont.

Japan

| New Left
Organisations | Repression
(from late 1968) | **Armed Clandestine
Groups** |

```
              ┌─────────────────┐        ┌─────────────────────┐
              │ Japan Communist │        │ Revolutionary Left  │
              │ Party Left Faction│─────▶│ Faction (1969–71)   │
              │ (Maoist) (1966) │        └─────────────────────┘
              └─────────────────┘                 │
                                                   ▼
                                          ┌──────────────────┐
                                          │ United Red Army  │
                                          │ (1971–2)         │
                                          └──────────────────┘
┌──────────────┐  ┌──────────────┐  ┌──────────────────┐
│ Communist    │  │ Communist    │  │ Red Army Faction │
│ League (First│─▶│ League       │─▶│ (1969–71)        │
│ Bund, 1958)  │  │ (Second Bund,│  └──────────────────┘
└──────────────┘  │ 1965)        │        ┌──────────────────┐
                  └──────────────┘        │ Yodogō Group     │
                                          │ in North Korea   │
                                          │ (1970)           │
                                          └──────────────────┘
```

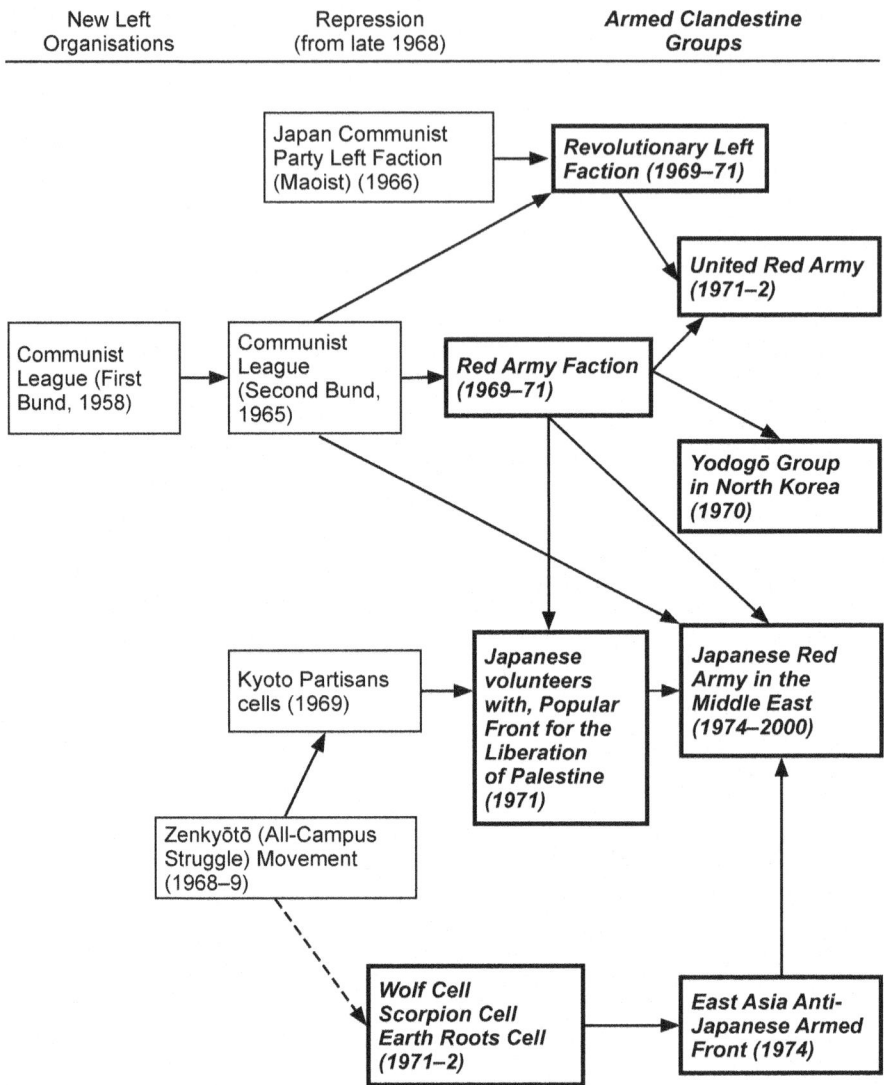

In the United States, because of the significant differences in the politics and priorities of each presidential administration (Nixon 1968–74; Ford 1974–5; Carter 1976–9; Reagan 1980–8), the adjudication of the political cases reflects policy changes, power plays, and resource reallocations that trickled down into reforms of the criminal justice system. The most dramatic of these shifts occurred in the 1980s when, during the Reagan administration, a relatively small number of actions involving political violence associated with earlier New Left protests were used to magnify the threat of a new wave of domestic terrorism. This led to enhanced funding and power for domestic intelligence agencies, including the Joint Terrorism Task Force; the creation of a new Senate Subcommittee on Security and Terrorism; the relaxation of guidelines for opening an internal security investigation; more restrictions on the qualifications for bail, and upgrades in security at state and federal correctional institutions. This shift also had an impact on Japan, when the Reagan administration pressed Japan and other countries to participate in a war on terror in the international sphere (Steinhoff and Zwerman 2013; Zwerman and Steinhoff 2012). Japan embraced the anti-terror war by stepping up efforts and seeking international cooperation to help locate and prosecute Japanese involved in clandestine political violence in exile. These investigations also resulted in increased funding and power for relevant domestic agencies, over and above the steady increases in security funding since the 1950s (Katzenstein and Tsujinaka 1991).

Criminal justice as a sequential process

Both countries gathered evidence through intense surveillance of known activists and suspected militants. Japan used close physical surveillance, while the US also utilised electronic surveillance. In some cases police and intelligence agents accompanied by paramilitary or riot personnel and equipment would forcibly arrest suspects. In both nations, elaborate vehicular security arrangements were used in moving the defendants from detention centres to court or from jail to jail. Many of the cases were sensationalised in the press and involved high profile defendants, and criminal justice agencies were able to capitalise on public interest and dramatise how they were protecting the public by prosecuting these very dangerous individuals.

In subsequent sections we compare our two samples systematically at each stage of the criminal justice process. This is an invariant sequence of stages that was applied to every case, but differences in the nature of the procedures in the two countries produced major temporal differences in the overall duration of the criminal justice process. We address these differentials as they arise in our comparative narrative, but in order to avoid confusion we postpone to a concluding discussion the theoretical analysis of temporal factors, along with a brief discussion of the role of spatial and milieu factors in these same cases.

Investigation and detention

Although the processes differed, both countries used enhanced tactics in order to obtain sufficient information to prosecute cases of clandestine political violence and to identify potential co-defendants. These enhanced techniques were in both countries carried out under conditions in which suspects did not have access to lawyers. However, in both countries, the legal support network helped activists to resist these pressures, although use of such defensive strategies was regarded as defiance of authority and had negative consequences for the suspect.

In Japan, initial police questioning and arrests led to extended periods of intensive interrogation with strong pressure to confess and, secondarily, to elicit information about other people. Moreover, in Japan, suspects do not write their own confession, it is the interrogator who constructs it to fit the prosecution's version of events. The suspect is then pressured to sign the confession. These confession statements are considered the most important form of evidence in the trial process (Foote 1995; Johnson 2002). Most criminal suspects confess within the first three days of interrogation (without counsel present). Suspects who do not confess within that time are taken to court to get a ten-day extension, which can be renewed once for a total of twenty-three days of interrogation. This can be further extended by brief release of the suspect, or by charging with one offence and then immediately rearresting on suspicion of another charge. The legal support network advocated the defensive strategy of exercising the right to remain silent during lengthy interrogations – a constitutional right that was not commonly invoked by suspects in criminal cases. This helps protect against confession, but it also marks the suspect as resistant and automatically increases the time in detention.

In the United States, protections for the constitutional rights of protesters were severely eroded during the Nixon presidency (1968–74). The principal tool for investigation, interrogation, and intimidation of political activists during this phase was the federal grand jury, a formal inquiry that could subpoena witnesses to testify about possible criminal activity. Activists who were issued a subpoena to a grand jury but refused to testify and who would not provide the government with information on specific organisations or individuals suspected of criminal activity could be jailed for civil contempt, a charge that carried a sentence of up to eighteen months. The legal support network responded by mounting a political campaign to encourage activists to, as a form of resistance, eschew any form of 'collaboration' with the grand jury. If a resister was jailed for refusing to cooperate, lawyers would then initiate a proceeding to have the subpoena quashed – to contend that no matter what pressure the government applied, the witness could not be coerced into supplying information. In that case the only purpose of incarcerating the witness was punitive and therefore illegal under the law governing grand juries.

The Carter administration (1976 through 1979) was marked by a relatively liberal orientation towards political dissent. The National Advisory Committee on Criminal Justice Standards and Goals – a major policy report issued during the first year of the Carter presidency (1976) – advocated 'sensitivity and restraint' on the part of the police, the courts, and correctional institutions in dealing with political offenders. The FBI was redirected away from interfering with freedom of political expression. Intrusive methods of surveillance on political groups could not be authorised on speculation. Numerous long-term investigations of radical organisations were terminated. Political fugitives were encouraged to surrender with the promise of receiving generous plea deals and light sentences.

However, when Ronald Reagan was elected president in 1980 the period of leniency came to an end. The FBI was authorised to open investigations on political organisations based on a 'reasonable indication' (including public statements) that the group intended to engage in criminal, subversive, or seditious activity.

The powers of the federal grand jury were enhanced. For the first time, activists who refused to testify could not only be jailed for civil contempt, but could be recalled and, if they still refused, charged with criminal contempt – a charge for which there is no maximum limit on sentences – for withholding information concerning 'terrorist' activity.

In both countries, persons arrested in clandestine political violence cases were routinely held in detention before, and often during, their trial, although the laws provide for release on bail. In Japan defendants in political cases were routinely denied bail on the legal grounds that they might flee or tamper with evidence, and were held in isolation cells in detention facilities. In the United States defendants are usually released on bail while awaiting trial, but can be denied bail if the defendant is deemed a flight risk or a danger to the community. During the Reagan administration the preventive detention law (1984) was passed for the federal criminal justice system. It gives judges the discretion to require pretrial detention for suspects who have been arrested in connection with any action associated with a terrorist group, even if the individual has no prior criminal record and is not being charged with an assaultive action. The conditions of detention are, in both countries, often more severe than the conditions of long-term incarceration. Isolation and communications restrictions, intrusive technology, and time and spatial limitations on visits cut political defendants off from other, non-political, detainees in the facility, inhibiting their interaction with co-defendants and obstructing the activities of the legal support network. While in the United States defence lawyers had some ability to alter the conditions of detention through court actions, in Japan they had very little power to do so and any resistance, such as refusing to cooperate in interrogation, resulted in increased severity of detention.

Charges for political violence

In both Japan and the United States, persons involved in clandestine political violence were often charged and prosecuted for criminal actions, such as weapons possession, harbouring a criminal or wanted person, aiding prison escapes, bank robbery, and murder. These might have been carried out either for direct political purposes or because of the exigencies of underground life (Zwerman and Steinhoff 2005). Many acts of political violence involved bombings. Some groups particularly focused on police or military personnel as targets, while in other cases police were killed in the course of other kinds of attacks. In addition, a surprising number of incidents of clandestine political violence did not go as planned and were either bungled or led to unexpected consequences. Suspects regarded these as unfortunate and unintentional accidents, while police and prosecutors saw them as evidence of the fundamentally criminal nature of the acts and their perpetrators. The government used these tactical errors to paint the defendants as ordinary criminals, to deny them any political legitimacy, and to further discredit and isolate them from the rest of the political movement. Both countries also had legal devices that could be used to increase the sentence. In the United States in the 1980s, the Racketeer Influenced and Corrupt Organizations (RICO) law – traditionally used to prosecute members of organised crime as racketeers – was used to prosecute groups engaged in clandestine political violence. The goal was to add time to sentences while accentuating the conspiratorial nature of the enterprise and erasing the political identities and histories of the defendants.

Prosecutors also brought charges that were implicitly or explicitly political. Charges of sedition, seditious conspiracy, or subversion were used in both countries. These broad-based political charges were often used to threaten and intimidate suspects, widen the search for accomplices, and to magnify the threat posed by defendants, as well as to lay the groundwork for very lengthy sentences. For instance, manufacture and/or use of explosives for political purposes on any scale are prosecuted in Japan under an explicitly political law that was passed over a hundred years ago to punish bomb-throwing anarchists. It carries penalties that extend all the way to the death penalty. Threatening to apply the explosives control law is thus a favourite device of prosecutors during interrogations, raising the spectre of the death penalty for relatively minor offences. The Japanese Anti-Subversive Activities Law also includes provisions to increase the penalty for other criminal acts if the defendant's motives are deemed to be subversive.

Most acts of clandestine political violence were planned and carried out by more than one person, in the name of an organisation, and broad-based charges such as subversion, sedition or RICO permit the government to charge anyone who had any involvement in planning, assisting, or carrying out a criminal act as a co-defendant in the case. In the initial stages of investigation and interrogation, the threat of being charged as a co-defendant was frequently a device for obtaining cooperation. Prosecutors in both countries often used the spectre of a broad-based charge as leverage to promise leniency, or in return for cooperation, but they did not necessarily follow through on such promises. Significantly, the charges for which these defendants were tried do not necessarily correlate with the sentences they later received. In general, in both countries prosecutors sought charges that would maximise the potential for long, punitive sentences, regardless of whether they had sufficient evidence to convict at the maximum level. The one exception was when the defendant was going to be openly rewarded for cooperation by being tried separately on reduced charges and/or (in the US) placed in a witness protection program. Since most charges were for group activities, there was some pressure within the group of defendants for everyone to stick together and participate in a group trial as an act of political solidarity. So unless a person had already broken with the group and supplied information about others to government agents, defendants were likely to remain in the group trial, facing potentially very severe punishment. In some instances in Japan, people participated in the group trial precisely because they had, during harsh interrogation, given evidence in a moment of weakness and later wanted to atone for it by remaining loyal to the group.

In the United States, charges may be reduced during preliminary hearings if a relatively minor defendant was willing to plead guilty to lesser charges, as long as the government expected that more serious charges could be levelled against those they perceived as leaders. By contrast, in Japan most of the charges were generic offences with a very wide range of potential sentences over which the trial judges had discretion, with prosecutors using their trial summation to demand the most severe penalty. We found limited change over time in the kinds of charges that were pressed, most of which reflected differences in the nature of the offences.

However, there is another temporal and spatial factor to consider. Some suspects were arrested during or soon after an act of clandestine political violence, when the incident was still fresh in public memory. Others remained at large for months, years, even decades. Some were hiding in plain sight under a different identity; others were leading an underground life in fear of arrest, while still others had gone into exile. In the Japanese sample, a Japanese group in exile carried out the second wave of clandestine political violence in the mid-1970s, with international attacks punishable under Japanese law. Conversely, persons who had gone into exile from the United States had been accepted by the host nation with restrictions preventing their continued political activity, and they could thus only be charged with the original airplane hijacking that had transported them into exile.

In the 1980s – with both countries renewing focus on earlier actions as part of anti-terrorism campaigns – much attention was directed at finding and prosecuting anyone who was known to have gone underground or to have been involved in any underground activity. Both countries' criminal justice systems presumed that anyone who had not yet been found and prosecuted was a continuing danger, and used the existence of such people to promote higher spending on anti-terrorism activities. Some people were put on wanted lists because of their political associations, without clear evidence of any criminal activity, while others had arrest warrants pending against them for specific incidents. In Japan, the apprehension of fugitives in exile was announced to the media as proof of both the need for and the effectiveness of the anti-terrorism campaign. Their long absence was regarded as defiance of the criminal justice system and they were treated harshly, regardless of what they had been doing in the interim and whether they expressed remorse. If they had been released abroad through 'free the guerrilla' action, their original trial was resumed after they were captured and returned to Japan. In the US, fugitives hiding underground were more likely to turn themselves in than to be found by law enforcement. In these cases, the individuals had already contacted attorneys who negotiated their pleas. Sentences were therefore likely to be shorter than they would have been had they been tried along with their compatriots. In reality, by the 1990s most of those who faced charges for actions committed years earlier had long since walked away from political violence (Zwerman and Steinhoff 2012).

The trial process and defence strategies

There is a fundamental temporal difference between criminal trials in the United States and Japan that has broad ramifications. In the United States, trials, once begun, are continuous until both sides rest their case and a verdict is reached. They are tried either before a single judge or a judge and a jury. Strong rules of discovery require the prosecution to share its evidence with the defence before the trial begins and both sides submit lists of witnesses who will be called to testify. The trial's focus is on the oral testimony of witnesses and cross-examination of their testimony, on exhibits that are entered into evidence, and on the persuasiveness of the arguments presented by the prosecution and defence. If there is a jury, it determines guilt or innocence, after which there is a sentencing hearing and the judge determines the sentence according to the legal requirements. However, the specification of the charges to the jury may incorporate decisions about whether the evidence meets the burden of proof for various levels of an offence, so this can also have a major impact on the determination of the sentence.

In Japan, contested criminal cases are tried before a panel of three professional judges of differing ranks.[1] The trial convenes intermittently, usually for half a day once or twice a month. The focus is on the compilation of a written documentary record that the judges can study between sessions, which forms the basis for oral testimony. Most oral arguments – including statements made by the defendant directly to the judges – are written and then read out in court, often at high speed, before being placed in evidence as written documents. There are virtually no rules of discovery, so the defence only knows about prosecution evidence when it is submitted to the court, and they do not know what other exculpatory evidence the prosecution might be withholding. As a result, prosecutors, defence lawyers, and judges only plan for a few trial sessions at a time, the first of which is generally taken up with the presentation of documents to be submitted in evidence and is an opportunity for objections by the other side.

This basic temporal difference in the two systems has several major implications. First, in Japan, defendants in clandestine political violence cases were generally held in solitary confinement in unconvicted detention during the long intermittent trial, although some of this time could at the judges' discretion later be credited against the sentence. It was not uncommon for such defendants to spend up to ten years in isolation cells in unconvicted detention. As communications restrictions to make the isolation more severe became commonplace, this incommunicado status also gradually came to be extended through the trial period.

Second, the discontinuity of the trials affects defence strategies. In the US system, the defence strategy is planned in advance by individual lawyers and defendants along with input from the legal support network. They are given some opportunity to meet together for that purpose before the trial even if the defendant is being held in detention. They can determine what evidence will be presented and how they can counter it, and can decide on each defendant's trial defence position. Defendants then proceed through the trial with a particular type of defence. This may be a conventional criminal defence that includes a not-guilty plea and a full trial by a criminal defence attorney not readily associated with the movements' legal support network; or it could be a defiant political defence in which defendants request to act as their own counsel, refuse to cooperate with the proceedings and use the court to advance the politics of their organisations; or a

---

1. Recent changes requiring some Japanese criminal trials to include lay judges do not apply to the trials in our sample. Similarly, some recent changes to the rules of discovery also do not apply to this set of cases.

quiet political defence in which the defendants will profess ideological support of the organisation and refuse to provide testimony harmful to others, but will accentuate the minimal role they played in illegal activity. The choice of defence strategy is a major factor in sentencing differentials.

Conversely, in the Japanese system co-defendants are held separately in isolation cells in a detention facility with a strict rule of silence. They are not permitted to meet except on trial days, when they are held together in a room when the court is not in session. Consequently, defence strategy has to be worked out through written communication, and through meetings between individual defendants and their lawyers or with members of the legal support network who visit them in detention. Defendant–lawyer communications are privileged, but any communications between co-defendants are sent by regular mail and read by censors at the detention facility. Defendants in unconvicted detention who are also under communications restrictions – which soon became standard for all clandestine political violence cases – cannot have visits with members of their legal support network. They are not allowed to communicate with one another by mail, and can only do so through their lawyers. Lawyers and their clients' ability to form a defence strategy is therefore limited and even deliberately obstructed. This procedural difference also has a clear spatial dimension since it involves the spatial isolation of the individual defendants from co-defendants and supporters.

Moreover, the intermittent, long-term nature of the Japanese criminal trial also alters the dynamic of a defence strategy. The defence does not know in advance what evidence the prosecution has and thus cannot plan a strategy around it. They only learn what the prosecution enters in evidence when it is submitted at particular points during the trial. Once they have seen what is being presented, the defence team has to scramble to find ways to counter it. If the defendants read the evidence during the trial session they may have some ideas about how to do so. Otherwise, it will be the defence team and the volunteer legal support network that try to find appropriate ways to counter it.

Japanese defendants do take a particular stance at the beginning of the trial, which parallels the options taken by US defendants. However, over the course of the long trial they may change their minds. The group that starts with a militant political defence frequently splits later because some defendants no longer want to stay with the militant position of their leaders, who have nothing to lose because they are going to get a severe sentence anyway. Judges in both the US and Japan may also split off individuals in order to consolidate their charges from some other trial into one sentence. If the group is divided from the very beginning, minor figures may be tried separately in a shorter trial for which they offer a defence of remorse and limited responsibility. This, too, adds a spatial dimension to the trial process.

Sentences and appeals

Although we began with cases of clandestine violence in Japan and the United States stemming from two parallel New Left protest cycles occurring in the same time period, there are some significant temporal differences in the overall span from the commission of acts of clandestine political violence to the end of their adjudication. The US cases of clandestine political violence stretched into the mid-1980s, but the trials were also concluded by the end of that decade. The Japanese acts of violence ended earlier, but it took much longer for all of the trials and appeals to end. Two factors are essential for explaining the temporal disparity of the Japanese case: long, discontinuous trials, and the delayed prosecution of returned exiles.

All of the acts of clandestine political violence for which people in the Japanese sample were prosecuted occurred between 1969 and 1977. The first trials for the original domestic cases ended in 1982, but it was not until 1993 that the appeals had been concluded and all sentence serving had begun. The exile group in the Middle East was responsible for two international hostage-taking incidents – in 1975 and 1977 – in which they successfully negotiated with the Japanese government to release several prisoners from the Japanese criminal justice system, including co-defendants in major ongoing trials. Their trials only resumed after they were found and deported back to Japan. All known members of the exile groups both in the Middle East and in North Korea – including those released from prison in Japan – were actively sought but out of reach until they could be found and brought to trial in Japan. The wave of trials involving exiles began in the late 1980s and only ended in 2010, substantially prolonging the criminal justice processes with delayed prosecutions for acts committed decades earlier. Delayed prosecution of out of reach exiles also adds a strong spatial element to the Japanese situation.

Although the range of charges is similar, the sentencing patterns are very different in Japan and the United States. There is a clear temporal pattern to sentencing in Japan: through 1976 there were many light sentences, and only two sentences to over fifteen years. After that point there were very few light sentences, many indefinite (life) sentences, and four death sentences. The earliest offences were less serious, but beginning in 1972 there were major incidents of clandestine political violence committed both in Japan and by exile groups. Because of long, discontinuous trials, the sentences through 1976 only covered parts of the trials even for the earliest incidents. The more severe sentences after 1976 reflect both the increased gravity of the offences and the steadily more punitive criminal justice system, which was influenced by international trends as well as by the transformative domestic event in 1972. We have found several examples of very similar acts receiving heavier sentences in later years, after they were redefined as 'terrorism'.

While sentences in both Japan and the United States were lengthy, in Japan, persons convicted for clandestine political violence ended up serving the full original sentences. At the end of the first trial a sentence would be handed down, with the most severe being either 'indefinite' – corresponding to life imprisonment – or death. Sentences of less than twenty years often included some credit corresponding to time spent in unconvicted detention, which could range from several months to several years. Both the prosecution and the defence would routinely appeal this lower-court decision for clandestine political violence. As in European civil law systems, the Japanese interpretation is that this is not double jeopardy because the lower court's decision is not final until it has been confirmed by a higher court: hence, both sides may appeal. Beginning in 1972, the prosecution would typically ask for as long a sentence as possible, particularly for unrepentant militant defendants and for those viewed as leaders. Judges frequently meted out sentences that were slightly lower, whereupon prosecutors would appeal. However, sentences were seldom lengthened as a result of a prosecutorial appeal. At the same time, the defence would appeal virtually any sentence for a simple reason: if the sentence is appealed, the defendant remains in unconvicted detention until the sentence is confirmed by a higher court, and all time spent in unconvicted detention counts against the overall sentence. While unconvicted detention in solitary confinement is difficult, it comes with much greater communications privileges than sentence serving in a regular Japanese prison. Persons awaiting the death penalty also face many years of imprisonment before the sentence is actually carried out, which they spend in isolation cells with limited communications privileges. As of 2014, out of the four death sentences for clandestine political violence that were originally handed down in 1979 and 1982, not one has been carried out, with one prisoner having died from a chronic illness.

By contrast, in the United States, the sentence handed down may bear little relation to the sentence served and – more significantly – may bear little relation to the specific role that the defendant played in the activity for which they were charged. Both aspects vary among apparently similar cases. Differences between the state and federal systems; the varied composition of the group on trial; differences in the priorities of subsequent administrations; differential access to an appeal process; political connections, and personal resources all produce wild discrepancies with respect to the actual length of time served. There is also a distinctive racial element at work in the American cases. The people who actually ended up serving extremely long sentences are African-American men who are still today serving long murder sentences handed down by state courts in the early 1970s. During that same early time period, white activists in the Weather Underground who had committed less serious acts of clandestine political violence received sentences of eight years or less, with the longest sentence served being three years. In the late 1970s and early 1980s, during the second wave of clandestine political violence in the United States, race recedes as a factor in sentencing. Variation in charges; differences between state and federal justice systems; the type of defence that the defendant mounts in court; the intensity of mobilisation on the part of counter-forces – such as police associations – as well as the time and the place where the defendant was apprehended in relation to the commission of the crime, are all factors that affect the sentencing structure and possibilities for parole, clemency, and pardon.

An interesting example of such disparity can be found in the case of the 1981 robbery of an armoured car undertaken by members of the Black Liberation Army and the May 19th Communist Organization (a successor group to the Weather Underground). The robbery went awry and one guard and two police officers were killed. Over a period of six years, sixteen people were arrested and tried on charges related to the incident. The sentencing outcomes vary wildly. At one end of the sentencing structure is an activist who served as a getaway driver for the robbery. She was apprehended a short time after the robbery, some distance away from the scene of the shoot-out. A state court charged her with three counts of felony murder. She mounted a defiant defence, and was sentenced to three sentences of twenty-five years to life, to be served consecutively (seventy-five years to life). By contrast, two defendants were apprehended months after the incident and charged with RICO in federal court. Although they were suspected of being among those who shot the police and accused of being among the robbers of the armoured truck, they were convicted only as accessories to the crime. They served seven and a half and five and a half years in prison respectively.

In other US cases, both principal and secondary players of violent action were swept into broad-based indictment, such as sedition or conspiracy, with defendants electing to mount defiant defences, in all cases resulting in severe sentences. The imbalance in the severity of sentences between major and minor players can only be corrected through dramatic action on the part of the government, such as a clemency or an executive pardon, or on the part of the defendant, such as an extradition application or a successful escape. In 1999, President Clinton granted clemency to a group of Puerto Rican nationalists who had been prosecuted during the Reagan era for a string of bombings carried out by the FALN, on condition that they renounce terrorism.

Time, space and milieu

In this study we have found similarities in the prosecution of clandestine political violence stemming from the New Left protest cycle of the late 1960s and early 1970s in the United States and Japan. The broad overall aims of the prosecutions are the same in both countries. Quite different, but functionally equivalent, procedures are used in the areas of investigation, detention, and charging of the cases. Trial procedures follow fundamentally different time patterns, which impacts on defence strategy and the length of time spent in unconvicted detention. There are similarities in the range of defence strategies used, but it is difficult to determine the impact of these strategies and other factors on actual sentences. We find a clear pattern of increased severity in sentencing over time in the more unitary and bureaucratic Japanese criminal justice system, whereas the US sentences varied wildly, for many structural, social, and political reasons that do not follow a clear temporal logic. Overall, the US groups were actively engaged in clandestine political violence for nearly a decade longer than the Japanese ones, but the prosecutions were completed much more quickly. The criminal justice process in Japan extended for over four decades due to lengthy discontinuous trial procedures and the delayed prosecution of returned exiles.

Time

We have found several distinct forms of temporality in this investigation, which are sometimes compounded with spatial or milieu effects. Some of these parallel the forms of temporality outlined by McAdam and Sewell (2001), while others do not.

Protest cycle temporal effects

In previous analyses we have located the New Left protest cycle of the late 1960s and early 1970s as nested in the larger political and social histories of Japan and the United States, and we have found parallel temporal effects within the protest cycles of the two countries. First, clandestine activity arose at a specific point in their respective New Left protest cycles, as a result of a sharp police crackdown on escalating violence. This had different effects on the more radical groups and led subgroups and individuals to break off and go underground or into exile, where they engaged in the clandestine political violence that is the focus of this chapter. Second, individuals came to participate in the protest cycle at different times. Second-generation activists, who joined the movement later, when repression of non-violent activism was at its peak, were less politically disciplined and disproportionately more willing to engage in violent actions. Third, the legal support network that had formed early in the cycle remained intact, sustaining connections between public activists, fugitives – underground and in exile – and prisoners. Interaction with legal support networks from the broader milieu facilitated continued resistance within the criminal justice system.

Temporal factors within the criminal justice process

The sequence of stages in the criminal justice system is basically the same in both countries and thus we have used it as the basic lens through which to compare the individual cases in our two samples. Despite parallel criminal justice system stages and a similarity of timing at the onset of underground political violence, the actual calendar time for the adjudication of underground political violence cases through the criminal justice system follows very different temporal patterns in the two cases.[2] Although underground political violence continued nearly a decade longer in the US, all prosecutions for these cases had concluded within four years of the last act of violence. By contrast, active prosecutions for the Japanese cases continued for two decades longer than in the US, and only ended in 2010 – thirty-three years after the last act of violence.

We attribute the longer time span in Japan to two factors. First, the stages of the criminal justice process move at very different speeds in Japan and the United States.

---

2. Of course, this does not eliminate the possibility of cases reopening in the future if members who are still at large and/or in exile return.

Each of the main stages of the process takes much longer in Japan, from the much longer time for interrogation before all charges are brought, through the radically different way that trials are carried out – intermittently and over a period of years – to the different way that appeals are treated in relation to serving the sentence. This structural difference affects all contested criminal cases, but the strategy for providing trial support for these political cases from within the New Left milieu ensures that virtually all cases are contested, which, in turn, ensures that the cases will take much longer to complete. The availability of sustained trial support makes it possible for the defendants to survive their long years of resistance within the criminal justice system. Hence, the extended timeframe is, in these cases, significantly confounded by the involvement of the broader New Left milieu.

The second factor is contingent and spatial, rather than structural. As noted above, the second wave of clandestine violence in the US was domestic, while in Japan it was international, with exile groups engaging in international attacks that they leveraged to gain responses from the Japanese and other governments. Although these acts took place outside the territorial boundaries of Japan, they were punishable under Japanese law and the statute of limitations was suspended until the perpetrators were brought back to Japan to stand trial. That took between one and two decades. Hence, it was a spatial factor that led to this temporal delay: suspects or defendants remained geographically out of reach of prosecution as a result of spending extended periods in exile.

Temporal factors in sentencing and transformative events

The temporal pattern of severity of punishment for acts of political violence is quite different in the two countries, and requires different explanatory concepts of temporality. Three different patterns are noteworthy. The US pattern shifts in accordance with changes in the political administration over a series of national election cycles, producing an alternation between tolerant and repressive periods that fits the traditional notion of cycles as wave-like and recurrent. This shift produced not only more punitive new sentences meted out during a conservative administration, but also the possibility of correction – by way of pardons or sentence reductions – by more liberal administrations. However, it only affected persons adjudicated under the federal system, not those handled in state courts, which were not subject to such federal intervention. This, in turn, underscores the critical spatial dimension affecting political violence convictions in the US due to states having separate legal systems that may vary considerably, plus the overarching federal system for cases crossing state borders.

In Japan, punishment became more severe over time, suggesting linearity. However, the transformative event (McAdam and Sewell 2001; Sewell 1996) of the United Red Army Incident in 1972 provided a turning point that was only evident in retrospect (Abbott 2001; Steinhoff 2013). Close examination of the cases that were pending when the United Red Army incident occurred, plus all subsequent cases, reveal a shift in prosecutorial attitude that eventually resulted in longer sentences.

The War on Terror, initiated by US President Reagan in 1980, affected prosecutions for political violence in both countries, and can be considered another transformative event with both prospective and retrospective impact. In the United States, the introduction of the War on Terror prompted a re-evaluation of old domestic cases rebranded as terrorism, with increased focus on finding and prosecuting the perpetrators. New cases were already from the outset labelled as terrorism. Significantly, at the time that acts of clandestine violence were committed – in the late 1960s and the 1970s in both countries – the term 'terrorism' was typically not applied even to international hijackings, embassy invasions, and politically motivated bank robberies. They were, instead, considered radical, militant, and 'extremist'. After 1980, the War on Terror provided the justification to pursue very old cases as well as new ones, and it served to demonise the New Left and its earliest legitimate social movement activities on the basis of what happened much later, after the protest cycle had been repressed.

Although the focus of our analysis is on prosecutions for clandestine violence and not directly on social movements, we suggest that the emergence of the term 'terrorism' in the early 1980s and its subsequent widespread application by states to virtually any contentious social movement activity that went against state interests may represent the onset of a new cultural epoch of contention, as McAdam and Sewell have theorised the concept. Although scholars have argued for decades that 'terrorism' is a political appellation reflecting the perspective of the state rather than a neutral social scientific concept, its recent application by autocratic rulers for demonising any political opposition suggests that it is a powerful state weapon against which protest movements in less democratic societies must now contend.

Space and milieu

We conclude by briefly pointing to the ways that spatial and milieu factors interact with temporality in this study. As noted at the outset, our research goes beyond the normal spaces of social movement activity to examine the submerged sites of clandestine activity as well as the various sites where the criminal justice process plays out in jails, courtrooms, and prisons. Beyond the obvious spatial factor of a binational comparative study, the existence of fifty different state criminal justice systems, plus a federal level that deals only with specified types of crimes, certainly complicates any analysis of temporal factors in the prosecution of clandestine political violence cases in the United States. By contrast, the unitary national criminal justice system in Japan administered by a national, elite career bureaucracy is much more predictable and easier to analyse. We found two distinctive spatial factors in our analysis of the Japanese case. First, the severe isolation of defendants held in solitary cells for years, prohibitions on co-defendants meeting together, and communications restrictions preventing support-group members from visiting those in unconvicted detention are all factors that obstruct trial preparations and produce spatial barriers separating individual political defendants from others, both inside and outside of the detention facility. Second, the already lengthy Japanese judicial process was further extended by the fact that wanted persons were in exile and thus geographically out of reach of the criminal justice system for long periods of time. It should also be noted that in some cases, after wanted exiles had been deported to Japan and put on trial, there was insufficient evidence to charge them with anything beyond passport violations. The passport violations occurred after they had been placed on the international wanted list, which left them unable to use their legal passports.

We emphasise the role that legal support networks played in both countries, helping persons arrested for clandestine political violence to navigate the criminal justice system as they move through its stages. As we have reported in more detail elsewhere (Steinhoff and Zwerman 2013; Zwerman and Steinhoff 2012) such legal support networks have historical roots in both countries. New Left and post-New Left clandestine political violence cases were reconfigured to bring together cause lawyers and volunteers from the broader New Left milieu, also encompassing volunteers outside the New Left who were committed to the social values of equality, civil liberties, and fair judicial procedures. The support networks made it possible for isolated defendants to sustain a movement identity throughout the criminal justice process and to maintain contact with activists on the outside as they continued to serve their sentences. The non-ideological nature of their support ultimately also helped militants to disengage from their commitment to violence while retaining their personal ties to the broader New Left social movement milieu in which they began their activist careers.

Our analysis illuminates many different forms of temporality, some intrinsic to the sequential nature of the criminal justice process in both countries, and others that affect the US and Japanese cases differently. In addition, we have shown that spatial and milieu factors interact with temporal factors in complex ways. Researchers who are committed to analysing political violence from a social movement perspective need to develop a model that captures the interaction between these factors.

References

Abbott, A. (1995a) 'A primer on sequence methods', in G. P. Huber and A. van de Ven (eds) *Longitudinal Field Research Methods: Studying Processes of Organization Change*, Thousand Oaks, CA: Sage Publishing, Inc., pp. 201–27.

— (1995b) 'Sequence analysis: New methods for old ideas', *Annual Review of Sociology*, 21: 93–113.

— (2001) *Time Matters*, Chicago: University of Chicago Press.

Foote, D (1995) 'Confessions and the right to silence in Japan', *Georgia Journal of International and Comparative Law*, 21(3): 415–88.

Gonoi, I. (2012) *Demo to ha Nanika? [What are Demonstrations About?]*, Tokyo: NHK Books.

Johnson, D. T. (2002) *The Japanese Way of Justice: Prosecuting Crime in Japan*, Oxford and New York: Oxford University Press.

Katzenstein, P. J. and Tsujinaka, Y. (1991) *Defending the Japanese State: Structures, Norms, and the Political Responses to Terrorism and Violent Social Protest in the 1970s and 1980s*, Ithaca, NY: East Asia Program, Cornell University.

McAdam, D. and Sewell, W. H. (2001) 'It's about time: Temporality in the study of social movements and revolutions', in R. R. Aminzade, J. A. Goldstone, D. McAdam, W. H. Sewell, E. J. Perry, S. Tarrow and C. Tilly (eds) *Silence and Voice in the Study of Contentious Politics,* Cambridge: Cambridge University Press, pp. 89–125.

Sewell, W. H. (1996) 'Historical events as transformations of structures: Invention revolution at the Bastille', *Theory and Society*, 25(6): 841–81.

Steinhoff, P. G. (1992) 'Death by defeatism and other fables: The social dynamics of the Rengo Sekigun purge', in T. S. Lebra (ed.) *Japanese Social Organization*, Honolulu: University of Hawaii Press, pp. 195–224.

— (2013) 'Memories of New Left protest', *Contemporary Japan, Journal of the German Institute for Japanese Studies*, 25(2): 127–65.

Steinhoff, P. G. and Zwerman, G. (2013) 'Passer puis renoncer à l'action violente: Les mouvements de la Nouvelle gauche aux États-Unis et au Japon face à la répression', *Cultures et Conflits*, 89: 71–92.

Tarrow, S. (2010) 'The strategy of paired comparison: Toward a theory of practice', *Comparative Political Studies,* 43(2): 230–59.

Zwerman, G. and Steinhoff, P. G. (2005) 'When activists ask for trouble: State-dissident interactions and the New Left cycle of resistance in the United States and Japan', in C. Davenport, H. Johnston and C. Mueller (eds) *Repression and Mobilization, Social Movements, Protest, and Contention*, Minneapolis: University of Minnesota Press, pp. 85–107.

— (2012) 'The remains of the movement: The role of legal support networks in leaving violence while sustaining movement identity', *Mobilization*, 17(1): 67–84.

Zwerman, G., Steinhoff, P. G. and della Porta, D. (2000) 'Disappearing social movements: Clandestinity in the cycle of New Left protest in the United States, Japan, Germany, and Italy', *Mobilization*, 5(1): 85–104.

Chapter Six

Remembering Violence: Four Cases of Contentious Memory in the Italian and Spanish Student Movements of the 1960s and 1970s

Lorenzo Zamponi

Political violence takes place in a symbolic environment that has been structured by the outcomes of previous events and cycles. Accordingly, understanding political violence in time requires understanding the way that past events shape outcomes in the present. The role of memory is crucial in this: the reproduction of an event through mnemonic practices extends the duration of the event and its outcomes. Through memory, contentious events can produce outcomes way beyond the end of the cycle of protest in which they are situated. How, then, do memories of violence impact on collective action? And, in particular, how do the different ways in which political violence is represented and reconstructed, through the mnemonic practices of different actors with divergent agendas, influence the public discourse that movements take part in, and the symbolic environment in which mobilisation takes place? The goal of this chapter is to contribute to answering these questions, through analysis of four cases of remembered political violence from the student movements of the 1960s and 1970s in Italy and Spain.

   Drawing on an analysis of media material and interviews with contemporary activists, I examine the impact of remembered violence on collective action, identifying key processes with regard to four different events: the battle of Valle Giulia in Rome 1968; the chase of Lama in Rome 1977; the Angelo Azzurro fire in Turin 1977, and the death of Enrique Ruano in Madrid 1969. I use the case of the battle of Valle Giulia to illustrate how strategic use of the memory of a violent event can serve as an identity-shaping device for the future development of mobilisation. In the case of the chase of Lama I stress how the memory of the 'years of lead' played a role in creating a filter between the past and the present, with the past being reinterpreted and reconstructed through the lens of the violence that occurred in the intervening years. The Angelo Azzurro case suggests that a dramatic episode of violence can take on the role of a proscription device in a local field of action, reproducing dynamics similar to those that characterise cultural traumas, but on a smaller scale. Finally, the analysis of the evolving representation of the death of Enrique Ruano illustrates how a process of depoliticisation can impact on the legitimacy of the memory of a violent event, in this case the police killing an activist.

Conflict in general, and political violence in particular, occupies a central place in the study of memory. 'It is traumatic memories, signalling the absent presence of violence, suffering, death and destruction, that have dominated scholarly discussion' (Bell 2009: 347). This consideration extends well beyond the academic context, proving even more prevalent in the media. The more contentious a story is, the more it will be told, retold and, therefore, remembered. It is not just that conflict dominates the news (Cohen, Adoni and Bantz 1990: 176), but conflict is also more likely than other social phenomena to be represented 'in relationship to other conflict items [...] connected to other events' and provided with 'historical background and context' (Cohen, Adoni and Bantz 1990: 177). The media tends to over-represent conflict and to represent any contentious episode as a newer version of something that has already happened in the past, providing the audience with a familiar reference to interpret something potentially unsettling and threatening, and thus contributing to the cultural construction of a set of canonical narrative conventions (Bird and Dardenne 1988; Cohen, Adoni and Bantz 1990; Edy 2006).

The way in which violence is remembered, retold, and interpreted produces related outcomes in the social-movement landscape, shaping, limiting, or enhancing different aspects of the episodes of contention that follow, both in the same cycle of protest and decades later. A general model of the impact of the memory of violence on future mobilisation is beyond the scope of this chapter. What I will do instead is analyse the interaction between different factors in four different cases. Three of these are cases of active violence, in the sense that the movement is using violent practices of contention, while in the fourth case a movement activist is the victim of the violence that is remembered. In two cases I analyse the way in which the memory of a certain event has an impact on future mobilisation, while in the other two cases I focus on the way in which changes in the social and cultural environment affect and reshape the memory of the events. These four examples stem from my research on the memory of the Italian and Spanish student movements of the 1960s and 70s and its impact on contemporary mobilisation. The work is based on two different sources: I have conducted a discourse analysis of media material, examining all newspaper articles from three Italian (*La Repubblica*, *La Stampa* and *Il Corriere della Sera*) and three Spanish (*El País*, *La Vanguardia* and *ABC*) mainstream newspapers citing relevant events of the student mobilisations of the 1960s and 1970s. I have also interviewed forty activists who have participated in student mobilisations of the last few years, asking them about their experience in the movement, treating their answers as texts in which I have identified and analysed all the implicit and explicit references to the past.

In this chapter I use part of this material in order to illustrate different processes through which political violence is remembered, through which its memory is narrated and reproduced, and through which it influences further mobilisation over time. For each of these processes I make use of one specific example from my research on the memory of the Italian and Spanish student movements.

This choice was made for reasons of clarity and does not mean that there is a precise one-to-one correspondence between the processes I am describing and the cases I chose. Different processes tend to be at work in different cases, with reciprocal and overlapping interactions. For example, the role of violence as an identity-shaping device is quite visible also in the case of the 'chase of Lama', which I have chosen to illustrate another process. Nevertheless, I refer one case to each of the processes I am interested in describing, with particular reference to some specific aspects of the public memory of that event in the context of its historical complexity.

In each of the following sections I describe one of the ways in which political violence is represented over time, how these representations interact with external factors, and how political violence impacts on future mobilisation through memory, with the particular aim to describe the interactions between some specific factors: the work of memory agents, the evolution of the cycles of protest, and the dynamics of the local and global public spheres.

My analysis is rooted in the sociological tradition of memory studies based on Maurice Halbwachs' seminal work, and on the literature on political violence and social movements – the reciprocal relationship of which I have explored elsewhere (Zamponi 2013). According to Halbwachs, 'no memory is possible outside frameworks used by people living in society to determine and retrieve their recollections' (Halbwachs 1992: 43). The field of public memory is structured by the conflict between different narratives of the past, each one aiming at hegemony. This conflict is not a sterile confrontation between different traditions, but a struggle for a group's position within the public sphere. If memory is strategic for setting the criteria of plausibility and relevance in the public sphere, then the narrative that succeeds in imposing itself can grant legitimacy and symbolic power to its group. From this point of view, the common notion of 'distortion' is nothing more than an ingenuous observation. Michael Schudon explains:

> Distortion is inevitable. Memory is distortion since memory is invariably and inevitably selective. A way of seeing is a way of not seeing, a way of remembering is a way of forgetting, too. If memory were only a kind of registration, a "true" memory might be possible. But memory is a process of encoding information, storing information, and strategically retrieving information, and there are social, psychological, and historical influences at each point. (Schudson 1995: 348)

The goal of the social researcher, therefore, is to analyse the processes of distortion that constitute memory in order to identify recurrent processes and agents involved in them. This distortion is sometimes part of a specific cultural and political project, but more often it is the result of a complex interaction between different factors, involving agents, each one carrying its own interests and goals. Collective memory is 'as much a result of conscious manipulation as unconscious absorption and it is always mediated' (Kansteiner 2002: 180).

Violence as an identity-shaping device: The battle of Valle Giulia

Rome, March 1, 1968. At 10 a.m. Several thousand students converged on Piazza di Spagna to protest against the police intervention to clear the occupation of the Roman university building by students. The Roman occupation and its counterparts all over Italy were part of a massive mobilization campaign for a reform of the university system. The march, joined by high school students, passed the headquarters of the RAI (the Italian public television broadcasting network) and the Christian Democratic daily, *Il Popolo*, and then reached Valle Giulia, where helmeted policemen armed with truncheons had garrisoned the faculty of architecture. The two sides confronted each other for a few minutes; then the fights, later known in the movement's mythology as 'The Battle of Valle Giulia', started. The clashes lasted for over three hours, in a dramatic escalation of violence. The police attacked with tear gas and water cannons; the students retaliated with eggs and stones. The police received reinforcements, and so did the students, while an enormous traffic jam blocked the entire city center. According to the police, the students built barricades with cars and destroyed police Jeeps. According to the demonstrators, the police acted with great brutality, charging to the command: 'Kill them'. The struggle, in which about 3,000 demonstrators and 2,000 policemen were involved, resulted in 211 injured (158 of them among the police), 228 arrested and 4 imprisoned. (della Porta 1995: xiv–xv)

The battle of Valle Giulia is an unquestionable symbol of the Italian '68 (della Porta 1995: xv; Passerini 1993: 383) and in particular of its relationship to violence, to the extent that it 'took on a legendary quality for Italian activists' (della Porta 2008a: 228). The core of this symbolic value is neatly summarised by Alessandro Portelli, in his well-known oral history of the event:

The battle of Valle Giulia was a traumatic experience, almost an initiation, for a generation of students. For many, it was the first confrontation with the police; for all, it was the first time that the student fought back. As Paolo Pietrangeli sang, 'Suddenly, a new thing happened: we didn't run, this time we didn't run' ('*non siam scappati più*'). (Portelli 1995: 192–3)

Valle Giulia is remembered as a symbol of violent resistance, as the start of a new phase in the trajectory of the movement, in which students would not passively tolerate police repression, but would instead achieve their goals – in this case, the occupation of the faculty of architecture – by any means necessary, even by employing actively violent tactics.

The process of acquiring a certain level of awareness of the movement's own means is a typical phase of radicalisation. But this process is mediated, and socially and narratively constructed. The possibility of the diffusion of the idea that 'a new thing happened' depends on the presence of social and narrative work: the production and reproduction of the story of this 'new thing'.

The case I am describing has two interesting characteristics: first, I am focusing on the memory of Valle Giulia in the weeks and months that followed the event – just after the 'battle'; second, I am referring to an event that occurred at the beginning of a cycle of protest, the so-called 'long 1968', which in Italy lasted until 1978 (Revelli 1995).

As regards the temporal proximity between the event and the mnemonic practices under analysis, it has to be said that it is a very peculiar kind of memory work that is involved in the construction and diffusion of narratives about very recent events. Memory work does not happen in a void, but is influenced both by the context in which it is situated and by the previous evolution of the narrative of the particular event. Many studies have underlined the path dependency of memory work (Spillman 1998) and the limited malleability of mnemonic material (Jansen 2007), and we can presume that the period of time immediately following an event corresponds to a very high level of malleability: since the story has never been told, it can be told with significant freedom of judgement. This does not automatically mean that the version of the story that is told first will be the one that persists for decades: public memory is a dynamic field, and competition between different narratives is always possible. But the importance of telling a story before anyone else for setting the terms of a specific narrative is undeniable.

Much has already been said about the peculiarity of events – and narratives of events – related to the beginning of a cycle of protest. The scholarship on social movements has debunked many myths of 'immaculate conception' (Taylor 1989) of protest, making clear that the element of surprise that characterises many protests is more related to a lack of information on the part of the observer than to the actual newness of movements, which are typically rooted in previous mobilisations (McAdam 1995). In particular, the construction of the perceived spontaneity with which protest is supposed to begin has been identified as a defining narrative act, necessary for legitimising the movement as something immediately linked to a social problem shared by a certain population, and not as a political process (Polletta 2006). In the case of the battle of Valle Giulia, the event is not considered the starting point of the Italian '68 – that symbolic role is traditionally played, in the Italian public memory, by the occupations of Palazzo Campana in Turin and of the Catholic University in Milan in November 1967 – but it is usually remembered as the turning point from the chaotic, transversal and fluid phase of the student mobilisation to a more ideologically defined and radical period of massive politicisation. The idea of the battle of Valle Giulia as a turning point that shaped the evolution of the cycle of protest of the Italian 1968 is so well rooted that Donatella della Porta cited this episode as one of her examples of events that 'remain impressed in the memory of the activists as emotionally charged events, but also represent important turning points for the organizational structures and strategies of the movements' (della Porta 2008b: 49). It is undeniable that the battle of Valle Giulia has proved to be an 'eventful protest', in della Porta's terms, capable of having a transformative effect on the movement itself. But the 'eventfulness' of a protest cannot be understood only as the result of some specific contextual factors, and della Porta has particularly underlined the role of long and plural preparatory processes, the relevance of communication, and the intensity of emotional experience. In fact, the sense that something new and historical – a fundamental turning point in the evolution of a movement – has happened, also needs an active process of social construction upon which the collective identity of the movement will also depend. This process is clearly visible in the case of the battle of Valle Giulia.

The first accounts of the episode contribute to the creation of the narrative of the 'battle', underlining the violent character of the event,[1] but are not prejudicial against the student movement. On the contrary, even after the most conflictual episode of the student mobilisation of '68, the press was sympathetic:

> [M]ost of the students are engaged in a wide debate on the general issues. There have been heated exchanges of ideas, but the discussion never departed far from a civil tone. But there are groups that have an interest in provoking incidents among the same students, in order to make impossible all the constructive debates aimed at building a consensus. And these cannot be other than the fascists.[2]

The word 'battle' is, then, present in the media reports already on the day following the event,[3] providing the potential for the creation of a certain narrative based on the active and violent resistance of the students against the police. The movement immediately exploits this chance, particularly the most revolutionary-leaning workerist groups – those parts of the movement that will, a few months later, begin to form Lotta Continua and Potere Operaio. The activists start to develop a specific mnemonic project, tending to make 'the battle of Valle Giulia' a symbol of a new, offensive attitude of the movement. During a demonstration in Pisa a couple of weeks after the event, the press reports, some people chanted 'Valle Giulia' and 'potere operaio'.[4]

This is an explicit act of memory work: memory agents retrieve symbolic material available in the public sphere – that already contains media accounts of a 'battle' in Valle Giulia – appropriating the representation of the event, attaching to it certain specific connotations and spreading the story as a narrative example of what the movement should become. Due to this work, the words 'Valle Giulia'

---

1. Giurato, L. (1968) 'Nuovi incidenti stamane davanti alla facoltà di Architettura Roma: dura battaglia a sassate fra migliaia di studenti e poliziotti', *Stampa sera*, 2 March, p. 1; my translation.

2. B., M. (1968) 'La facoltà d'Architettura a Roma incendiata da teppisti fascisti', *Stampa sera*, 15 March, p. 13; my translation.

3. Franci, G. (1968) 'Violenta battaglia nel centro di Roma fra studenti e polizia: centinaia di feriti', *La Stampa*, 2 March, p. 1; my translation.

4. N., G. (1968) 'A Pisa gli studenti entrano in stazione bloccano i treni, feriscono viaggiatori', *La Stampa*, 16 March, p. 17; my translation.

become directly associated not with a place in Rome but with a specific event, immediately historicised through narration.

In conducting this memory work, the movement also shows the capacity to use a wide set of means for cultural production. Already in May the press witnesses the organisation of movement events in which a self-made documentary on the 'battle of Valle Giulia' is screened:

> At the Unione Culturale (via Battisti 4) tonight at 9.30pm the 'Newsreel of the Student Movement number 1', a documentary on the events from March 1st to 15th, that means 'From Valle Giulia until the battle with the fascists in the Law Department' will be screened.[5]

In the weeks immediately following the event, the quite popular militant folk singer Paolo Pietrangeli writes a song entitled 'Valle Giulia' and he performs it in concerts and at festivals before publishing it in 1969 (Vettori 1975). The song contains a first-person narrative of the events of 1 March, climaxing towards the description of a fundamental turning point:

> They [the police] took their sticks in their hands
>
> and they beat us like they always do;
>
> but, suddenly, a new thing happened,
>
> a new thing, a new thing:
>
> we did not run away any more, we did not run away any more! (Pietrangeli 1969; my translation)

The song, which begins with a critique of the school system, goes through the experience of the battle against the police and – after celebrating the fact that this time it was the police who ran away – ends by rephrasing the initial critique, that no longer addresses the school system as such, but the ruling class in general. The mnemonic project is visible here. Valle Giulia is instrumental in shaping the identity of the movement in a specific direction: the project of radicalisation promoted by some of the most politicised parts of the movement. Valle Giulia becomes the symbol of those inside the movement who plan to stop 'running' away from the police and whose aim is, rather, to generalise a strategy of confrontation. To carry a sign with the words 'Valle Giulia' at a demonstration hundreds of kilometres from Rome, amounts to claiming responsibility for what the students did on 1 March, and to propose it should be done again. An event in this way becomes the symbol of an identity that is proposed for the movement as a whole; the symbol of a direction that – according to some – should be taken by the whole movement.

---

5.   Anonymous (1968) *Stampa sera*, 31 May, p. 2; my translation.

The movement has an active role in the field of public memory. It participates in the public debate; it promotes its own version of the recent past, and it uses technology to reinforce its narrative. Particularly some groups inside the movement carry on specific mnemonic projects. A recent past – and especially a contentious one – becomes a resource for the definition of identity. Therefore, the movement as a whole, as well as specific actors inside the movement, work to establish a certain representation of the past: a narrative capable of setting the borders of belonging.

And the results come in: less than a year later, when new occupations take place at the University of Rome, there are immediate references to 'the events of Valle Giulia'.[6] In time, the event becomes a reference for every episode of contention in the university: 'The incidents might be the worst happening in Rome since the episode of Valle Giulia.'[7]

It took only one year to complete the identification between the name of 'Valle Giulia', the place, and the events of 1 March 1968. Now, when a journalist writes 'Valle Giulia', the reader can assume that the article refers to that event, and not to a park in the centre of Rome, even if the context is not the student movement.[8] And the movement, meanwhile, has assumed Valle Giulia as a significant part of its own identity and development.

In this sense, the mnemonic practices of the public sphere's representation of the memory of the 'battle of Valle Giulia' transform this representation into an *identity-shaping device*: an instrumental tool in the evolution of the collective identity of the movement in the cycle of protest. An episode of political violence situated in 1968 produces outcomes in a long cycle of protest, through mnemonic practices and – in particular – through the strategic mnemonic work of movement actors.

Violence as filter: The 'chase of Lama' and the 'years of lead'

In February 1977 students occupied Rome University to protest against reform proposals made by the Education Minister Malfatti. The occupation quickly became a focal point for disaffection in the capital. [...] Luciano Lama, head of the CGIL[9], heavily protected by trade union and PCI[10] stewards, came to address the occupation. Both the 'creative' and 'militarist' wings of the

---

6.   Peroli (1969) 'Tensione all'ateneo di Roma Di nuovo in pericolo la riforma?', *La Stampa*, 13 February, p. 11; my translation.

7.   Zanotti, L. (1971) 'Duri scontri all'ateneo di Roma 60 feriti, tre agenti sequestrati', *La Stampa*, 3 February, p. 1; my translation.

8.   Fabbri, M. (1973) 'Merlino, imputato della strage di Milano indiziato con Preda per la "pista nera"', *La Stampa*, 31 July, p. 9; my translation.

9.   The largest Italian trade union confederation, then composed mainly of Communist and Socialist workers.

10.   The Italian Communist Party.

movement mobilized against him. In a tragic scene of mutual incomprehension, Lama was shouted down and violent clashes broke out between the Autonomi and the stewards of the PCI. A fortnight later, a demonstration of some 60,000 young people in the capital degenerated into a four-hour guerrilla battle with police. Shots were fired on both sides, and a part of the demonstrators chanted a macabre slogan in praise of the P38 pistol, the chosen weapon of the Autonomi. (Ginsborg 1990: 382)

The first representations of the facts on 17 February 1977 interpret the event as a sign of the crisis of the Italian Communist Party (PCI) – of its incapacity to speak to the youth and to keep up with the pace of a changing society.[11] The members of Autonomia Operaia[12] are credited with the attack, and they are immediately depicted as criminals[13], accused of '*squadristica* violence'[14], but there is more stress on the party debate than on that of the movement. The articles focus mainly on the difficulties of the PCI:[15] 'Not even the PCI, with its very receptive antennas, succeeds in picking up the moods of the youth?'[16], and '[a]n elderly man "always a PCI member" reflects aloud: "I have seen the comrades beating up autonomous brats. If our force – being 35% of the Italian voters – translates into such acts, then something is not working: we must have done something wrong."'[17]

Moderate union leaders explicitly criticise Lama, whose decision to give a speech at the occupied university is considered an arrogant attempt to subdue, instead of patiently listening to, the students:

[Macario, secretary general of the CISL[18]:] 'Patience, you need. And dialectic... This is a society that does not accept to be submitted, that does not tolerate imperialisms'.

11. Santini, F. (1977) 'Nella città più rossa la rivolta è perdente', *La Stampa*, 19 February, p. 3; my translation.
12. Post-workerist extra-parliamentary movement, led by Toni Negri, Franco 'Bifo' Beradi and others, active between 1976 and 1979. For historical references, see Sergio Bianchi and Lanfranco Caminiti 2007, 2008.
13. Anonymous (1977) 'Chi sono i provocatori', *Stampa sera*, 17 February, p. 2; my translation.
14. Scardocchia, G. (1977) 'Minuto per minuto, il comizio di Lama e la violenta battaglia all'Università', *La Stampa*, 19 February, p. 1; my translation.
15. Trovati, G. (1977) 'Giudizio politico', *La Stampa*, 4 March, p. 1; Trovati, G. (1977) 'La gravissima crisi rafforza il governo', *La Stampa*, 13 March, p. 1; R., S. (1977) 'Da contestazione a guerriglia un anno di Università a Roma', *La Stampa*, 22 April, p. 2; Gorresio, V. (1977) 'Annibale a Montecitorio', *La Stampa*, 18 May, p. 3; my translation.
16. Scardocchia, G. (1977) 'Minuto per minuto, il comizio di Lama e la violenta battaglia all'Università', *La Stampa*, 19 February, p. 1; my translation.
17. Madeo, L. (1977) 'Il disastro lasciato dagli occupanti', *La Stampa*, 19 February, p. 1; my translation.
18. The second largest Italian trade union confederation, composed mainly of Catholic workers.

[Benvenuto, secretary general of the UIL[19]:] 'We ought to have distanced ourselves from the idea that the unions, led by Lama, were going to the university to impose order on the students'.[20]

Even the quite conservative newspaper *La Stampa* is virtually taking the side of the students or – at the very least – strongly criticises Lama for his choice to address the movement in the occupied university with a unilateral act that was considered arrogant and paternalistic.

The event is considered a break-up between the student movement and the Communist Party[21] that was due to the fact that, for the first time in republican history, the PCI was not in opposition, in that the third Andreotti cabinet relied on abstention by Communist Members of Parliament. In that complex political phase, Lama's decision to give a speech at the occupied University is interpreted as a misplaced and arrogant way to establish a dialogue with the movement. Even inside the Communist Party there is a tendency to self-criticism for 'the lack of comprehension of the mood in the universities' and for the 'delay of the PCI and of the unions in addressing the issues of the youth'.[22] Lama himself claims that his was an attempt to establish 'a constructive dialogue', sabotaged by a violent minority of students.[23]

The narrative totally changes in correspondence with the so-called 'years of lead', an expression denoting the period of maximum intensity of political violence between 1977 and 1982, though it is sometimes used in a more general sense, to cover the whole of the 1970s (Betta 2009; Armani 2010).

Over time, the event becomes increasingly associated with terrorism,[24] especially[25] after 7 April 1979, when many of the leaders of Autonomia Operaia are arrested and charged with forming part of a single terrorist network together

---

19. The third largest Italian trade union confederation, composed mainly of Socialist, Social-Democratic and Republican workers.

20. S., R. (1977) 'Macario sul comizio di Lama', *La Stampa*, 22 February, p. 3; my translation.

21. Pucci, E. (1977) 'Insulti contro Scheda da ferrovieri del Sud', *La Stampa*, 2 August, p. 2; Casalegno, C. (1978) 'Un inedito di Casalegno', *La Stampa*, 10 June, p. 3; my translation.

22. Anonymous (1977) 'Università: autocritica comunista', *La Stampa*, 23 February, p. 4; my translation.

23. Pucci, E. (1977) 'Lama: occorre lavoro invece di assistenza', *La Stampa*, 14 April, p. 2; my translation.

24. Anonymous (1977) 'Non si può essere neutrali', *La Stampa*, 6 March, p. 21: R., S. (1977) 'Da contestazione a guerriglia un anno di Università a Roma', *La Stampa*, 22 April, p. 2; Tr., G. (1977) 'Perché contro la DC', *La Stampa*, 3 November, p. 1; my translation.

25. Giurato, L. (1979) 'Lama e Spriano ad Amendola Compagno, a sbagliare sei tu', *La Stampa*, 11 November, p. 2; Anonymous (1979) 'Tre storie, tre giovani uccisi perché tacessero', *La Stampa*, 29 December, p. 5; Fabbri, M. (1980) 'Gli operai dell'Alfa Le Br sono fra noi', *La Stampa*, 29 February, p. 7; Anonymous (1992) 'Quell'assalto a Lama aprì gli anni di piombo', *La Repubblica*, 23 September, p. 3; Castellano, C. (1997) 'Ma dire indulto non significa oblio', *La Repubblica*, 26 August, p. 13; my translation.

with the Brigate Rosse (Bocca 1980). This association grows stronger in the 1980s, when some former members of the BR start to say that they participated in the events on 17 February 1977.[26]

In the early 1980s – after the proper 'years of lead' – the memory of 1977 is filtered through the lens of terrorism. Lama, who in 1977 considered his speech as an attempt at dialogue, now exalts it as a bold antiterrorist action:

> We saw the P38 guns that day. [...] I still think I was right in going to the university: together with me, and through what happened to me, a part of the country realised what was going on, the danger that democracy was in.[27]

From this moment on, in every interview, Lama will portray himself as a lonely antiterrorism hero[28] and, after his death, this is how he is remembered.[29] Furthermore, the episode is mentioned, on various occasions, in interviews with trade union leaders after terrorist acts.[30]

The phenomenon is quite similar to one described by Giovanni De Luna in reference to cinematic representation of the 1970s, which has focused primarily on violence and terrorism, with

> a periodisation that flattened a whole decade into its second half, reducing the whole era into a unique tragic moment in which evil had converged. The before existed only as a premonition of the imminent catastrophe, the after was not interesting, and the during was flattened into the facts of the final years, above all on one event: the murder of Aldo Moro. (De Luna 2009: 142, my translation)

The filter of the 'years of lead' changes the memory of the 'chase of Lama': before, parts of the movement claimed to have participated in the event on the anti-Lama front in order to build an image of hard-core militancy; now, social and political actors claim not to have participated in the event on the anti-Lama front in order to

---

26. Anonymous (1982) 'Varisco sfuggì a molti agguati prima che le Br lo uccidessero', *La Stampa*, 9 April, p. 2; Anonymous (1983) 'Savasta carceriere di Dozier', *La Stampa*, 27 July, p. 3; Meletti, J. (2007) 'L'errore di noi brigatisti snobbare il Movimento', *La Repubblica*, 15 February, p. 9 (Bologna); my translation.

27. Tornabuoni, L. (1984) 'Lama: Per fortuna ho sbagliato', *La Stampa*, 6 January, p. 3; my translation.

28. Mieli, P., (1987) 'Lama: neanche Berlinguer mi capì', *La Stampa*, 11 January, p. 6; S., V. (1992) 'L'ex leader: "Spontanea? No, protesta orchestrata"', *La Repubblica*, 23 September, p. 3; my translation.

29. Scalfari, E. (1996) 'Quando mi disse 'austerità", *La Repubblica*, 1 June, p. 1; P., A. (1996) 'L'ultimo incontro 'fidatevi di Cofferati", *La Repubblica*, 1 June, p. 7; Caporale, A. (1996) 'Lama, l'ultima volta a San Giovanni', *La Repubblica*, 4 June, p. 6; Mafai, M. (2006) 'Lama, il cuore del riformismo', *La Repubblica*, 31 May, p. 50; my translation.

30. Giannini, M. (1999) 'Hanno voluto colpire la sinistra di governo', *La Repubblica*, 21 May, p. 8; Messina, S. (2002) 'La lezione di Andreotti I sindacati nostri alleati', *La Repubblica*, 27 March, p. 8; my translation.

build an image of commitment to antiterrorism. What in 1977 was considered an act of youthful turbulence provoked by the 'arrogance' of the Communist Party became, from the mid-1980s on, the incubator of murderous terrorism. To say that someone has participated in the chase of Lama is, in the 1980s, offensive – something that can be used as a powerful weapon in the public debate.

A particularly clear example comes from 1985, in the midst of the stormy debate on the abolition of the sliding wage scale proposed by the government, led by the head of the Socialist Party, Bettino Craxi. The proposal deeply divides the Socialists in government and the Communists in opposition, also cutting through the CGIL, which has both Communist and Socialist members. When the leader of the Socialist current of the union, Ottaviano Del Turco, needs to portray his Communist counterparts as extremists, he points out that the abolition of the sliding wage scale is also opposed by Mario Capanna – the secretary general of the radical left party *Democrazia Proletaria* – and 'leader of those who threw rocks against Lama at the University of Rome'.[31]

Interestingly enough, not only has this allegation nothing to do with the Communist members of the CGIL, but it is also based on a confusion: in fact, before becoming the secretary of *Democrazia Proletaria* Mario Capanna had been one of the best known and influential leaders of the 1968 protests in Milan, and in 1977 he was far too old to be at university. The story ends with Capanna bringing a lawsuit for defamation against Del Turco,[32] but what is relevant for the purposes of this chapter is that in this example we have a double rhetorical jump: not only are all those who participated in the 1977 protests now associated with political violence, but the same holds for those who protested in 1968. 'The chase of Lama' becomes both the metonymy of the whole cycle of protest of the 1960s and 1970s and a metaphor for political violence and murderous terrorism.

The instrumental use of the chase of Lama is also possible the other way around, as shown by an example from 1995: when Alberto Asor Rosa – famous literary critic and leftist intellectual, with strong credentials in the mainstream left of the 1990s – is accused of having been one of the inspirers of the Red Brigades by a disgraced former secret service agent, Rosa's answer starts by saying that, on 17 February 1977, he was physically on Lama's side: 'Lama? On that day I was in the university, next to the secretary of CGIL. And I risked having my bones broken.'[33]

In 1977, the press could have considered the act of standing at Lama's side as indicating Rosa's participation in the Communist Party's lack of understanding of 'the moods of the youth'. Now, after the 'years of lead', it has become a strong antiterrorism credential.

---

31. Devecchi, S. (1985) 'Del Turco: "Bastano i fatti a parlare in favore del no"', *La Stampa*, 6 June, p. 13; my translation.

32. Anonymous (1985) 'I sassi contro Lama', *La Stampa*, 8 June, p. 2; Anonymous (1987) 'Querela di Capanna processo a Torino', *La Stampa*, 22 January, p. 11; my translation.

33. Stella, G. A. (1995) 'Ma e' attendibile un colpevole di ladrocinio?', *Il Corriere della sera*, 9 March, p. 14; my translation.

The 'years of lead' occupy the field of public memory so heavily that they have become an irremovable filter between the present and everything that happened before 1978. The events of the 1970s – and in particular 1977 – are interpreted as merely instrumental to the explosion of political violence that followed. The presence of such a heavy memory of violence thus completely changes the representation of what happened before: as we have seen, the 'years of lead' reshaped the story of the chase of Lama in accordance with this narrative, the event now being interpreted as a build-up to political violence, portraying the same actors but in different roles. Competing narratives of political violence populate the field of public memory, reproducing in different ways the violence of the 1970s, and giving it the capacity to influence the public debate for decades afterwards.

Violence as a proscription device: The Angelo Azzurro fire

Neil Smelser – with amendment by Ron Eyerman – defines cultural trauma as:

> a memory accepted and publicly given credence by a relevant membership group and evoking an event or situation which is (a) laden with negative affect, (b) represented as indelible, and (c) regarded as threatening a society's existence or violating one or more of its fundamental cultural presuppositions or group's identity. (Smelser 2001: 44; Eyerman 2003: 2–3)

This concept is most useful for explanations of the role of big historical events – such as slavery in the American context (Eyerman 2003) or the Civil War in the Spanish one (Sánchez Mosquera 2008) – when the group to which the trauma refers can be identified with a whole national society or some relevant component of it. Relativising cultural trauma – identifying the borders of the social group for which a particular memory is traumatic and the relative levels of relevance that this memory occupies with respect to different social groups – is quite challenging and problematic. Nevertheless, the literature on cultural trauma is particularly useful in showing how a certain memory, if it gains a position of relevance in the public sphere, is able to shape the symbolic environment in which social actors are placed. The memory of certain events, narrated as characterised by negative effects, with an indelible nature and the capacity to violate a group's identity, can strongly contribute to setting symbolic limits and borders around a social actor. It can contribute to the establishment of certain prescriptions and proscriptions in a specific population, as Jeffrey Olick and Daniel Levy have shown with respect to the cultural constraints that the memory of the Holocaust has imposed on German politics (Olick and Levy 1997).

The case referred to in this section is far from comparable with slavery, civil war, and holocausts, but if we take the leftist movement milieu in Turin as the population of reference, it has assumed some of the main characteristics of a cultural trauma.

The Angelo Azzurro fire is one of the most traumatic events of the Italian youth mobilisation of 1977, for reasons connected both to the nature of the event – the accidental death of an innocent working class student – and to its public representation – the press publishing the picture of the dying victim.

On 1 October 1977 there was in Turin – as in many other Italian cities – an antifascist demonstration. These demonstrations had been organised by various groups of the revolutionary left in reaction to the killing of the communist militant Walter Rossi, who had been shot by far-right militants the day before, during an antifascist rally in Rome, in reaction to the killing of another leftist militant by fascists the day before, in an incredible chain of violence. During the demonstration in Turin, a group of activists attacked a bar, wrongly believed to be a meeting point for the fascist right, throwing Molotov cocktails. The twenty-two-year-old working class student Roberto Crescenzio was in the bar, did not manage to escape, and was burned to death. The picture of Crescenzio's stiff charred body, placed in a chair on the street as the ambulance arrived, made a huge impact in the public sphere. As Monica Galfré put it, the event, 'hushed the movement itself, marking a point of no return' (Galfré 2008: 129; my translation). This silence concerned not only the students of 1977. The persistence and reproduction of this memory in the local public sphere strongly influenced and shaped the symbolic environment of further activism in Turin. In particular, it had an effect on the level of violence tolerated by local public opinion – traditionally considered a key element of the political opportunity structure of any movement. It became more difficult for student activists in Turin to raise the level of contention, as vividly testified in this interview:

> My mother is extremely anxious about everything connected with street contention, because she is carrying the weight of the trauma of Angelo Azzurro in Turin [...] In 1977, during a demonstration, a Molotov Cocktail was thrown into a bar in Via Po, frequented by fascists, everyone escaped apart from a person who was in the bathroom and caught fire. There is this very famous image of this person, stiff, charred, sitting, with his rigid silhouette, on the street waiting for an ambulance. This thing constituted a very strong trauma for a whole generation in Turin, of which my mother is part.[34]

This is only one personal example of quite a large phenomenon that resonates strongly with both the literature on cultural trauma and with Olick and Levy's consideration of the prescriptive and proscriptive capacity of collective memory. In this case, a particularly morbid picture from a violent event in 1977 is able to play a relevant role in setting the limits of the repertoire of contention in 2014. This does not mean that Turin is condemned to respect these limits forever, given that 'the relationship between remembered pasts and constructed presents is one of perpetual but differentiated constraint and renegotiation over time, rather than pure strategic invention in the present or fidelity to (or inability to escape from)

---

34. Interview with student activist in Turin, 7 June 2013.

a monolithic legacy' (Olick and Levy 1997: 934). Nevertheless, remembered violence has a significant impact on contemporary mobilisation, acting as quite an effective *proscription device*, able to establish taboos that activists know they have to respect during street protests, unless they want to completely alienate public opinion.

Violence subject to depoliticisation: The death of Enrique Ruano

On the night of January 17th 1969, four young anti-Francoists were detained in Madrid. Three days later, one of them, Enrique Ruano Casanova, student of the Universidad Complutense and militant of the Popular Liberation Front would lose his life during the search of a flat in the city centre, while he was guarded by three agents of the state political police. (Domínguez Rama 2011a: back cover, my translation)

Shouting the slogan 'They murdered Enrique Ruano' the mobilisation in the university campuses of Madrid gradually grew until it provoked the almost total paralysis of academic life, involving strikes at most Spanish universities. Over the next few days, assemblies, incidents, and demonstrations at the university and in different places across the capital occurred as a sign of grief and protest. [...] On January 24th, the continuing student protest caused the academic authorities to close the University of Madrid, while the minister Fraga announced a state of exception in the whole of Spain for a period of three months. (Domínguez Rama 2011b: 44–6, my translation)

The memory of Ruano's killing is, until the beginning of the 1970s, internal to a cycle of a protest. It is related to an event that took place during a wave of mobilisation, directly involving an activist, and the movement appropriates it as a symbol of that which they are protesting against. After the end of the wave of student mobilisation, there is no social actor appropriating the memory of Ruano's death in order to develop a mnemonic project.

After the death of Franco and the transition to democracy, both the intrinsic characteristics of the story of Enrique Ruano and its immediate appropriation by the clandestine left and the student movement during a wave of mobilisation, makes it quite difficult to insert into the narrative of the Spanish transition to democracy, officially represented as a 'pacted rupture' (Linz 1992; my translation): a process of gradual change lead by the reformist sector of the Francoist elite under the supervision of the new king (Martín Villa 1985). Between 1975 and the 1982 electoral victory of the Socialist Party that put Franco's political heirs in the opposition for the first time, the Spanish press make scarce reference to how contributions from below led to the end of the regime. But the story of Enrique Ruano is still controversial later on, when the fact of having participated in anti-Francoist events, such as the 1966 *capuchinada* – a clandestine meeting of students in a convent in Barcelona, to found an alternative, democratic, student union – becomes a point of honour, a line on the CV that most politicians would be proud of. Not only did Ruano's story call attention to the excessive use of force on the part of the police – something that would be politically sensitive in any political regime, and that was particularly uncomfortable in a country characterised by strong tension between continuity and reform – but it also had as its protagonist a radical activist: a young revolutionary who looked more like those still protesting under the new democratic regime than the people now in government. Even if Ruano was, in fact, a victim of the violence of the regime, it was more difficult to represent him as an innocent victim than it would have been others, not only for his participation in a radical leftist group like the FLP but also for the connection between his death and the wave of student outrage that followed, set in a context that a Spanish historian described as characterised by a 'genetic fear of protest' (Sánchez Mosquera 2008; my translation).

The few references to Enrique Ruano's death in the 1980s (mostly in *El País*, as *ABC* and *La Vanguardia* chose silence) are strictly linked to the memory of anti-Francoism. Ruano is a controversial victim of the regime, whose memory became a mobilising symbol for students fighting against the dictatorship. The student movement of the 1960s and 1970s is represented through the lens of the struggle for democracy, and the idea of a 'Spanish 1968' is ridiculed even on the twenty-fifth anniversary of 1968. Interestingly enough, this article that denies the existence of a Spanish 1968 cites precisely those two events that will, in the following years, become the symbols of the Spanish 1968: the concert of Valencian singer Raimon, at the University of Madrid in 1968, and the 'obscure' death of Enrique Ruano in 1969.[35] But at this point it is still too soon: the memory of the student struggles goes under the master frame of Francoism, anti-Francoism, and transition, and Ruano sits uncomfortably in this narrative.

Even when, between 1992–6, Ruano's story emerges in the media in relation to a new trial concerning his death, those two traits are still visible: the anti-Francoist lens and the difficulty of portraying a militant as an innocent victim. Some articles reclaim truth and justice for Ruano, describing his death as 'one of the most sinister events of Francoism'[36], but the public recognition of Ruano as a victim is still controversial. The best example of this is probably an *ABC* article by Gregorio Peces-Barba, once Ruano's professor and now – in 1994 – rector of the Universidad Carlos III of Madrid. In the article,[37] Peces-Barba recognises the fact that 'bad memory' has been 'one of the keys of the political transition', and calls for an exception in Ruano's case, because 'this general principle, that counts for big collective decisions, would be unjust and petty if it became our attitude when people in flesh and blood are concerned'. This is an attempt to reconcile the request for truth, justice, and memory of the death of Enrique Ruano with the political,

---

35. Moran, G. (1993) '¿Existió aquel Mayo o lo imaginamos?', *La Vanguardia*, 24 April, p. 19; my translation.

36. Anonymous (1992) 'Enrique Ruano', *El País*, 14 July; my translation.

37. Peces-Barba, G. (1994) 'Enrique Ruano: recordando su vida y su muerte', *ABC*, 20 January, p. 3; my translation.

cultural, and judicial architecture of the transition, and it is quite a meaningful one, given that it is proposed by a man who personifies the transition. In fact, Gregorio Peces-Barba, after having defended anti-Francoist detainees as a lawyer during the dictatorship, was the representative for the Socialist Party in the committee that wrote the constitution and, in 1982, became president of the Spanish Congress. But the most interesting part of this article is where the author explains that Enrique Ruano's friends, 'who shared his ideas and his commitments, now live in the democratic society' as professionals, entrepreneurs and politicians, and that 'if Enrique had been able to develop that life that was cut off so early, he would now, like his friends and mates, be a good professional and a good citizen, and we cannot be haughty in contemplating the years and behaviours that frustrated many illusions and hopes of young people like Enrique Ruano'.

The author – a man who loved and respected Ruano and who is fighting for his memory – is, in a certain sense, asking for forgiveness of the victim, saying, yes, he was a revolutionary militant, but he was young, and look how important and respectable some of his fellow student activists have become – he could have been like them. Even in an article written by someone who loved Enrique Ruano and who is active in the struggle for giving him justice and memory, there is still the implicit concept that, even under a fascist regime, radical political activism is wrong. Or, at least, that within the master frame of peaceful transition it is very difficult to identify a revolutionary militant as an innocent victim of the violence of the regime.

The trial will end with the recognition that the official version of suicide was fabricated, but with the absolution of the three policemen, due to the disappearance of one of Ruano's bones, making it impossible to prove that he was killed.

The renewed popularity of Enrique Ruano's memory in the Spanish press is obviously linked to the work done by the media covering the trial, and by the debate in 2004–8 regarding the memory of the Civil War and the dictatorship that characterised Spanish politics (Aguilar 2008: 76–94). But there is something more: Ruano's memory becomes more legitimate and less controversial when freed from the frame of anti-Francoism and the transition. In fact, in the 2000s, there will be increased mention of Enrique Ruano's death in the context of a new narrative: that of the Spanish 1968, the existence of which had, until a few years before, been denied, but that finds legitimation in the public sphere after the normalisation of the Spanish political system. In many articles, Enrique Ruano becomes one of the two symbols of the Spanish 1968, together with the famous Raimon concert.[38]

This is not the only factor playing a role in this process, and many of the articles referring to Ruano's story are connected to the debate on memory mentioned above: denunciations of 'denied memory'; attacks on the PP for

---

38. Ordoñez, M. (2007) 'Aquel 'Marat-Sade' del 68', *El País*, 3 May; Savater, F. (2008) 'Un mes y cuarenta años', *El País*, 5 May; Fraguas, R. and Gisbert, P. (2008) 'Unas horas de libertad en el 68', *El País*, 23 May; Fraguas, R. (2008) 'Madrid vuelve a corear versos de Raimon', *El País*, 23 May; my translation.

its refusal to explicitly denounce Francoism, and pieces related to Judge Garzon's attempt to investigate Franco's crimes in spite of the Ley de Amnistia.[39] Nevertheless, there is a visible correlation between the gradual acceptance of Enrique Ruano in the canon of the victims of the dictatorship and the progressive 'sixty-eightisation' of the memory of the Spanish student movement. Specifically, in 2008, on the occasion of the fortieth anniversary of 1968, the memory of the student struggles of the 1960s and 1970s become for the first time completely integrated in the global narrative of 1968. On previous occasions, the press had always stressed the difference between what had happened in Spain and what had happened in the rest of the world, looking at the Spanish student movement as student opposition to Francoism, set in a context made exceptional by the presence of the dictatorship, rather than as a local instance of a global phenomenon. Now, the landscape has completely changed, and Enrique Ruano's death and Raimon's concert at the university become symbols of the Spanish 1968 movement. This seems to be quite a visible example of the processes of a globalisation of memory that the scholarship is beginning to address. As Philipps and Reyes have noted,

> [T]he dynamics of global forces can be seen as influencing and altering local and national memories and memory practices in ways that will be more intelligible when rendered within a framework of global memory than if understood solely in relation to local and national forces. (Phillips and Reyes 2011: 18)

Furthermore, '1968' is not a neutral label. To integrate the memory of the Spanish student movement in the global narrative of 1968 means to privilege, also in the Spanish context, the traits nowadays connected with the global narrative of 1968. As Daniel Bensaid wrote, this is 'a depoliticised and depoliticising reading' of 1968, in which the global student revolt is 'reduced [...] to the anti-authoritarian will and to the modernisation of lifestyle': a cultural reform rather than a political revolution (Bensaid 2008: 24). In a context such as this, in which the memory of a Spanish 1968 never developed due to the strength of the master frame of Francoism and the transition, to integrate the student movement into the framework of the global 1968 means importing a representation of 1968 that is based more on the American 'summer of love' than on the revolutionary attempts of European youth. Indeed, most of the articles published on the occasion of the fortieth anniversary tended to downplay the political aspects of the student struggle and to introduce – in a, for Spain, completely new fashion – anecdotes connected with cultural innovation, sexual liberation, generational change, lifestyle modernisation, etc.

---

39. Yañez-Barnuevo, L. (2005) '¡Ay de los vencidos!', *El País*, 12 October; Chicote Serna, E. (2006) 'Salvador', *El País*, 22 September; Berzosa, C. (2008) 'El olvido de la crueldad franquista', *El País*, 7 January; Elorza, A. (2009) 'Víctimas y verdugos', *El País*, 24 January; Altares, P. (2008) 'Progres apolillados y de pacotilla', *El País*, 11 December; my translation.

In this new context, the figure of Enrique Ruano becomes significantly less politically controversial and threatening. Paradoxically, while the politically charged memory of Enrique Ruano did not find a place in a very politicised context – the one hegemonised by the narrative of the transition – it found one in the new depoliticised framework of the Spanish 1968 where, together with Raimon's concert, it became a cultural symbol for a generational change. This particular act of violence, then, needed to be subject to depoliticisation in order to be legitimised in the field of public memory.

Conclusions

'The fugitive traces of memory long outlast the sound of the guns' (Bell 2009: 348). In the cases I have analysed in this paper, memory allowed the sound of the political violence of the 1960s and 70s to have a significant impact on an evolving landscape, from the immediacy of the cycle of protest that began in 1968, to the student protests of 2008 and 2010. The actors and events of this cycle of protest are no longer present, but new outcomes continue to be produced as long as mnemonic practices emulate the existence of those actors and those events.

Moreover, these cases quite clearly illustrate some of the dynamics of memory: the battle of Valle Giulia shows how an episode of contention – particularly a violent one – can become the object of the mnemonic project of a specific social actor who aims to shape the identity of the movement in a certain way; the impact of the 'years of lead' on the 'chase of Lama' shows how a phase of intense confrontation can – again, especially if violent – act as a filter between two historical phases, polarising the memory of everything that happened in the immediately preceding phase; the case of the Angelo Azzuro fire shows how a particularly unpopular act of violence can – especially if publicly represented with a sufficient amount of vividness and morbidity – act as a cultural trauma for a specific population, imposing proscriptions in the corresponding movement milieu; finally, in the case of the death of Enrique Ruano we see how public memory can first reject and then accept a victim as a popular symbol of a wave of mobilisation, depending on the evolution of the landscape of public memory, which is nowadays influenced not just by the traditional memory agents but also by waves and tendencies in the global memoryscape.

In addition to the active work of memory agents and the influence of the local and global political and cultural context, a significant role is played also by the evolution of cycles of protest. The memory work following the events in Valle Giulia would probably have produced different outcomes had the event not occurred at that precise moment in the protest cycle, that is, after months of student occupations had created the potential for a further development outside the universities. And Enrique Ruano's death would have taken on quite a different symbolic and mnemonic meaning had it not been the starting point of the most intense phase of student mobilisation of the Spanish 1960s and 1970s, leading to the last 'state of emergency' of the Francoist era.

The limited scope of these case studies, and the space constraint of a book chapter, does not allow for the level of comparative analysis necessary for wider generalisations. Nevertheless, these cases make visible the presence of specific mnemonic processes in relation to the contentious remembrance of episodes of political violence. They call for further research on this issue, especially in the context of the renewed interest in the study of collective memory and its relationship to contentious politics that characterises the current landscape of the social sciences.

References

Aguilar, P. (2008) *Políticas de la memoria y memorias de la política*, Madrid: Alianza Editorial.

Armani, B. (2010) 'La produzione storiografica, giornalistica e memoriale sugli anni di piombo', in M. Lazar and M. Matard-Bonucci (eds) *Il libro degli anni di piombo: storia e memoria del terrorismo italiano*, Milano: Rizzoli, pp. 207–26.

Bell, D. (2009) 'Introduction: Violence and memory', *Millennium – Journal of International Studies*, 38(2): 345–60.

Bensaid, D. (2008) '1968: finales y consequencias', in M. Gari Ramos, J. Pastor and M. Romero Baeza (eds) *1968: el mundo pudo cambiar de base*, Madrid: Viento Sur, pp. 19–28.

Betta, E. (2009) 'Memorie in conflitto: Autobiografie della lotta armata', *Contemporanea* XII(4): 673–703.

Bird, S. E. and Dardenne, R. W. (1988) 'Myth, chronicle, and story: Exploring the narrative qualities of news', in J. W. Carey (ed.) *Media, Myths and Narratives: Television and the Press*, London: Sage, pp. 67–88.

Bocca, G. (1980) *Il caso 7 aprile: Toni Negri e la grande inquisizione*, Milano: Feltrinelli.

Cohen, A. A., Adoni, H. and Bantz, C. R. (1990) *Social Conflict and Television News*, Newbury Park: Sage.

De Luna, G. (2009) *Le ragioni di un decennio, 1969–1979: Militanza, violenza, sconfitta, memoria*, Milano: Feltrinelli.

della Porta, D. (1995) *Social Movements, Political Violence, and the State: A Comparative Analysis of Italy and Germany*, Cambridge: Cambridge University Press.

—   (2008a) 'Research on social movements and political violence', *Qualitative Sociology*, 31(3): 221–30.

—   (2008b) 'Eventful protest, global conflicts', *Distinktion: Scandinavian Journal of Social Theory*, 17: 27–56.

Domínguez Rama, A. (ed.) (2011a) *Enrique Ruano: Memoria viva de la impunidad del franquismo*, Madrid: Editorial Complutense.

—   (2011b) '"A Enrique Ruano lo han asesinado": Un oscuro episodio de represión franquista nunca esclarecido', in A. Domínguez Rama (ed.) *Enrique Ruano: Memoria viva de la impunidad del franquismo*, Madrid: Editorial Complutense, pp. 33–58.

Durán Muñoz, R. (2000) *Contención y Transgresión: Las movilizaciones sociales y el Estado en las transiciones española y portoguesa*, Madrid: Centro de Estudios Políticos y Constitucionales.

Edy, J. A. (2006) *Troubled Pasts: News and the Collective Memory of Social Unrest*, Philadeplhia: Temple University Press.

Eyerman, R. (2003) *Cultural Trauma: Slavery and the Formation of African American Identity*, Cambridge: Cambridge University Press.

Galfré, M. (2008) 'L'insostenibile leggerezza del '77: Il trentennale tra nostalgia e demonizzazioni', *Passato e Presente*, 75: 117–33.

Ginsborg, P. (1990) *A History of Contemporary Italy: Society and Politics 1943–1988*, London: Penguin.

Halbwachs, M. (1992) *On Collective Memory*, Chicago: University of Chicago Press.

Jansen, R. S. (2007) 'Resurrection and appropriation: Reputational trajectories, memory work and the political use of historical figures', *American Journal of Sociology*, 112(4): 953–1007.

Kansteiner, W. (2002) 'Finding meaning in memory: A methodological critique of collective memory studies', *History and Theory*, 41(2), 179–97.

Linz, J. J. (1992) 'La transición a la democracia en España en perspectiva comparada', in R. Cotarelo (ed.) *Transición política y consolidación democrática. España (1975–1986)*, Madrid: CIS, pp. 431–57.

Martín Villa, R. (1985) *Al servicio del Estado*, Barcelona: Planeta.

McAdam, D. (1995) '"Initiator" and "spin-off" movements: Diffusion processes in protest cycles', in M. Traugott (ed.) *Repertoires and Cycles of Collective Action*, Durham, NC: Duke University Press, pp. 217–40.

Olick, J. K. and Levy, D. (1997) 'Collective memory and cultural constraint: Holocaust myth and rationality in German politics', *American Sociological Review*, 62(6): 921–36.

Passerini, L. (1993) 'Il '68', in M. Isnenghi (ed.) *I luoghi della memoria: personaggi e date dell'Italia unita*, Roma/Bari: Laterza, pp. 373–88.

Phillips, K. R. and Reyes, G. M. (2011) 'Introduction: Surveying global memoryscapes: The shifting terrain of public memory studies', in K. R. Phillips and G. M. Reyes (eds) *Global Memoryscapes: Contesting Remembrance in a Transnational Age*, Tuscaloosa: University of Alabama Press, pp. 1–26.

Polletta, F. (2006) *It Was Like a Fever: Storytelling in Protest and Politics*, Chicago: University of Chicago Press.

Portelli, A. (1995) *The Battle of Valle Giulia: Oral History and the Art of Dialogue*, Madison: University of Wisconsin Press.

Revelli, M. (1995) 'Movimenti sociali e spazio politico', in F. Barbagallo (ed.) *Storia dell'Italia repubblicana*, vol. II, part II, Torino: Einaudi, pp. 385–476.

Sánchez Mosquera, M. (2008) *Del miedo genético a la protesta: Memoria de los disidentes del franquismo*, Barcelona: Fundación Sindical de Estudios.

Schudson, M. (1995) 'Dynamics of distortion in collective memory', in D. Schachter (ed.) *Memory Distortion: How Minds, Brains, and Societies Reconstructs the Past*, Cambridge: Harvard University Press, pp. 346–64.

Smelser, N. (2001) 'Psychological trauma and cultural trauma', in J. Alexander, R. Eyerman, B. Giesen, N. Smelser and P. Sztompka (eds) *Cultural Trauma: Theory and Applications*, Berkeley: University of California Press, pp. 31–59.

Spillman, L. (1998) 'When do collective memories last? Founding moments in the United States and Australia', *Social Science History*, 22(4): 445–77.

Taylor, V. A. (1989) 'Social movement continuity: The women's movement in abeyance', *American Sociological Review*, 54(5): 761–75.

Vettori, G. (1975) *Canzoni italiane di protesta 1794–1974: dalla Rivoluzione Francese alla repressione cilena*, Roma: Newton Compton.

Zamponi, L. (2013) 'Collective memory and social movements', in D. A. Snow, D. della Porta, B. Klandermans and D. McAdam (eds) *The Wiley-Blackwell Encyclopedia of Social and Political Movements*, Chichester: Wiley-Blackwell, 225–9.

Newspaper articles

Altares, P. (2008) 'Progres apolillados y de pacotilla', *El País*, 11 December.

Anonymous (1968) *Stampa sera*, 31 May.

Anonymous (1977) 'Chi sono i provocatori', *Stampa sera*, 17 February.

Anonymous (1977) 'Università: autocritica comunista', *La Stampa*, 23 February.

Anonymous (1977) 'Non si può essere neutrali', *La Stampa*, 6 March.

Anonymous (1979) 'Tre storie, tre giovani uccisi perché tacessero', *La Stampa*, 29 December.

Anonymous (1982) 'Varisco sfuggì a molti agguati prima che le Br lo uccidessero', *La Stampa*, 9 April.

Anonymous (1983) 'Savasta carceriere di Dozier', *La Stampa*, 27 July.

Anonymous (1985) 'I sassi contro Lama', *La Stampa*, 8 June.

Anonymous (1987) 'Querela di Capanna processo a Torino', *La Stampa*, 22 January.

Anonymous (1992) 'Enrique Ruano', *El País*, 14 July.

Anonymous (1992) 'Quell'assalto a Lama aprì gli anni di piombo', *La Repubblica*, 23 September.

B., M. (1968) 'La facoltà d'Architettura a Roma incendiata da teppisti fascisti', *Stampa sera*, 15 March.

Berzosa, C. (2008) 'El olvido de la crueldad franquista', *El País*, 7 January.

Caporale, A. (1996) 'Lama, l'ultima volta a San Giovanni', *La Repubblica*, 4 June.

Casalegno, C. (1978) 'Un inedito di Casalegno', *La Stampa*, 10 June.

Castellano, C. (1997) 'Ma dire indulto non significa oblio', *La Repubblica*, 26 August.

Chicote Serna, E. (2006) 'Salvador', *El País*, 22 September.

Devecchi, S. (1985) 'Del Turco: "Bastano i fatti a parlare in favore del no"', *La Stampa*, 6 June.

Elorza, A. (2009) 'Víctimas y verdugos', *El Pais*, 24 January.

Fabbri, M. (1973) 'Merlino, imputato della strage di Milano indiziato con Preda per la 'pista nera'', *La Stampa*, 31 July.

— (1980) 'Gli operai dell'Alfa Le Br sono fra noi', *La Stampa*, 29 February.

Fraguas, R. (2008) 'Madrid vuelve a corear versos de Raimon', *El País*, 23 May.

Fraguas, R. and Gisbert, P. (2008) 'Unas horas de libertad en el 68', *El País*, 23 May.

Franci, G. (1968) 'Violenta battaglia nel centro di Roma fra studenti e polizia: centinaia di feriti', *La Stampa*, 2 March.

Giannini, M. (1999) 'Hanno voluto colpire la sinistra di governo', *La Repubblica*, 21 May.

Giurato, L. (1968) 'Nuovi incidenti stamane davanti alla facoltà di Architettura Roma: dura battaglia a sassate fra migliaia di studenti e poliziotti', *Stampa sera*, 2 March.

— (1979) 'Lama e Spriano ad Amendola Compagno, a sbagliare sei tu', *La Stampa*, 11 November.

Gorresio, V. (1977) 'Annibale a Montecitorio', *La Stampa*, 18 May.

Madeo, L. (1977) 'Il disastro lasciato dagli occupanti', *La Stampa*, 19 February.

Mafai, M. (2006) 'Lama, il cuore del riformismo', *La Repubblica*, 31 May.

Meletti, J. (2007) 'L'errore di noi brigatisti snobbare il Movimento', *La Repubblica*, 15 February.

Messina, S. (2002) 'La lezione di Andreotti I sindacati nostri alleati', *La Repubblica*, 27 March.

Moran, G. (1993) '¿Existió aquel Mayo o lo imaginamos?', *La Vanguardia*, 24 April.

Mieli, P., (1987) 'Lama: neanche Berlinguer mi capì', *La Stampa*, 11 January.

N., G. (1968) 'A Pisa gli studenti entrano in stazione bloccano i treni, feriscono viaggiatori', *La Stampa*, 16 March.

Ordoñez, M. (2007) 'Aquel 'Marat-Sade' del 68', *El País*, 3 May.

P., A. (1996) 'L'ultimo incontro 'fidatevi di Cofferati'', *La Repubblica*, 1 June.

Peces-Barba, G. (1994) 'Enrique Ruano: recordando su vida y su muerte', *ABC*, 20 January.

Peroli (1969) 'Tensione all'ateneo di Roma Di nuovo in pericolo la riforma?', *La Stampa*, 13 February.

Pucci, E. (1977) 'Lama: occorre lavoro invece di assistenza', *La Stampa*, 14 April.

— (1977) 'Insulti contro Scheda da ferrovieri del Sud', *La Stampa*, 2 August.

R., S. (1977) 'Da contestazione a guerriglia un anno di Università a Roma', *La Stampa*, 22 April.

S., R. (1977) 'Macario sul comizio di Lama', *La Stampa*, 22 February.

S., V. (1992) 'L'ex leader: "Spontanea? No, protesta orchestrata"', *La Repubblica*, 23 September.

Santini, F. (1977) 'Nella città più rossa la rivolta è perdente', *La Stampa*, 19 February.

Savater, F. (2008) 'Un mes y cuarenta años', *El País*, 5 May.

Scalfari, E. (1996) 'Quando mi disse 'austerità'', *La Repubblica*, 1 June.

Scardocchia, G. (1977) 'Minuto per minuto, il comizio di Lama e la violenta battaglia all'Università', *La Stampa*, 19 February.

Stella, G. A. (1995) 'Ma e' attendibile un colpevole di ladrocinio?', *Il Corriere della sera*, 9 March.

Tornabuoni, L. (1984) 'Lama: Per fortuna ho sbagliato', *La Stampa*, 6 January.

Trovati, G. (1977) 'Giudizio politico', *La Stampa*, 4 March.

— (1977) 'La gravissima crisi rafforza il governo', *La Stampa*, 13 March.

— (1977) 'Perché contro la DC', *La Stampa*, 3 November.

Yañez-Barnuevo, L. (2005) '¡Ay de los vencidos!', *El País*, 12 October.

Zanotti, L. (1971) 'Duri scontri all'ateneo di Roma 60 feriti, tre agenti sequestrati', *La Stampa*, 3 February.

PART TWO

SPACE

Chapter Seven

Spatial Contexts for Political Violence

Niall Ó Dochartaigh

Spatial contexts are not just a backdrop to violence. They are linked to political violence at a much deeper level and the penetration and defence of territorial boundaries is at the heart of organised violence and struggles for political control. Despite this, and despite the pronounced spatial turn in the social sciences in recent decades (Auyero 2006; Gieryn 2000; Massey 1992), spatial contexts are neglected in much of the literature on political violence. The strong focus in the terrorism literature on individual psychology and organisational structure, together with the practice of analysing violence through large-N comparative studies that treat sovereign states as unproblematic units of analysis are among the most important factors contributing to the marginalisation of space and its relatively underdeveloped theorisation in the political violence literature

Any analysis of the relationship between spatial contexts and political violence must proceed from an understanding of the modern state's project of territorial homogenisation (Agnew and Corbridge 1995; Elden 2009; Giddens 1996; Mann 1986, 1993; Tilly 1975). Political violence is defined by its relationship to the sovereign state, even in cases where violence by sub-state actors aims neither at secession nor at full control of the state. Safe spaces, oppositional spaces, 'ungoverned spaces' all present a challenge to the modern state's project of homogenising internal space and consolidating sovereign control. They are all defined by reference to the extent, character and effectiveness of the state's presence and influence in those spaces.

All spatial contexts below the level of the state have to be understood in terms of their relationship to the sovereign states in which they are located. In this respect, one of the most striking features of violent political movements with a global or transnational vision is how tightly structured they are by the spatial context of the nation states in which they operate. Whether communist revolutionaries in Vietnam or Islamic fundamentalists in Egypt, violent insurgent organisations with a global or transnational ideology are usually intensively nationalised in their organisational structures and political programmes, notwithstanding their cross-border relationships and activities. The exceptions, such as the 2014 Islamic State campaign that presented a united, centrally organised and simultaneous challenge to both the Syrian and Iraqi states, serve only to emphasise just how rarely such movements break free of the national cage. These primary spatial contexts have been so strongly reinforced and so intensively naturalised since the end of World War II that the political in all its forms – including its coercive and violent aspects – is now more rigidly territorially structured than in any previous era. Spatial contexts structure political violence more powerfully than ever before.

Despite the relative neglect in the literature, certain spatial dimensions of political violence have attracted increasing attention in recent years, including patterns of diffusion (O'Loughlin *et al.* 2010; Schutte and Weidmann 2011), intra-state variation in patterns of violence (Raleigh and Hegre 2009), and the relationship between boundaries and violence (Kalyvas 2006; Ron 2000, 2003; Staniland 2012). One of the most important strands in this spatially aware research is the recent work on geographically disaggregating patterns of violence (Cederman and Gleditsch, 2009; O'Loughlin and Raleigh 2008; Raleigh *et al.* 2010). For many years, the large-N quantitative work on violence sought to identify the causes of violence by correlating economic, social and political variables, using sovereign states as the unit of analysis. One of the earliest and best-known studies of this kind was Gurr's *Why Men Rebel* (1970). In one sense, this kind of work focused entirely on spatial context – the context of sovereign state territory – and the most influential recent work in this tradition focuses on the connections between economic development and political violence, correlating levels of violence with unemployment levels, GDP, age structure, natural resources and ethnonational diversity, among other things (Collier and Hoeffler 2004). This large-N work implicitly suggests that, when explaining the causes of violence, it is sufficient to analyse the correlates of violence at the national level.

A central difficulty with this approach is that spatial patterns of violence within states are often very uneven, with violence concentrated in just one or two regions, and often stretching across international boundaries. Sharp differences between regions within a state often create a political mismatch between the state and specific localities, which concentrates disaffection and facilitates mobilisation into violence. Unevenness in the distribution of violence is often strongly linked to other kinds of unevenness within states, including levels of economic development, deprivation, and ethnonational composition. The unevenness of violence provides a clear indication that spatial contexts below the level of the state are decisive in shaping patterns and levels of violence and that explanations that rely on national-level data are insufficient, even if the state remains a vitally important spatial context.

Duffy-Toft (2003), for example, has demonstrated that where an ethnonational minority is territorially concentrated within a state there is a much higher likelihood of a violent challenge associated with that group. Spaces where a national minority forms a regional, municipal or local majority present a challenge to the homogenising socio-spatial imperative of sovereign states. They also provide distinctive spatial contexts in which the predominance of social norms, attitudes and ideologies at variance with those dominant at the national scale combine to provide a supportive context for violent challenges to the state. Other recent work has identified additional aspects of spatial context that have a powerful effect on patterns of violence. Large-scale disaggregated research across a range of African states indicates, for example, that densely populated areas, areas close to international borders, and areas distant from the capital city all have a higher incidence of political violence. This research also identifies natural features of spatial contexts correlated with violence, such as deposits of precious gems or oil, and particular kinds of terrain, such as jungle or mountains (Le Billon 2007; Ross 2006).

While some of this disaggregated work has a tendency to marginalise human agency, some of the most intriguing and suggestive recent work at the micro level has reasserted the importance of the human dimension of local spatial contexts. For example, Zukerman Daly finds, in her work on Colombia (2012), that areas with a high concentration of demobilised combatants with prior involvement in conflict have a higher likelihood of renewed violence. Patterns of political violence are correlated much more strongly with local concentrations of these crucial social networks than with other variables, such as income, age profile, or terrain. This evidence suggests a strongly path-dependent character of spatial patterns of mobilisation for violence. Experience in clandestine organisation and in the use of confrontational tactics to challenge authority concentrate over time in particular local contexts, as do strong interpersonal networks marked by high levels of trust, ideological congruence and mutual understanding. All of these contribute to the establishment and perpetuation of distinctive local and regional contexts for action in which many of the factors facilitating militant mobilisation have been built up through experience of previous confrontations. This process can, of course, also work in contrary directions, whereby people in areas that have experienced severe, costly and unsuccessful violent struggles may be especially reluctant to begin such a cycle again (Kalyvas 2006).

There are increasing differences between powerful and weak states in the balance that they maintain between national and sub-national spatial contexts. Prosperous states use new technologies to increase their infrastructural power (Mann 1986) and to secure ever-tighter control of local spaces, thus shrinking the spaces available for violent challengers. At the same time, cheap new technologies offer ways to effectively coordinate violent challenges against weak states, resulting in many such states facing diminished control of territory. In a wide variety of developing countries new and powerfully institutionalised regional and local spaces have emerged that are in tension with the state and that, to one degree or another, exclude state forces. This is most dramatically evident in the case of Somalia where the spaces outside state control take several different forms. At one end of the spectrum, Somaliland in the north has declared independence as a sovereign state, unrecognised by the international community. Steering a course between formal secession and regional autonomy, the region of Puntland has unilaterally proclaimed its status as an autonomous region, enjoying many of the benefits of independence without presenting a formal challenge to Somali sovereignty. In addition to this, there are a wide variety of less rigidly demarcated and formalised spaces that are controlled by rebels and beyond the control of central government (Hagmann and Hoehne 2009; Renders and Terlinden 2010). In Somalia we see several different territorial projects underway, of which the central state's project to re-establish sovereign control is just one. All of the other projects present a challenge of one kind or another to the territorial project of the sovereign state. Somalia provides perhaps the clearest example of the way in which challenges to state authority are completely bound up with struggles to shape spatial contexts and territorial boundaries, both formal and informal.

The deeply spatialised and territorialised character of violent challenges to state authority is the central theme running through all of the chapters of this section. The links between the cases are most striking precisely because they deal with such different situations: a separatist movement in Xinjiang pushed back by intensive state surveillance to small and intimate spaces, and prevented from organising and consolidating at larger scales (Campana); Marxist revolutionaries seeking to take control of the Peruvian state and controlling and administering large rural areas of the country (De la Calle); a minor rebel group taking control of a section of the capital city in the midst of civil war in Côte D'Ivoire (Lomax); and the ostensibly apolitical urban gangs responsible for an ever increasing proportion of violent deaths worldwide (Carapic).

In all of these cases patterns of violence are deeply shaped by the spatial context of the sovereign state. And in each case meso-level territorial contexts play a powerful role in shaping violence, while micro-level contexts – at the level of urban neighbourhoods or even individual buildings – constitute both resources and objects of struggle.

In the case of Maoist rebel group Sendero Luminoso, the deeply uneven nature of both ethnonational distribution and economic development within Peru combined to create strong regional differences between economically marginal and less accessible areas of the state predominantly populated by an indigenous population on the one hand, and other areas of the state on the other. This created regional and local contexts that were much more conducive to mobilisation of the armed struggle of Sendero Luminoso and allowed the movement to establish powerful regional territorial bases. Once such bases were established the movement gained many of the advantages of a state, including the capacity to mobilise fighters through incentives and compulsion, and to provide a much stronger foundation for continuation of the campaign. Territorial control was both the object of the campaign and the means by which such a large-scale campaign was made possible.

De la Calle's chapter outlines how these varying territorial contexts within Peru shaped the tactics used by the movement. In areas where they enjoyed territorial control they deployed classic guerrilla warfare, ambushing troops and attacking military bases and police stations. In urban areas where they were not strongly identified with any local spaces at all, or where their territorial bases were at the micro level of small urban districts, they carried out the kinds of attacks usually described as 'terrorist', such as bombings. In this case the different spatial contexts helped to produce very different patterns of violence and quite a different repertoire of violent tactics used by the same organisation. It illustrates that we can explain forms of political violence partly in terms of levels of territorial control and the existence of distinctive spatial contexts at the regional and local levels.

Campana's study of spatial contexts for separatist mobilisation in Xinjiang illustrates the interrelated shaping power of national, regional and local contexts.

The province of Xinjiang is strongly naturalised and clearly delineated as a distinctive regional context for action, both because of the persistent, if weakening, predominance of the indigenous Uighur population and its official status as a culturally distinct administrative unit within the Chinese state. This regional spatial context has great potential to legitimise Uighur separatist demands. But while the regional context is a powerful legitimating resource, the infrastructural strength and surveillance capacities of the Chinese state ensure that this context cannot be effectively deployed as a basis for challenging the Chinese state. The regional context is utterly overwhelmed by the national. The influx of millions of Han migrants from other parts of China has eroded the distinctive ethnonational character of local spatial contexts such as cities and urban neighbourhoods. The consequence of the national overwhelming the regional in this way, and the penetration by the infrastructural capacity of the Chinese state, is that Uighur separatist movements have been pushed back into micro spaces. The spatially diffuse character of the militant campaign, as evidenced by the violent attacks by Uighur separatists in far-flung locations across China is indicative of the failure to establish a territorial base for a militant challenge to the state based on local or regional spaces in Xinjiang.

In Côte d'Ivoire, too, a meso-level regional division based on the ethnonational and economic unevenness of state territory (in this case between north and south) is linked upwards with high-level struggles over control of the state, and downwards with the micro-level dynamics of territorial control. Lomax's fine-grained study of the emergence, consolidation, and decline of a rebel territory in a northern suburb of the capital emphasises the importance of distinctive local populations in providing a spatial context conducive to challenging the state. Lomax shows how, in the case of the district of PK18, the presence of former rebel fighters, as well as the concentration, in this area, of northerners associated with the securely rebel-held territory in the north of the country, were both significant in allowing the Invisible Commando rebel group to establish and maintain this district as a territorial base. He also looks at the importance of protection in mobilising local youth into the group. His work emphasises the importance of distinctive local contexts in which particular kinds of networks, experiences, and affiliations are concentrated, but he also points out the significance of physical factors, such as the distance from the city centre and the relative inaccessibility of the area. While all of this illustrates the power that resides in particular local contexts as a resource for effectively challenging the state, the subsequent demise of this rebel zone is evidence of just how easily the wider national context can overwhelm such local factors. The success of the rebel movement as a whole produced immense and ultimately irresistible pressures on the Invisible Commando to accept the authority of that larger national movement, and brought a rapid end to their temporary enclave.

One of the most serious challenges to scholarship on political violence and to existing typologies is the intensification of lethal organised violence with no ostensible political goal, sometimes called social violence. In El Salvador, for example, more than 80,000 people were killed in a twelve-year civil war that ended in 1992 – a toll of several thousand a year (Seligson and McElhinny 1996). But some years after the war ended the annual murder toll began to relentlessly increase, rising to more than 4,300 in 2011. Gang-related violence had become almost as intense as the fighting of the civil war. The scale of the violence and its political importance was emphasised by gangs signing a truce in 2012, producing a sharp – albeit temporary – reduction in the rate of killing (Fox 2013).

While such violence has traditionally been excluded from debates on political violence, on the basis that it is criminal rather than political, the increasing scale of the violence and its high levels of structuring and organisation have prompted a rethinking of this strict division. It is useful, in this context, to recall that the boundary between gang violence and political violence has been somewhat blurred even in the most intensely ideological conflicts. To take just one example, the mobilisation of local youths into street battles between Nazis and communists on the streets of Berlin in the 1930s drew heavily on the local territorial loyalties of neighbourhood youth gangs (Rosenhaft 1983: 27–9).

Carapic's chapter analyses the spatial dimensions of this form of violence through the theoretical lens of urban theory, arguing for the distinctive character of urban violence. She illustrates the powerful spatial dimensions of urban violence in the establishment of 'ungoverned spaces', beyond state control. While the territories established by urban gangs involve the exclusion of state forces, they differ from the other cases here in that they do not seek sovereign control through secession or overthrowing a regime. They do, however, seek to clear localised spaces of state influence and authority in order to secure a territorial base for their own activities. The extent of their violence is often seen as a sign of their strength, but may in fact indicate the difficulty of securing and maintaining territorial control at this scale without being a part of a broader and more coherent territorial project at the national level. Kalyvas (2006) has pointed out that when one actor is in secure control of a territory, levels of civil war violence tend to be low. The intensity of the violence surrounding these territorial struggles by gangs is a sign of their difficulty in securing territorial control. It is one of the deeper ironies of the situation that these forms of violence are in a sense more tolerable to the state precisely because they are localised and do not aim to topple the government. The effective toleration of high levels of violence and gang activity within certain delimited spaces follows long-established patterns of state neglect and marginalisation of poorer areas, and a concern to insulate the rest of society from any overflow of violence from such areas.

One of the most important recent developments in research on spatial contexts for political violence is the work on hybrid and wartime political orders (Arjona 2014; Staniland 2012). This work focuses on the way in which non-state actors carve out spaces, and especially on the extent to which such processes may be managed in negotiation with the state both tacitly and explicitly. This process of engagement and negotiation produces what Staniland calls 'Wartime Political Orders': temporary territorial arrangements characterised by a certain degree of stability and mutual tolerance. The assumption of territorial control creates new challenges for anti-state actors who simultaneously work to challenge the state and to maintain order (Schlichte 2009; Malthaner 2011).

This work points away from traditional approaches that treat state borders as rigid frameworks for action and towards a newly complicated understanding of state territory and sovereignty. It strongly reinforces the point that states are not features of the natural landscape. They are social and political projects organised around a foundational territorial principle. States are centrally concerned to assert and enforce their monopoly on legitimate power as evenly as possible within a strictly delimited spatial context, even if few states come close to achieving this ideal. Political violence is at its most threatening to the state when it presents a significant challenge to this territorial project, and above all when oppositional militants are sufficiently powerful to secure local or regional territories of their own. At that stage they become a competing, but also – to some extent – a complementary source of order and social control, and states sometimes find it necessary to adapt by taking a more flexible and spatially variable approach to control of their sovereign territory. Territorial control becomes an object of engagement, compromise and negotiation between states and militant opponents. This is particularly important as a focus for future research because it highlights the very tight and direct relationship between sub-state struggles for territorial control and the global system of sovereign territorial states.

This increased awareness of the negotiated and contingent nature of territorial control of all kinds emphasises the need for work on political violence to be strongly underpinned by robust theoretical understandings of the connection between territory, power and coercion. There is a need for a conceptual framework that encompasses spatial contexts and territorial boundaries of all kinds – informal and formal, internal and international – and that conceives them as different but interrelated aspects of the same phenomenon. The fact that much of the work on political violence works with very powerful but unstated assumptions of the legitimacy and naturalness of the nation-state form, and the legitimacy of sovereign states facing armed challengers, presents a significant obstacle to such an understanding. However, if we are able to analyse the state as one territorial project among many – albeit the most spectacularly successful – new perspectives on the interrelations between those various projects will open up.

Perhaps the most urgent new research area is the role of new technologies in political violence. There is a great deal of research on certain aspects of the new technologies, focusing on the role of online interaction in the radicalisation of individuals, or analysing new forms of propaganda and new channels for its distribution. But the new information and communication technologies have altered spatial aspects of violent conflict at the deepest of levels and in ways that cannot be investigated solely by analysing browsing habits or patterns of online discussion. Remote-controlled technologies for territorial penetration and surveillance, technologies permitting direct communication with civilians in 'enemy' territory, and GPS technologies that permit the deployment of spatially concentrated violence at huge distances, are all factors that contribute to deep changes in patterns of political violence. The most powerful actors now have immensely greater capacity than ever before to penetrate, monitor, survey and shape behaviour within oppositional spaces in which they have no physical presence. This increased penetrability of oppositional spaces has, in turn, provoked deep shifts in material practices on the ground that impact on the internal spatial configurations of these contexts.

One of the clearest examples of the powerful material effects of these technological changes was provided by the 2014 conflict in Gaza. On the one hand, new technologies allowed the Israeli state to penetrate this territory in so comprehensive a fashion that it was possible to text the individual residents of buildings to inform them that their homes were about to be bombed from the air (Erlanger and Akramjuly 2014). Many of the advantages of securing a 'safe' territory beyond state control have been negated by the new technologies. This has not, however, led to less spatialised or deterritorialised forms of political violence. Instead, it has prompted a drastic reorganisation of space. Hamas – acting both as a militant group and the governing authority in Gaza – responded to this technologically-driven erosion of safe space with a drastic material reconfiguration of internal spaces: building a network of tunnels within the territory – many of them utilising domestic spaces – in order to retain some of the freedom of movement, supply, and internal communication that control of territory used to afford (Sherwood 2014). The new technologies had provoked a radical material alteration of the spatial context.

This is just one of the clearest examples of the deep and fundamental changes which new technologies work on the shaping of spatial contexts for political violence. Work has barely begun on how new technologies such as mobile phones, retina scanning, GPS tracking, CCTV, and electronically monitored barriers of all kinds are shaping and reshaping the territorial configuration of conflict.[1] This intersection between communication, territorial penetration, and political violence is perhaps the single most urgent and important area for future research on spatial contexts for political violence.

---

1. Some of this pioneering work is brought together in the *Journal of Peace Research* Special Issue on Communication, Technology, and Political Conflict, May 2015: 52(3).

References

Agnew, J. A. and Corbridge, S. (1995) *Mastering Space: Hegemony, Territory and International Political Economy*, London/New York: Routledge.

Arjona, A. (2014) 'Wartime institutions: A research agenda', *Journal of Conflict Resolution*, 58(8): 1360–89.

Auyero, J. (2006) 'Spaces and places as sites and objects of politics', in R. Goodin and C. Tilly (eds) *Oxford Handbook of Contextual Political Analysis*, Oxford: Oxford University Press, pp. 564–78.

Cederman, L. E. and Gleditsch, K. S. (2009) 'Introduction to special issue on disaggregating civil war', *Journal of Conflict Resolution*, 53(4): 487–95.

Collier, P. and Hoeffler, A. (2004) 'Greed and grievance in civil war', *Oxford Economic Papers*, 56(4): 563–95.

Duffy-Toft, M. (2003) *The Geography of Ethnic Violence: Identity, Interests, and the Indivisibility of Territory*, Princeton: Princeton University Press.

Elden, S. (2009) *Terror and Territory: The Spatial Extent of Sovereignty*, Minneapolis: University of Minnesota Press.

Erlanger, S. and Akramjuly, F. (2014) 'Israel warns Gaza targets by phone and leaflet', *New York Times*, http://www.nytimes.com/2014/07/09/world/ middleeast/by-phone-and-leaflet-israeli-attackers-warn-gazans.html?_ r=0, 8 July.

Fox, E. (2013) 'El Salvador Homicides Fell Over 40% in 2012', InSightCrime, http://www.insightcrime.org/news-briefs/el-salvador-homicides-fell-over-40-percent-2012. Accessed: 9 December 2014, 4 January.

Giddens, A. (1996) *The Nation-State and Violence*, Cambridge: Polity.

Gieryn, T. (2000) 'A space for place in sociology', *Annual Review of Sociology*, 26: 463–69.

Gurr, T. R. (1970) *Why Men Rebel*, Princeton: Princeton University Press.

Hagmann, T. and Hoehne, M. V. (2009) 'Failures of the state failure debate: Evidence from the Somali territories', *Journal of International Development*, 21(1): 42–57.

Kalyvas, S. (2006) *The Logic of Violence in Civil War*, Cambridge/New York: Cambridge University Press.

Le Billon, P. (2007) 'Geographies of war: Perspectives on 'resource wars'', *Geography Compass*, 1(2): 163–82.

Malthaner, S. (2011) *Mobilizing the Faithful: Militant Islamist Groups and Their Constituencies*, Frankfurt: Campus Verlag.

Mann, M. (1986) 'The autonomous power of the state: Its origins, mechanisms and results', in J. Hall (ed.) *States in History*, Oxford: Oxford University Press, pp. 109–36.

— (1993) *The Sources of Social Power, Volume II: The Rise of Classes and Nation-States, 1760–1914*, Cambridge: Cambridge University Press.

Massey, D. (1992) 'Politics and space/time', *New Left Review*, 196: 65–84.

O'Loughlin, J. and Raleigh, C. (2008) 'Spatial analysis of civil war violence', in K. Cox, M. Low and J. Robinson (eds) *The Sage Handbook of Political Geography*, London: Sage, pp. 493–508

O'Loughlin, J., Witmer, F. D. W. and Linke, A. M. (2010) 'The Afghanistan-Pakistan Wars, 2008–2009: Micro-geographies, conflict diffusion, and clusters of violence', *Eurasian Geography and Economics*, 51(4): 437–71.

Raleigh, C. and Hegre, H. (2009) 'Population size, Concentration, and civil war: A geographically disaggregated analysis', *Political Geography*, 28(4): 224–38.

Raleigh, C., Linke, A., Hegre, H. and Karlsen, J. (2010) 'Introducing ACLED: An armed conflict location and event dataset', *Journal of Peace Research*, 47(5): 651–60.

Renders, M. and Terlinden, U. (2010) 'Negotiating statehood in a hybrid political order: The case of Somaliland', *Development and Change*, 41(4): 723–46.

Ron, J. (2000) 'Boundaries and violence: Repertoires of state action along the Bosnia/Yugoslavia divide', *Theory and Society*, 29(5): 609–49.

— (2003) *Frontiers and Ghettos: State Violence in Serbia and Israel*, Berkeley: University of California Press.

Rosenhaft, E. (1983) *Beating the Fascists? The German Communists and Political Violence, 1929–1933*, Cambridge: Cambridge University Press.

Ross, M. (2006) 'A closer look at oil, diamonds, and civil war', *Annual Review of Political Science*, 9(1): 265–300.

Schlichte, K. (2009) *In The Shadow of Violence*, Frankfurt: Campus.

Schutte, S. and Weidmann, N. B. (2011) 'Diffusion patterns of violence in civil wars', *Political Geography*, 30(3): 143–52.

Seligson, M. A. and McElhinny, V. (1996) 'Low-intensity warfare, high-intensity death: The demographic impact of the wars in El Salvador and Nicaragua', *Canadian Journal of Latin American and Caribbean Studies*, 21(42): 211–41.

Sherwood, H. (2014) 'Inside the tunnels Hamas built: Israel's struggle against new tactic in Gaza War', *The Observer*, http://www.theguardian.com/world/2014/aug/02/tunnels-hamas-israel-struggle-gaza-war, 2 August.

Staniland, P. (2012) 'States, insurgents, and wartime political orders,' *Perspectives on Politics*, 10(02): 243–64.

Tilly, C. (ed.) (1975) *The Formation of National States in Western Europe*, Princeton: Princeton University Press.

Zukerman Daly, S. (2012) 'Organizational legacies of violence conditions favoring insurgency onset in Colombia, 1964–1984', *Journal of Peace Research*, 49(3): 473–91.

Chapter Eight

Fighting the War on Two Fronts: Shining Path and the Peruvian Civil War, 1980–95

Luis De la Calle

This chapter is about the tactical choices of rebel groups. In line with other chapters in this volume, I investigate the spatial and temporal patterns of tactical warfare, with special focus on the specific context of the internal conflict between the Peruvian state and Sendero Luminoso (or Shining Path, hereafter SP). Irregular wars are usually fought in two theatres: the countryside and in urban areas. My main claim is that rebels select tactics depending on which theatre sets the stage for their operations. For example, areas where the fight is for control of territory will see guerrilla-like attacks, while terrorist attacks are more likely in areas where the state holds sway. Territorial control is, in this way, key to understanding the tactics of insurgent groups, with temporal and spatial variation in patterns of control often determining changes in tactics.

We still know little about the repertoires of violence that insurgents select. Some rebels expend their resources on military encounters with state forces; others carry out terrorist attacks in the main cities, with no real chance of militarily defeating their enemies, while still others combine guerrilla actions with terrorist bombings in urban areas.

Long-lived insurgencies – such as the FARC in Colombia, and the Mujahedeen fighting the Soviets in Afghanistan – are good examples of the first category. They have largely given low priority to terrorist attacks. For groups involved in asymmetric, irregular civil wars (Kalyvas and Balcells 2010), the most relevant strategy has been to take territory from the government. Although rebels fighting for territorial control have obvious access to terroristic warfare techniques, they refrain from systematic exploitation of that option.

By contrast, armed groups without the capability of seizing territory from the state are forced to resort to terrorist warfare. ETA in Spain, the Tupamaros in Uruguay, and Uygur separatists are all instances of groups whose relative weakness in comparison to the enemy regimes have compelled them to carry out terrorist attacks, so as to increase the state's cost of not giving up. It is not that these groups could not count on a minority of supporters willing to give them logistical coverage and legitimise their methods and goals. But the strength of the Spanish state, the flatness of Uruguay, and the ruthlessness of China, respectively, gave these armed groups no option but to go on the run and fight their enemies clandestinely. These terrorist leaders would no doubt have preferred to play Fidel Castro. Instead, they had to go with Bin Laden.

Currently – and despite the recent successful experience of the National Liberation Army in Libya – new insurgencies are upgrading the importance of terrorist tactics in their broader warfare strategy. Recent Taliban unrest in Afghanistan and Pakistan shows a growing reliance on a mixed strategy of guerrilla warfare and terrorism. The conflict in Syria also attests to this, with rebels replacing risky defensive operations in liberated enclaves, such as Homs and portions of Aleppo, with the planting of bombs in the main cities and hit-and-run attacks in the countryside. The Islamic State in Iraq and the Levant's (ISIS) last offensive – as of March 2015 – in the Sunni-populated Iraqi Anbar province allowed the radical group to take over large swathes of territory. Yet, the group is still bleeding the largest cities of the country with suicide attacks and no-warning bombs.

This mixed warfare strategy is here to stay. Given that smart targeting technology allows incumbents to reduce the number of potential areas under rebel control, insurgents are forced to act in the capital cities, in order both to wear down the regime and to get publicity for their fight. This is not a new strategy. Armed groups have, in the past, practiced a similar combination of tactics. Hezbollah is a case in point with its twofold approach of putting pressure on Israel by running military operations in the Israeli-controlled areas bordering Lebanon while perpetrating terrorist attacks against Israeli interests abroad. Another remarkable case is SP – the Maoist armed group that declared war on the Peruvian state just when the latter had moved towards democracy.

In this chapter I present a detailed case study focusing on spatial and temporal variations of the repertoire of violence produced by the SP in Peru. To my knowledge, this is the first attempt to investigate this issue.[1] The Peruvian Civil War is a good test for checking how armed groups select their tactics and why it is that they resort to terrorism despite the fact that they keep fighting a war for territory. The Civil War lasted from 1980 until 1995, mainly pitting the SP against the Peruvian military and, according to the Comisión para la Verdad y la Reconciliación, causing around 69,000 deaths. All conflict datasets code the Peruvian case as a civil war, due to its lethality and the existence of rebels liberating some areas of the target country. However, the SP also ranks high in datasets on terrorist events. I investigate this apparent paradox by analysing the temporal and spatial distribution of SP choices of tactics, focusing on three types of warfare: guerrilla operations, bombings, and assassinations.

My claim is that the fight for territorial control has large implications for choice of tactics. I draw on previous work (Sánchez-Cuenca and De la Calle 2009; De la Calle and Sánchez-Cuenca 2011, 2012, 2014; De la Calle 2013) that has shown that the capacity of insurgents to seize and hold territory free from the state's grip has overwhelming effects on many features of

---

1. Although Ron's article (2001) discusses some tactical choices by the SP, its focus is more on strategies than on the repertoire of violence.

violent conflicts.[2] To begin with, insurgent lethality and – therefore – state repression both increase when rebels liberate territory, since rebels can use these areas to raise resources such as recruits, funds, and legitimacy, all of which sustain the fight. Second, wherever rebels control territory, they become the rulers. This implies that local dwellers' constraints on insurgent violence are not binding, since the rebels – as the only military authority in the liberated area – have the last word. In contrast, when rebels operate in state-controlled areas they must be very cautious about targeting, since their supporters could side with the government if they do not endorse the violence.

Finally, territorial control also determines tactics. When insurgents are able to control territory, they are better equipped to wage a guerrilla war. However, if insurgents do not liberate territory from the state's hands they must remain underground, and in those cases they cannot avoid relying on attacks that most people would identify as fully terrorist. It is a matter of resource constraint: groups with no territory usually run short on resources, and this forces them to maximise the impact of their limited number of attacks – achievable through the use of terrorist techniques. Conversely, groups with territorial control seek to wear out the enemy and consolidate their territorial positions, which is better accomplished through guerrilla-like actions. The implication is straightforward: on the one hand, guerrilla warfare should be more common in the areas where insurgents seize, hold, and fight for territory; on the other, urban areas – usually under state control – should be hit by the rebels through asymmetric tactics such as bombings and kidnappings.

In recent work (De la Calle and Sánchez-Cuenca 2014), we checked if the tactics of 122 armed groups around the world correlated with their capacity to liberate territory. Our results confirm that groups with territorial control relied very much on guerrilla attacks, while clandestine groups were more dependent on bombings. To avoid issues of endogeneity, we ran two additional tests to establish whether territorial groups mimicked clandestine group behaviour when operating in the largest cities of the country, and whether Hezbollah's variation in tactics over time could be accounted for by the territorial strength of the armed group. Although the two tests seem to confirm the theoretical expectation, a lack of yearly observations on territorial control by armed groups obscures the workings of the main mechanisms.

This is the reason that, in this chapter, I propose a longitudinal study of SP, with spatial as well as temporal disaggregation of the main indicators of control and violence. The rich dataset that I have gathered (1,800 districts over sixteen years – from 1980 to 1995) allows for a micro-level perspective analysis of

2. Needless to say, this theory relies on previous scholarship. For instance, Kalyvas's work on the importance of rebel control for patterns of targeting antedates our concern about rebel tactics (Kalyvas 2006). Furthermore, my understanding of terrorism echoes Crenshaw's view of terrorism as the weapon of the weak (Crenshaw 1981) and Merari's interpretation of terrorism as the warfare toolkit of clandestine insurgents (Merari 1993). For a full discussion of sources, see De la Calle and Sánchez-Cuenca (2014).

rebel choices of tactics. The dependent variable is the type of tactic used by the insurgents in the district. And as independent variables I measure SP's capacity to control territory in the district together with other correlates of violence, such as literacy rate, mountainous terrain, and state repression of local dwellers. By and large, the evidence supports the argument. SP's choice of tactics was mainly driven by its capacity to fight for territory. In the districts where SP could challenge state authority, it resorted to guerrilla warfare; in those where the state had a clear advantage, it was forced to rely on terrorist tactics.

This dual nature of the Maoist insurgency resonates well with the strikingly different testimonies about the conflict gathered from the rural areas and the capital city, Lima. While most Limeños experienced the conflict as a low-intensity terrorist conflict, the Andean departments underwent an extremely harmful civil war. This mixed repertoire of warfare also has implications for current conflicts, since it is becoming very common that insurgents resort to mixed tactics, with guerrilla operations in the rural areas and terrorist attacks in the safe state strongholds, as attested by the current conflict in Syria.

The rest of this chapter is organised as follows: in the second section, I present my main theoretical claim, namely that territorial control has large implications for the dynamics of rebel violence, and for tactic choice in particular; the third section describes the dataset, which includes 30,000 district years as units of observation; in the final section, I present statistical models to account for the spatial distribution of tactics. In a nutshell, areas under SP control were heavily affected by the war, with guerrilla warfare being the dominant tactic. By the same token, state-controlled areas did experience significantly more terrorist attacks than SP areas. These findings point to the need for further unpacking of the dynamics of civil war in order to understand the differential behaviour of the same insurgent group in different battlegrounds.

Territorial control and rebel tactics

The field of research on political violence has boomed during the last decade. Seminal works such as Fearon and Laitin's 'Ethnicity, Insurgency, and Civil War' (2003), and Kalyvas' *The Logic of Violence in Civil War* (2006) has led the way for more careful analyses of civil war onset and violence dynamics, respectively. Although Fearon and Laitin's article initially attracted most attention because of their arguably debatable findings, there has recently been progress also in the literature on the dynamics of conflict. There have been several efforts to explain the spatial distribution of rebel violence during civil wars, looking at patterns such as ethnic settlement (Costalli and Moro 2011, on Bosnia); land distribution (Gomes 2012, on the Naxalite rebellion in India); ideological voting patterns (Balcells 2011, on the Spanish Civil War), and colonial legacies (Mukherjee 2013, on India).

The analysis of target selection has also evolved. Research on underground groups has highlighted that civilian targeting in urban settings reduces the armed capacity of the insurgents (Condra and Shapiro 2012) ultimately leading to their defeat (Abrahms 2012). In the same vein, research on civil wars has also found that insurgents resort to civilian targeting when their capabilities are decreasing, their internal power structure is looser, and their territorial control more contested (Eck and Hultman 2007; Humphreys and Weinstein 2006; Kalyvas and Kocher 2010, Wood 2010).

Surprisingly, no similar empirical effort has been made with regard to the choice of tactics. Not only is there almost no empirical work on rebel tactics, but the existing body of research is overwhelmed by definitional issues, as testified by the huge literature on 'how to define terrorism'. This gap is more inexplicable when we consider that rebel tactics convey more information about the insurgents' strength than civilian targeting, which is pervasive in any violent conflict (De la Calle and Sánchez-Cuenca 2011).

In this chapter I seek to investigate how armed groups select their tactics. I draw on a theory that has been developed elsewhere (De la Calle and Sánchez-Cuenca 2014). To summarise, I assume that all insurgencies aspire to have the largest military power possible: the power to destroy the enemy and to seize the territory under dispute.[3] To that end, armed groups must organise like an army, with well-trained, heavily equipped personnel. This requires, among other things, camps or bases, funds to obtain weapons, and a large supply of recruits. The establishment of bases is easier if the country has rugged or forested terrain, but urban control is also plausible (Staniland 2010). Regarding funds, these may come from internal sources, such as domestic supporters, coerced revenues, and natural resources, or from external aid, such as diasporas and sponsor states. The recruitment capacity of the insurgency is a more complex issue: it depends on popular support for the insurgency, on the behaviour of the state, and also – endogenously – on the tactics and offensive power displayed by the insurgency itself.

Despite all rebel leaders wanting to maximise their military capabilities, they are frequently forced to run small armed campaigns, with little possibility of defeating the enemy. The main predictor of rebel strategy is not the leaders' propensity to follow one armed route or another, but the capabilities of the state they are fighting. Thus, the type of conflict we observe is largely determined by GDP: rebels operating in poor countries quickly make territorial inroads, fighting a guerrilla type of insurgency. By contrast, rebels operating in developing countries face stronger states preventing them from controlling territory, forcing them to operate clandestinely and carry out a lower-intensity sort of conflict. Rebels in rich countries usually have no chance, either because of lack of supporters, or because of highly sophisticated systems of state repression (De la Calle and Sánchez-Cuenca 2012).

---

3.   I do not here consider scenarios under which the rebels and the state cooperate in allocating the territory between themselves, and avoid fighting – as hypothesised in Staniland (2012). Providing that the state is interested in holding a monopoly of violence, these scenarios cannot stay in equilibrium for long.

Territorial control – the capacity of rebels to seize and hold portions of the country wherein they fight – makes the difference in rebel warfare. Rebels controlling territory try to expand their area of influence, with the ultimate aim of bringing about the collapse of the state. For that aim, rebels rely on guerrilla-like tactics such as raids, armed assaults, ambushes, targeted assassinations, and collective massacres. These tactics contribute to empowering rebel rule and therefore to attracting resources for the insurgency. On the other hand, rebels without territory use violence to mobilise the masses and to coerce the state. Because of the constraints imposed by clandestinity, underground groups are severely limited in their capacity to exert violence and can therefore only choose tactics that are compatible with their secretive nature. Their tactics tend to be those that allow the perpetrators to run away and hide after the attack. Car bombs set off by remote control and snipers shooting at their targets from hidden positions are tactics often adopted by underground armed groups.

There is a certain asymmetry between the two types of groups (Bueno de Mesquita 2013). In the case of territorial groups, if rebels decide to move the fight to the main capital, far away from their base, they will operate under constraints imposed by clandestinity, and their actions will therefore reproduce those of non-territorial groups. The argument, however, does not work in the opposite direction. Underground groups can hardly replicate the attacks of territorial groups, because they lack the necessary military power. Taking the case of SP, this has straightforward implications. Instead of expecting suicidal assaults against cities, or large indiscriminate attacks against civilians, insurgents operating beyond their strongholds will have to abide by the rules of clandestine warfare for fear of alienating potential urban supporters. Therefore, we should observe that rebels' tactics are determined by spatial and temporal variation in territorial control, with guerrilla warfare affecting war zone areas and terrorist tactics affecting state-controlled areas.

Some may argue that the causal argument is eroded by a problem of endogeneity, since it is quite plausible that in order for rebels to seize territory they must resort to guerrilla-like tactics. However, I do not here deal with the conditions under which rebels can liberate territory (for a thorough empirical investigation of this question, see De la Calle and Sánchez-Cuenca 2012). Instead, I investigate what the portfolio of rebel tactics looks like depending on whether rebels control territory or operate clandestinely. Endogeneity would be an issue when rebels have no idea where they are able to break ground, and they use tactics to figure that out.

The transition from clandestinity to territorial control usually spans a short period of time. When the state is strong, rebels quickly learn that liberating territory is impossible, and no transition takes place. Conversely, when the state is weak, territorial control is quickly achieved. If we look at the interior of the country, it is also possible to envision an insurgency that will control areas where the state is weak – usually in the countryside – while being unable to make territorial inroads in the better-guarded urban areas, with the capital city being the quintessential government fortress.

SP fits this stylised story well: it did control large areas of Ayacucho in its first year of armed activity, and fought for the neighbouring districts, but it never tried to seize territory in Lima, being well aware of the regime's logistical military advantage in the capital (McClintock 1995). Another example is rebel Islamists operating in Northern Mali who, after a few months of armed activity, had gained control of two thirds of the country. The intervention of French military troops forced rebels to flee and go underground. Suddenly, previously unseen suicide attacks were launched, for the sake of harassing French and African troops in charge of restoring peace (Teruel 2013). In brief, I do not deny that guerrilla tactics are necessary for liberating territory. The point is, rather, that these tactics cannot be extended through time unless the insurgency maintains some territorial base.

This chapter's main theoretical claim is that variation in rebel strength is related to variation in tactics, not only across space but also over time. Leaving aside the motivations for operating in safe state-controlled areas, insurgents carrying out attacks in these areas will mimic the tactics of purely clandestine groups. Relatedly, changes in territorial control should determine changes in tactics.

Another way to present this argument is through use of Kalyvas' five-zone continuum (2006). As is well known, Kalyvas defined territorial control by specifying a five-zone continuum: zone 1 is overwhelmingly controlled by the state; zone 2 is under the control of the state, but where rebels can operate clandestinely; zone 3 is the prototypical area under dispute, with contested authority over the district, with the army usually ruling during the day, and the rebels during the night; zone 4 is an area under rebel control, where the army can still make inroads; and finally, zone 5 is an area far from the reach of state forces.

Some scholars have argued that, in the case of the Peruvian Civil War, SP never had a safe rearguard into which the state could not penetrate (CVR 2003). My data confirms this, showing that there was not even one town where the rebels remained in charge throughout the whole cycle of violence. If there is no zone 5 in the data, this means that we will only be looking at the first four zones. For the sake of symmetry, I use a three-zone scale, where 1 is a safe/slightly contested state area, 2 is a contested area and 3 is an area under SP's hegemony (but not fully under its control).

The testable implications of my argument are straightforward:

1. Guerrilla warfare should be dominant in war zone areas (contested and rebel zones, according to Kalyvas' typology).
2. Terrorist warfare should be dominant in state-controlled areas (the provincial capital cities and districts in Lima province).
3. Sudden increases in rebel control should be related to more guerrilla warfare (although here the causal direction is not necessarily clear[4]).
4. Sudden decreases in rebel control should stand in relation to increases in terrorist warfare.

---

4. As mentioned above, territorial gains can be driven by the use of guerrilla warfare, but the opposite can also be true: territorial gains can boost guerrilla warfare.

Background

The Peruvian Civil War started on 17 May 1980, when several SP cadres broke the ballot boxes in Chuschi – a small town in Cangallo, in central Ayacucho. Driven by a fanatical understanding of Maoist Marxism, SP took advantage of decades of failed sociopolitical mobilisation to redress the political and economic grievances of the indigenous peoples of the Sierra (CVR 2003: vol. VIII; Koc-Menard 2007).

Violence initially spread quickly in the Andean triangle (Huancavelica–Ayacucho–Apurímac), with the region of Northern Ayacucho serving as SP's stronghold (Degregori 1986). The initial reluctance of Fernando Belaúnde's administration – the first democratic government since 1968 – to give exceptional powers to the military for dealing with the rebellion contributed to quickening the growth of SP (Gorriti 1990). When, in 1982, the army was called in, its tactics of indiscriminate repression further jeopardised the low levels of state legitimacy in the area (McClintock 1998). SP also took savage measures against local populations that stood up against its rule, as testified by the Lucanamarca massacre, in which SP guerrillas slaughtered sixty-nine farmers in reaction to the killing of two local SP cadres by local dwellers.

After consolidating its strongholds in the countryside, Sendero moved towards the Lima–Callao conurbation – home to of one third of the country's population – where they were also able to recruit many youngsters disappointed with the lack of opportunities and secular racial discrimination of the politico-economic establishment.[5] Taking advantage of the growing number of immigrants coming to Lima, and the creation of new shantytowns, SP set up urban commandos that carried out a permanent terrorist campaign against politicians and security forces in the safest areas of the country (Burt 1998).

During Alan García's term (1985–90), the army were given full powers to deal with the rebellion, as the government brought a large number of provinces under emergency law (Palmer 1995). SP was broadly damaged by the introduction of self-defense anti-SP militias in rural areas (Degregori 1998; Starn 1998), and launched the 'final offensive', intended to encircle Lima and force the downfall of the capital by cutting all supply lines from the countryside.

SP's final efforts to bring down the regime failed. The 'offensive' was a last attempt to mask SP's increasing weakness in the countryside, where many communities had set up government-backed self-defense squads. A higher reliance on terrorist tactics in Lima was countered by Fujimori's *autogolpe*. On 5 April 1992, Fujimori – president since July 1990 – dissolved Congress and empowered the military with all the resources needed to quash SP. A few months later, the arrest, in Lima, of Abimael Guzmán (*Comrade Gonzalo*) – the longtime leader of the group – gave Fujimori tremendous success and great popularity. By the end of 1993, only one year after the fall of Guzmán, SP was more or less finished. Guzmán's

---

5. According to Chávez (1989: 26), 80 per cent of the 183 SP prisoners sentenced in Lima before 1986 were thirty years old or younger.

arrest had dramatic effects on the morale of the SP militants, and many put down weapons and took recourse to the repentance law passed in 1992 (Bermúdez 1995). Guzman's later call for surrender simply copper-fastened the process.

Between SP, state repression, and the actions of minor groups, such as the MRTA, and the far-right Commandos Rodrigo Franco, the war had claimed 69,000 victims. Most of the violence was concentrated around the central Sierra region, with Ayacucho, Huancavelica and Apurímac as the deadliest departments, as well as the dangerous Huallaga corridor in Huánuco. It was not by chance that these areas experienced the largest presence of the insurgency. Only Lima showed a different pattern, with many attacks but with no open rebel control.

Data sources

In order to test the four aforementioned implications, I have created a dataset based on several sources of information. For the dependent variables – the levels of violence – I have relied on the GTD1 dataset. For the main independent factor – territorial control – I have relied on electoral data from municipal elections in Peru. I control for state repression with data from the CVR, and demographic and geographic data is taken from the 1981 national census.

The Global Terrorism Database (GTD) is the most comprehensive dataset on terrorism and political violence available today, totalling 61,637 incidents in its first wave (GTD1) (for a full description, see LaFree and Dugan 2007). It is based on the files collected by the Pinkerton Global Intelligence Service for the period 1970–97. GTD1 presents data at a high level of disaggregation, with the unit of analysis being a violent attack. The main advantage is that it provides detailed information about the nature and characteristics of the attack in terms of authorship, location, date, target, lethality, and type of action.

GTD1 relies on a loose definition of terrorism (namely: 'terrorism is the threatened or actual use of illegal force and violence to attain a political, economic, religious or social goal through fear, coercion or intimidation'), covering all types of political violence. In fact, eight out of the ten most violent groups included in the dataset were involved in civil wars, with SP and the FMLN (Farabundo Martí Front for National Liberation) heading the list (De la Calle and Sánchez-Cuenca 2011). GTD1 includes almost 4,000 attacks by SP.

In addition to counting yearly levels of violence at district level, GTD1 also allows for the categorisation of tactics. It distinguishes seven tactics: facility attack, bombing, assassination, kidnapping, hijacking, assault, and maiming. As the last four are marginal both regarding number of cases and relevance, I focus on the remaining three. Facility attacks are identified with large teams and with occupation of space, both of which are inherent characteristics of guerrilla activity. Given the requirements of this type of action, facility attacks are more likely to be observed when the insurgents have some territorial control. Bombings, by contrast, are not aimed at taking over a place, but at destroying it. And, as emphasised by the coders, the action of placing the bomb and making it explode is a clandestine one. Therefore, it is a tactic that should be adopted wherever the insurgency is forced to act underground. Assassinations are orthogonal to territorial control.

Another important source is the reports collected by the Comisión para la Verdad y la Reconciliación (CVR), a non-party group commissioned by the Peruvian Congress to investigate the origins, dynamics and consequences of the Civil War. The CVR dataset includes information on 16,383 deaths coded by location, date, status of the victim, and organisation responsible. No information about tactics is, however, available. According to the CVR, 8,631 victims were killed by SP, and the army was responsible for 5,690 deaths. I use these data to control for state repression in the districts.

The most critical variable for testing the theory is territorial control. Drawing on previous authors (McClintock 1998; Pareja and Torres 1989), in order to operationalise SP's presence[6] I exploit the variation in electoral outcomes at the district level. As the SP leadership always called on people to boycott elections in order to denounce the 'democratic farce', local elections were, in many districts, never held or else annulled afterwards on the basis of low turnout or failure of state authorities to oversee the election. In addition, many districts would see an extraordinarily high number of spoiled votes. Given that six local elections were held during the Civil War (in 1980, 1983, 1986, 1989, 1993, and 1995), we have enough data points to generate a credible proxy for territorial control.[7]

I consider a district to be under SP hegemony (zone 3 on my scale; zone 4 on Kalyvas') if the election was annulled or never held. I consider a district as contested (zone 2 on my scale; zone 3 on Kalyvas') when the election was held but the number of spoiled votes exceeded 50 per cent of the votes cast, on the basis that if the state is strong enough to run the election, but not strong enough to prevent SP from forcing or encouraging local citizens to cast a spoiled ballot, the situation resembles one of contested power. Finally, if the election ran smoothly, with few spoiled votes being cast, then the district belongs in zone 1 and is considered to be under secure state control (zones 1–2 on Kalyvas' scale). For inter-election years, the district maintains the value of the immediately preceding election.

A district is coded as 'decreasing control' when it has moved from zone 3 to zone 2; from zone 2 to zone 1, or from zone 3 to zone 1. Symmetrically, a district is coded as 'increasing control' when it has moved from zone 1 to zone 2; zone 2 to zone 3, or zone 1 to zone 3. These proxies are used to test the last two implications.

---

6. There are alternative ways to code territorial control, such as the use of average levels of violence at the district level (García 2009) and fixed administrative areas (Bhavnani *et al.* 2010). In my opinion, the electoral indication outperforms these as long as there are elections and the rebels call for people to boycott them.

7. I also gathered information about the local election held in 1966, just before the start of the Velasco dictatorship in 1968. Table 2 shows that the number of annulled elections, or elections with a high number of spoiled votes, was very low.

Table 8.1: Regional variation in SP's territorial control (row percentages)

Department	State Control	Contested Control	Sendero Control	Number of observations
Amazonas	86.5	7.7	5.8	1,263
Ancash	74.6	15.0	10.4	2,556
Apurímac	43.5	30.6	25.9	1,169
Arequipa	83.6	12.3	4.1	1,684
Ayacucho	39.8	25.0	35.2	1,592
Cajamarca	85.6	6.7	7.7	1,897
Callao	100			96
Cusco	82.8	11.7	5.5	1,654
Huancavelica	55.3	28.0	16.7	1,363
Huánuco	68.3	16.4	15.3	1,078
Ica	98.2	1.4	0.5	668
Junín	77.4	12.4	10.3	1,903
La Libertad	74.9	7.0	18.2	1,250
Lambayeque	96.9	1.2	1.9	523
Lima	85.2	7.0	7.9	2,606
Loreto	90.5	4.1	5.4	704
Madre De Dios	70.1	1.5	28.5	137
Moquegua	88.8	10.0	1.3	311
Pasco	68.3	23.2	8.5	422
Piura	97.5	1.9	0.6	1,011
Puno	78.2	14.6	7.2	1,654
San Martín	88.8	5.7	5.5	1,194
Tacna	84.5	3.5	12.0	399
Tumbes	98.4	0.0	1.6	189
Ucayali	79.1	0.0	20.9	177
National mean	77.2	12.2	10.7	
Observations	21,220	3,344	2,936	27,500

Tables 8.1 and 8.2 show variation in territorial control. On average, 20 per cent of the districts were either contested or under rebel control, with a peak in the three most affected war areas, Ayacucho, Apurímac, and Huancavelica (56, 52 and 41 per cent, respectively). The temporal variation also fits the narrative of the war, since SP triggered its last offensive in the late 1980s, bringing the democracy to the brink of breakdown in 1992. The successful arrest of Abimael Guzmán – SP's founder and sole leader – in September 1992 ended the campaign and caused the quick defeat and collapse of the insurgency.

Table 8.2: Temporal variation in SP's territorial control (row percentages)

Department	State Control	Contested Control	Sendero Control	Number of districts
1966*	98.6	0.6	0.8	1,558
1980	85.0	11.2	3.8	1,603
1981	88.1	11.1	0.8	1,648
1982	85.0	11.2	3.8	1,603
1983	77.1	11.0	11.9	1,752
1984	77.1	11.0	11.9	1,752
1985	79.0	12.3	8.7	1,803
1986	83.5	6.0	10.5	1,779
1987	84.4	6.5	9.0	1,803
1988	83.5	6.0	10.5	1,780
1989	59.9	14.5	25.7	1,719
1990	59.9	14.5	25.7	1,719
1991	62.7	17.9	19.4	1,802
1992	59.9	14.5	25.6	1,718
1993	77.2	22.8	0.0	1,624
1994	77.2	22.8	0.0	1,624
1995	95.9	3.1	1.1	1,771
Period mean	78.3	11.5	10.2	
Observations	22,756	3,354	2,948	29,058

* This year corresponds to the last local election before the onset of the military dictatorship headed by Velasco.

Additionally, in order to test the second implication I create a proxy for the districts belonging to the province of Lima, as well as for all provincial capital cities. I include a temporal control for the presidency tenure (Fernando Belaúnde 1980–85; Alan García 1985, 1990; Alberto Fujimori 1990, 1995).[8]

The result of all these sources of information is a dataset with around 30,000 observations (district–years), including 1,835 current districts and sixteen years (1980–95). In this chapter, I present results on the number of attacks in each district–year, broken down by tactics – facility, bombing, and assassination.

---

8. Additionally, I gathered data on geographic (altitude, size, population, distance to provincial capital), demographic (the number of non-Spanish speakers in the district and the percentage of the local population between twenty to twenty-nine years old, inclusively), and economic (share of poor families in the district) correlates from Peruvian censuses. I have not included these factors in the models used here, because they did not significantly alter the results and, on top of that, I do not see how they could impact on tactic choice through alternative channels to territorial control.

My focus is on investigating how rebels allocated their limited resources between this set of available tactics, and not on picking up general effects of the spread of violence. I therefore compare the share of tactics, rather than running separate regressions of the number of attacks carried out with each tactic.

Results

I open this section with some descriptive results. The main argument of this chapter is that state-controlled areas should see a predominant use of terroristic tactics, whereas guerrilla tactics should be more common in SP-controlled areas. According to GTD1 data, SP carried out a remarkably similar 39 per cent of its attacks through guerrilla (facility) actions and bombings. The remaining 22 per cent corresponded to assassinations. Table 8.3 unpacks these percentages by distinguishing between control zones and the three war presidencies.

Some comments are in order. First, a higher proportion of bombings always took place in state areas. Second, facility attacks were also more dominant in areas where the rebels operated openly, with the seeming emergence of a sort of inverted U-shaped pattern – the contested areas being the ones with more guerrilla attacks. Finally, temporal variation is also visible. During Alan García's presidential term, SP was on the verge of bringing down the regime, and we can see this in the data through a larger number of districts under SP fire, and a lower reliance on bombings. However, during Fujimori's presidency, the insurgency was effectively worn down, which slightly increased recourse to terrorist attacks.

I now turn to a more rigorous test of the model. The most important implication of the theory is the expectation that territorial control will drive the tactical choices made by the insurgent leadership. In areas where they control or are fighting for territory, they will rely on guerrilla warfare. By contrast, in areas far from their control – usually the main cities of the country – rebels will operate under the constraints of clandestinity, which means they will be forced to use terrorist tactics. In Table 8.4, I include three types of tactics as dependent variables: bombing, assassination, and facility as the base category.

Given that we are dealing with compositional data, the proper statistical technique for testing the theoretical claim is 'seemingly unrelated regressions' (SUREG), because the proportion of attacks carried out by an insurgency against one specific type of target is related to the proportion perpetrated against other targets.[9] Only observations with at least one attack are included, otherwise there would be zeros in the three proportions, and the log-ratios could not be calculated.

---

9. The basic idea is to run J-1 seemingly unrelated regressions (where J is the number of dependent variables: in this case, the three targets) transforming the dependent variables in additive log-ratios. Given this transformation, the resulting coefficients are not directly interpretable and have to be converted into the original proportions through simulation exercises (for an application of this technique to compositional data see Tomz, Tucker and Wittenberg 2002).

Table 8.3: Control zones and share of tactics by presidency (all attacks included)

Source		Control Zones: Belaúnde			Control Zones: García			Control Zones: Fujimori		
		State	Con-tested	Rebel	State	Contested	Rebel	State	Contested	Rebel
GTD1	Bombing	0.36	0.07	0.11	0.19	0.05	0.12	0.25	0.09	0.06
	Facility	0.51	0.69	0.66	0.46	0.58	0.54	0.41	0.43	0.55
	Assassination	0.13	0.23	0.22	0.34	0.36	0.33	0.33	0.55	0.38
	Number of towns	250	56	54	309	90	87	87	32	43

Table 8.4: Sendero tactics (only districts with at least one Sendero attack)

	ln(bombing/facility)	ln(assassination/facility)
Contested zone	-2.687*	-0.415
	(-2.47)	(-0.29)
Rebel zone	-1.766†	-0.729
	(-1.68)	(-0.52)
State repression	-0.0903*	-0.106*
	(-2.24)	(-2.26)
Province of Lima	9.727***	4.691**
	(4.87)	(3.02)
Provincial capitals	6.954***	1.821
	(6.09)	(1.85)
Increasing control	-1.925†	1.503
	(-1.80)	(1.02)
Decreasing control	-0.226	0.0608
	(-0.14)	(0.03)
Alan García	-0.277	3.893***
	(-0.34)	(4.34)
Fujimori	0.821	5.751***
	(0.73)	(4.59)
Constant	-7.898***	-7.564***
	(-9.18)	(-8.46)
p	0.13	0.04
N		975

t statistics in parentheses; † $p < 0.1$, $^*p < 0.05$, $^{**}p < 0.01$, $^{***}p < 0.001$

Table 8.5: Predicted proportions of violence by tactics (only districts with attacks are included)

Control Zones	Geography	Tactics		
		Facility	*Bombing*	*Assassination*
State	Countryside	0.99	0	0.01
	Provincial capitals	0.46	0.49	0.05
Contested	Countryside	0.99	0	0.01
	Provincial capitals	0.90	0.05	0.05
Rebel	Countryside	1	0	0
	Provincial capitals	0.84	0.13	0.03

The dependent variable is a log-ratio measuring the share in the town of each specific tactic compared to the base category (facility-guerrilla attacks). If the first two implications were correct, we should observe negative coefficients for 'contested' and 'rebel' zones in the first column –indicating that areas under SP control experience fewer bombings compared to guerrilla warfare – and positive coefficients for 'Lima Province' and 'provincial capitals', indicating that areas that are under the grip of the regime will experience more terroristic tactics. The four coefficients are statistically significant and correctly signed. The third implication also seems to be supported by the data: the territorial gains of the rebels correspond to an increase in guerrilla warfare. By contrast, rebel retrenchment does not prompt update of warfare in the short term. This seems to be a particular feature of SP's strategy: its eviction of populated areas and retreat to a densely forested jungle in the so-called VRAE (Valleys of Apurímac and Ene Rivers) signalled no rebel intention of complementing a lower presence with terrorist tactics.

As for the presidential terms, it is interesting to note an increase in assassinations compared to guerrilla attacks after Belaúnde had left office. The fact that García introduced emergency powers and Fujimori gave a free hand to the military prompted SP to divert resources from guerrilla actions to targeted assassinations. Thus, rebels may switch to targeted assassinations and ambushes to avoid highly asymmetrical military encounters.

As a simulation, I have plotted the predicted share of each type of attack depending on territorial control and whether the district was in the countryside, within Lima Province – the most populated province in the country – or in a provincial capital city. On the one hand, cities under safe state rule are expected to have the largest share of bombings (0.49). On the other, guerrilla warfare is concentrated in the countryside, regardless of which control zone insurgents were operating in. With all precautions, due to the model's over prediction of facility attacks, these two arguments brought together would point to the existence of two different logics of warfare in civil war: one in the countryside, where rebels try to capture territory, and another in those cities most important for the incumbent, where rebels are forced into underground fighting and search for legitimacy and support.

Conclusions

The spatial dynamics of violence are a booming subfield in the discipline of conflict. The collection of better datasets with micro-level information allows researchers to test fine-grained hypotheses about conflict features such as lethality, targeting, and tactic choice. In this chapter, I have focused on SP's selection of tactics during the Peruvian Civil War. Picking up the district as the unit of analysis, I take seriously the role of space, and investigate why armed groups should display different behaviours in different theatres of the conflict.

I have claimed that the capacity to seize and hold territory from the state is essential in understanding tactic choice. My expectation was that the prototypical repertoire of guerrilla warfare would be most concentrated in the areas where insurgents control territory. In these areas, the rebels gather more resources – funds, recruits, safe haven – allowing them to resort to high-lethality tactics such as guerrilla warfare and assassinations. Urban areas – which are usually under state control – should be hit by the rebels through indirect tactics such as bombings and assassinations. In the end, the map of tactics should be a good descriptor of the capabilities of the rebels.

The evidence partially supports this claim. SP's choice of tactics was largely driven by its capacity to fight for territory. In the districts where SP could challenge state authority, it resorted to guerrilla warfare; in those where the state had a clear advantage, SP was forced to rely on terrorist tactics. Furthermore, increasing rebel capabilities immediately corresponded to a larger reliance on guerrilla warfare. However, the opposite is not supported by the results: a shrinking of guerrilla forces does not immediately result in increased use of terrorist tactics.

This is quite an interesting non-finding. Another instance of this can be seen in the case of the Tamil Tigers in Sri Lanka, whose rapid territorial collapse did not result in a switch to terrorist tactics. By contrast, Islamist armed groups in Mali, Iraq and Yemen are examples of the opposite, with rebels who are losing ground quickly changing their tactics to terrorism. Perhaps it is a matter of ideology. Perhaps it depends on the reliance on terrorism during the previous stages of territorial fighting. Perhaps the explanation can be found in the origins of the insurgency, with groups originating in underground movements finding it less problematic to return to terroristic warfare. This no doubt calls for fascinating research into tactic escalation and de-escalation.

Peru has offered a useful testing ground for analysis of the spatial dynamics of violence. The results shed light on the extremely polarised views of the conflict found in Lima and the Andean regions. In the capital, politicians as well as pundits talk openly of SP as a terrorist group, while many people in Ayacucho still think of the conflict more as a sort of civil war than as a type of irrational Al-Qaeda style conflict. In broad terms, we can say that they are both right: SP ran a high-impact terrorist campaign in Lima, while launching a fully-fledged guerrilla war in the Andean corridor of the country. This brings us to the realisation that not only tactics, but also public interpretations of domestic conflicts, may be mediated by the relevance of symbolic spaces. In the end, winning the battle for public opinion is a necessary condition for political success, and the Peruvian state did not fully convince its citizens. Even if SP was militarily defeated, there are still latent pockets of SP supporters in Ayacucho, highly critical of the state due to its repressive record during the darker years of the war. These voters could be mobilised to support SP political candidates. But this is a different story: the one about what happens when the armed conflict is over.

References

Abrahms, M. (2012) 'The political effectiveness of terrorism revisited', *Comparative Political Studies,* 45(3): 366–93.

Balcells, L. (2011) 'Continuation of politics by two means: Direct and indirect violence in civil war', *Journal of Conflict Resolution,* 55(3): 397–422.

Bermúdez, Alejandro. 1995. "Los 'arrepentidos', una desbandada en Sendero." *Aceprensa,* 1 February 1995.

Bhavnani, R., Miodownik, D., and Choi, H. J. (2010) 'Three two tango: Territorial control and selective violence in Israel, the West Bank, and Gaza', *Journal of Conflict Resolution,* 55(1): 133–58.

Bueno de Mesquita, E. (2013) 'Rebel tactics', *Journal of Political Economy,* 121(2): 323–57.

Burt, J.-M. (1998) 'Shining Path and the "decisive battle" in Lima's *Barriadas*: The case of Villa El Salvador', in S. Stern (ed.) *Shining and Other Paths,* Durham: Duke University Press, pp. 267–305.

Chávez de Paz, D. (1989) *Juventud y terrorismo,* Lima: Instituto de Estudios Peruanos.

Condra, L. and Shapiro, J. (2012) 'Who takes the blame? The strategic effects of collateral damage', *American Journal of Political Science,* 56(1): 167–87.

Costalli, A. and Moro, F. (2011) 'The patterns of ethnic settlement and violence: A local-level quantitative analysis of the Bosnian War', *Ethnic and Racial Studies,* 34(12): 2096–114.

Crenshaw, M. (1981) 'The causes of terrorism', *Comparative Politics,* 13(4): 379–99.

Degregori, I. (1998) 'Harvesting storms: Peasant *rondas* and the defeat of Sendero Luminoso in Ayacucho', in S. Stern (ed.) *Shining and Other Paths,* Durham: Duke University Press, pp. 128–56.

—— (1986) *Sendero Luminoso: Los hondos y mortales desencuentros. Lucha armada y utopía autoritaria,* Instituto de Estudios Peruanos: Documentos de trabajo n° 4–6.

De la Calle, L. (2013) 'Civilian targeting in civil war: The case of Sendero Luminoso', paper presented at the OCV seminar series, New Haven, April 2013.

De la Calle, L. and Sánchez-Cuenca, I. (2014) 'How armed actors fight: Territorial control and rebel tactics', working paper, Madrid: Carlos III-Juan March Institute.

—— (2012) 'Rebels without a territory: An analysis of non-territorial conflicts in the world, 1970–1997', *Journal of Conflict Resolution,* 56 (4): 580–603.

—— (2011) 'What we talk about when we talk about terrorism', *Politics & Society;* 39(3): 451–72.

Downes, A. B. (2008) *Targeting Civilians in War,* Ithaca: Cornell University Press.

Eck, K. and Hultman, L. (2007) 'One-sided violence against civilians in war', *Journal of Peace Research,* 44(2): 233–46.

Fearon, J. D. and Laitin, D. D. (2003) 'Ethnicity, insurgency, and civil war', *American Political Science Review*, 97(1): 75–90.

García, M. (2009) *Political Violence and Electoral Democracy in Colombia: Participation and Voting Behavior in Violent Contexts*, unpublished thesis, Pittsburg University.

Gomes, J. (2012) *The Political Economy of the Maoist Conflict in India: An Empirical Analysis*, unpublished manuscript, Universidad Carlos III.

Goodwin, J. (2006) 'A theory of categorical terrorism', *Social Forces*, 84(4): 2027–46.

Gorriti, G. (1990) *Sendero: Historia de la guerra milenaria en el Perú*, Lima: Apoyo.

Humphreys, M. and Weinstein, J. M. (2006) 'Handling and manhandling civilians in civil war', *American Political Science Review*, 100(3): 429–47.

Kalyvas, S. (2006) *The Logic of Violence in Civil War*, Cambridge: Cambridge University Press.

Kalyvas, S. and Balcells, L. (2010) 'International system and technologies of rebellion: How the end of the Cold War shaped internal conflict', *American Political Science Review*, 104(3): 415–29.

Kalyvas, S. and Kocher, M. (2007) 'Ethnic cleavages and irregular war: Iraq and Vietnam', *Politics & Society*, 35(2): 183–223.

Koc-Menard, Sergio. 2007. 'Fragmented Sovereignty: Why Sendero Luminoso Consolidated in Some Regions of Peru but Not in Others", *Studies in Conflict and Terrorism* 30 (2): 173–206.

LaFree, G. and Dugan, L. (2007) 'Introducing the global terrorism database', *Terrorism and Political Violence*, 19(2): 181–204.

McClintock, C. (1998) *Revolutionary Movements in Latin America: El Salvador's FMLN and Peru's Shining Path*, Washington: US Institute of Peace Press.

Merari, A. (1993) 'Terrorism as a strategy of insurgency', *Terrorism and Political Violence*, 5(4): 213–51.

Mukherjee, S. (2013) *Colonial origins of Maoist insurgency in India: Long term effects of British indirect rule*, unpublished thesis, Yale University.

Palmer, D. (1995) 'The revolutionary terrorism of Peru's Shining Path', in M. Crenshaw (ed.) *Terrorism in Context*, University Park: Pennsylvania State University Press, pp. 249–309.

Pareja, P. and Torres, E. (1989) *Municipios y Terrorismo*, Lima: Camaquen.

Ron, J. (2001) 'Ideology in context: Explaining Sendero Luminoso's tactical escalation', *Journal of Peace Research*, 38(5): 569–92.

Sánchez-Cuenca, I. and De la Calle, L. (2009) 'Domestic terrorism: The hidden side of political violence', *Annual Review of Political Science*, 12(1): 31–49.

Staniland, P. (2012) 'States, insurgents, and wartime political orders', *Perspectives on Politics*, 10(2): 243–64.

— (2010) 'Cities on fire: Social mobilization, state policy and urban insurgency', *Comparative Political Studies*, 43(12): 1623–49.

Starn, O. (1998) 'Villagers at arms: War and counterrevolution in the Central-South Andes', in S. Stern (ed.) *Shining and Other Paths*, Durham: Duke University Press, pp. 224–59.

Teruel, A. (2013) 'Francia lanza una operación para evitar que resurja el terrorismo en Malí', *El País*, 24 October.

Tomz, M., Tucker, J. A., and Wittenberg, J. (2002) 'An easy and accurate regression model for multiparty electoral data', *Political Analysis,* 10(1): 66–83.

Wood, R. (2010) 'Rebel capability and strategic violence against civilians', *Journal of Peace Research,* 47(5): 601–14.

Chapter Nine

The Effects of Social and Spatial Control on the Dynamics of Contentious Politics in Xinjiang since the End of the 1990s

Aurélie Campana

Since the 1950s, the Chinese province of Xinjiang has been an arena for frequent outbursts of violence from Uighur clandestine groups opposing the Chinese state. There are numerous reasons behind this long-standing conflict, including nationalism, socio-economic deprivation, and cultural and religious discrimination. The kinds of violence employed by the Uighur groups ranges from riots to terrorist attacks and at times it spills over into other Chinese regions. Although official statistics[1] indicate that the number of violent incidents in Xinjiang has declined since 1997 (Millward 2004: 2), the Chinese government still considers the conflict in Xinjiang a threat to the security and integrity of the state. In response to this perceived security problem, Beijing has historically employed heavy-handed measures to suppress the Uighur movement. However, in the early 2000s, the state developed a new strategy for cutting the protesters off from their social base, comprised of both repression and socio-economic incentives. With the aim of Beijing achieving full control over the region, the strategy – the use of which has been extended in the aftermath of the 2009 Urumqi riots (Wine 2010) – comes with the strengthening of spatial and social control, such as daily surveillance, new restrictions on cultural and religious activities, and expansion of Han settlements.

This chapter examines the effects of these mechanisms of control on contentious politics, starting at the end of 1990. It argues that they strongly affect the dynamics of contention, as Beijing's measures draw new spatial and social boundaries and disrupt the traditional spaces in which the Uighur clandestine groups organise and recruit. To better understand how socio-spatial dimensions affect the dynamics of contention, this chapter relies on the concept of 'alternative space'. This concept aims to capture the influence that socio-spatial control exerts on the social environment in which the Uighur movement operates. Based on secondary sources, journalistic accounts, and fifteen interviews with members of

---

1.   Official figures and statistics are often conflicting and confusing, but show the same reduction in the number of violent incidents in Xinjiang after 1997 and the rise in protests, including violent ones, in other regions of China.

the Uighur diaspora who have recently emigrated from China,[2] this research shows that Beijing's spatial and social measures contribute to alter Uighur alternative spaces. This, in turn, strongly influences the Uighur movement, which would in the recent past use these spaces for mobilisation. The new conditions imposed by Beijing have resulted in the creation of fluid spatialities and a high level of compartmentalisation of the Uighur movement, and they have had a profound impact on its capacity to coordinate violent actions.

The Uighur question has been extensively addressed by nationalism scholars and, more recently, by terrorism experts, but only a few studies have analysed the dynamics of contentious politics in Xinjiang. These include Bovingdon (2010), Smith Finley (2013) and, to a certain extent, Hierman, (2007) and Zhao (2012). Moreover, students of Chinese contentious politics rarely focus on Xinjiang (Cai 2010; Chen 2011; O'Brien and Stern 2008). Indeed, the dynamics of the Xinjiang conflict differ from those shaping social unrest and protests in other Chinese provinces. O'Brien demonstrates how dissent groups have hijacked official institutional channels in order to advance their agenda (2003). As Chen puts it, China is a rare example of an authoritarian state that has 'accommodated or facilitated widespread and routinized popular collective action' (2011: 6). However, at least two provinces – Tibet and Xinjiang – have seen strong repression of popular collective action, amidst claims of 'separatism' or 'terrorism', and Uighur groups have never used official channels to voice their claims. Finally, authors studying Uighur collective action tend to overlook the spatial dimensions of the issue, and particularly the way that socio-spatial control affects the dynamics of contention. This chapter aims at bridging this gap. In addition, the empirical findings of the case study contribute to the theoretical debates on the role of space and alternative spaces in authoritarian-like environments.

The paper is organised into four parts. The first examines the role of the spatial and social contexts in contentious politics, broadening the discussion to include authoritarian regimes. The second part is a presentation of the history of contentious politics in Xinjiang. The third examines the recent evolutions of the socio-spatial dimensions of the conflict, and the role of Chinese 'modernising' policies in establishing strong social control over the Uighur minority. Finally, the fourth part provides an analysis of the ways in which the mechanisms of spatial and social control affect Uighur alternative spaces and the dynamics of contention in Xinjiang.

Socio-spatial environments and contentious politics in authoritarian contexts

Building on the contentious-politics approach to political mobilisation, many authors have recently analysed the role of both physical and social spaces in

---

2. My respondents are part of the Uighur diaspora living in France, Belgium, Turkey, USA, and Canada. They belong to three different categories: some are members of Uighur advocacy groups, supporting either Xinjiang's full independence from China or Xinjiang autonomy within a democratised China; some are involved in 'cultural' associations, the primary role of which is to preserve Uighur culture and language abroad; finally, some are Uighurs who fled China years or months ago and who are not formally involved in advocacy groups.

contentious politics (Sewell 2001; Martin and Miller 2003; Leitner, Sheppard and Sziarto 2008; Ó Dochartaigh and Bosi 2010; Bosi 2013; Nicholls *et al.* 2013). As Nicholls *et al.* has put it, recent research has underlined the 'centrality of spatial relations' in the dynamics of social movements (2013: 1). Space constitutes a central issue of contention, especially in a configuration of a nationalist movement opposing a state, with both claiming control over a contested territory (Tilly 2000: 149). Space also represents a context that structures and constrains physical and symbolic interactions. It affects, but could also be altered by, the dynamics of contention, as it is socially (re)produced through the practices of both state and non-state actors (Lefebvre 1991). At the same time, space is 'constitutive of dynamic processes of contention' (Martin and Miller 2003: 149), as it shapes the nature and content of contentious politics. Finally, space represents a 'source of power' (Ó Dochartaigh and Bosi 2010: 407–8): the attempt to establish alternative territorial and social control over constituencies brings empowerment to social movements challenging existing political and social orders.

Some authors highlight that in order to operate, organise, and recruit, social movements need to create 'free spaces' (Poletta 1999), 'safe spaces' (Sewell 2001), or 'safe territories' (Bosi 2013). Although the definition of these concepts varies from one author to another, they all capture the idea of social actions being embedded in dynamic social settings and in physical space. These spaces offer more than formal and informal infrastructures for organisation and mobilisation. They are built on a network of social relationships that contribute to shaping an alternative social order. While in democratic regimes the existence of these spaces and their role in contentious politics is well documented, that has not been the case in authoritarian-like contexts. Yet, Sewell contends that 'when the state is repressive and hostile […] the very survival of the movement depends on the creation or appropriation of safe spaces' (2001: 69). How, then, is it possible to create and maintain alternative spaces when repression renders direct claims on the state impossible, and where the closure of the political space reduces political opportunities, imposes severe constraints on mobilising structures, and prevents discursive frames from being propagated?

By 'alternative space' we mean space that offers some relief from crippling surveillance and repression, and in which individual and collective actors promote rules that differ from the ones governing the public spaces controlled by state authorities. Drawing on Giddens' concept of a 'social system', we define social space as 'reproduced relations between actors or collectivities, organized as regular social practices' (Giddens 1986: 25). This definition underlines the 'relational strategies of actors, their inter-subjective perceptions of the social reality, and the social links on both the normative and symbolic levels' (Campana and Ducol 2011: 401). The contention here is that alternative spaces work like semi-autonomous spaces, developing in the course of interactions with public spaces controlled by the authorities, as well as with other alternative spaces.

Alternative spaces are critical for social movements challenging an authoritarian state. Social movements need support from the constituency they claim to represent as they are forced to work underground and to counter the short and long-term consequences of repression as well as the state's strategies for deepening its influence over the contested group (Boudreau 2005: 35). They rely on a set of pre-existing social relationships, but they also contribute to reshaping them, especially in a context where both parties to the conflict employ violence to advance their agenda. From that perspective, when repression 'ignite[s] other forms of mobilization' or makes organisation more difficult, 'everyday resistance' is key (Davenport 2005: x). It plays a central role in fostering a sense of solidarity and supporting the creation and the continuation of alternative spaces. Behind-the-scenes activities are thus important as they increase political consciousness and 'contentiousness' (Johnston and Mueller 2001: 369). They also contribute to strengthening individual identification with the group's collective identity and spread a shared sense of grievances (Polleta 1999). Daily practices of resistance to power and to an imposed social order allow challengers of the state to 'appropriate space' (Pile 2012: 16) and create meaningful alternative social boundaries through 'less obtrusive contention and coded oppositional actions' (Johnston 2005: 109).

Nonetheless, in authoritarian-like political contexts, where spaces of freedom are limited, alternative spaces are extremely porous to political and social developments. We contend with Almeida that in authoritarian regimes, processes of contention 'tend to be much less homogeneous than [in] core democracies' (2003: 346). Given the high degree of uncertainty caused by repression and surveillance, alternative spaces are far less stable in an authoritarian environment than those created in a democratic environment. Their transformation could be either incremental and gradual or disruptive following, for instance, a violent crackdown. A repressive policy targeting certain social practices could lead to a redefinition of the alternative spaces, to an alteration of their symbolic and cultural boundaries, and – ultimately – to their suppression.

Alternative spaces could also be disrupted by internal contestation. The balance of power within a given alternative space is extremely fragile and depends not only on transactions taking place between the composite factions of the social movement, but also on the nature of the interactions with the state that is being challenged. For example, repression may affect the balance of power within the social movement, as it tends to either discourage the moderates – opening the floor to a more radical faction – or to radicalise them (della Porta 2013: 67). Ultimately, repression could lead to 'an organizational compartmentalization' and make underground organisations 'detach themselves from their external environment' (147). Under other circumstances, alliances between one or several of the factions composing the social movement and an external actor – such as a diaspora or a transnational terrorist group – could raise the profile of a faction, contributing to altering the rules that govern the alternative space as well as driving the state to increase its repressive measures.

Only few authors analyse the ways in which alternative spaces, once created, are transformed and adjusted in the course of interactions between different actors involved in contentious politics. This chapter focuses on this aspect. It shows how, over time, mechanisms of socio-spatial control put in place by the state to defeat a nationalist movement contribute to redraw the boundaries of traditional alternative spaces. In the case of the Uighur movement, this has led to a high degree of compartmentalisation. Before turning to an analysis of how the dynamics of contention are affected by competition over space, I will present a brief historical overview of the conflict.

A brief history of contentious politics in Xinjiang

The conflict in Xinjiang is deeply embedded in two larger parallel processes: the Chinese state-building process, and the nation-building process. 'Xinjiang' literarily means 'new frontier' or 'new dominion' in Chinese. Uighurs would rather describe it as 'East Turkestan', or use a more neutral term, like 'Uighur region'.[3] In 1949, the actual province of Xinjiang was officially incorporated into the newly born People's Republic of China (PRC), although the Chinese had controlled this territory since the late eighteenth century. In 1955, the region officially became the Xinjiang Uighur Autonomous Region (XUAR). The Uighurs were thus officially recognised as one of the Chinese nationalities.

However, the political autonomy granted to Xinjiang was artificial and all decisions were made in Beijing or by the local Communist Party, dominated by non-Uighur cadres. Uighur nationalist groups began to violently oppose Chinese and communist rule soon after 1949. The origin of the modern separatist movement dates back to the period 1944–9, when the East Turkestan Republic (ETR) was established, in the Ili region in the southern part of Xinjiang. ETR was based on a Pan-Turkish ideology and had the support of the Soviet Union (Rudelson 1997: 29). From 1949 and until the early 1980s, the scope and scale of violence was limited. The causes of violence ranged from the desire to secede to resistance to the cultural policy. Another cause of violence was the growing interethnic tensions between Uighurs and Hans, who emigrated en masse to the Uighur region from 1949 onwards[4] (Millward 2004: 6). In the late 1970s, Deng Xiaoping initiated a set of economic and social reforms that translated into an economic boom in Xinjiang, stimulated by the oil, gas, and raw materials industries (Starr 2004: 4). These reforms came with a new influx of Han settlers, who largely benefited from the economic dynamism, while the Uighurs remained socio-economically deprived. Although sporadic uprisings and riots occurred – such as the ones that rocked the cities of Aksu, Urumqi, and Kashgar in 1980–1 – the situation in Xinjiang stabilised as a result of the relaxation of the 'more assimilationist aspects of cultural policy' (Millward 2004: 8). There was no political autonomy, but minorities, including Uighurs, were granted the rights to follow their own religion and to use their own language.

In the mid-1980s, student mobilisation occurred in Xinjiang as it did in other parts of China, but the slogans chanted by Uighur protesters were not simply about openness and democracy. They called for 'the end of what they described

---

3. Interviewee L, August 2013.
4. Patterns of Han migration changed over time: some were forced to move to Xinjiang; others answered to the CCP calls; and still others settled voluntarily in the XUAR in the hope of getting a better job.

as 'discrimination' (Millward 2004; Bovingdon 2004: 179), with a specific emphasis on family-planning policies, and some claimed independence. There was a re-organisation of some clandestine separatist groups, instigated by some of the young Uighurs who had participated in the student movement. Some were influenced by the events in the neighbouring Afghanistan and adopted a religious agenda. One such example is the group headed by Zahideen Yusuf, who was accused of being responsible for the 1990 riots in the city of Baren (Mackerras 2001: 291). Other major outbursts of violence – interethnic clashes; demonstrations calling for independence and the end of the 'Han domination', and protests denouncing police practices or social policies – occurred on a regular basis across the whole region (for reliable lists, see Bovingdon 2004: 174–90; and Roberts 2012). The 1990s was Xinjiang's most violent decade, with official reports of more than 200 violent incidents (Information Office of the State Council of the PRC 2002).[5] The reasons for these violent incidents were extremely diverse, including both intraethnic and intrareligious violence,[6] but all incidents were repressed and framed as manifestations of 'separatism'.

The Chinese government's answer to the violence was multifaceted. It first focused on the suppression of 'separatist activities'. The 'Strike Hard' campaign, launched in 1996 against 'separatists, splittists, extremists', brought heavy-handed and indiscriminate repression (Amnesty International 1999). It imposed new restrictions on religious and cultural rights and encouraged more Hans to emigrate to the province. At the end of the 1990s, China engaged in a consolidation strategy. In the second half of 1999 China started a campaign called 'Open up the West', designed to develop the more backward regions, to increase state capacity, and to enhance the ongoing nation-building process (Goodman 2004: 318). Since then, economic incentives have become the 'largest tool in the central government's policies toward Xinjiang and the Uighurs' (Van Wie Davis 2008: 19). In the same vein, the 'New Deal' of 2010 gave priority to the development of the 'livelihood of all ethnic groups' (Cuifen 2012: 62). Both campaigns also meant new waves of Han migration to Xinjiang.

The consolidation phase came with a new upsurge in repression against 'Uighur separatists' – from 2001 labelled 'Uighur terrorists'. Indeed, China promptly adopted the 'War on Terror' rhetoric to legitimate its heavy-handed approach towards Uighurs. The Chinese discourse points to the alleged connections established between Uighur groups, the Taliban and Al-Qaeda (Information Office of the State Council of the PRC 2002), although the evidence for this is extremely weak, not to say inexistent (Roberts 2012). It was in this tense context that Beijing imposed new restrictions on religious and linguistics rights, reinforcing social control over the Uighur minority.

The crackdown on clandestine Uighur groups had dramatic consequences for the Uighur movement, which suffered increasing repression at the end of the 1990s and throughout the 2000s. The number of protests and violent confrontations

---

5. Official figures still need to be treated with caution. Non-violent protests also occurred on a regular basis.

6. Interview with D, Turkey, December 2009.

declined, but sporadic violent incidents still occurred on a rather regular basis. The 2009 Urumqi riots were the most deadly since the 1990s (Watts 2009; Emet 2009; World Uighur Congress 2009) and represent a turning point. At the same time, the implementation of new social measures to accelerate the 'integration' of Xinjiang into the Chinese state and nation strongly affected the socio-spatial dimensions of the conflict.

The Beijing strategies between control of XUAR territory and transformation of the public space

Beijing's strategy for separating the Uighur clandestine groups from their social base has, since the early 2000s, placed economic incentives at its centre. The rationale behind this policy underlines the socio-economically deprived Uighur minority's need for work in order to improve quality of life and buy social stability. However, it is also part of the larger Chinese nation and state-building processes. As such, it contributes to fuel resentment, as 'modernisation' comes with the implementation of new mechanisms of spatial and social control resulting in tightened control of Uighurs in public space, alteration of the spatial ethnic distribution, and transformation of public space itself.

Surveillance strategies and appropriation of Xinjiang public space

Since the onset of the 'Strike Hard' campaign, both Beijing and the XUAR government have increased state surveillance. As one of the respondents put it, 'some kind of structured opposition exists in Xinjiang, but people fear surveillance from the government. Cell phones are tapped. Intelligence services monitor everybody all the time. Everyone has the impression of being under constant surveillance.'[7] Traditional techniques of surveillance – extended since 2009 – are heavily used to lock down XUAR territory and to establish strong control over the public space. For instance, in the aftermath of the deadly 2009 Urumqi riots thousands of surveillance cameras were installed in the streets, on buses and in the shopping centres of the main cities (Moore 2010). In 2010, some 5,000 policemen have been recruited to patrol the streets in Urumqi alone (Xinhua 2010). Furthermore, in early 2014, CPP leaders announced the strengthening of spatial and social control, dispatching 200,000 high-level Party cadres 'to live and work in grassroot communities for a year at a time' (Leibold 2014: 3). These cadres are in charge of assisting local authorities but also of gathering intelligence and preventing flare-ups of a social and ethnic nature. The rationale behind this strategy, labelled 'grid-style social management system' – employed also in other parts of China – is to lock down and control all settlements of population, with strong emphasis on the Uighur minority. As Zhang Chunzian, the Communist Party chief in XUAR, put it in March 2014, '[we must] thoroughly enter and

---

7.   Interview with K, France, December 2012. My translation.

garrison [Xinjiang society] in order that no blank spaces are left behind' (quoted in *Ibid.*: 5). Accordingly, Beijing and the XUAR have made surveillance one of their main strategies for penetrating all parts of XUAR and asserting their control over both territory and society.

These surveillance techniques contribute to the drawing of new social boundaries, as they bring further restrictions upon Uighurs. Scores of measures have been adopted to establish stronger control over the public space and to discourage informal gathering – for instance in a street or in a park. One of the respondents notes that, since 2009, Uighurs are not allowed to gather in public spaces. According to him, those who infringe on this informal rule may face intimidation at best and, at worst, arrest.[8] These practices have been extended to Uighur private houses, which policemen can raid at any time to check whether an informal meeting is under way.[9] Restrictions also concern religious practices: neither members of the Chinese Communist Party; Uighurs working for the government; women; Uighurs under the age of eighteen, nor university students are allowed into mosques.[10]

Other religious restrictions – in place to prevent 'social disorder' – enforce new informal norms and are designed to weaken Uighurs' appropriation of space. For instance, it is for this reason that Uighurs are regularly prevented from celebrating religious festivals. On 7 August 2013 police brutally intervened in Akyol, Aksu prefecture, to stop Uighurs from gathering on the eve of the Eid al-Fitr festival, organised to celebrate the end of the holy month of Ramadan (Hoshur and Turdush 2013). In the same vein, in the name of the 'fight against extremism' Uighurs have seen a decrease in their rights to exteriorise their religiosity. For instance, it is forbidden for men under the age of forty to grow a beard, and those who do not conform to this could be subjected to harassment in the streets. Veiled women face the same threat.[11] The 2013 Turpan riots occurred after a woman had been prevented from wearing a full veil (Patience 2013). The implementation of daily surveillance measures on such a large scale prevents the Uighurs from expressing their religious identity in public spaces. It comes with the Sinicisation of XUAR public spaces – a process furthered by the massive Han migration and supported by a top-down redefinition of social and spatial boundaries.

Alteration of the ethnic distribution and the transformation of public space

Beijing control has also accelerated the appropriation of Xinjiang territory, a process that comes with rapid alteration of the ethnic spatial distribution as well as transformation of the public space in both rural and urban areas. Beijing's migration policies have completely changed the ethnic landscape of Xinjiang. While the

---

8. Interview with A, Turkey, December 2012.
9. Interview with C, Turkey, December 2012.
10. Interview with K, France, December 2012.
11. Interview with D and E, Turkey, December 2012.

Uighurs represented 75 per cent of the Xinjiang inhabitants in 1949, today they make up roughly 45 per cent (nine million) of the total XUAR population.[12] The proportion of Hans has dramatically increased, from 6.7 per cent in 1949 to 40.6 per cent today (Howell and Fan 2011: 119). According to the 2003 census, 82 per cent of the Uighurs live in the southern part of XUAR. The Han migration has, nevertheless, progressively altered the patterns of population distribution. Hans first settled in the cities of the northern part of Xinjiang, and especially in Urumqi, where, in 2000, they made up 75 per cent of the population (Hasmath 2012: 5). They also actively participated in the creation of new settlements, built by the Xinjiang Production and Construction Corps (XPCC). Established in 1954 and composed of an overwhelming majority of Hans, the XPCC constitutes a powerful 'state within a state' (Cliff 2009), which controls large parts of the territory and which, in 2012, produced nearly one-sixth of Xinjiang's GDP (*The Economist* 2013). The Corps has become a very powerful corporation and a 'central organisation for the PRC's control of Xinjiang' (Olgaard and Nils 2012: 29). It has recently expanded its activities to the southern part of Xinjiang, where Uighurs represent a majority. The Corps has historically been present in the rural parts of Xinjiang, but recently it began to create new settlements in urban centres, further altering the spatial distribution of ethnic groups.

This geographical expansion of Han settlements, in addition to Beijing's policies of 'ethnic mingling' (Leibold 2014), and promoting Uighur migration to other parts of China, results in the acceleration of the Sinicisation process and in the radical transformation of public space, also in cities historically with a majority population of Uighurs. For instance, in Urumqi, the street names have been Sinicised, making Uighur elders – who for most part do not read nor speak Mandarin – strangers in their own city.[13] These developments, which go hand in hand with land expropriation and the destruction of traditional Uighur houses in some XUAR cities, fuel interethnic tensions, even though Uighurs and Hans remain spatially divided in most of Xinjiang's urban centres. The transformations in Kashgar – an historical city populated by a majority of Uighurs – illustrate the consequences of these 'modernising' policies with about 85 per cent of the traditional Uighur houses having been destroyed. Uighur families, evicted from their property, have been forced to settle in the recently constructed buildings in the Kashgar suburbs – the financial compensation for their old homes being far

---

12. Uncorroborated and unofficial estimates speak of twenty to thirty-three and even forty-five million Uighurs (interview with G and C, Turkey, December 2012). Three of my respondents say that China attempts to minimise the demographic weight of Uighurs. Although these figures should be regarded with the same level of caution as the official statistics, one point is worth mentioning: official statistics do not take into account illegal children. However, most Uighur families do not respect the family-planning policy and have more than two children. These children are illegal and cannot be registered, except if the family pays a fee or bribe the officials in charge of delivering the registration permits. Illegal, or 'black', children have no documents and cannot attend schools. Today, all ethnic groups – also the Han – face this problem.

13. Interview with G, Turkey, December 2012.

too small to buy plots in the city centre. The only traditional Uighur houses that have been preserved have been transformed into tourist attractions (Tassy 2011). It is no surprise that, forced to live in a new environment, some Uighurs feel cut off from their communities.[14] This new reality contributes to the weakening of local Uighur cohesion and redraws spatial and social boundaries between Han and Uighur communities, as well as within Uighur communities now dispersed in different parts of the city. It is also a component of Beijing's 'ethnic mingling' policy, which aims at erasing ethnic boundaries, both physically and symbolically. This decompartmentalisation clearly promotes ethnic homogenisation and the Sinicisation of space and people, and illustrates the way in which control of physical and social spaces has become a major component of this protracted conflict. The Uighurs, lacking in resources when pitted against the Chinese steamroller, seem unable to adapt to this development.

Competition over space and disruption of the Uighur traditional alternative spaces

Chinese 'modernising' policies create new spatial and social boundaries, as they disrupt the physical and social spaces in which Uighurs live. Yet, for recruitment and mobilisation, the Uighur movement has historically relied on Uighur alternative spaces. The alteration of the socio-spatial environment in which it had operated for decades has completely transformed the rules of the game, as the measures of control and surveillance adopted in the early 2000s – tightened after the 2009 Urumqi riots – put Uighur alternative spaces under constant pressure. This affects the dynamics of contention in that it forces Uighur activists to constantly adjust to the new conditions created by Chinese policies.

The transformation of Uighur alternative spaces

In China – as in other authoritarian-like contexts – networks based on horizontal and personal relationships are crucial in creating alternative spaces that nurture active and passive resistance strategies (Pain 2005). O'Brien and Stern note that in China proper, pre-existing social networks 'incubate resistance' (2008: 17). In Xinjiang, given the multiple stratifications of Uighur society, these alternative spaces were based on religious, local and occupational ties. In the 1970s and the 1980s, the Uighur groups composing the Uighur movement relied mostly on pre-existing networks, including large family/clan networks and Sufi brotherhoods. Naby shows that Uighur religious elites used the Sufi brotherhood networks and/or the network of mosques to communicate and cooperate (1986), while secular Uighurs, living predominantly in urban centres, were more reliant on networks based on occupational ties. Dillon notes the importance of religious elites for establishing connections between groups and for winning popular

---

14. Interview with G, Turkey, December 2012.

support (2006: 103). Sufi brotherhoods, which had a strong social function in that they provided welfare to their members (Dillon 2009), were at the centre of religious and social life. At the same time, mosques, being loosely controlled, were strategic places for activists to meet and mobilise their constituency. In order not to be detected, they operated only through interpersonal contact and word of mouth (Dillon 2006: 107).

The recent restrictions on religious rights, state surveillance, and the existence of state-sponsored Islam seem to have disrupted these alternative spaces. As a matter of fact, since 1999, a training program for Muslim clerics – officially registered and recognised by the state – has been enforced to increase control of religious clerics (Dillon, 2004: 129). Moreover, the state directly funds mosques and finances the education of new clerics in order to better monitor their activities and the message they spread when preaching (Hasmath 2014). The existence of this 'official Islam' creates intra-ethnic tensions and is one of the causes of violence in Xinjiang (Hoshur 2013a). The control established by the state over the mosques and other forms of Uighur sociability – such as networks based on occupational ties – disrupts Uighur alternative spaces that in a recent past operated as instances for mobilisation and milieus of socialisation to an alternative Uighur social order.

These circumstances have forced Uighur groups contesting the government to shrink and go deeper underground, but also to adjust their strategies to this new context. As mosques are no longer safe places, some Uighur groups convene informal meetings in private houses.[15] This strategy contributes to moving alternative spaces from Uighur public places of sociability to private ones. This results in a high degree of fragmentation, as survival strategies call for discretion and scaling down of the movement's activities. The pressure that Chinese authorities place on communications – mobile phone tapping, limited access to the Internet, and complete blackouts – makes coordination difficult, leading to almost complete atomisation of the Uighur movement.

In addition, in a context of religious renewal and constant attacks on Uighur traditional alternative spaces, new alternative spaces are emerging. Labelled Islamist, they are slowly contributing to the transformation of the social environment in which Uighur clandestine groups operate. While traditional Sufi brotherhoods have either been co-opted or put under strict surveillance, the underground Islamic schools that have flourished in the 2000s have become alternative spaces where activists organise collective action (Lee 2014: 4). The role played by underground Islamic madrassas provides supporters of radical Islam with a new audience within the population. This process comes with a partial redrawing of symbolic Uighur alternative spaces and fuels the intra-religious competition between Sufi – both officially recognised and underground – and non-Sufi brotherhoods. These conditions make coordination between the different groups that constitute the Uighur movement extremely difficult.

---

15. Interview with D, Turkey, December 2012.

The high compartmentalisation of the Uyghur movement

It should be emphasised that the conditions imposed through strong repression and tightened control only accelerated a process already underway since the birth of the Uighur nationalist movement, namely its compartmentalisation. Indeed, the Uighur movement, presented by Chinese official discourse as homogenous and well-coordinated, has always been strongly divided, loosely organised and with no real central leadership. Some coordinated actions were undertaken in the 1990s, but they were often carried out at the local level, in district, cities, or administrative regions of XUAR. Since the onset of the 'Strike Hard' campaign, the separatist movement has gone completely underground (Dillon 2004: 110). More or less isolated groups are still operative, and some activists are said to have created armed groups hiding in the mountainous areas of Xinjiang (Dillon 2006: 110). Any attempts to get more accurate information on their membership, structuration, and the support they enjoy within the population have so far failed.[16]

The high level of repression partly explains why, over time, the Uighur movement has adopted loose, not to say almost non-existent, organisational structures: a loose organisation minimises the costs of repression in the short and medium term. From this perspective, the adoption of strategies of survival in an authoritarian political environment requires continuous adjustments and leads to a high degree of compartmentalisation of the movement. Violent groups are certainly those most affected by this dynamic. Van Wie Davis remarks that the groups that 'claim responsibility [for violent actions in Xinjiang] are frequently splintering, merging and collapsing' (2012: 29). Beijing's increasingly repressive stance towards Uighurs since the end of the 1990s has only contributed to further this trend. Indiscriminate repression, widespread arrests, and death sentences of Uighurs play a critical role in this process, as do daily surveillance practices, which prove to be extremely destructive as they create a climate of mistrust and suspicion within the Uighur community.

The intensification of the social and spatial fragmentation and the localisation of groups and factions that compose the movement impose a restructuring of

---

16. The official information on violent events in Xinjiang is strongly biased. Indeed, the Chinese government strongly controls the discourse on violent organisations in Xinjiang. According to the official framing, the East Turkestan Islamist Movement (ETIM) – accused of being a 'major component of the terrorist network headed by Osama bin Laden' (Permanent Mission of the People's Republic of China to the United Nations 2001) – has been responsible for the violent incidents that occurred in Xinjiang since its creation in 2001. The Chinese diplomatic offensive on the international scene in the aftermaths of the 9/11 attacks bore some fruit, as in 2002 both the UN and the US added ETIM to their lists of terrorist organisations. Although doubts persist about the very existence of this organisation (Roberts 2012), the accusations levelled against ETIM by the Chinese government have largely contributed to assimilate Uighur separatism and discontent with terrorism. To speak of clandestine groups is a very sensitive issue, now more than ever. This aspect explains why most of my respondents categorically refused to discuss clandestine violent groups. Only two acknowledged the existence of such groups, but both strongly insisted on the fact that they only represent a minority (interview with K, France, December 2012; interview with G, Turkey, December 2012).

resistance at the micro level. Although official information coming from this region should be treated with extreme caution, it allows for drawing some hypotheses on the structuration of Uighur clandestine groups: they are small groups, of about ten young men, who act very locally (Hoshur 2013b). Most of the time, these groups seem to have no formal relationships with other clandestine groups active in other parts of Xinjiang. In this context, the Uighur movement has proven incapable of capitalising on very tense interethnic relations (Smith Finley 2000) and to frame the socio-economic discontent in such a way as to create new opportunities to connect the different groups composing the movement.

On the one hand, social and ideological divisions remain significant and are an impediment to large-scale social action. On the other, as traditional alternative spaces are being redefined around new solidarities, repression and widespread surveillance dramatically reduce the capabilities and capacities of the Uighur movement to raise ethnic consciousness and contentiousness amongst Uighurs. In a context in which it is extremely difficult to mobilise and organise protests, everyday acts of resistance remain the main acts of contention.

'Everyday resistance' as the main acts of contention

Politically active Uighurs represent a tiny minority among the minority of Uighurs that support independence from, or increased autonomy within, China (Starr 2010: 23). Nevertheless, as Bovingdon (2010), Smith Finley (2007; 2013) and others convincingly show, daily activities are pervaded by resistance to the Chinese social order, despites a high degree of political, social and cultural fragmentation within the Uighur society (Rudelson 1997; Fuller and Starr 2004). This everyday resistance takes several forms, contributing to strengthen individual identification to the group's collective identity and to spread a shared sense of grievances. All the respondents agreed that the practice of the Uighur language in both private and public spaces is certainly the most visible form of resistance, in that it draws clear ethnic and spatial boundaries and helps to raise ethnic consciousness and 'contentiousness'. Bovingdon (2010) and Smith Finley (2013) demonstrate that, in a context where the political field is completely closed to any form of opposition, popular culture has been one of the most efficient vehicles for everyday resistance. It diffuses subtle critical attitudes of an imposed social order, and negative stereotypes of Hans, as well as serving to counter-balance Chinese propaganda (Bovingdon 2010: 88–94; Smith Finley 2007: 628).

Since the 1990s, religion has become a stronger identity marker in differentiating Uighurs from Hans. Before the crackdown on religious activities in 2009, observers remarked on a rise in the frequentation of mosques, in the celebration of religious festivals, and in the number of places of worship (Smith Finley 2007). Most of the interviewees agreed that this development is deep-rooted and concerns above all the urban youth.[17] One respondent emphasised

---

17. Interview with H, Belgium, December 2012.

that an increasing number of women are wearing the veil, even in Urumqi.[18] The tightened surveillance decreed by Beijing in the aftermath of the 2009 Urumqi riots seems only to have strengthened the role of Islam as an identity marker. Indeed, the repeated attacks against religious practices faces strong resistance, at least in the cities: women regularly challenge the ban on their attending the mosque;[19] religious gatherings are discreetly organised for very small groups in private houses, despite these practices can being potentially costly as police officers may at any time raid houses in search of the Koran.[20]

Even if ordinary Uighurs seem to exhibit an apparent lack of interest in issues related to resistance to Chinese rule (Lasserre 2010), a majority of them adopt daily attitudes that seek to preserve and affirm Uighur distinctiveness even in those public spaces where Uighur identity is regularly attacked. Such an attitude creates fluid spatialities, the boundaries of which are defined in the course of the interactions with other Uighurs or with Hans. These spatialities contribute to foster a sense of solidarity and help shape and reproduce rules that support an alternative social order. As the Uighur movement has lost most of its capacities to mobilise at a national level, and local groups remain loosely organised and uncoordinated, everyday resistance remains the main vehicle for opposition to Chinese rule.

Conclusion

The chapter stresses the central role of social and spatial contexts in the dynamics of contention in authoritarian regimes. Relying on the concept of alternative spaces, it analyses the critical role of these spaces for social movements in an authoritarian environment. It shows, specifically, that Uighur capacities to mobilise, recruit and coordinate actions are strongly undermined by direct attacks, targeting traditional Uighur alternative spaces through social policies, repression, and surveillance. Control of space has recently become a central component of Chinese policies in Xinjiang. Serving to enhance the nation and state-building processes, this Chinese strategy also puts unprecedented pressure on the Uighur movement. Repression, state surveillance, and social policies imposing stronger social control over the Uighur minority disrupt traditional solidarity networks and Uighur alternative spaces. Homogenisation and assimilation policies fracture and compartmentalise geographical as well as social spaces, while imposing Beijing's power over Uighurs. These spatial and social strategies contribute to weaken a movement that has always been divided and that seems to grow increasingly detached from its local constituencies. Repression institutes a climate of fear, but daily state surveillance proves to have longer-term effects than repression in that it establishes a climate of mistrust within the boundaries of the ethnic group.

---

18. Interview with F, Turkey, December 2012.
19. Photos of women climbing the locked portal of a mosque, shown by anonymous interviewee (E), Turkey, December 2012.
20. Interview with D, Turkey, December 2012.

Nevertheless, the consequences of repression and state surveillance on mobilisation can only be understood in relation to societal changes and, more specifically, the religious revival and renewal that have been affecting Uighur society since the early 1990s. The alteration of the traditional Uighur alternative spaces results in their ongoing redefinition. This remains difficult to assess with any certainty, given the scarcity and poor quality of sources. Nevertheless, religion seems to play a structuring role again, but intra-religious competition makes this process much more complex than it was in the 1980s. Moreover, the redefinition of alternatives spaces, and the current challenges facing the Uighur social movement as a whole make networking and coordination a more difficult task than ever. In this context, everyday resistance plays a central role in the preservation of an alternative social order that strongly differs from the one imposed by Chinese policies.

Acknowledgements

I would like to thank the editors of this volume, Dr. Lorenzo Bosi, Dr Niall Ó Dochartaigh, Dr. Daniela Pisoiu, and my colleague Dr. Francesco Cavatorta, for their valuable comments and suggestions on earlier drafts of this article.

References

Almeida, P. (2003) 'Opportunity organizations and threat-induced contention: Protest waves in authoritarian settings', *American Journal of Sociology*, 109(2): 345–400.

Amnesty International (1999) *People's Republic of China: Gross Violations of Human Rights in the Xinjiang Uighur Autonomous Region*, 1 April, ASA 17/18/99.

Bosi, L. (2013) 'Safe territories and violent political organizations', *Nationalism and Ethnic Politics*, 19(1): 80–101.

Boudreau, V. (2005) 'Precarious regimes, protest repression and their interaction', in C. Davenport, H. Johnston and C. Mueller (eds) *Repression and Mobilization*, Minneapolis: University of Minnesota Press, pp. 33–57.

Bovingdon, G. (2010) *The Uyghurs: Strangers in Their Own Land*, New York: Columbia University Press.

—— (2004) *Autonomy in Xinjiang: Han Nationalist Imperatives and Uyghur Discontent*, Washington D.C.: East-West Center Washington.

Cai, Y. (2010) *Collective Resistance in China: Why Popular Protests Succeed or Fail*, Stanford: Stanford University Press.

Campana, A. and Ducol, B. (2011) 'Rethinking terrorist safe havens: Beyond a state-centric approach', *Civil Wars*, 13(4): 396–413.

Chen, X. (2011) *Social Protest and Contentious Authoritarianism in China*, Cambridge: Cambridge University Press.

Chung, C. (2004) 'The Shanghai cooperation organization: China's changing influence in Central Asia', *The China Quarterly*, 180: 989–1009.

Clarke, M. (2010) 'Widening the net: China's anti-terror laws and human rights in the Xinjiang Uyghur Autonomous Region', *The International Journal of Human Rights*, 14(4): 542–58.

Cliff, J. (2009) 'Neo oasis: The Xinjiang Bingtuan in the twenty-first century', *Asian Studies Review*, 33(1): 83–106.

Davenport, C. (2005) 'Introduction. Repression and mobilization: Insights from political science and sociology', in C. Davenport, H. Johnston and C. Mueller (eds) *Repression and Mobilization*, Minneapolis: University of Minnesota Press, pp. vii–xli.

della Porta, D. (2013) *Clandestine Political Violence*, Cambridge: Cambridge University Press.

Dillon, M. (2004) *Xinjiang: China's Muslim Far Northwest*, London, New York: Routledge Curzon.

—— (2006) 'Uyghur separatism and nationalism in Xinjiang', in B. Cole (ed.) *Conflict, Terrorism and the Media in Asia*, London: Routledge, pp. 98–115.

—— (2009) 'Uighur resentment at Beijing's rule', *BBC News*, 6 July, http://news.bbc.co.uk/2/hi/asia-pacific/8137206.stm (accessed 7 March 2014).

The Economist (2013) 'Settlers in Xinjiang. Circling the wagons' http://www.economist.com/news/china/21578433-region-plagued-ethnic-strife-growth-immigrant-dominated-settlements-adding (accessed 20 August 2013).

Emet, E. (2009) *5 Temmuz: Urumçi Olayı ve Doğu Türkestan*, Ankara: Grafiker.

Fuller, G. and Starr, F. (2004) *The Xinjiang Problem*, Washington D.C.: Central Asia-Caucasus Institute, Paul H. Nitze School of Advanced International Studies, Johns Hopkins University.

Giddens, A. (1986) *The Constitution of Society: Outline of the Theory of Structuration*, Berkeley: University Press of California.

Goodman, D. (2004) 'The campaign to 'open up the west': National, provincial level and local perspectives', *The China Quarterly,* 178: 317–34.

Hasmath, R. (2012) 'Migration, labour and the rise of ethno-religious consciousness among Uyghurs in urban Xinjiang', *Journal of Sociology*, DOI1440783312459101, first published 3 October 2012.

—   (2014) 'What explains a rise of ethnic minority tensions in China?', paper presented at the American Sociological Association Annual Meeting, San Francisco, August 2014.

Hierman, B. (2007) 'The pacification of Xinjiang Uighur protest and the Chinese state, 1988–2002', *Problems of Post-Communism,* 54(3): 48–62.

Hoshur, S. (2013a) 'Imam stabbed to death after supporting crackdown against Uighurs', *Radio Free Asia*, 16 August, http://www.rfa.org/english/news/ Uighur/imam-08162013200309.html (accessed 6 March 2014).

—   (2013b) 'Uyghurs killed in police raids part of 'separatist bomb plot'', *Radio Free Asia*, 24 October, http://www.rfa.org/english/news/uyghur/ plot-10242013183820.html (accessed 6 March 2014).

Hoshur, S. and Turdush, R. (2013) 'Three Uyghurs shot dead, 20 injured in Eid eve clashes', *Radio Free Asia*, 10 August, http://www.rfa.org/english/ news/uyghur/clashes-08102013000244.html (accessed 12 August 2013).

Howell, A. and Fan, C. (2011) 'Migration and inequality in Xinjiang: A survey of Han and Uyghur migrants in Urumqi', *Eurasian Geography and Economics*, 52(1): 119–39.

Information Office of the State Council of the PRC (2002) *East Turkistan Forces Cannot Get Away with Impunity,* 21 January, reproduced and translated into English on www.china.org.cn. Available at: http://www.china.org. cn/english/2002/Jan/25582.htm (accessed 30 July 2013).

Johnston, H. (2005) 'Talking the walk: Speech acts and resistance in authoritarian regimes', in C. Davenport, H. Johnston, and C. Mueller (eds) *Repression and Mobilization*, Minneapolis: University of Minnesota Press, pp. 109–37.

—   (2006) 'Let's get small: The dynamics of (small) contention in repressive states', *Mobilization: An International Journal*, 11(2): 195–212.

Johnston, H. and Mueller, C. (2001) 'Unobtrusive practices of contention in Leninist regimes', *Sociological Perspectives,* 44(3): 351–75.

Kriesi, H. (2004) 'Political context and opportunity', in D. Snow, S. Soule and H. Kriesi (eds) *The Blackwell Companion to Social Movements,* Malden and Oxford: Blackwell Publishing, pp. 65–90.

Lasserre, S. (2010) *Voyage au pays des Ouïghours (Turkestan chinois, début du XXIe siècle)*, Paris: Éditions Cartouche.

Lee, R. (2014) 'Unrest in Xinjiang, Uyghur Province in China', Aljazeera Center for Studies, http://studies.aljazeera.net/en/reports/2014/02/201421281846110687.htm (accessed 3 October 2014).

Lefebvre, H. (1991) *The Production of Space*, Malden and Oxford: Wiley-Blackwell.

Leibold, J. (2014) 'Xinjiang work forum marks new policy of "ethnic mingling"', *China Brief*, 14(12), 19 June, http://www.jamestown.org/regions/chinaasiapacific/single/?tx_ttnews%5Btt_news%5D=42518&tx_ttnews%5BbackPid%5D=52&cHash=e382c60e99ad9bfe6cd7453376dc25a0#.VC1zzvl5N8E (accessed 3 October 2014).

Leitner, H., Sheppard, E. and Sziarto, K. (2008) 'The spatialities of contentious politics', *Transactions of Institute of British Geographers*, 33(2): 157–72.

Mackerras, C. (2001) 'Xinjiang at the turn of the century: The causes of separatism', *Central Asian Survey*, 20(3) 289–303.

Martin, D., and Miller, B. (2003) 'Space and contentious politics', *Mobilization: An International Journal*, 8(2): 143–56.

Millward, J. (2004) 'Violent separatism in Xinjiang: A critical assessment', *Policy Studies*, no. 6, Washington D. C.: East-West Center.

Moore, M. (2010) 'China installs 40,000 CCTV cameras in Xinjiang ahead of anniversary of deadly ethnic riots', *The Telegraph*, 2 July, http://www.telegraph.co.uk/news/worldnews/asia/china/7867536/China-installs-40000-CCTV-cameras-in-Xinjiang-ahead-of-anniversary-of-deadly-riots.html (accessed 5 March 2014).

Naby, E. (1986) 'Uighur elites in Xinjiang', *Central Asian Survey*, 5(3/4): 241–54.

Nicholls, W., Miller, B. and Beaumont, J. (2013) 'Introduction: Conceptualizing the spatialities of social movements', in W. Nicholls, B. Miller, and J. Beaumont (eds) *Spaces of Contention*, Aldershot: Ashgate Publishing, pp. 1–25.

O'Brien, K. (2003) 'Neither transgressive nor contained: Boundary-spanning contention in China', *Mobilization*, 8(1): 51–64.

O'Brien, K. and Stern, R. (2008) 'Introduction: Studying contention in contemporary China', in K. O'Brien (ed.), *Popular Protest in China*, Cambridge: Harvard University Press, pp. 11–25.

Ó Dochartaigh, N. and Bosi, L. (2010) 'Territoriality and mobilization: The civil rights campaign in Northern Ireland', *Mobilization*, 15(4): 404–25.

Pain, E. (2005) 'Moscow's North Caucasus policy backfires', *Central Asia-Caucasus Analyst*, 29 June, http://www.cacianalyst.org/?q=node/3151, (accessed 1 July 2005).

Patience, M. (2013) 'China Xinjiang riots toll "rises to 35"', *BBC News*, 28 June, http://www.bbc.co.uk/news/world-asia-china-23093714 (accessed 2 July 2013).

Permanent Mission of the People's Republic of China to the United Nations (2001) 'Terrorist activities perpetrated by "Eastern Turkistan" organizations and their ties with Osama bin Laden and the Taliban', *Permanent Mission of the People's Republic of China to the United Nations,* November 29, http://www.china-un.org/eng/zt/fk/t28937.htm (accessed 3 July 2013).

Pile, S. (2012) 'Introduction: Opposition, political identities and spaces of resistance', in S. Pile and M. Keith (eds), *Geographies of Resistance,* New York: Routledge, pp. 1–31.

Poletta, F. (1999) "Free spaces' in collective action', *Theory and Society,* 28(1): 1–38.

Roberts, S. (2012) *Imaginary Terrorism? The Global War on Terror and the Narrative of the Uyghur Terrorist Threat,* Washington: Ponars Eurasia Working Paper.

Rudelson, J. (1997) *Oasis Identities: Uyghur Nationalism Along China's Silk Road.* New York: Columbia University Press.

Scott, J. (1985) *Weapons of the Weak: Everyday Forms of Peasant Resistance,* New Haven: Yale University Press.

Sewell, W. (2001) 'Space in contentious politics', in R. Aminzade, J. Goldstone, D. McAdam, E. Perry, W. Sewell, S. Tarrow and C. Tilly (eds), *Silence and Voice in the Study of Contentious Politics,* Cambridge, Cambridge University Press, pp. 51–88.

Smith Finley, J. (2000) 'Four generations of Uighurs: The shift towards ethno-political identities among Xinjiang's youth', *Inner Asia,* 2(2): 195–224.

— (2007) 'Chinese oppression in Xinjiang, Middle Eastern conflicts and global Islamic solidarities among the Uyghurs', *Journal of Contemporary China,* 16(53): 627–54.

— (2013) *The Art of Symbolic Resistance: Uyghur Identities and Uyghur-Han Relations in Contemporary Xinjiang,* Leiden/Boston: Brill.

Starr, F. (2004) 'Introduction', in F. Starr (ed.) *Xinjiang: China's Muslim Borderland,* New York: Central Asia-Caucus Institute.

Tarrow, S. (2008) 'Prologue: The new contentious politics in China: Poor and blank or rich and complex', in K. O'Brien (ed.) *Popular Protest in China,* Cambridge: Harvard University Press, pp. 1–11.

Tassy, E. (2011) 'Chine: Au Xinjiang, Kashgar à la croisée des chemins', *Le Monde,* 2 December, http://www.lemonde.fr/voyage/article/2011/12/02/au-xinjiang-kashgar-a-la-croisee-des-chemins_1612531_3546.html (accessed 5 March 2014).

Tilly, C. (2000) 'Spaces of contention', *Mobilization: An International Journal,* 5(2): 135–59.

Van Wie Davis, E. (2008) 'Uyghur Muslim ethnic separatism in Xinjiang, China', *Asian Affairs: An American Review,* 35(1): 15–30.

— (2012) *Ruling, Resources and Religion in China: Managing the Multiethnic State in China. Managing the Multiethnic State in the 21st Century,* New York: Palgrave Macmillan.

Watts, J. (2009) 'Old suspicions magnified mistrust into ethnic riots in Urumqi', *The Guardian,* 10 July, http://www.theguardian.com/world/2009/jul/10/china-riots-uighurs-han-urumqi (accessed 30 July 2013).

World Uyghur Congress (2009) *The Urumqi Massacre*, July 2009. Available at: http://www.uyghurcongress.org/en/?cat=255 (accessed 10 August 2013).

Xinhua (2010) 'Security camera blanket covers Urumqi', *China Daily*, 2 July, http://www.chinadaily.com.cn/china/2010-07/02/content_10050565.htm (accessed 5 March 2014).

Zang, X. (2012) 'Scaling the socioeconomic ladder: Uyghur perceptions of class status', *Journal of Contemporary China*, 21(78): 1029–43.

Zhao, T. (2010) 'Social cohesion and Islamic radicalization: Implications from the Uighur insurgency', *Journal of Strategic Security*, 3(3): 39–52.

Chapter Ten

Invisible Commandos, Visible Violence: Protection and Control in the Autonomous Republic of PK18

Jake Lomax

The processes by which rebel movements emerge and are extinguished have interested scholars as part of the growing civil wars literature, but clear answers remain elusive. By analysing a case of rapid emergence and demise of a rebel group within a single suburb of post-election-crisis Abidjan, this chapter analyses how control of territory, and attempts to control territory, shape the threat environment. The protective decisions made by individuals and armed groups within this environment are here analysed with a focus on their complex interaction. The aim is to investigate how control, contestation, and protection interact in order to inform the understanding of the success or otherwise of rebel movements.

In mid-December 2010 the Invisible Commandos commenced an urban guerrilla campaign against Ivorian President Laurent Gbagbo, from PK18, a remote suburb of Abidjan. After quickly establishing control of central PK18, at the end of February 2011 they won the key battle of 'Black Saturday', which removed Gbagbo's forces from the periphery of PK18 and put the Commandos in control, and the 'Autonomous Republic of PK18' was announced shortly thereafter. But a little over six weeks later, Gbagbo had been arrested, the Invisible Commandos disbanded, and their charismatic leader Ibrahim Coulibaly had been shot dead by troops loyal to the new President Alassane Ouatarra.

So, in a period of rapid change following the 2010 elections in Côte d'Ivoire, just four months saw the emergence, rapid growth, and even more rapid demise of the shadowy rebel group. During these four months, many PK18 residents faced risks to their lives from shelling, stray bullets, targeted threats, and killings, as well as a lack of food, water, electricity, and income. This chapter analyses the short life cycle of this rebel group in order to explore the complex relationship between contestation and control of armed groups and associated civilian decision-making. It addresses how the Invisible Commandos shaped, and were shaped by, the socio-spatial wartime environment of PK18, with emphasis throughout on the decisions made by Commandos and associated civilians. While the focus is spatial, the structure of this chapter is broadly temporal, following the short timeframe from the emergence of the Invisible Commandos through to their demise in April 2011.

Concepts and literature

Recent years have seen an increased prominence of the element of space for understanding political violence. Among the most influential contributions in explaining wartime violence against civilians is Kalyvas' (2006) theory of territorial contestation and control. One particular contribution of the theory is its emphasis on the importance of the agency of civilians, as not just passive victims of violence but influential actors in their own right, able to use the presence of armed groups to serve their own ends. For Kalyvas, the role of information is central, inasmuch as this is the main resource that civilians have recourse to: they may know who amongst them is supporting the opposition, and so denounce them to the controlling armed group, enabling that armed group to target violence effectively. Focusing on the deeper relational factors that underlie the establishment of rebel strongholds, Bosi (2013) discusses the importance of 'safe territories' that provide armed rebel groups with the physical space within which 'social networks develop over time and shape formal and informal infrastructures of support that maintain dense affective, familial, and personal relations between armed activists and their local constituencies' (2013: 81). By establishing control over territory, an armed group may develop 'infrastructures of support' that may help them challenge the state. This suggests a stronger, long-term tie between armed groups and civilian constituencies than that suggested in Kalyvas' theoretical model, which assumes that civilians ally themselves with whichever military force is the stronger, regardless of factors such as identity or ethnicity. Zukerman-Daly's (2012) analysis of Colombia shows that the locations in which insurgencies occur do not correspond well to the traditional correlates of violence but, rather, occur where there are 'organisational legacies' of war, especially the presence of former rebels. This highlights the importance of human resources available in the territory, rather than the physical resources that have dominated much analysis. Ó Dochartaigh (2013) emphasises how boundaries form around territorial spaces, changing behaviour and expectations of combatants and civilians in those areas and indeed resulting in wholly spatially defined perceptions of threat. Ó Dochartaigh builds on the work of Ron (2000), who emphasises how very different social spaces may evolve in similar and proximate terrain through changes in the norms and rules that shape the behaviour of armed actors.

These concepts are here applied to a situation where the formation and eradication of boundaries took place over a matter of months, and across a single, narrowly defined territorial space. This chapter discusses the implications of weak state control over territory during a period of war. It is argued that weak control and – importantly – government attempts to establish better control, led to a cycle of boundary formation, local mobilisation and military strengthening that allowed the Invisible Commandos to build support and military capacity such that they quickly became an important threat to Laurent Gbagbo. This highlights some important aspects about control and contestation not found in present models, and the discussion centres on the importance of protective motivations, particularly for mobilisation.

Bosi and della Porta (2012) analyse the 'micro-mobilisation' processes by which people join armed groups. They distinguish between individual-level motivations for joining, organisational-level 'meso' factors, and situational 'macro' factors, highlighting that it is the interaction between these levels that makes understanding mobilisation so complex a task. Guichaoua (2010) demonstrates how protection from threats is an important motivation for joining the Oodua People's Congress in Nigeria. This chapter takes a similar approach to Bosi and della Porta (2012) in its focus on the interactions between levels, but threat is taken to be an important motivating factor for individual and group decisions at all three levels. While significant progress is being made in the literature in understanding violence, participation, and other decisions made by civilians and armed groups, the complexity of the interrelationships between these decisions is underexplored.

The book of which this chapter forms part is a significant step in contributing to building a systematic understanding of this contextual complexity, and this chapter supports this effort through an illustrative example of the causes, consequences and complexities of militia control and contestation. Because the subject of analysis is the whole life cycle of a rebellion, the contribution is not narrowed down to one particular aspect of political violence, but the discussion centres primarily on the territorial dynamics of protection and control. To take such a holistic empirical approach is challenging, especially as regards the many conflicts that last for years or decades and that are spread across huge expanses of territory. This chapter's approach allows for the in-depth exploration of context by taking an extremely localised micro view of part of a very short war.

The chapter proceeds as follows. The remainder of this introduction outlines the wider political context. The second section provides some background information on the Invisible Commandos (IC) and PK18, and details the battle of Black Saturday, which represents the main instance of contestation during the period. The third section, 'Building boundaries', details how threats to the founders of the IC drove them to protect themselves by gathering together in PK18, and how ongoing attempts to defeat the IC in fact strengthened them and assisted in the formation of the safe territory. The focus is on micro-level decisions. The fourth section, 'Contesting boundaries', examines how this meso-level contest over control of PK18 increased threat to the civilian population due to the protective motivations of armed actors. The fifth section details the macro-political shift that led to the fall of the IC, and the sixth section draws these themes together in a conclusion.

Context

For much of its post-independence history, Côte d'Ivoire was one of Africa's economic success stories. In the 1970s and 80s, with relatively effective governance and booming exports of cocoa and coffee, Côte d'Ivoire attracted large-scale immigration from other countries in the region. This was encouraged by the state as it meant a supply of labour for agricultural work. But in the 1990s the economy began to stagnate, and interethnic tensions emerged. This coincided with the end of the thirty-three year long Houphouët-Boigny rule, and the new generation of political leaders exploited these tensions.

The first Ivorian Civil War started in 2002 when, on 19 September, troops in the north of the country mutinied. The failure of the rebel forces to secure Abidjan led to a stalemate in which the north of the country was run by the rebels while the south remained under the authority of the state, run by President Laurent Gbagbo. Long delayed elections were eventually held to end the impasse in the autumn of 2010 and were supposed to reunite the country. But when, in October 2010, the close-run second round confirmed Alassane Ouattara as President (ICG March 2011), Gbagbo disputed the outcome and refused to leave his post. There followed several months of tension, with escalating violence, especially in the west of the country. As the rebel army moved down from the north towards the capital, the national army (FDS) divided, with many supporting Gbagbo, and pro-Gbagbo youth militias mobilised in Abidjan. A French-led UN force patrolled the capital and defended Ouattara, but had no mandate to effectively intervene until the end of March, when UN Resolution 1975 was passed.

In December 2010, amidst this tense standoff, a shadowy Abidjan-based rebel group began fighting against Gbagbo. Known as the Invisible Commandos (IC), they fought a guerrilla campaign from PK18 – a remote suburb in the north of Abidjan. Before describing the Commandos and PK18, I will briefly outline the other main armed actors. The Forces Nouvelles (FN) was the rebel army that had controlled the north of the country for the last decade. They were led by Guillaume Soro – prime minister and Ouattara's ally. On 18 March 2011 they merged into a new army – the Forces Républicaines de Côte d'Ivoire (FRCI) – alongside parts of the FDS that had defected to Ouattara's side. The FN made up the majority of the new FRCI, and the new force, like the FN, suffered from a weak decentralised command structure (ICG August 2011). For the sake of simplicity I refer to Ouattara's military support during the crisis as 'FRCI' throughout. Also on the side of the FRCI were the French, and the French-led UN forces in Côte d'Ivoire, although they did not have much of an offensive military role until the very end of the crisis.

Unless otherwise stated, 'FDS' refers to that majority within the state army that had stayed loyal to Gbagbo when part of it had splintered to support Ouattara. The FDS operated from several bases across Abidjan, including Camp Commando in Abobo. Also on Gbagbo's side were CECOS[1] – a special security command police force – a number of Liberian mercenaries, and the Jeunes Patriotes (young patriots) youth militia. These young patriots – primarily southern Christian male youths strongly supportive of Gbagbo – were mobilised by their leader, Gbagbo ally Charles Blé Goudé, and were eventually armed by the Gbagbo side to help shore up the forces attempting to keep him in power.

Somewhere between these two coalitions were the Invisible Commandos. Although, like the FRCI, they were fighting to oust Gbagbo, they were led by a

---

1. CECOS stands for the *Centre de Commandement des Opérations de Sécurité*.

long-standing rival of the FRCI leader Soro. They seemingly came from nowhere to become one of the most effective fighting forces in Abidjan during the early days of the crisis, taking control of PK18 by early March, declaring it the 'Autonomous Republic of PK18' (*The Daily Telegraph* 2011), before disappearing just as quickly.

Methods

The data analysed for this chapter stems in large part from unstructured interviews with four ex-Invisible Commando combatants, and thirty-two structured and semi-structured interviews with civilians. The data was collected in a series of phases, with some structured interviews conducted by telephone and semi-structured interviews conducted in person. The civilian interviews were for the most part relatively brief – lasting fifteen minutes or less – and covered perceptions of, and relationships with, armed groups, as well as self-protection strategies. Several civilian interviews were much longer, lasting an hour or more. Ex-combatant interviews lasted several hours and covered the same range of topics. These – like the longer civilian interviews – went into more detail on the precise micro-dynamics of control and contestation. All interviews were conducted in French, with the interviewer or research assistant taking notes that were written up immediately after. Due to the sensitive topics under discussion, no recording of interviews was possible – quotes presented here are accurate summaries of the discussion and not the exact phrasings used. All phases of primary data collection are underpinned by online research of local and international media reports in French and English, and the only major western published source on the topic is Varenne (2012). The data was collected to support the design of a survey of 715 households, focusing on displacement decisions. The survey data is not analysed here, though some references are made to it.

The Invisible Commandos

Following a failed attempt on the life of the prime minister Guillaume Soro, in 2007, and the 'Christmas in Abidjan' coup plot later that year, a small group of former rebel soldiers were exiled to Benin. They were a group close to Ibrahim Coulibaly (commonly referred to as 'IB'), who had, many years before, worked as a bodyguard for Alassanne Ouattara while he served as prime minister. IB had risen rapidly from bodyguard to a position of influence thanks, in part, to his involvement in the 1999 coup d'etat. However, his involvements in later coup attempts were much less successful. He directed military operations in the failed coup of 2002, which led to the division of Côte d'Ivoire with the rebels controlling the north of the country. IB was absent as they took control, and it was in this power vacuum that Guillaume Soro took control of the north and unified the rebel forces. In 2004, clashes between IB's and Soro's men in the northern rebel capital Bouaké led to a permanent rift between the two that left IB in political exile. In 2008, IB was tried and convicted in absentia in France, and he was served with an international arrest warrant. But two years later preparations began for another attempt to regain political power. According to one of the ex-combatants interviewed in Abidjan, this core group returned from exile in 2009, on IB's instruction, in order to plot to overthrow Laurent Gbagbo following the 2010 elections, whatever the result. Parts of the group initially based themselves in Bingerville, on the eastern side of Abidjan, but during the early stages of the crisis they settled in PK18.

There were eventually about twelve loosely organised collectives across Abobo that were referred to as the Invisible Commandos (Ben Rassoul 2012). The main faction – that discussed in this chapter – was based in PK18. They were led by Inza Karamoko, also known as 'Colonel Bauer' – a name borrowed from the television series *24* – who was previously a com'zone commander in the rebel-controlled north of Côte d'Ivoire (Ben Rassoul 2012). Karamoko was the military commander of the Invisible Commandos, and represented the Commandos in press interviews prior to IB joining his forces in Abidjan.

PK18

PK18 – abbreviation of Point Kilometre 18, in reference to its distance from a location at the centre of Abidjan – is one of several unusually named quartiers of the northern Abidjan suburb of Abobo. Abobo is sprawling and working class, home to 1.5 million of Abidjan's 6.4 million inhabitants, many of whom are immigrants or northerners. It contains major transport hubs of Abidjan, including its train station, which connects to the north of the country and to Burkina Faso, where much of the immigrant population is from. Abobo forms a large part of northern Abidjan and as it is located north and east of the Banco forest it is relatively isolated from the rest of Abidjan. PK18 is the most remote part of Abobo. The map below shows PK18 outlined in black through Abobo and north of the large expanse that is the Banco National Park.

The map shows how remote PK18 is from the centre of Abidjan, with the central business district of Plateau located by the lagoon. The presidential palace is south of the UNOCI base, in Plateau, but Gbagbo's residence was east of the centre, on the lagoon. A few miles further east is the Golf Hotel, where Ouattara's camp set up during the crisis.

Abobo was, during the crisis, considered a pro-Ouattara stronghold. Certainly it was home to many ethnic northerners and immigrants viewed as Ouattara supporters, and it was, overall, supportive of Ouattara in the 2010 elections. But Abobo cannot be viewed as simply opposed to Gbagbo. It had also previously elected Simone Gbagbo – the wife of Ouattara's rival – to office, and the loyalties of the population there were far from unanimous. Still, it was an attractive location for an armed group opposed to Gbagbo because, apart from the presence of potentially sympathetic ethnicities in the local population, there were, more importantly, a significant number of ex-members of northern rebel groups living in that area of Abidjan. As a result of having associates who had been residents of and worked in PK18 for years – many as taxi drivers – the Invisible Commandos had a level of pre-existing knowledge of who in the community was sympathetic to or working for the Gbagbo regime. The presence of ex-soldiers also meant there

Figure 10.1: Map of Abidjan area showing location of PK18 relative to important locations

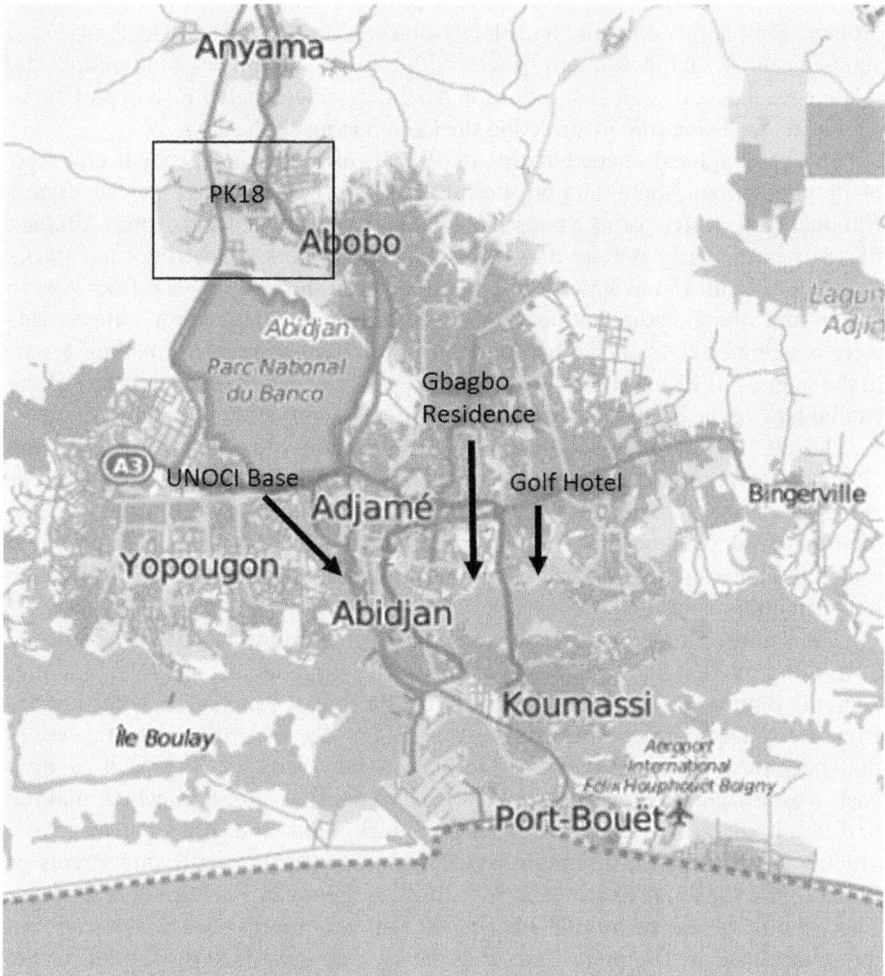

Map © OpenStreetMap.org contributors.

was a pool of potential recruits with previous experience of handling weapons and with social contacts in the rebel forces. The imported local knowledge enabled the Commandos to combine the military efficiency of trained soldiers with local knowledge, targeting policemen and other members of the state apparatus so as to build up their weapons supply in the early days of their operations.

Many Abobo residents consider their quartier to be different to the rest of Abidjan, regarding it, in some way, less part of the state. The Town Hall has limited influence and there are frequent demonstrations and resistance to state authority. Perhaps in order to compensate for this, Abobo has seen the erection of state institutions, including Camp Commando – a military base – and Cité de Police – a modern, luxurious and tarmacked housing development for police officers, built amidst the mud and shanty housing of PK18. The MACA prison is situated nearby, on the southern fringes of the suburb. Despite these measures, the relative weakness of state institutions in Abobo in general, and PK18 in particular, may have had some role in attracting the Commandos to the area.

The geographical characteristics of PK18 mirror the independent character of its population: Abobo sits on the northern and eastern fringes of the Banco National Park, which forms a natural barrier between the area and central Abidjan. PK18 is particularly remote and its haphazard network of narrow mud tracks makes it difficult to navigate. While two roads run through it – one from Abobo to Anyama, and the other up the western side of Banco, to the north – these roads were not connected to each other with tarmac until after the crisis, making access to the interior of PK18 difficult. The map shows how, while urban and part of the capital city, to the north and west, PK18 borders countryside.

Despite its relative isolation, PK18's proximity to central Abidjan and Gbagbo's forces also contributed to make it a strategic location. Rebel forces stationed here, at the edge of the de facto capital, would be influential due to their potential to engage government troops and attack key state apparatus, while remaining far enough away from the opposition forces and key strategic assets to make attaining control realistic.

The satellite image below shows some key locations in this early episode of fighting in what became known as the Battle for Abidjan. The IC had, under General Bauer, set up their main military base at a very small hotel not far from the N'Dotre junction to the west of PK18. It was a little west of a school that later became an IC training facility for new recruits. The road running east–west through the centre of PK18 was, at the time, not tarmacked, making it difficult for armed vehicles to enter. Checkpoints and other barriers were quickly established on this main road, beginning on the small side streets of PK18, particularly at Pharmacie Safi, midway between N'Dotre and Agripac. The zone of influence around Pharmacie Safi was relatively uncontested, but the area closer to the main base at N'Dotre was very heavily shelled in the week running up to Black Saturday, with Gbagbo's tanks firing from the road running north to N'Dotre from the western edge of the Banco forest. The main access road on the eastern edge of PK18 had always had a government forces checkpoint at Agripac, the junction between the cross road and the main Abobo–Anyama road.

Building boundaries

So, PK18 was an attractive location for the IC, and this section details how they came to be there and how they progressed from a largely unarmed group of ex-rebel soldiers into a considerable fighting force that controlled PK18 and much of

Figure 10.2: Satellite image of PK18 showing key conflict locations

Image © 2011 DigitalGlobe, Inc.

the rest of Abobo. An important reason, I shall argue, was their desire to protect themselves, and the ongoing failed attempts to suppress them.

Varenne (2012) concludes that the Invisible Commandos were the self-defence militias of Abobo, and to a large extent this was indeed the case.[2] However, there were three main categories of 'members' of the Invisible Commandos in PK18. First, there were the initial instigators of the IC, which was the core group, close to IB. Second, there were former rebel fighters of various allegiances who had military training and social connections to the rebel networks. Since Abobo is traditionally home to migrants from the north of Côte d'Ivoire, where the main rebel movement was based, the presence of rebels and those with connections to rebels is unsurprising. Third, also joining the PK18 IC were untrained *'jeunes du quartier'* – or neighbourhood youths. Apart from those inducted into the Commandos, there were other youths forming checkpoints and operating within the protective sphere of the Commandos without being part of the organisation. The argument of this chapter is that protection played some role in the mobilisation process at each of these levels of the organisation, and that the levels of mobilisation and protection are interconnected.

A year after the death of IB, his private secretary gave a media interview that shed some light on the emergence of the Commandos. In late 2010, the Commandos were in Abidjan but were dispersed around the capital, and under

_____

2.   This will be addressed in more detail in section five.

suspicion. They were effectively unarmed, though they had military training, and many were known to the security authorities:

> We had fighters [...] in the ten municipalities of Abidjan and Anyama. Since the CECOS had heard that ex-combatants lived in parts of the economic capital, it was deemed appropriate to relocate many of them. We grouped in Abobo PK 18 where [...] Colonel Bauer lived. In other municipalities, CECOS removed our men who never come back (Ben Rassoul 2012).

The Invisible Commandos had, then, been spatially quite a disparate group that had, under threat from CECOS, gathered together in one of the most remote parts of Abidjan, home of one senior member. While effectively civilians they were vulnerable to attack when isolated, so what Ben Rassoul describes as a 'sleeper cell' was forced into active mobilisation due to the targeted threat they faced as individuals. According to the same interview, they became armed actors on 16 December 2010, when they used a borrowed Kalashnikov rifle to surprise those policing the installation of a new director general of the public radio and television authority, RTI. That day they acquired nine more Kalashnikovs from the fleeing police. A few days later, they obtained more from troops coming to find them, and so it went on: 'Gradually, we built an arsenal of combat' (Ben Rassoul 2012).

It was through such failed attempts from Gbagbo's side to maintain control of Abobo and PK18 that the IC gained most of their weapons. The legacy of state attempts to control Abobo – the official residences for police and other pro-Gbagbo institutions – were initially a major source of weapons. These had in large part been deserted following the emergence of the IC, so weapons could easily be taken. Second, ongoing attempts to maintain control through armoured vehicle patrols, as well as attempts to find the leader of the Commandos, provided ambush targets for the IC, which they successfully exploited. In this way they acquired increasingly heavy weapons and armed vehicles – the process of attempts to maintain control of Abobo and to destroy the Commandos backfired, serving instead to strengthen them. One author on the online news source Abidjan.net entitled his article 'Repeated attacks on Abobo: How Gbagbo arms the Invisible Commandos' (2011). The account of Black Saturday provided by a senior ex-combatant also emphasised the importance of arms gained during the battle. Once they had driven the FDS back from Agripac, they were able to access a large arms cache at Depot 9, just south of the checkpoint, which turned the battle decisively in their favour. Contestation, then, is not only about territory but it also has important consequences for military resources and the fighting capacity of rebel groups.

As detailed in the previous section, the PK18 territory was – with the existing rebel networks and favourable geographical factors – an IC resource before they moved there. Yet it was not only the weakness of state control that made the territory a resource. The historic and ongoing state attempts to retain, and then regain, control provided the IC with both weaponry and attractive headquarters.

Mobilisation created boundaries in that it quickly exposed the weakness of the state in the area, prompting many police and pro-Gbagbo residents to abandon their homes and residences. At this stage the IC were left in control of central PK18, while the periphery was controlled by Gbagbo-loyalists. The process was assisted by the situation of a chaotic macro-level stand-off that may have distracted state military attention, even if little overt fighting was taking place elsewhere in Abidjan at the time.

Protection formed part of the mobilisation process for the central command element of the Commandos, and the same held for junior and peripheral members. While there was no pay for the Commandos, they were cooked for by women volunteers. Some sections of the Commandos requested small, and seemingly genuinely voluntary contributions at checkpoints and civilian houses in order to purchase water, tea and coffee. There is little evidence that mobilisation was motivated by financial gain, but rather for self-protection, community protection, and the desire to oust Gbagbo:

> In the Invisible Commandos, there was no recruitment but memberships. People have voluntarily agreed to join the movement. There were no wages, youth did not require payment or even the promise of payment. (Senior ex-combatant)

The process of the formation of the enclave made it dangerous to leave because of open fighting in the streets, the risks of passing through the loosely defined and fluid spaces between the IC and the FDS, and the targeted violence across Abidjan that many Dioula[3] feared upon leaving Abobo. One ex-IC combatant who lived just outside PK18 in an area with many Gbagbo loyalists described how this situation led him to participate:

> Since 2002, I had contact with the New Forces in Bouaké but I was not a fighter. I attended their camp but I did not have access to weapons. During the post-election crisis, some dissidents of the New Forces were in Abobo. Those I knew in this group told me to be ready and they will sign me to fight. But with all the attacks against the people of the north, I decided with my brother to flee Abobo. We failed because the young people who manned the checkpoints were checking identity cards, so it was risky for us to cross. Having not succeeded, we decided to reconnect with our former Forces Nouvelles friends, to see if we can join them. After several refusals (because we were too young), we insisted until we managed to join the Invisible Commando. Also it should be noted that the injustice suffered by many Dioula motivated our choice. (Regular ex-combatant)

Because PK18 was becoming a space that provided some measure of protection for northerners, even during the violent process of establishing full control, this encouraged recruitment into the Commandos. This particular combatant's decision

---

3. An ethnicity broadly associated with opposition to Gbagbo.

on whether to flee or participate was clearly strongly influenced by existing social networks, and he was permitted to join the Commandos in a proper fighting capacity.

An important factor in the mobilisation of local youths without close personal connection to the IC was undoubtedly the control of territory that the Commandos were already beginning to establish. The actions of the Commandos, combined with the physical features of PK18, had already made FDS penetration into the interior of PK18 difficult at the beginning of mobilisation. Youths formed gangs and checkpoints on the smaller mud tracks in the knowledge that a trained military force was backing them up, possibly following the example set by the Commandos themselves with their checkpoints on the main central road of PK18. While the contestation over control created major threats of indiscriminate violence directed against PK18 residents, the presence of the IC also protected the majority of civilians of 'northern' identities in PK18 from targeted threats in the home and at checkpoints. Such threats came, generally speaking, from youth militias and mercenaries operating through much of the rest of Abidjan, which was under Gbagbo-loyalist control. While such groups operated on the peripheries of PK18 – especially from the Ebrie Village of Anonkoua-Kouté on the south-eastern edge – and attacked PK18 civilians surveyed near the area, such groups were generally rare in PK18 and Abobo. This was in part due to the overall ethnic composition and political tendencies of the population, and in part to the emergence and eventual controlling presence of the Invisible Commandos.

> Because many soldiers had deserted, the FDS were aided by youth militia, and it was these people who were very dangerous for the population. [...] the militia killed many of the Dioula ethnic group. When youth militias met a Dioula, they assumed them to be supporters of Ouattara or ICs, and they may be killed without justification. These militias were many in Yopougon but very few in Abobo. (Civilian Interviewee 23 October)

Youths were able to mobilise to protect themselves against attacks from Anonkoua Kouté youths, because – due to IC control – such small-scale mobilisation could not be targeted for punishment by more powerful armed actors, such as the FDS or CECOS. Other areas of Abidjan had opposed Gbagbo in the elections but were overrun by the FDS and pro-Gbagbo youth due – at least in part – to the absence of an effective opposition force to provide protection for those willing to mobilise. Of course, the youth mobilisation across Abobo also supported the control exercised by the IC central command, and so the mobilisation of the core group of Commandos and the peripheral mobilisation of youth militia created a two-way protective relationship under their sphere of influence.

This section of the analysis has argued that the foundation of the IC stronghold in PK18, and their subsequent success in mobilising local youth to the cause of ousting Gbagbo, were due to the protection afforded by the creation and maintenance of the safe territory. The natural benefits of PK18 were augmented by failed attempts to exercise state control, which strengthened the Commandos.

The next section analyses the main attempt to regain control – the battle of Black Saturday – and its implications for civilians.

Contesting boundaries

The previous section outlined how the IC gaining control of PK18 had some positive effects on the protection of parts of the civilian population due to the prevention of selectively targeted violence by pro-Gbagbo forces. I now turn to analyse violent acts between armed groups, how these relate to changing patterns of control, and how they change the dynamics between armed groups and civilians. Central to the emergence of the Autonomous Republic of PK18 are the events of the week running up to the battle of Black Saturday. The battle denotes the intense fight between Gbagbo loyalist troops – CECOS and FDS – and the Invisible Commandos, which provoked massive civilian displacement. The main threat to PK18 civilians was spatially targeted violence, especially FDS shelling from the periphery after they had lost control of PK18.

Unsurprisingly, the IC's success had brought increased pro-Gbagbo FDS presence to the periphery, aiming to contain and defeat the rebels. As the military capacity of the IC increased, the FDS lost the ability to travel in safety beyond their checkpoints. This helped to create the boundaries of the enclave and produced the feeling that PK18 was 'under siege'. The Agripac checkpoint formed a centre for Gbagbo's influence in PK18, but the FDS rarely moved past this point. Even during the massive incursion of Black Saturday, the considerable force sent to defeat the IC apparently did not dare to move far past the Agripac checkpoint.

The FDS being pushed to the periphery meant it was now the IC that could search for weapons in people's homes, while the FDS, due to lack of information, lost the capacity to target individuals. Abobo had been declared a 'red zone' and the Gbagbo regime had broadcast their intention to destroy it, but relatively little violence was observed until 22 February. That day, armoured CECOS vehicles ventured past Agripac and onto PK18's main east–west road. They were ambushed on the main road of Abobo's Derrière Pont, at Carrefour Diallio. The killing of at least ten people (ICG March 2011, Abidjan.net 2011[4]) in this incident ensured that the Gbagbo loyalist forces began to take the threat of the Invisible Commandos seriously. That day, and for the following two days, there was intense fighting between the IC and FDS, including extensive use of heavy weapons and shelling. There was some respite on the Friday, but the following day came to be known as Black Saturday due to the intensity of the fighting when a large ground force was sent to defeat the Commandos. One ex-IC member described the experience:

The Wednesday[5] before that Saturday, we had killed an army officer in combat, and the Saturday, it was like a revenge that the FDS were coming to take.

---

4.   http://news.abidjan.net/h/392498.html.
5.   Media reports and other interviews suggested this ambush occurred on the Tuesday.

They were heavily armed (twenty-two tanks and nearly 3,000 men) and led an assault on PK18. They succeeded in pushing us back and we had to desert the checkpoints that we had. We retreated as far as Unicafé. The FDS stopped their assault at Agripac, and they did not progress any further. But still they fired shells towards our position. We had to call on the old men with mystic power to help us out of the situation. There were five mystics there. Their actions made the shells stop exploding when they landed. That helped us a lot. And we began to plan ambushes against the FDS to the point that they were forced to retreat back to Abobo centre. That was how we regained our checkpoints and retook the ground. (senior ex-combatant)

The account reflects the deep belief in mysticism held by many in the Commandos, their opponents, and the civilian population in general. Late on Black Saturday, the IC took advantage of abandoned FDS weapons caches south of the Agripac checkpoint and rapidly turned the battle against the government forces, pushing them much further east, towards the centre of Abobo.

It thus appears that, despite a concerted effort to remove the Invisible Commandos through a ground and artillery offensive, the IC ultimately came out victorious, and from then on they enjoyed unchallenged control of PK18 with the FDS having been pushed back to the area in and around their base, Camp Commando, in the centre of Abobo. Black Saturday – or 'Samedi Noir' – was well known by the residents of PK18 and Abobo, but did not seem widely known in other areas of Abidjan and – despite being a key turning point in the Battle for Abidjan – was not widely reported in the media as a conflict event.

Nevertheless, media documentation of clashes and mass outflows of civilians on the Saturday and Sunday are in evidence, and the events triangulate with the testimony of a Médecins Sans Frontières (MSF) representative working in Abobo as well as interviews with civilians in PK18. On 28 February, MSF set up their Abobo hospital. MSF could not access PK18 due to the intense fighting, and on 28 February they began to receive wounded individuals from that area. That day, 115 patients were received, 45 per cent of these had bullet wounds; others had shrapnel or knife wounds (MSF pers. comm. 2012).

While it is difficult to define exactly where fighting occurred, the overall impression of the survey enumerators was that the mid-week battles took place around the east–west road through Derrière Pont (literally, 'behind the bridge', referring to the bridge over the train track immediately west of Agripac), especially between N'Dotre and Diallio, while Black Saturday fighting extended further east, especially between Agripac and Unicafé. For PK18 civilians, these four days of particularly intense conflict across the five-day period produced the greatest threat of the crisis. The Gbagbo side found their inability to control the territory intolerable, and they justifiably feared that the Commandos would strengthen within a safe territory and become an existential threat to the Gbagbo side. What follows is a brief outline of how threat to armed groups, shaped by control and contestation of territory, may affect civilians.

Kalyvas (2006: 69), in summarising how new forms of war are thought to result in violence, speaks of 'the acute feeling of vulnerability that combatants experience in the context of irregular war'. To this he attributes killing of civilians, due either to inability or deliberate failure to differentiate between civilians and rebels. Following Kalyvas, I argue that threat to an armed force may have two effects: first, threat to armed groups may increase their propensity to use violence, when the payoff of using violence includes the immediate possibility of saving one's own life or the life of comrades. Contestation between armed groups thus increases the use of 'indiscriminate' violence against civilians due to the troops' instincts of self-protection when under fire or operating in the opposition's safe territories. Second, increased 'indiscriminate' violence occurs under these conditions of pitched battle when forces – for strategic or personal reasons – may seek to avoid personal threat exposure. This could be observed on Black Saturday when FDS troops refused to go beyond the Agripac checkpoint to take on the Commandos, choosing instead to shell their presumed positions from the checkpoint, thus allowing the IC time to regroup and eventually win the battle, as well as increasing threat to civilians in the area. In this way, being under threat from another armed force restricts targeting capacity in that armed actors cannot see their targets when located far away or behind shelter, resulting in loss of capacity to target on the basis of identity or behaviour. Also, longer-range weapons may be inherently inaccurate.

Both these 'trigger happy' and 'shooting blind' effects would suggest that during high levels of contestation, targeting criteria may be largely location-based. Associated increase in 'indiscriminate' threat to civilians, then, stems from the self-protection of armed actors, rather than from a lack of information. Contrary to Kalyvas' (2006) 'hedging bets' motivation, it may be that, in some contexts, and for certain periods, what drives civilian failure to share information is the wish to avoid indiscriminate violence. It may be that, in such cases, indiscriminate violence causes the failure of civilians to communicate information, as well as the other way round. This makes some sense given the PK18 context. Certainly in those few days of intense fighting, civilians were for the most part hiding indoors, rather than seeking interaction with combatants: 'The intensity of the fighting was such that civilians did not have the courage to take action against one of the two forces fighting each other' (Civilian Interviewee 30 October).

I now turn to discuss the consequences of contestation for protection strategies in more detail, including how armed actors try to protect civilians, and the overlaps between threat and protection. Where violence is indiscriminate and perpetrated from a distance, the protection payoff for civilian mobilisation is less than when violence is face-to-face and conducted by actors who lack a considerable military advantage. In the face of the shelling and street-to-street fighting, the protection strategy adopted by most was displacement. Of the households surveyed, 85 per cent displaced in whole or in part, and the overwhelming majority of these displacement actions took place in the week of Black Saturday (from the Monday before until the Monday after). The IC tried to protect the civilian population by communicating the start of the fighting between themselves and the Gbagbo loyalists, which helped civilians to access food and other essentials during periods of relative safety:

> When the bombing began, people were afraid because of the intensity of the fighting [...] Later, the IC gave signals that announced when we should stay indoors: there were three shots (firing heavy weapons) that announced the fighting. This allowed people to leave in the morning to get supplies to the market and once heard the third shot, they hurried to the church or to their homes. (Civilian Interviewee 29 Oct 2012 B)

Armed actors sharing information with civilians may be of formal or informal character. Many households had contacts in the FDS and the police who were able to warn them when attacks were to be launched against PK18.

> Personally, I have friends of the Gbagbo clan who came to tell me that the situation would get worse and I had to go out with my family. They themselves have received information during their various political meetings and wanted to warn me. (Civilian Interviewee, 29 October 2012)

Such informal information sharing through personal contacts may be viewed as unambiguously protective. However, it is difficult to distinguish formal threat-communication – such as the declaration of Abobo as a 'red zone' – from formal information-sharing to protect civilians. Telling civilians of an impending attack on an area and encouraging them to leave may be loosely termed a protective action, but the removal of civilians also serves a strategic purpose in that it isolates rebels from the civilian population. Invisible Commando actions protecting civilians staying in PK18 could be seen as more benevolent but, of course, these also served a strategic purpose in that they helping the IC to avoid isolation. These meso-to-micro attempts to shape behaviour may, then, be both well-intentioned and strategic.

This section has illustrated how – for a short time – contestation between groups over the territory made the 'safe space' far from safe for civilians and armed groups alike. Threats to armed groups from other armed groups also increased the threat to civilians in PK18, due to those groups trying to protect themselves during combat. Nevertheless, within this environment in which the armed actors presented a great threat to civilians, both sides attempted – formally or informally – to protect civilians in some way, albeit in whole or in part to serve their own strategic objectives.

This concerted attempt to remove the boundaries partly formed by the presence of the Invisible Commandos failed, and like earlier, weaker, attempts to defeat the IC it ended up strengthening them. Through the battle of Black Saturday, the IC consolidated control over the centre of PK18 and pushed the FDS further away from the periphery. They gained control of the key checkpoints on arterial roads at Agripac and N'Dotre, and so were better able to prevent the FDS from firing shells at the population. After the IC had gained full control of PK18 – following Black Saturday – the IC was accused of attacking Anokoua-Kouté, as well as of committing human rights abuses (HRW).[6] This attack seemingly removed the threat that had been posed by informal armed groups operating from the village, affecting northern civilians in the southern fringes of PK18. But while Black Saturday undoubtedly strengthened the IC, it also sowed the seeds of their downfall, which is the subject of the next section.

The end of the republic

Protection and the desire to oust Gbagbo were unifying drivers of mobilisation across all levels of the IC. But the central group of IB loyalists also had another important incentive to participate. Their motivation was rooted in long-standing relationships, and their wish was to further the political agenda of their leader in his attempt to be reinstated in the Ivorian political landscape after years in exile. This separate reason at the heart of the Invisible Commandos ultimately contributed to the violent nature of its demise, since once Gbagbo was ousted and with the FRCI effectively in control, the threat that had driven mobilisation amongst all but the core central 'sleeper cell' was diminished, while the threat to that core remained, alongside their desire for political influence. This diminished the organisational capacity of the group as they lost the ability to mobilise their forces.

I will now address this issue of the organisational capacity of the Commandos, and how it was affected by control of territory and external political events. After winning the battle of Black Saturday, IC control was established at the key Agripac checkpoint and the arterial roads. IB then came to PK18, from near the Ghanaian border, and the IC's approach to the civilian population changed significantly. IB set up headquarters in the Cité de Police – the relatively grand former police residential development – and began trying to leverage the success of the Commandos into realising his own political ambitions. He took local civilian relationships more seriously than the Commandos had done up to that point, setting up a civilian–military liaison committee, which began to distribute food in the community, organising press conferences and regular public meetings with the local population, held in front of the main villa in the Cité de Police. Although the crisis had seen a significant decrease in the PK18 population, IB seemingly set out to establish some forms of local governance that might add to his political credibility.

In some ways, the IC became a stronger organisation during this time. Gbagbo's forces no longer posed a threat in PK18, and IB brought with him experienced loyal soldiers from his home area, as well as forces liberated from the Maca prison. The public appearance of the Commandos became increasingly that of a formal armed force. Images from this period show an increasing number of uniformed men, and balaclavas were no longer worn, since there was no longer a need for

---

6. This narrative is disputed in Varenne (2012). However, the debate concerns the identity of the perpetrators rather than whether or not abuses occurred.

Figure 10.3: Satellite image of Cité de Police

The red roofs and tarmacked roads of the modern police quarter in PK18 (highlighted in white) contrast with the iron roofs and mud roads of surrounding buildings. Image © 2011 DigitalGlobe, Inc.

fighters to hide their identities. Meanwhile, the position of Gbagbo loyalist forces in Abidjan, and particularly in Abobo, were getting weaker as they lost battles to the Commandos and as the FRCI forces advanced from the north.

Although the IC were becoming a stronger force and their territorial control was expanding, the FRCI arriving in Abidjan represented another, larger, force fighting against Gbagbo. And because they were under the control of presidential challenger Ouattara and the prime minister Guillaume Soro, the FRCI had much greater legitimacy than the IC in the eyes of the international community as well as for the majority of the Abidjan population opposed to Gbagbo. On 11 April, in an operation directed by French UN troops, the Forces Nouvelles arrested Gbagbo. This completely changed the external political environment for the IC, and removed the reason for participation for the vast majority of its members.

Second, the strengthening of the IC coincided with the undermining of its community foundations. IB's leadership was divisive within the community and the Commandos. It had not been obvious to members drawn from the local youth that that the central unit of the IC existed in great part to achieve IB's personal ambitions, and for much of the period some were unaware that IB was involved at all. So IB's arrival in PK18 at the end of March, and his political statements regarding his intention to rule a transitional military government – thus threatening Ouattara's position – were viewed as something of a breach of trust by those who thought they had been fighting to replace Gbagbo with the electoral victor Ouattara. The regular ex-combatant interviewed said he felt betrayed once he realised that IB was pushing for political influence, but that he carried on fighting. Others did not: 'when people knew that IB's fighting was personal many of its members deserted the ranks, and IB had to bring youths from his village to help in the fight.' (Civilian interviewee, 29 October)

Third, the establishment of total control in PK18, and the increasing FRCI and IC control in other areas of Abidjan, greatly diminished the threat to Dioula and other northerners. The extension of the safe territory to the south and east made households in PK18 relatively safe from violence. The removal of the possibility of targeted attacks from CECOS, the FDS, or Anokoua-Kouté youth, meant removal of the micro-protection motivation of being part of the IC. Hence, the protective role of the IC was no longer relevant for any but the core central group. Due to the long-standing rivalry between IB and Soro, for those close to IB, the FRCI being in control under Guillaume Soro was perhaps as great a threat as they faced with Gbagbo still in charge. At this time, the existence of the Commandos as a significant fighting force may have been necessary for keeping IB and his associates alive, and so the calls on IB to disarm the Commandos were met with hesitation.

Once Gbagbo was arrested, the internal tensions of the IC led to its swift demise. At the time of the Autonomous Republic of PK18, IB was claiming in the media that the IC comprised 5,000 men, though he had clear incentives to exaggerate his own influence, and other estimates from within the Commandos peaked closer to 3,000.[7] Once Gbagbo had been deposed, there was no reason for most of these men to fight the FRCI – indeed, many favoured Ouattara over IB. The boundaries of the safe territory were simultaneously weakened at the micro-level within, and the macro-level without. This left a relatively small group of IB's close affiliates quite exposed in a PK18 with a sparse local population largely indifferent to his presence and broadly supportive of his political opponent.

After the arrest of Gbagbo, Ouattara's new regime called on IB to disband the Commandos and join the new national army, the FRCI. IB resisted these calls, stalled disarmament, and held out for a direct meeting with Ouattara. This resulted in a stand-off, and on 20 April, the Forces Republicaines de Côte d'Ivoire troops – or, FRCI, formerly Forces Nouvelles – attacked PK18 and were repelled after a short battle. They returned the following week and, on the evening of 27 April 2011, the FRCI shot IB dead. The Commandos were ultimately defeated by a relatively small group of FRCI soldiers, succeeding where a combined force of thousands of men with tanks had failed just two months previously.

---

7. In mid-April 2011, journalists of the Associated Press estimated that fewer than 1,000 men were present, http://www.nytimes.com/2011/04/24/world/africa/24ivory.html?_r=0.

Conclusion

This chapter has outlined the life cycle of a short-lived rebel group, which fought to establish control of a safe territory but which ultimately failed to perpetuate the group or to fulfil the core objective of their leadership, although the two other aims – the removal of Gbagbo, and the protection of the ethnic northerners from targeted violence – were at least partially successful. The main aim of the chapter has been to demonstrate how protection and control interact through the creation, maintenance, and erosion of territorial boundaries.

The chapter has provided some background to the Invisible Commandos and descriptions of the natural attributes of PK18 that made it an attractive location for a base, and that ultimately contributed to it becoming a safe rebel territory. The chapter then highlighted the role of protective motivations on the part of various core and peripheral members of the Commandos, and how these were driving in the formation of territorial boundaries. Protective motivations, and the territory as a 'resource' provides explanation for how both mobilisation and the legacy of state attempts to control Abobo helped the IC to grow so rapidly and to take control of a substantial area of the economic capital. The chapter analysed some aspects of the impact on the protective relationship between civilians and the armed group brought on by a concerted attempt on the part of the state forces to destroy the Commandos. In this case, contestation between armed groups, and the involvement of widespread indiscriminate violence, had the – perhaps intended – effect of significantly depopulating the safe territory as the state forces protected themselves at the expense of PK18 civilians. However, ultimately, the intensive use of violence backfired in the same way that less intensive violence had before, serving to cement the IC's control of territory. Yet the expansion of the safe territory and the increased control meant that protection was no longer necessary. This, in parallel with shifts in the macro environment, undermined the IC's local legitimacy and led to their downfall.

Finally, the case analysis highlights the importance of the interaction between contestation, control, and protection in the formation and end of armed movements. Control may create a virtuous cycle with protection facilitating rapid mobilisation within a defined space, but in the absence of shared protection objectives, or shared political objectives, the legitimacy of rebel movements may be lost just as quickly.

References

Ben Rassoul, T. (2012) 'Côte d'Ivoire: Un an après retour sur 'le commando invisible' Des nouvelles révélations sur la mort d'IB', interview by Félix D. Bony, *Over-blog.fr*, 27 August, http://cotedivoire-lavraie.over-blog.fr/article-cote-d-ivoire-un-an-apres-retour-sur-le-commando-invisible-des-nouvelles-revelations-sur-la-mo-104151180.html (accessed 27 April 2012).

Bosi, L. (2013) 'Safe territories and violent political organizations', *Nationalism and Ethnic Politics*, 19(1): 80–101.

Bosi, L. and della Porta, D. (2012) 'Micro-mobilization into armed groups: Ideological, instrumental and solidaristic paths', *Qualitative Sociology*, 35(4): 361–83.

The Daily Telegraph (2011) 'Soldiers open fire on women protest in Ivory Coast', 4 March, http://www.telegraph.co.uk/news/worldnews/africaandindianocean/cotedivoire/8360781/Soldiers-open-fire-on-women-protest-in-Ivory-Coast.html (accessed 21 October 2014).

Guichaoua, Y. (2010) 'How do ethnic militias perpetuate in Nigeria? A micro-level perspective on the Oodua People's Congress', *World Development*, 38(11): 1657–66.

International Crisis Group (ICG) (2011) 'Côte d'Ivoire: Is war the only option?', Africa Report No. 171. 3 March.

— (2011) 'A critical period for ensuring stability in Côte d'Ivoire', Africa Report No. 176. 1 August.

Kalyvas, S. N. (2006) *The Logic of Violence in Civil War*, New York: Cambridge University Press.

Médecins Sans Frontières (MSF) (2012) personal email correspondence on MSF work in PK18,,31 October.

Ó Dochartaigh, N. (2013) 'Bounded by violence: Institutionalizing local territories in the north of Ireland', *Nationalism and Ethnic Politics*, 19(1): 119–39.

Ron, J. (2000) 'Boundaries and violence: Repertoires of state action along the Bosnia/Yugoslavia divide', *Theory and Society*, 29(5): 609–49.

Varenne, L. (2012) *Abobo-la-guerre: Côte d'Ivoire, terrain de jeu de la France et de l'ONU*, Paris: Mille et une Nuits.

Zukerman-Daly, S. (2012) 'Organizational legacies of violence: Conditions favoring insurgency onset in Colombia, 1964–1984', *Journal of Peace Research*, 49(3): 473–91.

Chapter Eleven

Armed Urbanism: Political Violence and Contestation in Conflict and 'Non-Conflict' Cities

Jovana Carapic

Empirical observations suggest that political violence and contestation is increasingly an urban phenomenon. But what role do cities play in the emergence and proliferation of different forms of armed urbanism, such as urban insurgencies and gang warfare? Recent studies in the field of urban sociology offer valuable insights. This literature has examined the processes and mechanisms that allow for the development of various forms of contentious politics taking place in cities. These include socially positive ones – such as peaceful protests, boycotts, and public campaigns – but also those of a more sinister nature, such as organised crime, gangs, riots, rebellions, terrorism, and urban insurgencies.

It is useful to elaborate on the specific qualities that differentiate cities from other sociopolitical scales of organisation. All sociopolitical forms of organisation are defined by the degree to which they combine social space – characterised by the everyday relations among the local population, societal groups, and state institutions – and physical space, that is, the actual spatial layout of the territory that the organisation occupies (Bosi 2013: 83). What differentiates cities from other sociopolitical forms of organisation, however, is the extent to which they intertwine social and physical space. This is evident in the classic conceptualisation of cities as provided by Wirth (1938: 8), who defined them as 'relatively large, dense, and permanent settlement[s] of socially heterogeneous individuals'.

What is most interesting about Wirth's definition is that it seeks to link the socio-physical organisation of the city to modern forms of urban life, or what he called 'urbanism' (Wirth 1938: 3). Specifically, and as Rodgers notes (2010: 3), the aim was to describe 'the way in which urban environments universally determine the actions of individual agents'. Most recently, and echoing Wirth's conceptualisation of cities, the focus has been on cities as constitutive for the emergence and evolution of political contestation (Nicholls 2008), as well as on urban forms of violence (Rodgers 2010).

Building on this literature, this chapter develops the notion of 'armed urbanism' – a conceptual lens for understanding how the socio-physical organisation of cities gives rise to similar types of armed groups in times of conflict, and in so-called non-conflict settings: urban insurgencies and gangs, respectively. The chapter proceeds in three steps. First, it provides empirical evidence to support the argument that the nature of armed conflict is changing, with the location of political violence and contestation becoming increasingly urban.

It will consequently be argued that scholars of political violence and contestation need to take urban politics, civic conflicts, and the related urban sociology literature into account. Second – and building on urban sociology literature – the chapter develops the notion of armed urbanism and illustrates it by making theoretical comparisons between urban insurgencies and gangs. The chapter then provides empirical examples of cases of armed urbanism from around the globe.

The changing nature of armed conflict: urbanity rising?

The past twenty-five years have witnessed not only a decline in the number of armed conflicts (Sundberg *et al.* 2012), but also a drop in their intensity (Themnér and Wallensteen 2013: 511). The Geneva Declaration's *Global Burden of Armed Violence* report has found that 526,000 individuals die annually as a result of violence. Only 10 per cent of these can be labelled as conflict-related deaths, while the rest is the result of violence that takes place in 'peaceful' or 'non-conflict settings' (GBAV 2011: 43). To put these figures into perspective, between 2004 and 2009 'the people of El Salvador were more at risk of dying violently (a death rate of 61.9 per 100,000) than any population around the world', including Iraq, which during the same period had a death rate of 54.9 per 100,000 (GBAV 2011: 52, 55).

There has also been a change in where armed conflict occurs. Although the number of urban armed conflicts is small compared to the instances of inter or intra-state wars, it has been argued that its importance in modern-day sub-national warfare is likely to increase (Harroff-Tavel 2010; Rosenau 1997; US Government 2011). Part of the reason for this simply has to do with demographics. In the words of John L. Sorenson (1965: 8), 'there are far more cities today than a hundred years ago, and a larger number of potential rebels live in them'. This statement is even more valid today when, for the first time in history, the majority of the world's population is living in urban centres, and current projections indicate that two-thirds of the global population will be living in cities by 2050 (UN-Habitat 2013). While urban population growth has historically been linked to development and consolidation of political control (Tilly 1992), it has also been associated with increased political contestation and violence.

O'Sullivan and Miller (1983: 127) – scholars of insurgency during the Cold War period – argued that central to the success of an insurgency is the political and territorial control of territory, which, in turn, is best controlled by 'holding its urban foci', making urban settlements the primary targets in wartime. In addition, the authors argued that, along with increased urbanisation levels, 'any conflict involving or seeking the interest of the mass of the population is bound to take place in the cities' (1983: 137). A number of recent studies find that urban and densely populated places are more prone to armed conflict and violence than less densely populated peripheral or rural areas (Raleigh *et al.* 2010; Sundberg and Melander 2013). This is echoed in the work of military theorists and military doctrine, both of which increasingly emphasise the notion of 'battlespace', which, as Graham (2009: 279) points out, entails 'a conception of military matters that includes absolutely everything [...] [including] everyday sites, spaces and experiences of city life'.

Another reason for the likely increase in urban conflict is that in an era of asymmetric warfare the urban environment is seen to act as a 'force multiplier' by providing armed groups with ease of access to protection and resources (le Blanc 2013: 805; US Government 2011: 9). Both the infrastructure and the densely populated environment in urban spaces allow armed groups ease of movement, camouflage, protection, and the ability to resort to irregular fighting tactics when engaging the formal security apparatus (Dawson 2007; Graham 2009). Together these factors create a situation in which even a militarily weak armed group could have the possibility to not only cause a significant amount of damage to the urban infrastructure, the urban population, and state institutions, but also to attract local and international media coverage (Ibrahim 2011: 121). Finally, urban environments are more likely to provide armed groups with greater resources, including finances – obtained through criminal activities such as extortion, robbing banks, or kidnapping – a higher probability of acquiring weapons and explosives, and secure anonymity by mingling with the civilian population (le Blanc 2013; Ibrahim 2011; Russell and Hildner 1971).

The 'urban' nature of organised violence is also evident in non-conflict settings. Urban violence in Central America and Latin America – especially in Brazil, El Salvador, Guatemala, Honduras, and Jamaica – is so intense that in terms of 'body count', death rates have surpassed those experienced in many intra-state conflicts (Rodgers and Baird forthcoming). This has led some analysts to draw parallels between the dynamics of urban violence and full-scale armed conflict (Manwaring 2007). In the early 2000s, the nature and distribution of violence in the city of Rio de Janeiro, for instance, was often described in terms usually reserved for situations of armed conflict: 'armed factions, with military weapons, controlling territory, people and/or resources within the favelas and operating within a command structure' (Dowdney 2003: 10). Although much of the urban violence in Central and Latin America is attributed to gangs and organised crime, a significant portion of it is 'state-based' and is most often perpetrated by police officers (Ahnen 2007; French 2013; Willis 2013a). Again taking Brazil as an illustration, in 2012 at least 1,890 individuals died during police interventions, which translates into an average of five people killed by police officers each day, with the majority of deaths occurring in urbanised areas, such as São Paulo, Rio de Janeiro, Bahia, and Paraná (Fórum Brasileiro 2013: 8, 126).

Similar trends have been documented in Africa, although research there suffers from a significant dearth of data and statistics. That being said, the recent UCDP Georeferenced Event Dataset has compiled information on violence at the event level for the time period 1989–2010. The database divides the African continent by population density, and codes 'urban' areas as those that 'contain at least one urban location with at least 100,000 inhabitants', with all other coded 'rural' (Sundberg and Melander 2013: 529). Despite the low threshold for 'urbanity', the study found that only about 13 per cent of the continent was coded as urban. Nevertheless, about half of all fatalities occurred in urban settings, with localities characterised by medium-level population density being relatively more prone to violence than more densely populated urban areas and rural areas (Sundberg and Melander 2013: 530). As in Central and Latin America, the most 'urbanised' type of violence is one-sided violence, defined as 'the use of armed force by the government of a state or by a formally organised group against civilians' (Sundberg and Melander 2013: 525; Eck and Hultman 2007: 235).

The above observations raise doubts as to whether the state continues to be the appropriate reference object in the study of political violence and contestation. Yet much of the scholarly literature on the subject continues to view only violence directed against the state – in the sense that it entails contestation over national territory or institutions – as political violence (Themnér and Wallensteen 2013: 509). As Kalyvas argues (2006: 19), most revolutions, sustained peasant insurrections, 'revolutionary' or ethnic insurgencies, anticolonial uprisings, and resistance wars against foreign occupiers are included in the analysis of armed conflict and political violence and contestation; all other forms of violence, such as 'violent protests, riots, crime, and low-level banditry, all of which leave sovereignty pretty much intact' are excluded from the category. Even when the role or importance of cities in conflict is acknowledged, it is only seen as a means to an end, so that control over a city, especially if it is the capital, is directly linked to obtaining political authority (Kalyvas 2006: 133; Landau-Wells 2008; Sorenson 1965: 8).

Political violence as urban violence

By ignoring those forms of violence that are *not* directed against the state and *do not* aim to control it, scholars not only misrepresent the nature of armed conflict in particular cases, as well as globally, but they also limit their understanding of political violence and contestation more generally. Specifically, the focus on the level of the state obscures the numerous 'civic conflicts' that take place around the globe, and that are often characterised by high levels of violence. While these 'civic conflicts' often do not aim to take control of the state, they are not necessarily any less political.

Beall *et al.* (2013: 5) define civic conflict as the 'violent expression of grievances (which may be social, political, or economic) *vis-à-vis* the state or other actors'. Specifically, the term refers to diverse forms of violence – such as organised crime, gang warfare, terrorism, religious and sectarian rebellions, or riots – which seem to have two things in common: a) they all tend to take place in urban settings, and b) they do not aim to take control of the state. Although civic conflict is linked to state or municipal weakness and often involves economic motivation on the part of the violent forms of organisation engaged in them, they are not a simple by-product of weakness or financial desire. Rather, civic conflict is the violent expression of daily urban politics – attempts by the urban population to alter the power relationships within cities.

The issues underpinning the emergence of violent civic conflict are thus social issues related to the nature of cities – such as density, diversity, and compressed inequality – and to demands for citizenship rights in urban areas (Lefebvre [1967] 1996). In other words, if the avenues for non-violent contestation over civic issues – i.e. 'generative civic engagements' – are blocked, there is a possibility for contestation to transform into violent civic conflict (Beall *et al.* 2013: 12; UN-Habitat 2013: 135). This is especially so in view of the claim that 'political violence often spreads during periods of protests. It frequently develops inside social movements and is indeed (although not often) a (most visible) by-product of their actions' (della Porta 2014: 163). Despite being economic and social, many civic conflicts are therefore also inherently political (Beall *et al.* 2013: 5). This raises some questions: what can social movements tell us about political violence and contestation in conflict and non-conflict cities? What insights do we obtain regarding the formation and evolution of armed groups in urban settings?

Urban politics: from social movements to urban violence

Societal groups are usually found at the micro-level of the city, i.e., within a territorially delimited neighbourhood. This observation has led to the characterisation of urban space as a conglomeration of 'urban villages' (Gans 1962) that are often inhabited by a large number of individuals of a particular group, often possessing the same set of beliefs, providing the 'critical mass' needed for the formation of particular forms of societal organisation (Firth 1975). More precisely, these urban villages tend to be neighbourhoods which in themselves are 'safe territories' within the city, i.e., areas where particular societal groups develop and foster relationships among their members and the local population (Bosi 2013). The presence of safe territories produces forms of societal organisation characterised by 'strong ties', which, in turn, result from frequent or repeated interaction between individuals who are involved in an intimate and reciprocal interpersonal relationship, such as close friends, kinship groups, ethnic groups, or ideologically-based groups (Bosi 2013: 81, 82–3; Granoveter 1973, 1983).

It is this aspect of cities – the presence of safe territories which, in turn, foster the creation of societal groups – that enables them to play the role of 'incubator' for the emergence of social movements, but also of armed groups, as discussed below. Given the multiplicity of villages in the city, societal forms of organisation are likely to face common grievances *vis-à-vis* the municipal government. The existence of common grievances allows for a possibility for different societal groups from different parts of the city to create networks of 'resistance', by pooling resources and devising common strategies – often even creating a common front – when dealing with urban political elites (della Porta and Diani 2006: 159). In essence, societal groups begin forming a network maintained through the creation of 'weak ties', defined as relationships that result from infrequent meetings, low emotional attachment and intimacy, and asymmetric exchange of services and goods between individuals or groups (Granoveter 1973, 1983).

While strong ties may characterise life at a neighbourhood or community level, weak ties are those superficial, anonymous, and impersonal relationships that shape urban life at the level of the city. Although some urban sociologists have seen these weak ties as drivers of problems that face the urban landscape (such as crime and delinquency, see Wirth 1938), Granovetter (1983) argued that they are actually vital for the emergence and crystallisation of social movements, precisely because 'the success of an individual group depends on its ability to draw in the support of other marginal groups in the city' (Miller and Nicholls 2013: 459).

Any discussion of the city as a place conducive to the emergence and development of social movements must be complemented with a view of the city as the locus of state control (Ó Dochartaigh 2013; Uitermark et al. 2012: 2550). State control mechanisms – an indication of state strength at the municipal level – have been found to be a key factor in the consolidation and evolution of societal organisations into social movements and armed groups, and the *modus operandi* of both (Holston 2008; Nicholls 2008). State strength is conceptualised not only as the presence and degree of sedimentation of state institutions in the city, but also as their ability to incorporate societal groups (see Saunders 1981; Katznelson 1981; Castells 1983). When the state is weak at the city level, i.e., when it is not able to foster political inclusion by either co-opting certain societal groups or channelling their discontent into local state institutions, space opens up for the creation of weak ties across societal groups and the emergence of social movements (Uitermark et al. 2012: 2551).

Drawing on della Porta (2014: 164), policing strategies in a city can be taken as a barometer both for the political opportunities available to societal groups to either work with state institutions or to form coalitions with other societal groups, and the kinds of protest tactics (violent or non-violent) they will adopt when trying to renegotiate the social arrangements of the city. The police is one of the key state institutions responsible for creating law and order in the city, yet empirical evidence suggests that in many parts of the world it is also one of the most notorious perpetrators of urban violence (Moncada 2013: 8). In the Global North, where much of the research on policing comes from, police violence is spontaneous and rare. Conversely, in many parts of the Global South, the police are often extremely violent, relying on policies of control and repression, which can on the one hand be traced back to the leftover practices from authoritarian pasts (Ahnen 2007), but which are perhaps also due to a lack of skills and capacity necessary for the proper implementation of investigative policing, e.g., forensics. The ultimate result is that 'torture, extortion, and police killings continue seemingly unabated, while prisons have become spaces where rights are systematically violated as they overflow their capacity' (Willis 2013b: 86).

This chapter proposes the notion of *armed urbanism* as a means of relating the various empirical observations to the literature on civic conflicts and urban social moments. Inherent in the concept of armed urbanism is the notion of *convergent evolution*, defined as a process 'whereby social contexts around the world give rise to similar social phenomena' (Rodgers and Hazen 2014: 1). Building on this insight, armed urbanism reflects the way in which the socio-physical characteristics of the urban environment foster the emergence and evolution of armed groups in the city. Given the fact that urban settings are likely to concentrate populations within a particular physical space – i.e. safe spaces – which, in turn, fosters the development of dense relationships between individuals – i.e. strong ties – they are likely to lead to the production of locally-based and relatively cohesive armed groups. The state's recognition of the existence of these safe spaces and their relationship to a particular armed group fosters the creation of state policies – often repressive police tactics – that aim to reassert the state's monopoly on the use of force in the city. Inadvertently, however, these policies also allow for the consolidation of the armed group and for the creation of links between the armed group and other societal groups and movements in the city – i.e. weak ties.

Armed urbanism: urban insurgency and gang warfare

According to the US army doctrine on urban warfare (US Government 2011: 34), different types of armed groups are likely to be operational in cities, including conventional forces (especially in the form of motorised or mechanised rifle battalions); light infantry battalions, or semi-military groups; personal armies of warlords (groups that rally around single individuals); and unconventional or semi-organised forces such as gangs, urban insurgencies, and terrorist groups. For the purposes of this chapter, which takes a uniform approach to violence – in the sense of a violence continuum from conflict to non-conflict violence – the focus will be on urban insurgencies and gangs.

Urban insurgency

Up until now, the phenomenon of 'urban violence' has been a marginal issue within the literature of political violence and contestation. That being said, the changing nature of armed conflict is slowly placing the 'urban question' more centrally within the debate. According to Staniland (2010: 1627), urban insurgency can be seen as different from both civil war – which is often fought in rural areas – and revolutions – which happen rather quickly – and can be defined as a form of political violence that '(a) originates and is sustained in urban settings, (b) is waged by organised non-state actors using irregular tactics, and (c) reaches the level of casualties to be included as a case of civil war.'

One of the inherent assumptions in the study of political violence and contestation is that war generates a particular form of spatial organisation, one where cities are controlled by the state (Fearon and Laitin 2003; Kalyvas 2006: 133; Kocher 2004: 24–6). The sedimentation of state institutions in cities – especially those related to the provision of law and order – provides municipal and national governments with a significant advantage when it comes to the control of urban territory and its population. The continued presence of the state, and the effectiveness of its security infrastructure in cities, exerts a significant limitation on urban insurgencies, especially in terms of organisational structure, membership and mobilisation, and overall tactics.

Yet while state control over urban areas tends to be more acute, it is never total (Ó Dochartaigh 2013: 124), instead producing 'safe territories' – in both physical and sociopolitical space (Bosi 2013) – for urban insurgencies to emerge (US Government, 2011: 9). Nevertheless, the continuous presence and threat stemming from the state creates a situation in which urban insurgencies are, at least initially, forced to 'go underground', i.e., to become clandestine organisations and to act in relative isolation from the urban population (Bosi 2013: 86). The 'father' of urban guerrilla warfare, Carlos Marighella (1982: 80), went so far as to suggest that urban insurgencies themselves should be isolated and of a fragmented nature: 'in order to function, the urban guerrilla must be organised in small groups. A group of no more than four or five is called the firing group. A minimum of two firing groups, separated and sealed off from other firing groups, directed and coordinated by one or two persons, this is what makes up a firing team.' Consequently, the urban insurgency becomes a small group based on strong ties, with the group members being 'the only source of information, the only source of confirmation, and, in the face of external danger and pursuit, the only source of security' (le Blanc 2013: 811).

There are at least three consequences of an organisational structure based on strong ties. First, it makes interaction with the general population difficult, as insurgents cannot publically lobby for popular support. Second, it creates a 'recruitment dilemma' for the armed group, as it is difficult to distinguish genuine supporters of the insurgency from traitors or even state informants (US Government 1992). Specifically, the literature on urban forms of warfare echo the studies on societal groups that are highly specialised and based on strong ties, and suggests that urban insurgencies lack the necessary information to make ties with individuals and groups in the broader urban community, fearing that they would be infiltrated by state informants and thus exposed, arrested, or killed (le Blanc 2013: 811). Third, such strong ties within the group produce an increased sense of militarisation and elitism within the insurgency, so that the preservation of the group becomes the primary purpose (Bosi 2013: 86). This in itself leads to more violent actions taken on the part of the group, which not only further isolate it from the general population, but are also more likely to initiate a repressive reprisal from the state (le Blanc 2013: 811).

Thus, while strong ties within urban insurgencies actually increase the cohesiveness of the group and its ability to act collectively to inflict damage on the state, they also limit the chances of success. In order to be successful, urban insurgencies must be able to go beyond the membership base and foster weak ties with local communities (Staniland 2010: 1629). But since open mobilisation is difficult in the city, urban insurgencies seek to foster relationships with pre-existing societal groups or social movements (le Blanc 2013). Most often, insurgents reach out to disgruntled groups that have already established themselves in the urban environment, such as radical students, intellectual elements in society, poor and socially excluded youths, or religious and ethnic minorities (Russell and Hildner 1971). Such groups are likely to accept urban insurgents into their fold if generative civic engagement is blocked, and if they thus see the use of force as a legitimate option (Sorenson 1965).

If the rights of particular societal groups in the 'urban village' are continuously undermined, they are likely to publically voice their discontent and demand a change in the social and political arrangements and institutions governing the city and the distribution of resources. However, if avenues for generative civic engagement are blocked, societal groups may welcome the use of force. Urban insurgencies, then, can 'cloak themselves' with the grievances of these groups and in the process legitimise their organisations (Staniland 2010: 1629). In some cases, insurgents may even 'foster' the creation of weak ties with these groups by increasing their violent activity with the hope of inducing a repressive response from the state (le Blanc 2013: 810). Legitimation of urban insurgency is not the only side effect of the creation of weak ties to the local community and its related societal groups. Such a relationship also serves to mitigate the level of radicalism of the urban insurgency, for the latter's success and status is now tied to the desires and support of the community (Bosi 2013: 86).

While urban community structures determine where insurgency is possible, they are not able to tell us when sustained insurgency in cities will occur. Rather – like the crystallisation of social movements – the state's disposition towards urban insurgencies, that is, its attempts to avoid, contain, or repress the threat, has been found to be one of the main driving factors behind their emergence (Sorenson 1965). This is especially so if the state's response is highly repressive and targets not only the armed group but also a specific societal group or community. As Staniland (2010: 1630) explains, this implies that in order 'to understand how rebellion is sustained at the threshold of insurgency, we need to look at counterinsurgency policy'.

The state's counterinsurgency policy can be taken as a frame for understanding not only the strength of the state, but also the opportunities available to urban insurgencies. On the one hand, the response from the state may be so strong that it wipes out the urban insurgency, along with a sizable portion of the urban population. This is an extreme case that has been referred to as 'urbicide' – a form of political violence that is 'intentionally designed to erase or "'kill"' cities', and to 'displace dissent and resistance' (Graham 2010: 84, 86). In such circumstances, the development of urban insurgency is severely hindered. On the other hand, if the state is weak the likely outcome is not insurgency, but the rapid overthrow of state power in the form of a revolution (Staniland 2010: 1630). Since the threat of the state is no longer present, armed groups are not only able to publically mobilise for support, but may also carry out their attacks without much pushback from the state.

However, most counterinsurgency techniques are not this drastic and fall in between the all-out assault on the city and the complete lack of engagement from the state. Echoing the discussion on the role of the state in the development of social movements, this middle space has been termed 'coercive governance', and refers to a situation in which a 'capable state [...] aims to retain control of a city in the face of socially mobilised insurgency but without using urban annihilation' (Staniland 2010: 1630). When do capable states engage in coercive governance and what does this mean in practice? Evidence suggests that states prefer to 'manage' urban insurgency when they are concerned with their international image and when the regime depends on support from the population of the city where the insurgency has taken root. In addition, the ties that urban insurgents and their allied societal groups make with political elites and security forces in the city are also likely to prevent acutely repressive tactics or at least limit their use and spread (Staniland 2010: 1631).

Counterinsurgency policies and their effects on the opportunities available to urban insurgents echo the way in which municipal and national governments deal with social movements in non-conflict settings, such as through inclusion in the state institutions. The difference, however, is that while inclusion in state institutions leads to a slowing down in the development of social movements, when it comes to urban insurgency it actually fosters its development.

Gangs

Despite the fact that gangs are seen to be one of the major security threats in places like Central and Latin America (Rodgers and Baird, forthcoming), they continue to be excluded from theoretical debates on political violence and contestation. But given the changes in the nature of armed conflict and organised violence globally, this chapter argues that gangs need to be considered as a form of armed urbanism.

There are various definitions of gangs,[1] but for the purposes of this chapter I follow Rodgers (2006: 272) and define the term broadly to encompass 'a very definite social institution, consisting of a variably sized group of generally male youths [...] who engage in illicit and violent behaviour – although not all their activities are illicit or violent'. Moreover, gangs tend to have a particular territorial dynamic in the sense that they tend to be associated with 'a specific urban neighbourhood, although larger neighbourhoods often have more than one gang and not all have one, as there clearly needs to be a critical mass of youth in a neighbourhood for a gang to emerge, and they tend not to develop in richer neighbourhoods' (*Ibid.*). This definition of gangs is useful since the emphasis on territory, a young membership base, and the reliance of the use of violence places the gang phenomenon squarely within the broader category of armed groups, and so within the scope of study of political violence and contestation.

Central to an armed group's ability to control territory is the notion of 'ungoverned spaces', which refers to neighbourhoods, semi-urban areas, and large parts of the countryside where the state has little, if any, reach or influence (Clunan and Trinkunas 2010). In the city, ungoverned space often refers to those 'interstitial spaces' that frequently overlap with particular neighbourhoods that

---

1. The most comprehensive definition of gangs was provided by Frederic Thrasher (1927: 46). According to him, 'gangs emerge as spontaneous peer groups that operate in interstitial spaces of the city and become gangs only through conflict with other gangs or societal groups. It is through conflict that gangs then develop organisational structure, solidify the boundaries of belonging and behaviour, and narrow down their activities.

the police does not enter, and where gangs hold territory and exert social control (Hagedorn 2008: 7; Muggah and Mulli 2011: 63). These neighbourhoods are also areas where urbanisation, and social, economic, and political exclusion is experienced most intensely. Such ungoverned or interstitial spaces are synonymous with the 'safe territories' necessary for the emergence of various social and armed groups (Bosi 2013). As such, 'gangs are not a unique form but one of the many kinds of armed groups that occupy the uncontrolled spaces of the "world's slums"' (Hagedorn 2008: xxiv).

As with other types of armed groups, the establishment of territorial control is paramount to the success of the gang. This in itself does not occur spontaneously, but is a process that sees gangs evolve from youth peer groups to more institutionalised territorial organisations, to 'violence entrepreneurs', and finally into institutionalised societal organisations capable of controlling territory and creating localised social order (Stephenson 2011, 2012). Yet unlike other types of armed groups that may aim to control large swathes of territory,[2] gangs tend to be more 'local', associating themselves with specific neighbourhoods. This association not only delineates the physical boundaries of the territory under their control (Skaperdas and Syropoulos 1995: 62), it also places 'membership' criteria on the gang. Ultimately, the ideas of 'neighbourhood' and 'gang' collapse into one (Moore 1978: 35) with the gang often emerging as the sole provider of social order (Rodgers 2006).

The central feature of territory for the emergence and development of gangs also has the effect of structuring violence in the city. Specifically, 'gang warfare' is shaped by the relationship between neighbourhoods and their associated gangs, since the territorial boundaries become the places where violence is most likely to occur (Brantingham *et al.* 2012: 856–79; Campbell 1984: 286; McDonald 2003: 67; Rodgers 2006: 277). This argument is echoed in the civil wars literature, which emphasises that variations in the control over territory by armed groups and state forces foster distinct patterns of violence: violence is highest in contested areas and lowest in areas where either the state or the armed group has control (Kalyvas 2006; Kalyvas and Kocher 2009).

While the above paragraphs illustrate *where* gangs are likely to emerge, they do not specify *when* gang violence will become so intense as to present a considerable security threat to the state. However, it appears that, just as state repression is taken to be an indicator of when an urban insurgency is likely to occur, a fundamental reason underpinning the emergence of gangs is the state's lack of capacity to obtain a monopoly on violence in the urban terrain, combined with heavy-handed approaches aimed at (re)asserting this monopoly. One example was the increase in the levels of urban violence and gang sophistication in the various Mano Dura (literally, 'iron fist') counter-gang initiatives implemented in Central America (Jütersonke *et al.* 2009). Rather than reducing the level of gang

---

2.   Either for the purposes of creating a counter-state (as rebels or insurgency groups do), or for controlling a certain market (as in the case of organised crime).

activity and violence in the country, these policies had the adverse effect, and ended up increasing *mara* organisation and sophistication as well as raising the levels of gang violence in society (Jütersonke *et al.* 2009: 12).

El Salvador is a case in point. During the 1990s, cities such as the capital San Salvador were characterised by a proliferation of gangs and gang-related violence. In order to tackle this threat, in the summer of 2003 the Salvadorian government initiated its Mano Dura policy, which allowed for the immediate imprisonment – for up to five years – of anyone who displayed gang-related tattoos or showed gang signs and symbols in public (Hume 2007). In the one-year period following its institution, the policy resulted in the imprisonment of about 20,000 individuals. The policy was highly controversial, primarily because most of those arrested were minors. Consequently, when the Salvadoran Supreme Court found the policy to be in violation of the United Nations Convention on the Rights of the Child (Jütersonke *et al.* 2009: 10), almost all of those arrested were released. Although it aimed to mitigate the level of gang-related crime and violence in the country, the Mano Dura policies ultimately led to the evolution and sophistication of gangs, in particular the Mara Salvatrucha and Mara-18 (Wolf 2012).

From gangs to urban insurgencies, and back again?

The similarities between urban insurgency and gangs are such that in many parts of the world it is difficult to separate the two (Hagedorn 2008: 37), lending further credence to the argument that the gang phenomenon should be included not only in the broader study of armed groups (Hazen 2010; Rodgers and Muggah 2009) but also within the category of armed urbanism. Several examples serve to illustrate this point.

In Sierra Leone, gangs have existed since at least the turn of the twentieth century, initially emerging as peer groups made up of young unemployed or working-class men forming societal groups known as 'odley societies' (dancing clubs). These groups would frequently meet at public events and engage in dance competitions that often resulted in violence. Such episodes of violence fostered the evolution of these societal groups from dance clubs made up of peers into gangs, locally referred to as 'the rarri boys'. Yet the evolution of the gangs did not stop there. With the sociopolitical changes taking place in the late 1950s and early 1960s, the rarri boys became increasingly associated with political elites and their protesting base. By the time of independence, in 1961, the rarri boys had effectively 'transitioned from random individual violence to collective social violence in the name of an idea' – i.e., they had became part of a politically motivated social movement (Abdullah 2002: 28).

The evolution of Sierra Leone's rarri boys continued also after independence. During the 1970s and 1980s, due to the lack of job opportunities in the country at the time, the membership base of the rarri boys and odley societies became increasingly educated and aware of the political and social problems in the country. These new 'generations' started calling for a revolution, and some groups within the broader rarri boys phenomenon were able to organise themselves politically, and in 1991, an insurgency movement was formed. This insurgency was followed by a coup d'état by young military officers, in 1992. As the levels of political violence escalated, rarri boys were increasingly incorporated into the Civil War, now assuming the role of 'child soldiers' (Abdullah 2002: 28–35).[3] Following the cessation of conflict, most of the individuals who had participated in violence returned to urban settings, where they either formed their own gangs or joined pre-established ones (Strattan Guerra 2013).

Distinguishing between different types of armed actors was difficult also in Indonesia during and after the Suharto New Order regime (Bertrand 2004). Although most analysts are quick to point to the wearing away of the state's monopoly on violence following the 1998 fall of the Suharto regime, in reality the state had always shared use of violence with various other armed actors. Although gangs had already existed in Indonesia during the Dutch colonial period, it was during the independence struggle of the 1940s that these gangs first created links with the Indonesian state and its security forces, in order to aid it in providing goods needed for the struggle. Under the New Order regime the relationship between the state, its security apparatus, and various gangs became more institutionalised, and under the 'System for the Protection of the Environment' (*Siskamling*) it was made almost legal (Bertrand 2004: 338).

This close relationship between the state and the various gangs was beneficial to both actors. The former was able to exert influence in areas where it might not have – or should not have – had reach, while the latter obtained an avenue for social and economic advancement by joining civil and paramilitary forces, and even entering politics. In the sociopolitical environment of post-Suharto Indonesia, the various gangs continue to exist and influence social life both locally – by being able to control territory and the distribution of goods, legitimising their action through identity appeal – and nationally – by offering their services to political parties (Bertrand 2004: 338–9; Wilson 2006).

Post-independence East Timor is another example of this inability to separate gangs from other types of armed groups, often associated with civil war or high levels of insecurity. In the post-conflict environment, various types of gangs proliferated on the small island nation. During the 2006–7 crisis, it became evident that they had become a major force in society, playing a role in the near collapse of the state (Carapic and Jütersonke 2012). Although many international observers were quick to blame the post-independence sociopolitical environment for the emergence of the various gangs – and even blaming them for the near collapse of the state during the 2006–7 crisis – in reality, most of the groups had their origins in the armed resistance movements against the Indonesian Occupation. The ritual arts and martial arts groups, and in particular the veteran's organisation, originated within the clandestine, student, and armed fronts, respectively (Carapic 2014).

---

3. It should be noted that not all 'child soldiers' in the Sierra Leone conflict were former gang members, see Hoffman (2011).

Due to the similarities between urban insurgent groups and gangs – the environment within which they emerge, their relations with the local population, and the occasional difficulty of distinguishing between the two groups – some scholars have argued that the two are in fact the same phenomenon, both in terms of their overall aims to control (urban) territory and in their ultimate goal of taking over the state (Manwaring 2005). This is paralleled in the policing sector, where, even though it is recognised that 'criminal street members are not insurgents, and street gangs are not insurgencies', there is nevertheless sufficient similarity between the two to warrant comparable state responses (Bertetto 2013). According to Bertetto (2013), a member of the Chicago Police Department, the common denominator is that both types of armed groups engage in activities that 'hold the population hostage': while they further their goals by relying on the support – provided both by will and by coercion – of the population, and depend on the recruitment of the local population in order to expand their 'operation', they nevertheless use violence against any person in the population who they consider a threat (Bertetto 2013).

These enumerated similarities between insurgencies and gangs have been used as a justification not only for including the gang phenomenon in the broader study of armed groups, but also for transforming the way that the state tackles the issue of armed groups in urban settings. In places like Colombia, Brazil, Haiti, and South Africa, the similarity between gangs and urban insurgencies has recently been taken as an invitation to utilise military strategy in dealing with 'law and order' issues (Becker 2011; Jensen 2010; Muggah and Souza Mulli 2012). Similarly, in Afghanistan and Iraq, policing strategies have been incorporated into military doctrine and directed against insurgents or rebels operating in urban areas (Musa *et al.* 2011; Quinn 2012; US Government 2011). The inherent assumption here is that '[counterinsurgency] guidelines intend to reach the same end state as urban policing does: a safe and secure population' (Freeman and Rothstein 2011: 13).

Conclusion

In his review of Warren Magnusson's *Seeing Like a City* (2011), the political theorist Loren King (2013: 804–5) asks 'why we ought to privilege *any* spatial, civic, or imaginative scale in asking questions about political concepts, processes, and practices'. King's answer is not rooted in the ontology of political concepts, processes, and practices, but in their real world relevance. Consequently, he argues that 'the analytic frameworks we adopt ought typically to reflect the nature of what we are examining, and the questions we seek to answer' (King 2013: 805). The central claim of this chapter echoes King's sentiment, and submits that in an increasingly urbanised world where traditional forms of armed conflict appear to be on the decline, contemporary analyses of political violence and contestation need to take urban politics seriously.

The first part of the chapter highlighted a number of empirical observations that point to evidence that there has been a significant change in the nature of armed conflict, both in terms of where it is being fought and with what intensity.

This changes the way in which we conceptualise conflict, political violence, and contestation. Specifically, political violence and contestation is not solely about disputes over state borders and territorial control. Rather, in today's rapidly urbanising world it often has more to do with tensions around particular social arrangements, such as social, economic, and political inclusion. These social tensions have been referred to as civic conflicts, and although they have the potential to escalate into organised forms of violence, they do not necessarily undermine the sovereignty – and thus the integrity – of the state. Understanding civic conflicts is paramount, and one entry point for this is the notion of armed urbanism. Taking up some of the key insights from the field of urban sociology, armed urbanism is put forth as a conceptual lens for understanding urban political violence and contestation, the social and physical organisation of the city (Wirth 1938), and how this fosters the emergence and evolution of armed groups in conflict and non-conflict settings.

On the one hand, the concept of armed urbanism emphasises the social life of the city, both the strong ties dominant at the neighbourhood level, within the armed group, and among the local population, and the weak ties characteristic at the city level, exemplified by links made between the armed group and other societal groups, social movements, and even the state. On the other hand, it highlights the physical aspects of the city and the impact these have on the formation and spread of armed groups. The presence of 'ungoverned' or 'safe spaces' that provide the opportunity for the armed group to consolidate and evolve is key here. Safe spaces are inherently 'known' to the state, as it is aware of its lack of influence in the territory. This, in turn, means that any attempts by the state to reassert its monopoly on the use of force is directed at these spaces and the armed groups that occupy them. Attempts to reassert control often involve repressive policing or military strategies, which, even if accompanied also by softer tactics, have the negative side effect of alienating the local population and consolidating the position of the armed group. This chapter has illustrated the notion of armed urbanism by drawing on examples from various contexts in order to highlight the similarities between urban insurgencies and gangs, while also emphasising our inability to separate the two.

References

Abdullah, I. (2002) 'Youth culture and rebellion: Understanding Sierra Leone's wasted decade', *Critical Arts: South-North Cultural and Media Studies*, 16(2): 19–37.

Ahnen, R. E. (2007) 'The politics of police violence in democratic Brazil', *Latin American Politics and Society*, 49(1): 141–64.

Baras, R. (2014) 'Gangs and insurgencies: A comparative analysis', in M. S. Paul and K. J. Finkenbinder (eds) *Preventing And Managing Conflict In An Unstable World*, Carlisle: Peacekeeping and Stability Operations Institute, pp. 313–56.

Beall, J. (2006) 'Cities, terrorism, and development', *Journal of International Development*, 18(1): 105–20.

Beall, J., Goodfellow, T. and Rodgers, D. (2013) 'Cities and conflict in fragile states in the developing world', *Urban Studies*, 50(15): 3065–83.

Becker, D. C. (2011) 'Gangs, netwar, and community counterinsurgency in Haiti', *Prism*, 2(3): 139–42.

Bertetto, J. A. (2013) 'Countering criminal street gangs: Lessons from counter insurgent battlespace', *Small Wars Journal*, http://www.smallwarsjournal. com/Jrnl/Art/Countering-Criminal-Street-Gangs-Lessons-From-The-Counterinsurgent-Battlespace (accessed 17 April 2014).

Bertrand, R. (2004) ''Behave like enraged lions': Civil militias, the army and the criminalisation of politics in Indonesia', *Global Crime*, 6(3/4): 325–44.

Bosi, L. (2013) 'Safe territories and violent political organizations', *Nationalism and Ethnic Politics*, 19(1): 80–101.

Brantingham, J. P., Tita, G. E., Short, M. B. and Reid, S. E. (2012) 'The ecology of gang territorial boundaries', *American Society of Criminology*, 50(3): 851–85.

Campbell, A. (1984) *The Girls in the Gang*, Oxford: Basil Blackwell.

Carapic, J. (2014) *Order and Authority Within and Beyond the State*, unpublished thesis, Geneva Graduate Institute of International and Development Studies.

Carapic, J. and Jütersonke, O. (2012) *Understanding the Tipping Point of Urban Conflict: the Case of Dili, Timor-Leste*, Working Paper No. 4 in Working Paper Series *Understanding the Tipping Point of Urban Conflict: Violence, Cities and Poverty Reduction in the Developing World*, The University of Manchester, May 2012.

Castells, M. (1983) *The City and the Grass-Roots: A Cross-cultural Theory of Urban Social Movements*, London: Edward Arnold.

Clunan, A. and Trinkunas, H. A. (eds) (2010) *Ungoverned Spaces: Alternatives to State Authority in an Era of Softened Sovereignty*, Stanford: Stanford University Press.

Dawson, A. (2007) 'Combat in hell: Cities as the Achilles' heel of US imperial hegemony', *Social Text*, 25.2(91): 169–80.

Dowdney, L. (2003) *Children of the Drug Trade: A Case Study of Children in Organised Armed Violence in Rio de Janeiro*, Rio de Janeiro: 7 Letras.

della Porta, D. (2014) 'On violence and repression: A relational approach (*The Government and Opposition*/Leonard Schapiro Memorial Lecture, 2013)', *Government and Opposition*, 49(2): 159–87.

della Porta, D. and Diani, M. (2006) *Social Movements: An Introduction*, Malden: Blackwell Publishing.

Eck, K. and Hultman, L. (2007) 'One-sided violence against civilians in war: Insights from new fatality data', *Journal of Peace Research*, 44(2), 233–46.

Fearon, J. D. and Laitin, D. D. (2003) 'Ethnicity, insurgency, and civil war', *American Political Science Review*, 97(1): 75–90.

Firth, R. (1975) 'An appraisal of modern social anthropology', *Annual Review of Anthropology* 4(1): 1–26.

Fórum Brasileiro de Segurança Pública (2013) *Anuário Brasileiro de Segurança Pública ano 7 2013*, São Paulo: Fórum Brasileiro de Segurança Pública.

Freeman, M. and Rothstein, H. (2011) 'Introduction', in M. Freeman and H. Rothstein (eds), *Gangs and Guerrillas: Ideas from Counterinsurgency and Counterterrorism*, Monterey: Naval Postgraduate School, p. 13.

French, J. H. (2013) 'Rethinking police violence in Brazil: Unmasking the public secret of race', *Latin American Politics and Society*, 55(4): 161–81.

Gans, H. J. (1962) *The Urban Villagers: Group and Class in the Life of Italian-Americans*, New York: Free Press.

Global Burden of Armed Violence (GBAV) (2011) *Global Burden Of Armed Violence 2011: Lethal Encounters*, Geneva: Geneva Declaration Secretariat.

Graham, S. (2010) *Cities Under Siege*, London: Verso.

——— (2009) 'The urban battle space?', *Theory, Culture, Society*, 26(1): 278–88.

Granovetter, M. (1973) 'The strength of weak ties', *The American Journal of Sociology*, 78(5): 1360–80.

——— (1983) 'The strength of weak ties: A network theory revisited', *Sociological Theory*, 1(1): 201–33.

Hagedorn, J. M. (2008) *A World of Gangs: Armed Young Men and Gangsta Culture*, Minnesota: University of Minnesota Press.

Harroff-Tavel, M. (2010) 'Violence and humanitarian action in urban areas: New challenges, new approaches', *International Review of the Red Cross* 92(878): 329–350.

Hazen, J. M. (2010) 'Understanding gangs as armed groups', *International Review of the Red Cross*, 92(878): 369–86.

Hoffman, D. (2011) *The War Machines: Young Men and Violence In Sierra Leone And Liberia*, Durham: Duke University Press.

Hume, M. (2007) 'Mano dura: El Salvador responds to gangs', *Development In Practice*, 17(6): 739–51.

Ibrahim, A. (2011) 'Conceptualisation of guerrilla warfare', *Small Wars and Insurgencies*, 15(3): 112–24.

Jensen, S. (2010) 'The security and development nexus in Cape Town: War on gangs, counterinsurgency and citizenship', *Security Dialogue*, 41(1): 77–247.

Jütersonke, O., Muggah, R., and Rodgers, D. (2009) 'Gangs, urban violence, and security interventions in Central America', *Security Dialogue,* 40(4–5): 373–97.

Kalyvas, S. N. (2006) *The Logic Of Violence In Civil War,* Cambridge: Cambridge University Press.

Kalyvas, S. N., and Kocher, M. A. (2009) 'The dynamics of violence in Vietnam: An analysis of the hamlet evaluation system (HES)', *Journal of Peace Research,* 46(3): 335–55.

Katznelson, I. (1981) *Marxism and the City,* Oxford: Clarendon Press.

King, L. (2013) 'Seeing like a theorist', *International Journal of Urban and Regional Research,* 37(2): 804–14.

Kocher, M. A. (2004) *The Human Ecology of Civil War,* unpublished thesis, University of Chicago.

Krause, K. (2009) 'Beyond definition: Violence in a global perspective', *Global Crime,* 10(4): 337–55.

Landau-Wells, M. (2008) *Capital Cities in Civil Wars: The Locational Dimension of Sovereign Authority,* London: Crisis States Research Centre.

Le Blanc, J. (2013) 'The urban environment and its influences on insurgent campaigns', *Terrorism and Political Violence,* 25(5): 798–819.

Lefebvre, H. ([1967] 1996) 'The right to the city', in E. Kofmanj and E. Lebas (eds), *Henri Lefebvre: Writings on Cities,* Oxford: Blackwell, pp. 147–59.

Magnusson, W. (2011) *Politics of Urbanism: Seeing Like a City,* Abingdon: Routledge.

Manwaring, M. G. (2007) *A Contemporary Challenge to State Sovereignty: Gangs and Other Illicit Transnational Criminal Organisations in Central America, El Salvador, Mexico, Jamaica, and Brazil,* Carlisle, PA: Army War College, Strategic Studies Institute.

—— (2005) *Street Gangs: The New Urban Insurgency,* Carlisle, PA: Army War College, Strategic Studies Institute.

Marighella, C. (1982) 'Minimanual of the urban guerrilla', in M. Jay (ed.) *Terror and Urban Guerrillas: A Study of Tactics and Documents,* Coral Gables: University of Miami Press, pp. 67–115.

McDonald, K. (2003) 'Marginal youth, personal identity, and the contemporary gang: Reconstructing the social world?', in K. Louis and B. Luis (eds) *Gangs and Society: Alternative Perspectives,* New York: Columbia University Press.

Miller, B. and Nicholls, W. (2013) 'Social movements in urban society: The city as a space of politicization', *Urban Geography* 34(4): 452–473.

Moncada, E. (2013) 'The politics of urban violence: Challenges for development in the Global South', *Studies in Comparative International Development,* 48(3): 217–39.

Moore, J.W. (1978) *Homeboys: Gangs, Drugs and Prison in the Barrios of Los Angeles,* Philadelphia, PA: Temple University Press.

Muggah, R. and Souza Mulli, A. (2012) 'Rio tries counterinsurgency', *Current History,* 111(742): 62–6.

Musa, S., Morgan, J. and Keegan, M. (2011) *Policing and COIN Operations: Lessons Learned, Strategies, and Future Operations.* Washington: National Defence University.

Nicholls, W. J. (2008) 'The urban question: The importance of cities for social movements', *International Journal Of Urban And Regional Research,* 32(4): 841–59.

Ó Dochartaigh, N. (2013) 'Bounded by violence: Institutionalizing local territories in the North of Ireland', *Nationalism and Ethnic Politics,* 19(1): 119–39.

O'Sullivan, P. and Miller, J. W. (1983) *The Geography of Warfare,* New York: St Martin's Press, Inc.

Quinn, R. B. (2012) *Combat Policing: The Application of Selected Law Enforcement Techniques to Enhance Infantry Operations,* Quantico: Marine Corps University.

Raleigh, C., Linke, A., Hegre, H. and Karlsen, J. (2010) 'Introducing ACLED: An armed conflict location and event dataset: Special data feature', *Journal of Peace Research,* 47(5): 651–60.

Rodgers, D. (2006) 'Living in the shadow of death: Gangs, violence and social order in urban Nicaragua, 1996–2002', *Journal Of Latin American Studies,* 38(2): 267–92.

—   (2009) 'Slum wars of the 21st century: Gangs, mano dura and the new urban geography of conflict in Central America', *Development and Change,* 40(5): 949–76.

—   (2010) *Urban Violence is Not (necessarily) a Way of Life: Towards a Political Economy of Conflict in Cities.* Working Paper No. 20, World Institute for Development Economics Research.

Rodgers, D. and Baird, A. (forthcoming) 'Understanding gangs in contemporary Latin America', in S. H. Decker and D. C. Pyrooz (eds) *Handbook of Gangs and Gang Responses,* New York: Wiley.

Rodgers, D. and Hazen, J. M. (2014) 'Gangs in a global comparative perspective', in J. M. Hazen and D. Rodgers (eds) *Global Gangs: Street Violence Across the World,* Minneapolis: University of Minnesota Press, pp. 1–25.

Rodgers, D. and Muggah, R. (2009) 'Gangs as non-state armed groups: The Central American case', *Contemporary Security Policy,* 30(2): 301–17.

Rosenau, W. G. (1997) "Every room is a new battle': The lessons of modern urban warfare', *Studies in Conflict & Terrorism,* 20(4): 371–94.

Russell, C. and Hildner, R. E. (1971) 'Urban insurgency in Latin America: Its implications for the future' *Air University Review,* 22(6): 1–11.

Saunders, P. (1981) *Social Theory and the Urban Question,* London: Hutchinson & Co.

Skaperdas, S. and Syropoulos, C. (1995) 'Gangs as primitive states', in G. Fiorentini and S. Peltzman (eds) *The Economics of Organized Crime,* Cambridge: Cambridge University Press, pp. 61–81.

Sorenson, J. L. (1965) *Urban Insurgency Cases.* No. Drc-Imr-176, Santa Barbara: Defense Research Corp.

Staniland, P. (2010) 'Cities on fire: Social mobilization, state policy, and urban insurgency', *Comparative Political Studies,* 43(12): 1628–31.

Stephenson, S. (2011) 'The Kazan leviathan: Russian street gangs as agents of social order', *The Sociological Review,* 59(2): 324–47.

—— (2012) 'The violent practices of youth territorial groups in Moscow', *Europe-Asia Studies,* 63(1): 69–90.

Strattan Guerra, V. (2013) 'Child soldiers, gang members: Reconceptualising urban violence in America', Unpublished Paper.

Sundberg, R. and Melander, E. (2013) 'Introducing the UCDP georeferenced event dataset', *Journal of Peace Research,* 50(4): 523–32.

Sundberg, R., Eck, K. and Kreutz, J. (2012) 'Introducing the UCDP non-state conflict dataset', *Journal of Peace Research,* 49(2): 351–62.

Taw, J. and Hoffman, B. (1994) *The Urbanization Of Insurgency: The Potential Challenge To US Army Operations,* Santa Monica: Rand Corporation.

Themnér, L. and Wallensteen, P. (2013) 'Armed conflicts, 1946–2012', *Journal Of Peace Research,* 50(4): 509–21.

Thrasher, F M. (1927) *The Gang: A Study Of 1,313 Gangs In Chicago,* Chicago: University of Chicago Press.

Tilly, C. (1992) *Coercion, Capital, and European States, AD 990–1992,* Oxford: Blackwell.

Uitermark, J., Nicholls, N. and Loopmans, M. (2012) 'Cities and social movements: Theorizing beyond the right to the city', *Environment and Planning A,* 44(11): 2546–54.

United Nations Human Settlements Programme (UN-Habitat) (2013) *State of the Worlds Cities, 2012/2013: Prosperity of Cities,* New York: UN-Habitat.

United States (US) Government (2011) *FM-3-06.11: Combined Arms Operations In Urban Terrain,* Washington: Headquarters Department of the Army.

—— (1992) 'Appendix A: The urban insurgent', in *FM 7-98: Operations in Low Intensity Conflict,* Washington: Headquarters Department of the Army.

Willis, G. D. (2013a) 'Antagonistic authorities and the civil police in São Paulo, Brazil', *Latin American Research Review,* 49(1): 3–22.

—— (2013b) *The Killing Consensus: Police Detectives, Police that Kill and Organized Crime in Sao Paulo, Brazil,* unpublished thesis, MIT.

Wilson, I. D. (2006) 'Continuity and change: The changing contours of organized violence in post-new order Indonesia', *Critical Asian Studies,* 38(2): 265–97.

Wirth, L. (1938) 'Urbanism as a way of life', *American Journal of Sociology,* 44(1): 1–24.

Wolf, S. (2012) 'Mara Salvatrucha: The most dangerous street gang in the Americas?', *Latin American Politics and Society,* 54(1): 65–99.

PART THREE

MILIEU

Chapter Twelve

Political Violence in its Milieu

Daniela Pisoiu

The fact that groups and organisations involved in political violence do not emerge and function in an isolated manner but are closely interrelated with the broader social milieu of sympathisers, helpers, and prospective recruits is, in the social movement and the terrorism literature, considered self-evident. Indeed, particularly relational approaches to the study of political violence outline the parallels between violent political action and other types of political activism and protest both in terms of mechanisms of emergence and the individual life stories of the participants. Yet it is only recently that scholars have begun to express a particular interest in the conceptualisation of this broader social environment and its relationship to violent political entities. The so-called 'radical milieu' has been found to entertain various facets and relates in multiple ways to the self-understanding and actions of violent political groups and organisations, thus playing an important role in the overall dynamic of political violence. The previous sections of this volume have contributed to this area of research, and the chapters of the present section turn explicitly in this direction.

The concept of 'milieu' is a novel and welcome addition to the conceptual arsenal of the political violence field of study – a field that is increasingly moving away from simple and deterministic relationships of cause and effect, aiming instead towards an understanding of political violence as a process involving various actors, dynamics, and levels of analysis. The recent 'discovery' of the importance of milieu may be surprising, since it should indeed be self-evident. The utilisation of milieu is typically rationalised through the idea that terrorist and other violent groups do not develop and act in a vacuum, but are already and always embedded in certain social environments. Nevertheless, this intuitively palpable aspect tends to disappear in practical analytical work, whereby media reports and the academic literature gravitate towards assumptions of abnormality and isolation. In other words, explanatory paradigms consistently search for features specific to certain individuals, groups or cultures that tend to determine involvement in political violence, all the while focusing on these units of analysis in isolation from their broader environment. We are thus faced with a situation in which something that should be obvious to the naked eye needs to be substantiated and presented to the world as new.

Malthaner and Waldmann (2014) have done wonderful work in applying the concept of 'milieu'. They begin by noting how 'terrorist groups should not be regarded as completely isolated, socially "free-floating" entities' (2014: 1), and go on to place this concept within the broader process-oriented and interactive paradigm of the study of political violence:

Not only do they [terrorist groups] develop in the context of escalating interactions between social movements, political opponents, and state actors. Terrorist groups also emerge from and operate within a specific, more immediate social environment – which we call the *radical milieu* – which shares their perspective and objectives, approves of certain forms of violence, and (at least to a certain extent) supports the violent group morally and logistically. (*Ibid.*)

There are, therefore, two major dimensions and functions of the radical milieu: as a pool of emergence, and, at a later stage, as ideational and logistical support for terrorist entities. Importantly, milieu does not simply refer to the social aspect of groups or communities, but also to their discursive and symbolic dimensions. The groups and their social environments 'share experiences, symbols, narratives, and frameworks of interpretation with this milieu and the armed groups are – at least to a certain extent – linked to (or part of) its social networks' (Malthaner and Waldmann 2014: 7). The authors identify three types of dynamics present in the relationship between the radical milieu and the terrorist entity or clandestine group: the terrorist group can emerge from the radical milieu during a process of gradual radicalisation; the two can emerge at the same time, independently from each other; or the radical milieu can emerge afterwards, as a consequence of a strategic move to create support groups.

The first type of dynamic – the emergence of a terrorist group out of the broader radical milieu – can be found in previous literature on social movements and terrorism, where it has been empirically applied to a variety of ideological orientations and various levels of analysis. At the individual level, della Porta has found that, in the case of left-wing terrorism in the 1970s, 'those who joined the armed struggle had already been involved, often for many years, in legal radical Left organizations' (1992: 261). The literature on right-wing extremism has consistently recorded transitions from subcultural right-wing milieus towards more radical right-wing movements, as in the case of skinheads developing into neo-Nazis (Bjørgo 1993; Sprinzak 1995; Dobratz and Shanks-Meile 1997; Van Dyke and Soule 2002; Schäfer-Vogel 2007), and from such movements and groups to terror cells. A connection between jihadi terrorists and previous membership in non-violent Islamist organisations – such as Hisbut-Tahrir, or Tabligh – has also been observed (Barnes 2006; Beyler 2006; Hoffman 2009). Not necessarily a research finding yet, in a sense, illustrating common-sense knowledge in the field, Sageman (2011) stated that '[t]errorism emerges out of a political subculture [...] Just as these terrorists emerge from a neo-jihadi subculture rejecting the values of the West, so did Breivik emerge out of an Islamophobic subculture rejecting the immigration of Muslims to the West.'

In terms of conceptualisation, there have been precursors to the use of 'milieu', with concepts such as 'supporters', 'sympathisers', and 'subculture' denoting related aspects. In terms of definition, 'milieu' is broader and more inclusive than either of these three. 'Supporters', for example, specifically refers to a group of individuals offering operational support to a terrorist organisation. For example, Horgan and Taylor (1997), taking the case of PIRA (the Provisional Irish Republican Army), differentiate between active or operational membership, on the one hand, and the support network, or non-operational membership, on the other.

While the former take part in actual armed attacks, as part of the 'Active Service Units', the latter fulfil other supporting roles, such as hiding weapons or offering safe houses (Horgan and Taylor 1997: 3). They further suggest that, given security concerns, recruitment would usually be sourced within this community. In the pyramid model of radicalisation (McCauley and Moskalenko 2008), 'sympathisers' form the initial layer of involvement, in terms of beliefs, feelings and behaviour, whereby individuals simply 'sympathize with the goals the terrorists say they are fighting for' (1997: 417).

The concept of 'subculture' originates in criminology and refers to an autonomous normative system and social values distinguishing certain minority groups: a way of life that somewhat draws on – but is fundamentally different from – the 'mainstream' (Cohen 1997; Gordon 1997). Within the literature, 'subculture' has also been used to depict the broader activist social environment (della Porta 1992), but its usage more frequently refers to specific sections, or 'scenes', of the radical or extremist spectrum, such as right-wing skinheads or left-wing autonomists. In this context, the classic conceptualisation of subculture has been that of socially marginal groups emerging from disadvantaged socio-economic layers, powerfully driven by the pursuit of a certain lifestyle and the enjoyment of particular music and clothing and with only a slight interest in politics. More recent conceptualisations have moved away from this idea in two important ways: in relation to contemporary jihadism in Europe, authors have argued that 'subculture' denotes the terrorist cells and individuals themselves, rather than some precursors in the radicalisation process (Horsburgh and Jordan 2004; Cottee 2011). The rationale for this would be, on the one hand, the idea of core characteristics of subcultures forming autonomous systems of norms and values radically opposed to the mainstream, and, on the other, the explanation for the emergence of subcultures, namely status frustration. Without necessarily agreeing with the latter, some authors have argued that 'subculture' is a more adequate conceptualisation of contemporary forms of political extremism and terrorism, precisely due to the contemporary prevalence of style and lifestyle in the self-understanding of individual activists of all ideological colours, as well as in the strategies that groups use for attracting new adherents (Pisoiu 2015).

The chapters of this section discuss, apply, and expand the concept of the radical milieu by in-depth analysis of a variety of case studies. Jérôme Drevon unpacks the radical milieu itself with reference to the case of radical Salafism in Egypt and through the use of conceptual tools derived from framing theory in social movements. In particular, Drevon finds that the nature, characteristics and effects of the radical Salafi milieu in Egypt have differed over time depending on variations in degree of organisational centralisation and control, which, in turn, have had an effect on the ways in which radical frames have been diffused and legitimated. Niall Ó Dochartaigh focuses on the relationship between the republican milieu in Ireland and the process of mass mobilisation into militant Irish republican organisations from 1969 onwards. In particular, he argues that this is a fourth type of dynamic between the supportive radical milieu and the organisation, whereby a political crisis was transformed and overwhelmed to the extent that a new milieu was eventually established, with the original one growing hostile to the new mass mobilisation. In a detailed historical case study of left-wing political violence in Italy in the 1970s, Luca Falciola observes that the relationship between groups and milieu is not always one of support, as these relations can also be characterised by disapproval and even opposition to the actions of armed groups. His chapter is thus a detailed examination of the conditions under which such support initially emerged, and the factors that eventually led to its deterioration and dissolution. Finally, in his case study of the al-Jamaa al-Islamiyya, Stefan Malthaner elaborates on the process of violent escalation from the perspective of a triangular relationship between the militant group, its social environment, and state repression, thus developing the original process model of escalating policing. In particular, he outlines two sources and subsequent dynamics of violent escalation: an agenda of social and cultural islamisation, met with resentment on the part of the target population and followed by attempts to impose the new order by force; and repressive intervention on the part of the state, triggering withdrawal of support for the militants, which, in turn, led to a reaction of coercion and terror exercised by the latter on the local communities. The chapters in this section thus offer inquisitive and innovative approaches to both the concept of milieu and the phenomenology of its interaction with violent political actors.

Although not principally focused on milieu, some of the chapters in the previous two sections on time and space explicitly reference milieu as an important component of the overall dynamic of political violence. Steinhoff and Zwermann, for example, found that legal support networks had two types of effects on New Left and post-New Left clandestine political violence cases in Japan and the United States between 1970 and 2010. Defendants were, due to their involvement, on the one hand able to sustain their resistance throughout the legal process of prosecution, trial, and sentence, while, helping militants to disengage and reconnect with the broader, non-violent social movement milieu on the other. And Lorenzo Zamponi outlines the effects of specific acts of violence on the movement milieu in his chapter on contentious memory and the Italian and Spanish student movements.

To conclude these introductory notes on milieu, it needs to be pointed out that, given the relative novelty of the problematic, further avenues of investigation are necessary in order to complete and elaborate on the picture of these dynamics. Given that, so far, the focus has been on single-case studies and ideologically uniform cases, a logical step forward would be to turn to cross-ideological comparative studies. Beyond the slick differentiation between support and approval, more granular studies could examine in further detail the various kinds of relationships that exist between milieu and violent political entities, particularly as they unfold along the process of involvement in political violence. The seemingly atypical case of European homegrown jihadism, which emerged as peaks of violent activity in the absence of a broader, local social movement, and in the presence of isolated pockets of 'milieu', requires an evidence-based examination that tests and possibly adapts the initial model of the relationship between social movement, milieu and terrorist organisation. Finally, as applied to contemporary and 'new' forms of political protest and violence, a more general examination and testing of existing social movements' process conceptualisations of emerging political violence is in order.

References

Barnes, H. (2006) *Born in the UK: Young Muslims in Britain*, London: Foreign Policy Centre.

Beyler, C. (2006) 'The jihadist threat in France', in H. Fradkin, H. Haqqani and E. Brown (eds) *Current Trends in Islamist Ideology,* Vol. 3, Washington: Hudson Institute, pp. 89–113.

Bjørgo, T. (1993) 'Militant neo-Nazism in Sweden', *Terrorism and Political Violence,* 5(3): 28–57.

Cohen, A. K. (1997) 'A general theory of subcultures', in K. Gelder and S. Thornton (eds) *The Subcultures Reader,* London, New York: Routledge, pp. 44–54.

Cottee, S. (2011) 'Jihadism as a subcultural response to social strain: Extending Marc Sageman's 'bunch of guys' thesis', *Terrorism and Political Violence,* 23(5): 730–51.

della Porta, D. 1992. 'Political socialization in left-wing underground organizations: Biographies of Italian and German militants', in D. della Porta (ed.) *Social Movements and Violence: Participation in Underground Organizations,* Greenwich, London: JAI Press, pp. 259–90.

Gordon, M. M. (1997) 'The concept of the sub-culture and its application', in K. Gelder and S. Thornton (eds) *The Subcultures Reader,* London, New York: Routledge, pp. 40–3.

Hoffman, B. (2009) 'Radicalization and subversion: Al Qaeda and the 7 July 2005 bombings and the 2006 airline bombing plot', *Studies in Conflict and Terrorism,* 32(12): 1100–16.

Horgan, J. and Taylor, M. (1997) 'The provisional Irish republican army: Command and functional structure', *Terrorism and Political Violence,* 9(3): 1–32.

Horsburgh, N. and Jordan, J. (2004) 'Jihadist subculture of terrorism in Spain', *5th Global Conference Interdisciplinary.net,* https://www.inter-disciplinary.net/ati/violence/v5/horsburgh%20paper.pdf (accessed 26 March 2015).

Malthaner, S. and Waldmann, P. (2014) 'The radical milieu: Conceptualizing the supportive social environment of terrorist groups', *Studies in Conflict & Terrorism,* 37(12): 979–98.

McCauley, C. and Moskalenko, S. (2008) 'Mechanisms of political radicalization: Pathways toward terrorism', *Terrorism and Political Violence,* 20(3): 415–33.

Pisoiu, D. (2015) 'Subcultural theory, jihadi and right-wing radicalization in Germany', *Terrorism and Political Violence,* 27(1): 9–28.

Sageman, M. (2011) 'Why do extremists like Breivik turn to violence?', 1 August, http://globalpublicsquare.blogs.cnn.com/2011/08/01/why-do-extremists-like-breivik-turn-to-violence/ (accessed 29 August 2011).

Schäfer-Vogel, G. (2007) *Gewalttätige Jugendkulturen – Symptom der Erosion kommunikativer Strukturen,* Berlin: Duncker & Humblot.

Sprinzak, E. (1995) 'Right-wing terrorism in a comparative perspective: The case of split delegitimization', *Terrorism and Political Violence*, 7(1): 17–43.

Van Dyke, N. and Soule, S. A. (2002) 'Structural social change and the mobilizing effect of threat: Explaining levels of patriot and militia organizing in the United States', *Social Problems*, 49(4): 497–520.

Chapter Thirteen

The Emergence and Construction of the Radical Salafi Milieu in Egypt

Jérôme Drevon

Contextualisation of political violence has recently gained prominence in the literature.[1] This development has followed decades of criticism – from both insiders and outsiders – as regards the ontological, epistemological, and methodological foundations of this field.[2] These reconsiderations have influenced the study of political violence and encouraged increasingly rich and intricate research projects that reject the understanding of violence as the outcome of isolated psycho-pathological factors, radical ideologies, or solely as the product of structural factors.[3] The emerging consensus on political violence advocates for an understanding of it as a dynamic, interactive, constructed, and emergent process (della Porta 2013) caused by a myriad of mutually constituted multi-level factors. This consensus generally favours the study of processes and causal mechanisms based on rich and contextualised qualitative case studies.[4]

The contextualisation of political violence presented in this book pertains specifically to time, space, and milieu. The study of milieu combines many distinctive approaches. A prevailing angle focuses on milieu as the social environment in which violent movements emerge and develop. To use an analogy favoured by Mao Zedong, this social environment is the sea in which revolutionary guerrillas swim (Hilsman 1968: 271). The characteristics of the milieu can create an array of opportunities for militant and insurgent groups to mobilise and achieve significant levels of popular support for the completion of their tactical and strategic objectives. At the same time, their milieu can also hinder activities and limit available options.[5] A focus on social environment includes, for example, evolving mechanisms of popular support in civil war settings (Malthaner 2011; Wood 2003). Contextualised studies of political violence generally demonstrate that radical groups cannot be studied in isolation from the milieu in which they evolve.

---

1. This research was made possible by a grant from the Swiss National Science Foundation (SNSF).
2. Major criticisms of terrorism studies have recently been re-articulated by scholars of critical terrorism studies (e.g., Jackson, Smyth and Gunning 2009). For a recent debate on the state of research on terrorism studies, see *Terrorism and Political Violence* 26(4).
3. Some of these criticisms were developed, for instance, in della Porta 2013; Hafez 2003; Pape 2006; Sageman 2004, 2008.
4. See e.g., della Porta 2013; Kalyvas 2006; Malthaner 2011; Weinstein 2007; Wood 2003.
5. One expanding branch of the literature focuses on the role of popular support in the use of certain repertoires, such as suicide bombings (e.g., Bloom 2004, 2007).

The study of violence in Islamic settings has seen increasing coverage of the development of Salafi jihadism. This terminology describes Muslims who legitimise the use of violence against nominally Muslim heads of state, but there are secondary disagreements among scholars over what exactly Salafi jihadism entails in terms of political behaviour and religious creed (Hegghammer 2009; Wagemakers 2012; Wiktorowicz 2006). Rich studies of Salafi jihadi groups show how scholars regularly fail to contextualise these actors within their milieu. However, just as holds for other, non-Islamic settings, it can be assumed that Salafi jihadi actors cannot be isolated from the broader environment in which they flourish, and which can both constrain and sustain their development.

This chapter investigates the emergence and evolution of the Salafi radical milieu in Egypt. This is defined as the social structures composed of supporters and sympathisers of the militant groups, providing them with both logistic and moral support. It is the setting from which these groups emerge and to which they remain connected (Malthaner 2014: 639; Waldmann 2010). This chapter argues that the internal characteristics of the radical milieu should be studied through the analysis of the diffusion of Salafi jihadi frames, at both micro and meso levels. It demonstrates that different types of frame diffusion – relational and non-relational – are related to fundamentally different networking structures. Relational diffusion of Salafi jihadi frames materialises through intermediaries at the micro and meso levels. This type of diffusion is mediated by different networking structures determining the level of internal control over its development. Conversely, non-relational diffusion occurs through global communication and creates a diversified radical milieu characterised by the absence of internal control.

This chapter establishes that the Egyptian Salafi radical milieu has been constructed in two successive phases. The first takes place between the 1970s and the 1990s. During this time, milieu-construction is better understood through meso-level study of its composite networks and organisations, since these had a virtual monopoly on the relational diffusion of frames and on micro-mobilisation. The second phase is set in the 2000s, with non-relational diffusion of radical frames through new means of communication fundamentally affecting the expansion of its milieu, and informing its development as internally more diverse and individualised. This came to subsequently shape the post-2011 developments.

This study is based on eighteen months of intensive field research, undertaken in Cairo between 2011 and 2014. The research includes a prolonged political ethnography with diverse groups of Salafi jihadi supporters in Egypt, as well as semi-structured interviews with leaders and members of two former militant groups in Egypt: the Islamic Group and the Jihad Group, and of their political parties.

An organisational study of Salafi jihadi networks

Modern Salafism is considered a contemporary revivalist religious movement defined by the specificity of its religious approach to Islam, which nevertheless contains acute internal political diversity. The Salafi approach to Islam (*al-manhaj al-salafi*) mostly diverges from non-Salafi Islam in the method of interpretation of Islamic sources. Salafi Muslims reject what they consider to be a blind following of the four canonical Islamic schools of law (Meijer 2009:4) and insist on the need to return to the two fundamentals sources in Islam – the Qur'an and the Sunna (the practice of the Prophet) (Haykel 2009: 38–9). Salafis promote a specific creed (*'aqida*), which is not shared by the majority of Muslims, and they insist on the necessity to purify Islam, ridding it of any innovation deemed un-Islamic (*bida'*), and from remnants of polytheist beliefs and practices (denounced as *shirk* in Arabic).[6] The political preferences of Salafis diverge substantially, however, with the trend including supporters of the status quo, proponents of political participation, and radicals, who legitimise the use of violence against Muslim leaders who do not rule exclusively with Islamic law (Hegghammer 2009; Wagemakers 2012; Wiktorowicz 2006).

The academic study of Salafi jihadism is relatively elitist and actor centred. Most research projects focus on specific case studies of Salafi jihadi groups and scholars to investigate their idiosyncratic evolution.[7] Despite their valuable explorations of internal Salafi jihadi debates,[8] their limited elitist focus fails to account for the interactions between these groups and scholars, on the one hand, and the radical milieu in which they evolve, on the other. They generally understand the evolution of Salafi jihadism from the point of view of its prominent armed group leaders and religious scholars, and are virtually silent on the articulation of these debates on the micro and meso levels. Moreover, they generally overlook internal organisational dynamics and neglect to study the important networking structures of the groups.

The interactions between Salafi jihadi leaders and their followers have mostly been investigated from a social movement perspective.[9] The prevailing perspective resorts to framing studies to unpack the interactions between the Salafi jihadi elite and its followers (Meijer 2007; Wagemakers 2008, 2011, 2012; Wiktorowicz 2004). These studies explore the ideological articulation of Salafi jihadi thought and its adoption at a micro level with the tools commonly used for framing studies (including frame alignment and frame resonance).[10] Despite their multi-level objectives, however, these studies often reproduce the same elitist bias centered on ideological construction rather than on its micro reception, with a few exceptions (Wagemakers 2012; Wiktorowicz 2005).

More comprehensive multi-level research on the interactions between Salafi jihadi leaders and groups, and their followers, has adopted a meso-level focus. These studies question the organisational make-up of Salafi jihadi groups, from

---

6. For general academic literature on Salafism, see Meijer 2009; Rougier 2008.

7. A non-exhaustive representative list of studies of Salafi Jjihadi groups and scholars include Brachman 2008; Gerges 2011; Lia 2008; Tawil 2011; Wagemakers 2012.

8. See for instance Lahoud, 2012, 2013; Moghadam and Fishman 2011; Ryan 2013.

9. See e.g., Hegghammer 2010; Wiktorowicz 2000, 2001, 2005.

10. On framing, see Benford and Snow 2000; Johnston and Noakes 2013; Snow and Benford 1988; Snow, Rochford Jr, Worden and Benford 1986; Snow 2014.

organised entities to loose networking structures, and the impact of these on micro-mobilisation and on the diffusion of ideas. They notably argue that group socialisation is crucial to the adoption of Salafi jihadism (Sageman 2004, 2008; Wiktorowicz 2005). In this regard, they stress the role of pre-existing ties between members of Salafi jihadi networks, and the importance of the meso-level processes leading to the adoption of violence. This corpus, therefore, follows the lead of established studies of political violence, emphasising the role of small-group dynamics.[11] More recently, they have been further supplemented by an emerging focus on the impact of the radical milieu (Malthaner 2014; Waldmann 2010).

Informed by the diverse scholarship on Salafi jihadism, this chapter focuses on the meso-level organisations and networks that structure the Salafi radical milieu. More specifically, this approach justifies the central assertion of this chapter that in Egypt, there are two main types of frame diffusion that have led to the socialisation of the radical milieu, and the subsequent adoption of Salafi jihadism. The first type of diffusion is relational and materialises through personal contacts and intermediaries, while the second type of diffusion is non-relational and occurs through new means of communication such as the Internet.

The central argument of this chapter is that different types of frame diffusion are aligned with different networking structures. The corollary of this argument is that specific networking structures have certain implications on the internal level of control over the ideological and organisational development of the radical milieu. In the case of non-relational diffusion, the argument is rather straightforward. The non-relational diffusion of Salafi jihadism creates a diversified radical milieu through new means of global communication, characterised by the absence of central internal control over its ideological and organisational development. New followers of Salafi jihadism shape their own intellectual and religious understanding of this trend, which is not contingent on their inclusion into specific radical networks that could enjoy a monopoly on ideological articulation and organisational make-up.

In the case of the relational diffusion of Salafi jihadism, the argument is more sophisticated. The level of internal control over the development of the radical milieu, relationally diffused, is contingent on the structures of the meso organisations that compose it. Structured, cohesive, and integrated groups are more likely to expand their social networks while simultaneously maintaining a high level of internal control over their organisational and ideational developments. Conversely, divided groups with poor local anchorage are less likely to manage to expand their networks while maintaining a stronger internal control over their developments. Analytically, the study of the meso dynamics of militant groups should focus on the type of ties uniting their leaders; their leaders and followers, and these groups and their broader social networks.[12]

---

11. See Crenshaw 1987; della Porta 1995.
12. This analytical perspective draws on Staniland's 2014 study of armed groups' embeddedness within their broader social networks.

The emergence of Salafism in Egypt and the inception of its jihadi offshoot in the 1970s

Salafism emerged in Egypt at the beginning of the twentieth century. The first influential association promoting Salafi views – *al-jam'ia al-shari'a lil al-'amilin bil al-kitab wal-sunna al-muhammadiyya* (the lawful association for those who behave according to the Book [the Qur'an] and Muhammad's tradition) – was created by Sheikh Mahmud Khattab al-Sobki in 1912. The association has, since then, been engaged in social work in the fields of preaching, education, and health (Faid 2014: 52).[13] Egypt's second main Salafi association emerged from a split in *al-jam'ia al-shari'a*. In 1926, Sheikh Muhammad Hamed al-Fiqi created *jam'ia ansar al-sunna al-muhammadiyya* (Association of the Partisans of Muhammad's Tradition), which has since followed the Salafi approach to Islam (Faid 2014: 54). These associations have since their inception developed an important network in Egypt, even if they had relatively limited political influence until the 1960s.

Since the 1970s, Salafism has spread considerably in Egypt due to a variety of factors. Regionally and internationally, this period marked a renewed influence of religion in the Middle East caused by the loss of Jerusalem in 1967, the relative demise of Arab nationalist ideologies after the 1967 Arab defeat, and the growing influence of the Gulf countries. In Egypt, the death of former president Jamal Abd al-Nasser in 1970 was followed by Anwar Sadat's accession to power. Sadat departed from the stance of his predecessor and changed Egypt's regional alliances (Thompson 2008: 317; Kandil 2013: 99). Domestically, he benefited from the religious revival, portraying himself as the 'believer president' against his nationalist and socialist political opponents (Esposito 1998; Zaman 2010: 146). He alleviated the pressure on the Islamist trend and released thousands of members of the Muslim Brotherhood from prison (Zollner 2008: 48). The liberalisation of the 1970s generally facilitated the expansion of religion in the public sphere.

The legitimisation of Islamist violence appeared gradually and distinctively, in three groups whose diverging patterns of mobilisation came to impact on the emerging networking topography of Egypt's radical milieu. Initially, the growing religiousisation of the public sphere, and the political and social consensus regarding the role of Islam in society, was not associated with theological justification of the use of violence. The relatively liberal political system was fairly inclusive, allowing for the development of religious groups. The legitimisation of violence among Islamist groups emerged as part of three different trends. Their respective influence and roles substantially diverged, however, and the following analysis will trace their origins and interactions with the broader radical milieu, as mediated by their organisational structures.

---

13. Many observers do not consider this association to be Salafi *per se*. It is included here due to the increasing importance of Salafism among its members.

The first violent Islamist group was a sectarian epiphenomenon of the repression of the Muslim Brotherhood under Nasser. *Jama'a al-muslimun* (Society of Muslims)[14] was founded and led by Shukri Mustafa, following his release from prison in 1971. Mustafa adopted the ideas of Muslim Brotherhood intellectual Sayyid Qutb, who was radicalised in prison before his execution in 1966 (Calvert 2010; Musallam 2005; Toth 2013). Until the dissolution of his group, in 1978, Mustafa recruited young followers, and advocated for isolation from the allegedly un-Islamic influence of Egyptian society.[15] *Jama'a al-muslimun* was primarily a product of the harsh detention of Muslim Brotherhood members in prison, rather than of Sadat's political system.

This group was characterised by peculiar sectarian and authoritarian internal dynamics that isolated it from society and hindered the development of a supportive environment. This group was mostly based on prison ties, and its rejection of other Muslims on theological grounds later obstructed its local expansion. Frame diffusion at a local level was therefore extremely limited and this group had, during its short existence, the characteristics of a cult organised around an authoritarian leader.[16] Leaders and other prominent members of the Islamic Group and the Jihad Group claim in interviews that they often tried to convince the followers of *jama'a al-muslimun* to revise their views, without significant success.[17] The group had no substantial role in the expansion and development of Egypt's radical milieu in the 1970s.

The second essential component of the Salafi radical milieu was the nebula commonly referred to as the Jihad Groups (*jama'at al-jihad*). This designates loosely related cells united by their eagerness to replace the regime with an Islamic state, although they frequently disagreed on tactical issues. Multiple interviews with former members and leaders of these cells indicate that their adoption of violence was not directly informed by Sadat's policies or by a process of radicalisation in prison, as in the case of Shukri Mustafa. These youths were from religious backgrounds and were recruited individually through social networks that had developed inside mainstream Salafi associations – most notably *ansar al-sunna* – and through family ties and acquaintances. Their adoption of a violent form of Salafism was a result of the local jihadi leaders successfully framing the creation of an Islamic state in Egypt as the sole remedy to multiple domestic and international grievances. These grievances were wide-ranging and stretched from the liberation of Jerusalem to the creation of an Islamic utopia.[18]

---

14. This group has often been referred to as *takfir wal-hijra* (Excommunication and Exile) even though it never used this appellation.

15. Studies of this group include Ansari 1984; Cozzens 2009; Ibrahim 1982, 1988; Kepel 1993.

16. See fn. 14.

17. According to my interviews with members of the JG and of the IG in the 1970s, including Abd al-Rawf Amir al Jaysh, Kamal Habib, Osama Hafez, Najih Ibrahim and Rifai Taha.

18. Interviews with Abd al-Rawf Amir al Jaysh, Ali Faraj, Kamal Habib, Salih Jahin, Nabil Na'im and Osama Qassem.

The networking mode of organisation of these cells and their early adoption of violence explains the types of framing used, their relational pattern of micro-mobilisation, and their circumscribed expansion. These cells centred around nodes of distinctive leaders who recruited through relational framing within their close surroundings – in Salafi institutions and among their own friends and family members. Their early adoption of violence meant that being a member entailed personal pitfalls akin to high-risk activities. These networks could not recruit publicly, and trust and security issues limited their expansion. The coordination between their cells was therefore limited and they generally suffered from internal competition between individual leaders.[19] As a result, while these networks enjoyed some level of embeddedness in mainstream Salafi associations, they did not manage to expand in the wider society or create a substantial supportive milieu outside of their local ties.

The last essential component of the violent Salafi milieu in Egypt in the 1970s is *al-jama'a al-islamiyya*, or the Islamic Group (henceforth IG). This movement emerged in universities in Upper Egypt, and initially it merely strived to teach and spread Islam in society. In its conception as a student group, it did not follow a specific political agenda, and its religious framework was not clearly articulated. According to its leaders, the Salafi approach to Islam was adopted only later, towards the end of the 1970s. Eventually, it became a dominant force in Upper Egyptian universities, increasingly providing essential support to the students (Abdo 2002: 125; Kepel 1993). Its members gradually confronted their leftist and nationalist opponents and the group radicalised as a result. The closing of political opportunities in Egypt served to fuel the radicalisation process, as did Sadat's new international outlook and his rapprochement with the United States and Israel. From a comparative perspective, the radicalisation of this group was therefore more closely related to Sadat's political choices and to the contentious conflict with political opponents than were the jihad groups.[20]

The organisational development of the IG thus differed substantially from that of the jihad groups. The emergence of the IG as a non-violent movement reinforced the strong ties between its leaders and facilitated the mobilisation of its followers and the constitution of a broad constituency before the beginning of the contentious conflict. Joining the IG was initially akin to joining a low-risk activity. IG leaders therefore had time to define the group's internal mode of organisation, and managed to make a consensual decision over the ideational and strategic developments of the group. Moreover, the IG was initially embedded in the social structures of the Egyptian South and engaged in public work, which eased the micro-mobilisation of a diversified membership. The adoption of violence in the aftermath of these organisational developments meant that the larger constituency of the IG shaped the foundations of an incorporated radical milieu controlled by IG leaders.

---

19. *See* fn. 18.

20. Interviews with Osama Hafez, Abd al-Akhr Hamad, Najih Ibrahim and Rifai Taha.

By the end of the 1970s, the closing of political opportunities in Egypt led to a rapprochement between some cells of the jihad groups and the Islamic Group in the South. Discussions were followed by agreement on a plan to topple the regime with a popular revolution combined with a military coup.[21] However, this new alliance did not take any further steps towards a violent removal of the regime, and the assassination of Anwar Sadat in October 1981 was first and foremost a hastened response to the large-scale arrests ordered by the latter during the month leading up to his death.

The reconstruction of the Salafi radical milieu in the 1980s and the 1990s

Following Sadat's killing, further development of the Egyptian radical milieu was disturbed by the arrest of most members of radical groups and networks. During these massive waves of arrest, radical group members who escaped arrest left the country or became clandestine. The radical Salafi milieu was virtually decimated with the groups being relocated to prison, where they used their detention to re-evaluate their choices and determine their future. While they initially believed that they would be executed by the regime, the relative clemency of the judiciary prompted new discussions about the future. Negotiations regarding the consolidation of a united group failed to yield a positive outcome and personal conflicts between IG and jihadi group leaders caused a split, leading to the emergence of two distinct groups: the Islamic Group and the Jihad Group.[22]

The IG now materialised as a structured organisation with a well-defined leadership. In prison, a consensual direction constituted by its four main leaders was named to design the group's ideology and strategic vision for the future. This leadership – subsequently referred to as the historical leadership – was composed of the main founders of the group, whose pre-existing positions and organisational authority was formally acknowledged. In prison, they published several books that epitomised and summarised the ideology and tenets of the IG.[23] The already strong ties between its leaders facilitated the survival of the group and the reaffirmation of its consensual nature.

In 1984, IG leaders benefited from the liberation of many second-tier leaders and members, and the group's infrastructure in Upper Egypt could be revived. The strong legitimacy and unity of its imprisoned leadership helped to promote its views on the ground and to recreate pre-1981 social networks. The group took advantage of a phase of relative political liberalisation to recruit new members and to socialise them into the group's ideological tenets through a relational diffusion of the new frames developed in jail.[24] The IG reproduced pre-1981

---

21. Interviews with Abd al-Rawf Amir al Jaysh, Kamal Habib, Najih Ibrahim and Rifai Taha.

22. Interviews with Osama Hafez, Nabil Na'im, Osama Qassem and Rifai Taha.

23. Interviews with Osama Hafez, Abd al-Akhr Hamad and Nahim Ibrahim.

24. Interview with Rifai Taha.

micro-mobilisation patterns, assimilable to the joining of a low-risk activity – as argued above – and recreated a broad supportive environment and milieu in the south. This milieu was ideologically coherent and well structured around local IG leaders.

The Jihad Group (henceforth JG), on the other hand, did not come out of prison as a united entity. Its leadership was plagued by internal divisions and conflicts over which strategy to adopt.[25] These divisions did not occur in a vacuum but generally reflected the pre-1981 divisions between differentiated networks. Eventually – from 1984 onwards – the progressive liberation of second-tier leaders and members only worsened the internal divide. Many members and leaders of this group – including Ayman al-Zawahiri and Sayyid Imam – used this opportunity to go to Afghanistan to train fellow members. In prison, its leaders became increasingly isolated and, according to imprisoned leaders, the ties with the Afghan-based leadership were then severed.[26]

As a result, in the 1980s, the JG reproduced pre-1981 micro-mobilisation patterns, failing to overcome previous impediments to its expansion. In prison, JG leaders did not manage to clearly define the ideological and strategic views of the group, publishing only a few leaflets representing the individual position of some members. The JG failed to establish any sustainable coordinated networks on the ground, and its members merely managed to mobilise individuals located around them, in limited social networks. Despite the relatively open political environment, the JG's secret nature and internal divisions hindered the constitution of a strong supportive milieu.

From a comparative perspective, after 1984 the reconstruction of the radical milieu in Egypt followed two distinctive organisational patterns. In the South, the IG successfully reconstituted its former networks and structured them around a cluster of trusted leaders. Due to the relatively free political environment this revived radical milieu expanded relatively rapidly and attracted many new followers that could be socialised into the group's ideological tenets and identity. This mode of organisation afforded the IG strong internal control over its radical milieu as well as a substantial level of local embeddedness in society. Conversely, JG-affiliated cells suffered from the divisions of the leadership in prison and abroad and reproduced pre-1981 patterns of socialisation. Its local networks were divided, secret, and lacked the coordination and control that the IG enjoyed. The JG's ideological tenets were only marginally spread at a local level, through family ties and acquaintances. This comparison between the IG and the JG demonstrates that relational diffusion of radical frames was differently negotiated by these groups' respective modes of micro-mobilisation.

Eventually, the cycle of contention between the security services and the followers of the violent Salafi milieu, triggered in Egypt in 1987, was not the outcome of deliberate strategic or tactical choices made by the leadership of

---

25. Interview with Nabil Na'im.
26. Interview with Salih Jahin and Osama Qassem.

these groups. It mostly resulted from changing state policies towards the Islamist radical milieu – represented chiefly by the IG and the JG – and from the wave of repression launched by the new Egyptian minister of the interior, Zaki Badr (Awwa 2006; Haenni 2005; Malthaner 2011). The IG and JG leaderships considered an armed confrontation as inevitable, but thought that the time had not arrived for a militarisation of their conflict with the state.[27]

These groups, and the radical milieu around them, managed state repression in different ways. The IG managed to preserve internal control over its followers and limited the use of violence at a local level during the first two years (i.e., before the disintegration of its leadership on the ground).[28] It benefited from growing sympathy from the population in some neighbourhoods of the Egyptian capital Cairo, and managed to further mobilise new followers. Initially, the group's support networks grew as a result of the contentious conflict with the state, which strengthened the local radical milieu forming around them. By contrast, the JG's organisational weakness and limited local anchorage prevented it from unifying and controlling new sympathisers. Interviews with some of the latter reveal that the group suffered from divisions among local JG leaders, and failed to unite their ranks. JG cells acted independently and resorted to selective violence against security forces, without regard of strategic objectives. These two cases thus demonstrate that the radical milieu formed around these groups reacted differently to state repression depending on the level of internal control and on their respective networking topographies. After a few years, they nonetheless suffered the same fate. The organisational structures of the IG and the JG were decimated on the ground level, with their leadership suffering imprisonment or exile. The remaining radical milieu became isolated from society, until it disappeared at the end of the 1990s.

In the meantime, the ideological construction of Egyptian militant groups was, paradoxically, consolidated thousands of kilometres away, in the Pakistani city of Peshawar. In the 1980s, the arrival of thousands of Arab volunteers for the Afghan Jihad (Anas 2002; Hegghammer 2010: 38; Salah 2001) created an environment in which Islamists from the Muslim Brotherhood, Salafi associations, and militant groups from diverse countries – notably Egypt and Syria – discussed and exchanged ideas. This relational diffusion of new ideas had a prominent role in the ideological shaping of the violent Salafi trend drawn from the Salafi creed and from the violent and militant approach to political action of Egyptians and Syrian militant groups. Egyptian leaders of the Jihad Group – including Sayyid Imam and Ayman al-Zawahiri – played a crucial role in this new ideological orientation. Other Salafi jihadi ideologues – such as Abu Muhammad al-Maqdissi and Abu Musab al-Suri – went on to become prominent representatives of this trend (Lia 2008; Wagemakers 2012).

---

27. Interviews with Abd al-Akhr Hamad and Rifai Taha.
28. Interview with Maher Farghali.

The radical milieu around the IG and the JG was not immune to these ideological developments nor to this relational diffusion of new ideas. Many prominent members and leaders residing in Peshawar and in the Afghan training camps contributed to discussions and debates.[29] In order to understand the integration of the new ideas in these groups' ideologies it is nonetheless necessary to first understand the organisational mediation presented by specific group dynamics and by the general characteristics of the Egyptian Salafi radical milieu. In particular, it reveals that the latter could not have been acquainted with these ideological developments prior to the 2000s, when these groups had organisationally disappeared in Egypt.

On the one hand, in Peshawar, leaders of the IG recognised the primacy of their imprisoned leaders in shaping the group's ideology and for its strategic decision-making.[30] Hence, while some of the Peshawar leaders grew closer to the Salafi jihadi approach to political action, they still delegated the direction of the movement to the imprisoned leadership. Conversely, the rupture between the JG in Peshawar and its leaders in prison gave more leeway to its leaders abroad. Some of these leaders' adoption of the Salafi jihadi approach to Islam therefore had an incomparable impact on the ideological construction of this group, in this case leading to a wider adoption of these ideas by group members, facilitated by their isolation from the group's imprisoned leadership.

Neither the groups' followers in Egypt nor the Salafi radical milieu was influenced by these ideological developments, due to the impossibility to reach them either relationally or non-relationally. The expatriate leadership of the IG and the JG recognise that they did not then have the means to communicate easily with their followers in Egypt, nor to disseminate their new literature, published abroad.[31] Similarly, members in Egypt and in prison maintain that they only had sporadic access to this new written corpus and add that they only became acquainted with it after their liberation from prison in the 2000s.[32] The evolving complexity of the ideological construction of the IG and the JG abroad was thus, in the 1990s, only marginally distributed among supporters of the groups, and inside the violent Egyptian Salafi radical milieu.

The 1990s marked the end of the cycle of violence in Egypt. IG leaders – notably Karam Zuhdi and Najih Ibrahim – directed a unilateral initiative to end violence in Egypt.[33] In 1997, after intense internal discussions and a few unsuccessful attempts (Ashour 2009; Awwa 2006), they managed to declare a unilateral ceasefire for the group. They also succeeded in convincing their followers in prison to accept this new decision and to lay down their weapons.

---

29. Interviews with Abd al-Akhr Hamad, Nabil Na'im, Muhammad Omar Abd al-Rahman and Rifai Taha.

30. *See* fn. 29.

31. Interview with Abd al-Akhr Hamad and Rifai Taha.

32. Interview with Salih Jahin and Majdi Salem.

33. Interview with Osama Hafez and Najih Ibrahim.

Eventually, the imprisoned leadership of the IG led a process of ideological revisions, amending several violent ideological tenets laid down in the literature of the group. Similar steps were also partially taken by followers of the JG, who pronounced a unilateral ceasefire in 1995, before revising some of their ideological tenets in 2007 (Ashour 2009).

The development of a diversified and individualised Salafi radical milieu in the 2000s

The construction of the Salafi radical milieu metamorphosed during the decade that preceded the 2011 Egyptian uprising. The two main factors influencing its constitution were the growing individualisation of religiosity in Egypt – reinforced by the development of new means of communication – and the framing of new international grievances. In combination with the organisational disappearance of the IG and the JG, this contributed to the expansion of Salafism in Egypt and to the end of these groups' relative monopoly on the development of the Salafi radical milieu. This milieu eventually became associated with the Salafi jihadi trend, which grew as a diverse and individualistic approach to radical Islamic activism.

The expansion of new media in the 2000s played a crucial role in the development of the religious field in Egypt. The proliferation of satellite TV channels, Egyptian households having increasing access to the Internet, combined with a marketisation of religion, promoted a new individualistic approach to Islam in Egyptian society (Haenni 2005; Roy 2012). This diversification of the religious field was reinforced by the growing disrepute of the religious establishment and by its inability to fulfil religious expectations at the level of the individual (Roy 2012). This individualisation of religion is reflected in the marginalisation of traditional and institutionalised forms of religiosity, which was progressively replaced by an individuality-driven selectivity among an array of religious sources (Roy 2012).

This setting provided fertile ground for the diffusion of new forms of Salafism. Salafi preachers increasingly relied on new religious TV channels and on the Internet, rather than on Salafi associations, for spreading the Salafi approach to Islam (Field and Hamam 2009). This new mode of socialisation shaped Salafism's new organisational and ideological make-up. While previously, Salafi Muslims in Egypt would primarily be socialised in Salafi institutions around specific religious scholars, this new socialisation, through the Internet and satellite TV, individualised the new generation's religious approach, allowing people to make an eclectic selection from diverse sources.

By the early 2000s, the former militant groups had formally disappeared in Egypt. The IG and the JG had no organisational presence and their members remained scattered abroad, primarily in Iran, Pakistan, and Europe.[34] In Egypt, the ideological revisions of the IG and factions of the JG gradually paved the way for the liberation of thousands of prisoners under the condition that they refrain from any public activity. Most of them were subsequently placed under the

---

34. Interview with Muhammad Omar Abd al-Rahman.

surveillance of the State Security Investigation Service (*mabahith amn al-dawla*), which maintained tight control of their interactions with other Egyptians. Leaders of both groups – notably Osama Qassem and Abd al Akhr Hamad[35] – recognise that this particular setting prevented them from reaching out to the new Salafi jihadi generation that, according to the IG religious mufti, Sheikh Abd al Akhr Hamad, was mostly socialised on the Internet, with Sheikh Google.

The propagation of Salafism and the absence of organised militant groups in Egypt are not, however, sufficient to explain the expansion of the violent Salafi milieu. The crucial element triggering its expansion in the 2000s is epitomised by the wars launched by the United States in Afghanistan in 2001, and in Iraq in 2003. While the post-9/11 invasion of Afghanistan and the subsequent replacement of the Taliban regime initially enjoyed a degree of international legitimacy also among prominent Muslim religious scholars, the Iraq War was a game changer. Many Middle Eastern countries were quick to perceive its lack of legitimacy and its framing as a remnant of old Christian crusades in the Middle East. The armed opposition to US-led forces was similarly legitimised among mainstream Muslims, easing the transition of young Salafi's adopting violent frames.

At a micro level, a political ethnography with several groups of Salafi jihadi youths revealed that a majority had defined themselves as Salafi Muslims before accepting the religious justifications of violence framed by jihadi ideologues. They stress their genuine consternation at the Iraq War and argue that it nourished a personal, political, and religious quest. As individuals, they were looking for indigenous answers to these external threats against the Muslim world. They claim that the inability of mainstream Salafi preachers to adequately respond to the attacks against the Muslim world urged them to explore other alternatives. The main theological Islamic discourse of armed defence of the Muslim world was the growing jihadi corpus available on the Internet, particularly on the website of prominent Salafi jihadi ideologue Abu Muhammad al-Maqdissi.[36]

The new individual adoption of Salafi jihadi frames through non-relational diffusion online was of tremendous importance for the construction of the new radical milieu, which significantly contrasted with the past. In the 1980s and the 1990s, the construction of Egypt's violent milieu essentially occurred inside and around the IG and the JG. Conversely, the socialisation into violent frames in the 2000s was primarily non-relational, and taking place online. Members of the new Salafi jihadi milieu socialised individually and without intermediaries. They shaped a new individualised radical milieu that did not enjoy the topographical characteristics of former IG and JG-related networks. This individualistic approach, combined with access to a wide literature, facilitated new supporters personally interpreting the meaning of Salafi jihadism. This new pattern of socialisation eroded the control that militant groups had had over the ideological construction of the new violent milieu, inexorably broadening its ideological foundations.

---

35. Interview with Abd al-Akhr Hamad and Osama Qassem.

36. *Minbar tawheed wal jihad*, www.tahwed.ws. For more information, see Wagemakers 2011.

This peculiar socialisation into the violent milieu has also meant that the distinction between different trends of Salafism, based on their political approaches – referred to as politico, scientific, and jihadi in the literature – has become more blurred than expected. These distinctions do not adequately reflect the experiences of Salafi jihadi individuals and the internal diversity of this new radical milieu. Hence, even if new Salafi jihadi supporters mostly agree on the illegitimacy of current Muslim rulers, and on the necessity to oppose foreign occupation of Muslim lands, there is wide disagreement regarding subsidiary issues. For instance, they quarrel on the legitimacy of mainstream Egyptian preachers such as Muhammad Hassan and Muhammad Hussein Yaqub, and of scholars affiliated to Saudi Arabia, such as former mufti Ibn Baz. These extensive divisions – which reflect wider divisions between realists and purists (Moghadam and Fishman 2011) – were relatively inconspicuous prior to 2011.

The impact of the 2011 Arab Spring on the Egyptian Salafi radical milieu

In 2011, the Egyptian uprising inaugurated an unprecedented era for Egyptian Salafism and for the Salafi radical milieu. The opening of political opportunity after the resignation of former president Hosni Mubarak challenged the existing Salafi status quo and presented a new reality. The Egyptian military authorities liberalised participation in the political process and shortly after the uprising an array of new parties had appeared. Existing constraints on public activities were lifted, at least informally. Moreover, the new authorities gradually released thousands of Egyptians affiliated to the Salafi radical milieu, including members and leaders of the IG and the JG. This opening of political opportunities thus presented many challenges and opportunities to the Salafi radical milieu, which was reflected in their ideational and organisational implications.

The first notable ideational challenge to the Salafi radical milieu pertained to the legitimacy of political violence in Muslim countries. This issue was a dividing line that had formerly affected the development of mainstream Salafism and its radical fringe. Before 2011, Egyptian Salafis consistently agreed that Islamic law should be comprehensively applied in Muslim countries, and their disagreement mainly consisted in the question of the legitimacy of using violence for reaching this outcome. The IG and the JG had historically legitimised the use of armed force to topple the regime, before renouncing this with the publication of their theological revisions in 2001 and 2007. The Salafi jihadi trend, on the other hand, was essentially defined by its support of armed violence against Muslim leaders who did not fully apply Islamic law. After 2011, however, its self-proclaimed representative in Egypt rebutted this claim and publicly announced that they would thenceforth only focus on public preaching. This new understanding of the legitimacy of political violence thus blurred this first division between mainstream and jihadi Salafism.

The delegitimisation of violence as a means to implement Islamic law in a Muslim country did not, however, comprehensively dissipate the use of violence in the Salafi discourse. The deterioration of the Syrian Civil War and the militarisation of a mostly non-violent uprising of the Syrian population gathered a significant sector of Egyptian Salafism behind the legitimisation of armed resistance to the regime of Bashar al-Asad. This support was reflected in the favourable public stance adopted by non-jihadi preachers and politicians, on television as well as in public demonstrations.[37] Paradoxically, while the renunciation of the use of violence in Egypt suggests that radical Salafis grew closer to mainstream Salafis, the Syrian War signalled that this rapprochement was not unidirectional, but led also to mainstream Salafis supporting the legitimisation of violence in other contexts.

The second main ideological challenge of the aftermath of the 2011 uprising concerned democracy and the legitimacy of political participation in the electoral process. In the past, the broadly defined Egyptian Salafi social movement family widely rejected democracy as a system of governance based on the sovereignty of the people.[38] This theological stance differentiated Salafis from many Islamist competitors, most prominently the Muslim Brotherhood. The Salafi position was further reinforced by the absence of free and fair elections in Egypt and by the official ban on religious political parties. After 2011, however, the political transition that followed the removal of Hosni Mubarak encouraged many sectors of the Salafi social movement to reconsider their position. Influenced by the Kuwaiti precedent and by the emergence of various Egyptian Islamist parties, many Salafi political parties mushroomed. Despite internal political divergences, most Salafis eventually legitimised participation in the political process.

These two ideational reconsiderations considerably affected the Salafi radical milieu after the 2011 uprising. The previous section demonstrated that the pre-2011 radical milieu was marked by its individualised and diffused networking topography and by the absence of internal structures that could regulate its ideational development. Being Salafi jihadi was primarily an ideational stance that did not necessarily entail a particular organisational belonging. This specificity signifies that the Salafi radical milieu was volatile and susceptible to external stimuli such as the Arab Spring. Discussions on political violence in Muslim countries and on the participation in the political process therefore transformed what it meant to be Salafi jihadi in Egypt. Field research has shown that, after 2011, Salafi jihadism broke up into three directions: the first group accepted the legitimacy of the political process as a means to implement Islamic law, and coalesced with mainstream Salafism. During the 2012 elections, many of its members supported the candidature of the Salafi preacher Hazem Abu Ismail. The second group maintained its theological rejection of the political process without excommunicating its proponents. The last group denounced political participation and excommunicated its advocates.

---

37. According to the author's field research.
38. See al-Anani and Malik 2013; Al-Anani 2012; Lacroix 2012; McCants 2012; Utvik 2014.

The apparition of new ideational divergences, combined with a relatively permissive political environment after 2011, was conducive to the transformation of the organisational make-up of Salafi networks. The new political environment was favourable to public demonstrations, which proliferated in support of the Syrian jihad and of the application of Islamic law in Egypt. Thousands of Salafis of all ideological persuasions conglomerated and paved the way for flourishing interactions between previously isolated individuals and trends. This synergy produced new formal and informal networks and groupings, including *ansar al-shari'a* (Partisans of Sharia), *al-haraka al-islamiya li tatbiq shar' Allah* (the Islamic Movement for the Application of God's Law), and *al-tayyar al-salafi al-jihadi* (the Salafi Jihadi Trend), among others. These labels do not refer to clearly defined entities but designate, rather, informal groups of Salafis who gathered after the 2011 uprising. In addition, the unity of the Salafi social movement family regarding the legitimacy of the Syrian Civil War, and its popularity among Salafi youths, led to the emergence of covert social networks. The relatively easy access to Syria through Turkey, and the willingness of many youths to join the armed opposition to Bashar al-Asad, led to the emergence of numerous informal networks in Egypt. These networks essentially facilitated the procurement of visas, passports, funds, and contacts abroad.

The post-2011 developments consequently demonstrate the vulnerability of the individualised Salafi radical milieu, which expanded non-relationally in the 2000s through new means of communication. In contrast to former IG and JG-related networks – which had some level of internal control over their respective milieus – the new Salafi jihadi milieu is characterised by the absence of internal control over its ideational and organisational development. The opening up of political opportunity, therefore, effectively transformed its defining characteristics. Political developments in Egypt switched the dividing line between jihadi and mainstream Salafis and led to the inclusion of a substantial share of the former in the latter. In addition, this relatively free environment promoted internal discussions and led to the development of new networks whose future cannot yet be ascertained.

Conclusion

The study of milieu is fundamental to the contextualisation of political violence. This object of study has nonetheless long been marginalised in the literature, despite its valuable contribution to the multi-level study of violent forms of contention. The radical milieu is defined as the social structures of supporters and sympathisers of insurgent and armed groups providing them with essential logistic and moral support. This chapter premised that the characteristics of the radical milieu could empower or obstruct militant groups' abilities to function and accomplish their tactical and strategic objectives.

This chapter explored the construction of the radical Salafi milieu in Egypt, with particular focus on the study of the evolution of its networking structures. It argued that the evolving topography of radical networks can be uncovered through the study of the diffusion of radical frames at the micro and meso levels.

The main argument was that different types of frame diffusion are aligned with different networking structures, and that specific networking structures have specific repercussions on the level of internal control over the ideological and organisational development of the radical milieu.

The chapter demonstrated that the radical milieu in Egypt expanded through two types of frame diffusion: the first type, in the 2000s, was essentially non-relational. Salafi jihadi frames were diffused through new means of communication, such as the Internet, and were individually adopted by newcomers to the radical milieu. This type of frame diffusion facilitated a faster and broader expansion of the radical milieu, which was nevertheless not subjected to any organisational internal control due to of the facultative embeddeness of its members. After the 2011 uprising, this radical milieu appeared to be strikingly susceptible to macro changes, such as an opening up of opportunity. In Egypt, it led to the redefinition of the essential characteristics of the radical milieu, both ideationally and organisationally.

The other type of frame diffusion in Egypt was essentially relational. In this case, relational diffusion designates the relational adoption of radical frames. This chapter has demonstrated that a study of relational diffusion necessitates the uncovering of the internal structures of radical networks, in order to assess the level of internal control over members of the radical milieu. The relevant factors pertain specifically to the type of ties present between the leaders of militant groups, between leaders and followers, and between the groups and their constituencies.

References

Abdo, G. (2002) *No God but God: Egypt and the Triumph of Islam*, Oxford: Oxford University Press.

al-Anani, K. (2012) 'Islamist parties post-Arab Spring', *Mediterranean Politics*, 17(3), 466–72.

al-Anani, K. and Malik, M. (2013) 'Pious way to politics: The rise of political Salafism in post-Mubarak Egypt', *Digest of Middle East Studies*, 22(1), 57–73.

Anas, A. (2002) *Walada Al-Afghan Al-'Arab Sira 'Abd Allah Anas Bayn Mas'ud Wa 'Abd Allah 'Azam*, London: Dar Al-Saqi.

Ansari, H. (1984) 'The Islamic militants in Egyptian politics', *International Journal of Middle East Studies*, 16(1), 123–44.

Ashour, O. (2009) *The De-Radicalization of Jihadists: Transforming Armed Islamist Movements*, Taylor & Francis e-Library.

Awwa, S. M. (2006) *Al-Jama'ah Al-Islamiyah Al-Musallahah Fi Misr, 1974–2004*, al-Qahirah: Maktabat al-Shuruq al-Dawliyah.

Benford, R., and Snow, D. A. (2000) 'Framing processes and social movements: An overview and assessment', *Annual Review of Sociology*, 26: 611–39.

Bloom, M. M. (2004) 'Palestinian suicide bombing: Public support, market share, and outbidding', *Political Science Quarterly*, 119(1), 61–88.

—— (2007) *Dying to Kill: The Allure of Suicide Terror*, New York: Columbia University Press.

Brachman, J. (2008) 'Leading Egyptian jihadist Sayyid Imam renounces violence', *CTC Sentinel*, 1(1), https://www.ctc.usma.edu/posts/leading-egyptian-jihadist-sayyid-imam-renounces-violence (accessed 20 May 2015)

Calvert, J. (2010) *Sayyid Qutb and the Origins of Radical Islamism*, New York: Columbia University Press.

Cozzens, J. B. (2009) 'Al-Takfir wa'l Hijra: Unpacking an enigma', *Studies in Conflict & Terrorism*, 32(6), 489–510.

Crenshaw, M. (1987) 'Theories of terrorism: Instrumental and organizational approaches', *Journal of Strategic Studies*, 10(4), 13–31.

della Porta, D. (1995) *Social Movements, Political Violence, and the State: A Comparative Analysis of Italy and Germany*, Cambridge: Cambridge University Press.

—— (2013) *Clandestine Political Violence*, Cambridge: Cambridge University Press.

Esposito, J. L. (1998) *Islam and Politics*, Syracuse: Syracuse University Press.

Faid, 'A. (2014) Al-Salafiyyun Fi Misr: Min Shari'a Al-Fatwa Ila Shari'a Al-Intikhabat in Nafi', B., al-Mawla, 'I & Taqiyya, A. *Al-Dhahira Al-Salafiyya Al-Ta'adudiyya Al-Tandhimiyya Wal-Siyasiyya*, Doha: Markaz Al-Jazeera Lil-Dirasat, pp.49–74.

Field, N., and Hamam, A. (2009) 'Salafi satellite TV in Egypt', *Arab Media and Society*, 8, 1–11.

Gerges, F. A. (2011) *The Rise and Fall of Al-Qaeda*, Oxford: Oxford University Press.

Haenni, P. (2005) *L'ordre des caïds: Conjurer la dissidence urbaine au Caire*, Paris: Karthala.

Hafez, M. M. (2003) *Why Muslims Rebel: Repression and Resistance in the Islamic World*, Boulder: Lynne Rienner Pub.

Hegghammer, T. (2009) 'Jihadi Salafis or revolutionaries? On religion and politics in the study of militant Islamism', in Meijer, R (ed.) *Global Salafism: Islam's new Religious Movement*, Oxford: Oxford University Press, pp. 244–66.

— (2010) *Jihad in Saudi Arabia: Violence and Pan-Islamism since 1979*, Cambridge: Cambridge University Press.

Hilsman, R. (1968) 'Two American Counter-strategies to Guerrilla Warfare: The Case of Vietnam' in Tang Tsou (ed.), *Crisis in China*, vol. 2, *China's Policies in Asia and America's Alternatives*, Chicago, IL: University of Chicago Press, pp. 269–70.

Ibrahim, S. E. (1982) 'Egypt's Islamic militants', *Merip Reports*, 103(2): 5–14.

— (1988) 'Egypt's Islamic activism in the 1980s', *Third World Quarterly*, 10(2), 632–57.

Jackson, R., Smyth, M., and Gunning, J. (2009) *Critical Terrorism Studies: A New Research Agenda*, New York: Taylor & Francis.

Johnston, H. and Noakes, J. A. (2013) *Frames of Protest: Social Movements and the Framing Perspective*, Lanham: Rowman & Littlefield Publishers.

Kalyvas, S. N. (2006) *The Logic of Violence in Civil War*, Cambridge: Cambridge University Press.

Kandil, H. (2013) *Soldiers, Spies and Statesmen: Egypt's Road to Revolt*, London: Verso Books.

Kepel, G. (1993) *Le Prophète et Pharaon: Aux sources des mouvements islamistes*, Paris: Seuil.

Lacroix, S. (2012) *Sheikhs and Politicians: Inside the New Egyptian Salafism*, Washington D. C.: Brookings Doha Center.

Lahoud, N. (2012) 'Beware of imitators: Al-Qa'ida through the lens of its confidential secretary', *New York: The Combating Terrorism Center at West Point*.

— (2013) 'Jihadi discourse in the wake of the Arab Spring', *New York: The Combating Terrorism Center at West Point*.

Lia, B. (2008) *Architect of Global Jihad: The Life of Al Qaeda Strategist Abu Mus'ab Al-Suri* (Reprint), New York: Columbia University Press.

Malthaner, S. (2011) *Mobilizing the Faithful: Militant Islamist Groups and their Constituencies*, Frankfurt: Campus.

— (2014) 'Contextualizing radicalization: The emergence of the 'Sauerland-Cell' from radical networks and the *Salafist* movement', *Studies in Conflict & Terrorism*, 37(8): 638–53.

McCants, W. (2012) 'The lesser of two evils: The Salafi turn to party politics in Egypt', *Brookings Middle East Memo*, (23): 1–7.

Meijer, R. (2007) 'Yūsuf al-'Uyairī and the making of a revolutionary Salafi praxis', *Die Welt Des Islams*, 47(3), 422–59.

—   (2009) *Global Salafism: Islam's New Religious Movement*, New York: Columbia University Press.

Moghadam, A. and Fishman, B. (2011) *Fault Lines in Global Jihad: Organizational, Strategic, and Ideological Fissures* (1st ed.), New York: Routledge.

Musallam, A. (2005) *From Secularism to Jihad: Sayyid Qutb and the Foundations of Radical Islamism*, Westport: Praeger.

Pape, R. (2006) *Dying to Win: The Strategic Logic of Suicide Terrorism*, New York: Random House Trade Paperbacks.

Rougier, B. (2008) *Qu'est-ce que le salafisme?*, Paris: Presses Universitaires de France.

Roy, O. (2012) 'The transformation of the Arab world', *Journal of Democracy*, 23(3), 5–18.

Ryan, M. W. S. (2013) *Decoding Al-Qaeda's Strategy: The Deep Battle Against America*, New York: Columbia University Press.

Sageman, M. (2004) *Understanding Terror Networks*, Philadelphia: University of Pennsylvania Press.

—   (2008) *Leaderless Jihad: Terror Networks in the Twenty-First Century*, Philadelphia: University of Pennsylvania Press.

Salah, M. (2001). *Waqai' Sanawat Al-Jihad: Rihla Al-Afghan Al-'Arab*, al-Qahirah: Khulud lil-Nashr.

Snow, D. A. (2014) 'The emergence, development, and future of the framing perspective: 25+ years since 'frame alignment'', *Mobilization: An International Journal*, 19(1), 23–45.

Snow, D. A. and Benford, R. (1988) 'Ideology, frame resonance, and participant mobilization', *International Social Movement Research*, 1(1): 197–217.

Snow, D. A., Rochford Jr., E. B., Worden, S. K. and Benford, R. (1986) 'Frame alignment processes, micromobilization, and movement participation', *American Sociological Review*, 51(4), 464–81.

Staniland, P. (2014) *Networks of Rebellion: Explaining Insurgent Cohesion and Collapse*, Ithaca, New York: Cornell University Press.

Tawil, C. (2011) *Brothers In Arms: The Story of al-Qa'ida and the Arab Jihadists*, London: Saqi Books.

Thompson, J. (2008) *A History of Egypt: From Earliest Times to the Present*, Harpswell: Anchor.

Toth, J. (2013) *Sayyid Qutb: The Life and Legacy of a Radical Islamic Intellectual*, Oxford: Oxford University Press.

Utvik, B. O. (2014) 'The Ikhwanization of the Salafis: Piety in the politics of Egypt and Kuwait', *Middle East Critique*, 23(1), 5–27.

Wagemakers, J. (2008) 'Framing the threat to Islam: Al-wala' wa al-bara' in Salafi discourse', *Arab Studies Quarterly*, 30(4), 1–22.

—   (2011) 'Protecting jihad: The Sharia council of the Minbar al-Tawhid wa-l-Jihad', *Middle East Policy*, 18(2), 148–62.

—   (2012) *A Quietist Jihadi: The Ideology and Influence of Abu Muhammad al-Maqdisi*, Cambridge: Cambridge University Press.

Waldmann, P. (2010) 'The radical milieu: The under-investigated relationship between terrorists and sympathetic communities', *Perspectives on Terrorism*, 9(2): 25–7.

Weinstein, J. M. (2007) *Inside Rebellion: The Politics of Insurgent Violence*, Cambridge: Cambridge University Press.

Wiktorowicz, Q. (2000) 'The Salafi movement in Jordan', *International Journal of Middle East Studies*, 32(2), 219–40.

— (2001) *The Management of Islamic Activism: Salafis, the Muslim Brotherhood, and State Power in Jordan*, New York: State University of New York Press.

— (2004) 'Framing jihad: Intramovement framing contests and al-Qaeda's struggle for sacred authority', *International Review of Social History*, 49(S12): 159–77.

— (2005) *Radical Islam Rising: Muslim Extremism in the West*, Lanham: Rowman & Littlefield Pub Inc.

— (2006) 'Anatomy of the Salafi movement', *Studies in Conflict & Terrorism*, 29(3), 207–39.

Wood, E. J. (2003) *Insurgent Collective Action and Civil War in El Salvador*, Cambridge: Cambridge University Press.

Zaman, M. Q. (2010) *The Ulama in Contemporary Islam: Custodians of Change*, Princeton: Princeton University Press.

Zollner, B. (2008) *The Muslim Brotherhood: Hasan al-Hudaybi and Ideology*, New York: Routledge.

Chapter Fourteen

The Radical Milieu and Mass Mobilisation in the Northern Ireland Conflict

Niall Ó Dochartaigh

This paper extends existing work on the radical milieu by examining the way in which relations between a militant group and its milieu are affected by transformations in the broader political context. Specifically, it examines how transformative events (Sewell 2005), the associated expansion of the radical milieu, and mass mobilisation into militant organisations serve to transform both milieu and militant groups.

Radical milieus are often characterised as the crucial supportive context from which violent militant challenges to the state emerge, serving also to sustain such challenges. Mass mobilisation is often characterised as an expansion and broadening of the radical milieu. This chapter emphasises, instead, how mass mobilisation challenges and disrupts existing radical milieus and militant organisations. It outlines the serious tensions between existing militant organisations and the newly expanded milieu, and explains how militant leaderships may even come to reject and oppose the mass mobilisation.

The chapter addresses these key questions through a study of a long established but politically marginal republican milieu in Ireland, and the process of mobilisation into militant Irish republican organisations from 1969 onwards. It outlines how a small and densely-networked radical milieu – and the militant organisation it sustained – responded to, and influenced, a mobilisation that stretched far beyond the tightly-drawn boundaries of that radical milieu, and how it was to a great extent driven by contingent transformative events. It begins by outlining the importance of the pre-existing milieu in providing organisational frameworks, dense social networks and interpretive frames that channelled and structured mass mobilisation. It moves on to analyse the ways in which those who were part of the existing radical milieu and of militant republican organisations adapted to this new context, examining the shaping force that mass mobilisation exerted on these organisations. It explains the paradoxical process by which leading segments of the original milieu rejected the mobilisation, finding themselves politically marginalised in key local centres of mobilisation as a consequence. Some of the most important militant republican leaders would ultimately reject the new mobilisation. By the 1980s, senior republican leaders – who had by then transformed the Official IRA and Official *Sinn Féin* into the Workers Party – would offer strong support for state efforts to repress the new militant groups. The chapter also looks at the way in which other segments of that pre-existing milieu and of the IRA adapted and repositioned themselves in response to the mass mobilisation.

The Irish republican/radical milieu before mass mobilisation

The radical republican milieu that existed in Ireland in the 1950s and 60s was small and politically marginal, but deeply-rooted, quite clearly defined, and marked by a great degree of continuity in terms of personnel and territorial concentrations of activism and support. It had its origins in the mid-1920s, when the vast majority of those in the republican movement decided to play a full part in the new Irish state and moved into mainstream electoral politics. At this point, a small rump of republicans continued to reject the legitimacy of the new Irish Free State on the basis that it was not a fully independent republic and that it comprised only twenty-six of Ireland's thirty-two counties. This rump organisation, consisting of both a political party – *Sinn Féin* – and an armed IRA, was from the beginning uneasily connected to forces on the left who sought to steer this rejectionist attitude to the Irish state in a socially radical direction. This was despite the fact that many in *Sinn Féin* and the IRA were strongly conservative (Patterson 1989). These organisations were embedded in a broader republican/radical political milieu that had significant cultural and social expression and involved a wider support base.

In territorial terms this milieu was a kind of archipelago, consisting of a number of small locally concentrated clusters of sympathy and support. The distribution of these territorial bases derived in part from local concentrations of radical and rejectionist republicanism that had been established during the Irish Civil War and consolidated into the 1920s. Thus, there were clusters of support in certain areas of the southern counties of Kerry and Cork where IRA violence had been most intense during the Irish War of Independence, and where civil war violence that pitted republicans against the Free State forces had been marked by its intensity and by reprisal killings (Coogan 1987: 61–2). There were clusters of support, too, in certain working-class areas of Dublin, from which key leaders and activists of the movement – such as Cathal Goulding – were drawn (Sweetman 1972: 135–48). Clusters of sympathy and support existed also in other areas, where prominent local figures had in the 1920s made the decision to continue to reject the treaty settlement, and in parts of the border counties of Leitrim, Louth, Donegal and Monaghan where proximity to the border and cross-border interaction with the security forces in Northern Ireland helped to sustain radical attitudes.

North of the Irish border this radical project faced not an Irish state but a pro-British Unionist regional government within the UK. South of the border rejectionist republicans were a marginal faction. North of the border, however, where the Catholic and nationalist community formed one third of the population, the Unionist government excluded all sections of this community from political power and republicans had quite a different relationship to the mainstream politics of the nationalist minority. They were not a tiny rejectionist rump, but part of the mainstream northern nationalist politics, a fact that was evident in the northern Nationalist Party's willingness to make occasional electoral pacts with them (Farrell 1980). A faction in the Northern IRA felt that the movement as a whole should recognise the Irish government and focus its efforts on ending partition rather than rejecting the independent Irish state. Some of them formed a breakaway group called *Saor Uladh* (Free Ulster). They launched armed attacks against security forces in the North in the 1950s but did not reject the authority of the Irish state (Bowyer Bell 1972: 302–3, 325–6). There was thus a certain disjuncture between the IRA south of the border – where it centred on key ideological positions that were rejected by the bulk of the Irish people – and north of the border, where its rejection of an exclusionary Unionist state continued to resonate with large sections of the nationalist minority. Subsequent tensions between the core leadership and the new mass mobilisation in the North derived in part from this disjuncture in the movement's relationship to the wider societal context in the two jurisdictions.

The small number of active republicans in the North operated, from the 1920s onwards, in a sympathetic milieu in the majority of the overwhelmingly Catholic and nationalist areas, including urban areas such as the Lower Falls in West Belfast, and Derry's Bogside. A supportive milieu also existed in rural areas with a strong republican tradition, such as East Tyrone and South County Derry.

The strong local presence in certain areas was reproduced and sustained through commemorations and parades that served to publicly assert and demonstrate the support for republicans in particular local spaces, at events such as the annual Easter commemorations of the 1916 Rising (Daly and O'Callaghan 2007; O'Callaghan and Daly 2007). Many of these events were held not in urban civic centres or in the most populous locations in the countryside but in areas where there was a supportive local milieu, including local neighbourhoods such as the Falls Road in Belfast and Derry's Bogside.

In addition to this, a number of important national commemorations drew people together from all over Ireland, notably the annual commemoration of eighteenth century republican rebel Wolfe Tone, at Bodenstown near Dublin. Particularly from the mid-1960s, this commemoration provided an occasion for groups from the radical left to parade alongside the republicans (Hanley and Millar 2010) and contributed to sustaining and reproducing a radical milieu on a national level, linking core members of the movement with sympathisers and activists from related organisations. For republicans scattered around the country it provided a chance to get a strong sense of a national milieu, rather than simply a locally supportive milieu. This milieu was sustained by key focal points for social interaction, including venues such as the Felons' Club (for republican ex-prisoners), and Dwyer's Gaelic Athletic Club on Belfast's Falls Road. In Dublin, republicans socialised in bars such as Slattery's on Capel Street, or O'Donoghue's on Merrion Row (Hanley and Millar 2010: 34, 82). Other venues identified with the movement were scattered around the country. These venues were associated with present or former members of the movement, but drew in a wider public that formed part of the republican and – in many cases – radical left-wing milieu, providing locations for the reproduction of a broader resistant republican identity beyond the formal organisations.

As the republican leadership built stronger links with the radical left, in the mid and late 1960s, this milieu expanded. It was also thickened up by the Wolfe Tone Societies which were established as a focus for intellectual exchange, drawing together radical republicans, communists, and others on the left, creating a new institutional focus for interaction (Bowyer Bell 1972: 402–9; English 2004: 82–92; Purdie 1990: 122–9).

This milieu had a complex relationship with violent militants. The IRA had, in 1956, launched an armed campaign against British sovereignty in Northern Ireland, calling it off in 1962 when they failed to gain significant support from northern nationalists. During the campaign – which saw four *Sinn Féin* candidates elected to the Irish parliament – the broader republican milieu had been important in the provision of safe houses, logistical support, and election campaigning (Bowyer Bell 1972; Coogan 1987). Even after the campaign ended the republican movement continued to reject the legitimacy of both the Irish government and of British sovereignty in the North. The IRA continued to recruit and train, and the movement reserved the right to deploy violence in pursuit of Irish self-determination, although it eschewed the use of violence against the security forces of the Irish state (Bowyer Bell 1972: 402–9; Hanley and Millar 2010: 58–60; Purdie 1990: 122–9). During this period, there were intermittent violent IRA attacks against property and in support of workers' strike action, including the 1968 bombing of an American-owned fishing trawler in the western port of Rossaveal, on the grounds that foreign-owned fishing vessels represented a threat to Irish fishermen (Hanley and Millar 2010: 66–7). Thus, even during this quiet period before the 1969 outbreak of violence in the North, this radical republican milieu was associated with a secretly organised militant organisation that continued to recruit and train its members in the use of arms and to carry out occasional attacks against property. The great majority of those in the milieu were not, however, members of the IRA, or even supporters of violent action. Many of the leaders who were most politically active in the mid and late 1960s had nonetheless been directly involved in the IRA campaign of the 1950s.

Over the course of the 1960s, the leadership of the republican movement built strong alliances on the left, with communists and Labour Party radicals. They shifted the emphasis of the movement from Irish sovereignty and reunification to social issues on both sides of the Irish border. They re-established the pre-eminence of a long-submerged tradition of socialist republicanism that had first been asserted in the 1930s (Bowyer Bell 1972: 402–9; Hanley and Millar 2010: 27–32; Patterson 1989). Several vehicles for cooperation between republicans and others on the left were established during the 1960s, broadening the republican milieu by drawing in activists who were primarily concerned with social change. New Housing Action Committees in Derry, Belfast, and Dublin agitated on housing issues and brought together Labour Party, communist, and republican activists who in some cases used tactics of civil disobedience, including sit-downs and direct resistance to evictions (Purdie 1990: 122–9; Hanley and Millar 2010; Ó Dochartaigh 2004). Another key organisation was the Northern Ireland Civil Rights Association. It aimed to create pressure for reform and an end to police repression in the North. It had a broad base and the republicans neither dominated nor controlled it. Nonetheless, the idea for the civil rights association originated in internal republican discussions on alliance-building and on ways to exert political pressure for change, and they played a key role in its establishment (Bosi 2006, 2007, 2008; Maney 2008, 2012; De Fazio 2009; Purdie 1990; Hanley and Millar 2010: 85–6). IRA units were directed towards housing activism and direct action on social issues and away from the 'mindless militarism' of armed campaigns against state forces. When the Housing Action Committees and the civil rights movement took to the streets, members of the IRA played key roles in both. For example, an internal IRA report states that the majority of those who resisted an eviction in Derry, in 1967, were IRA members (Ó Dochartaigh 1999). When the first civil rights marches began, IRA members acted as stewards and took part in banned marches, and young republicans were among the first people to be arrested for staging sit-down protests (Hanley and Millar 2010: 84–6, 103; Ó Dochartaigh 1999; Purdie 1990: 122–9). They also took part in the squatting of houses in both Irish jurisdictions. Despite the fact that this activism did not involve armed attacks on the state, it was directly connected to the IRA's tradition of illegal, direct action. The fact that IRA members were willing to break the law and run the risk of being arrested made them a significant resource for the civil rights movement, which pursued a strategy of civil disobedience. The important point is that, throughout the 1960s, when republicans were cooperating with forces on the left and while they had rejected the 'mindless militarism' of the 1950s campaign, they nonetheless remained distinctive in their willingness to use physical force, break the law, and challenge and confront state forces through direct action. The movement did not, during this period, reject the use of force but they sought to redirect it towards social activism and the pursuit of political reform (Bowyer Bell 1972, 402–9; Hanley and Millar 2010: 58–9; Patterson 1989: 84–110; Purdie 1990: 122–9).

When violence broke out around some of the early civil rights marches, and when this was followed by rioting and – ultimately – by a sustained campaign of violent action by the Provisional IRA that would last for more than thirty years, it seemed obvious to many that the crisis had been generated by this radical milieu.[1] Many unionists argued strongly that the radical and republican milieu, and the organisations that it sustained, were the central cause of the violence (Purdie 1988). Indeed, the strongest intellectual critics of the Provisional IRA argued that the violence was crucially connected to the existence of a broader sympathetic republican and nationalist milieu that was 'ambiguous' about violence. Figures such as Conor Cruise O'Brien indicted those who formed this mileu as much as he indicted the IRA itself, and saw the solution to the violence in condemning sympathisers and those who expressed solidarity, marginalising and isolating anyone who formed part of a broader supportive milieu (O'Brien 1972). People living in districts where the IRA was strong came to be regarded as tainted by, and responsible for, violence. According to this analysis, the central cause of violent conflict was a culture of extremism and violence embodied in organisations and facilitated by a wider supportive milieu.

---

1. The Provisional IRA broke away from the Official IRA in 1970 on the basis that the leadership of the movement was not militant enough and had failed to 'defend' nationalist areas of Belfast.

Within a few years of the outbreak of the conflict, many of the pivotal figures who had been at the heart of the milieu in the mid 1960s had become fierce critics of the Provisional IRA's campaign of violence, denouncing them as 'terrorists' and accusing them of 'vicious sectarian nationalism' (Hanley and Millar 2010: 394, 498). South of the Irish border, a large proportion of those involved in the republican activism of the mid-1960s would become ever more critical of republican violence in the North. The Official Republican movement would ultimately offer strong support for repression of the IRA by the British Army and the RUC, while continuing to assert its republican credentials and fealty to the tradition of radical republicanism (Hanley and Millar 2010: 387). They included figures such as Cathal Goulding and Sean Garland, who had themselves taken part in earlier IRA campaigns and who had, in the 1960s, been central to this milieu. In condemning the Provisional IRA and opposing an armed campaign to reunite Ireland, they did not reject the use of revolutionary violence in principle, continuing to argue that it would ultimately be necessary for overthrowing capitalism.

It is widely assumed that a radical milieu is crucial for the emergence and sustaining of a campaign of political violence, but this alienation and opposition between core components of the radical republican milieu in Ireland in the 1960s, and the mass mobilisation into violence at the end of that decade, calls the nature of this relationship into question. It indicates that mass mobilisation into violence, rather than simply emerging from a milieu, can be a source of extreme tension between newly mobilised activists and their supporters on the one hand, and those who constitute the original organisation and milieu on the other.

Crisis and mobilisation

Mass mobilisation was initially generated by the civil rights marches of late 1968, during which there were violent confrontations with the police force in the North. This brought the issue of repression and the relationship between the state and the minority nationalist community to the top of the agenda (Ó Dochartaigh 2004). Repression and unionist domination of the northern state became the central focus for the movement. This broad mobilisation among the nationalist minority saw increased support for the republican movement in the North, particularly because republicans had been active and prominent in the civil rights campaign. Prior to 1969, the republican Easter parades in Derry and Belfast had generally been small – occasionally tiny – events, but the Derry Easter parade of 1969 attracted thousands of people (Ó Dochartaigh 2013). This fact points to a dramatic expansion of the supportive milieu for republicans in Derry and in Belfast. The continuities with the civil rights marches were very important in this regard. The civil rights movement had mobilised a population that had been politically quiescent for decades. Once mobilised, many people were willing to offer some support to the republican movement because, like the civil rights movement, it was a strong oppositional force seeking to exert pressure on the state.

The Easter marches of 1970 were just as large as those in 1969, bringing thousands onto the streets. They now included large numbers of uniformed members of the republican Scouting and Girl Guide organisations, indicating a significant influx of new members (Ó Dochartaigh 2013). At this stage, neither wing of the republican movement had begun a violent campaign, and the extensive participation in the marches did not represent endorsement of such a campaign. It is important to note, too, that many of those who joined the Scouting wing of the movement never progressed to membership of the IRA. Nonetheless, the numbers demonstrate that the civil rights mobilisation and the associated disorder on the streets had generated an unprecedented mass mobilisation into the republican organisations. It also indicated that the expanded milieu remained intensely localised in the urban working-class areas and the rural areas where it had previously existed in much weaker form.

The pre-existing republican milieu and organisations decisively structured this new mobilisation in many ways. They provided organisational structures for people to join, arranged events and marches where people could show support, and – most importantly – set out a political vision and ideological analysis that seemed to provide a clear and straightforward programme for transformative political change. But by the mid 1970s, just a few years after the Official Republican leadership had led a march of thousands through the streets of Derry, their support in the city had dwindled to almost nothing. Those who controlled the pre-existing leadership and structures, and who had been at the centre of the radical milieu, and had benefited most from this initial wave of enthusiasm and mobilisation, had by this time become almost completely alienated and detached from the newly expanded milieu.

Pre-existing structures and milieu were important, but even more important in shaping the mobilisation and this newly expanded milieu was the contemporary political context for mobilisation: the sense of an opening in the political opportunity structure, and the increasing hostility and confrontation between state security forces and young nationalists on the streets. This context created pressures that would ultimately overwhelm those who had dominated the movement in the 1960s. In a sense, this new mobilisation displaced – as much as it augmented – the existing radical republican milieu.

New milieu, new movement

> Sometime in the autumn of 1971, I opened the front door of Patsy Murphy's house in Hatch Place [in Dublin] to find Cathal Goulding, the chief of staff of the Official IRA, standing there. He asked could he come in and talk [...] I ushered him in. He wanted to know about the men in the Derry branch of his army. Their numbers had grown considerably, and he had no idea who the new men were or what they were like. (Dublin-based journalist Nell McCafferty, originally from Derry, cited in White 2006: 250–2)

Long a marginal and cloistered tradition, the republican movement experienced an expansion, both in formal membership and in the supportive milieu over the course of 1969 and early 1970. In August 1969, in Belfast, disturbances escalated to shootings in which several people died, and there was large-scale sectarian rioting in which nationalist minority areas came under attack. This led to much broader support for the use of weapons for defensive purposes. After British troops were deployed that same month they gradually came into conflict with nationalists on the streets and radicalisation spread further into nationalist rural and urban areas that had been quiet up until then.

The expansion of the republican milieu was generated by direct experience of confrontation with the state; by the widespread sentiment that the republican movement was necessary for the defence of nationalist areas, both against state forces and loyalist sectarian attacks; and by the sense of the political opportunity afforded by a historic crisis in which there was the possibility of transformation of the political system that marginalised and excluded the nationalist minority. Importantly, mass mobilisation and the expansion of the supportive milieu took place before republicans launched armed campaigns against the state. This newly expanded milieu would help to set the pace and shape the form of those campaigns. The contrast with the previous IRA campaign in the 1950s is instructive. In 1956 the IRA's national leadership had launched Operation Harvest, a centrally organised and coordinated attack on security forces in the North, deploying volunteers from all over Ireland, most of them operating outside their home areas (Bowyer Bell 1972; Coogan 1987). The campaign was planned, initiated, and eventually called off by the leadership. The crucial decisions in relation to the campaign were made by a national leadership whose main constituency was the IRA membership. Those members, in turn, were part of a small radical milieu that was tightly clustered around the organisational structures of the movement. The escalation and termination of the campaign were both under the direct control of the national leadership.

The mass mobilisation of 1969 and 1970, however, was so extensive and so driven by circumstances beyond the control of the republican leadership that it quickly created forces that stretched beyond their control. A small radical milieu that had supported a marginal and relatively ineffective armed organisation had been swamped by a new mass mobilisation and a massively expanded supportive milieu. The pre-existing radical milieu and organisation gave shape to the new mobilisation and tried hard to assimilate it to existing organisational goals. But it was not in control of it and it presented major challenges to the movement. The new milieu expanded in such a way that the bulk of those who had been mobilised turned against the leadership who had led the movement in the 1960s and who had been at the centre of the republican and radical milieu prior to mass mobilisation.

The escalating violence in the North generated a flood of recruits for the movement, but as contextual factors generated pressure for intensified action it became impossible for the movement to hold on to them. The new context and the new milieu generated pressure on the movement in two ways. The first was through processes of competitive escalation. The context of a wider crisis of authority generates pressure for intensified violent action that organisations cannot afford to ignore because, if they do, these newly mobilised activists will help to strengthen opposing organisations that draw on the same recruitment pool. In large part as a consequence of these pressures the IRA leadership in 1969 recruited heavily for the IRA, stockpiled arms, trained, and prepared to act in defence and retaliation, moving much closer towards an offensive armed campaign than the core leadership group had ever intended to. We can see this intensified militarisation and movement towards an armed campaign and expansion of the IRA in 1969 and the early 1970s as a development driven to a great extent by the new mass mobilisation.

Many within the movement itself were critical of the leadership's slow response to the escalating violence, and its perceived incompetence in deploying physical force. In late 1969, an alliance of disgruntled republicans – drawing together some who had stayed within the movement but were uneasy with its moves towards electoral politics and Marxism, and others who had dropped out of the movement after the 1950s campaign – established a Provisional IRA and Provisional *Sinn Féin*, and claimed the mantle of the Republican movement. They were dissatisfied with the leadership's hesitant and cautious approach to the mass mobilisation and the violence on the streets. They aimed to take a much more assertive approach, to arm and expand in order to protect nationalist urban areas against state forces and loyalists, but also to try to use the crisis to advance the goal of a united Ireland. They became the chief competitors to those who remained with the Official movement.

This new organisation was much more open to the newly mobilised youth. Although its key leaders were firmly embedded in the existing republican radical milieu, it was the context of escalating violence, mass mobilisation, and rapid political change that impelled them in this more militant direction. The fact that this new faction was oriented to the changed context, and saw the new mobilisation as a resource rather than a problem to be managed and restrained, made them more attractive to many of those who had been newly mobilised. Thus, Martin McGuinness, whose family was not part of the existing republican milieu, initially joined the Official IRA. Finding that they were hesitant to provide weapons or carry out attacks, he moved to the Provisional IRA, becoming a key leadership figure (Bishop and Mallie 1988: 155–6).

This put pressure for increased militancy on the Official Republican leadership. But even the Provisional IRA found itself subject to significant shaping pressures from this newly mobilised milieu. They too found the violence moving beyond their control and escaping the intentions and aims of the leadership.

New recruits within the movement also applied pressure for intensified action. One new recruit in Derry recalled how they repeatedly pressed their reluctant commander to allow them to escalate their attacks, and defied his authority (O'Doherty 1993). When, in 1971, the president of Provisional *Sinn Féin* offered a mild rebuke to IRA units who had fired at workers coming from a factory where the workforce was predominantly Protestant, he was sharply rebuked by the Belfast IRA (White 2006: 180–1). When, also in 1971, the IRA chief of staff Sean MacStiofain went to meet volunteers in Belfast he sought to exert his authority and assert the position of the national leadership by disciplining an IRA volunteer for losing his weapon. The assembled volunteers effectively mutinied, saying they would resign en masse if the penalty was enforced. The chief of staff was forced to back down (Bradley and Feeney 2009: 107–8). These tensions were even more intense within the Official IRA where one prominent militant Belfast IRA member, Joe McCann, was repeatedly called to disciplinary hearings but simply ignored the attempts by the IRA hierarchy to control his actions (Hanley and Millar 2010: 173). One senior IRA member who operated north and south of the border, in counties Tyrone and Kerry, respectively, has outlined how, in the early 1970s, the traditionalist founders of the Provisional IRA in those two areas were pushed aside by younger and more radical members frustrated by the reluctance to escalate (O'Callaghan 1999: 73, 115).

The extent of the popular radicalisation in northern nationalist areas in the early 1970s is well captured by the comment of one British army journalist reporting on a working-class nationalist area in 1974. He wrote that 'every man, woman and child seem to object to the presence of the army' and that 'friendly contact with the local people is virtually non-existent' (Ó Dochartaigh 1997: 288). This broad-based radicalisation created a much wider supportive milieu for the IRA than had ever existed before, but in the process the movement itself was transformed and had to adapt to the demands of this new support pool.

The tension between this newly expanded milieu and the republican leadership figures who had emerged from the pre-existing milieu is strikingly expressed in an appeal to the Provisional IRA Army Council, written by a republican Women's Action Committee in West Belfast as violence began to intensify in the spring of 1971. IRA members were under strict orders to refuse to recognise the jurisdiction of the courts in order to assert the illegitimacy of the jurisdictions created by the partition settlement. Recognising a court was a serious disciplinary offence. One consequence of this was that IRA members were being jailed because they could not contest the charges brought against them. The authors of the letter emphasised the disastrous effect of this insistence on political principle, stating that,

> We recognise the principles on which the Republican movement is founded but nevertheless feel that this policy of non-recognition in these times is really ineffective and is considered by the general public [i.e. the nationalist community] as playing into the hands of the enemy.

They also emphasised that the new supportive milieu could not be taken for granted and warned that:

> The whims of people are unpredictable [...] and support readily and easily given to a justifiable cause can just as swiftly be withdrawn. Always remember that not every supporter of the Movement is a Republican.[2]

---

2.   Daithí Ó Conaill Papers, in the Seán O'Mahony Papers, MS 44, 169/4, National Library of Ireland.

That is, the new expanded milieu was quite different from the more ideologically committed milieu of the previous decades. This applied to the newly expanded Official IRA as well. Hanley and Millar (2010: 175), for example, report the story that 'when one Official [IRA] prisoner was told to go to an education class, he responded: "Education for fucking what? I joined to defend my area and you told me I could."'

This new milieu was supportive of the IRA in a context of large-scale violence on the streets and attacks both from the army and from loyalists. It was not concerned with the finer points of republican ideological purity. Motivated by opposition to state repression and the need for defence they pressured the movement towards altering ideological positions in order to combat the state more effectively.

One other sphere in which the movement adapted to this newly expanded milieu was in the maintenance of internal order. As time progressed, the Provisional IRA became involved in the punishment of suspected criminals through beatings, shootings, and expulsions. This was to a great extent driven by local demand (Collins and McGovern 1997; Moloney 2002: 152–3) and was a significant innovation for the IRA, one that diluted the organisation's primary function of attacking the state. These expanded functions were a direct result of expansion in the supportive milieu, which then produced pressures for the IRA to maintain social order in the absence of state security forces.

A leadership rejecting mass mobilisation

The most striking aspect of this expanded milieu is its relationship to the Official Republican leadership – those who had been the driving force and the ideological heart of the movement in the years immediately preceding mass mobilisation. The key leadership figures in this group did not join the Provisionals, and a large proportion of key IRA commanders on the ground stayed with the Official movement too. This Official leadership took a very cautious approach to the use of violence but as conflict escalated in the early 1970s they authorised its use for defence and retaliation against the British Army. The leadership took the earliest opportunity it could to call an indefinite ceasefire in 1972. While the Official IRA would be active in feuds with the Provisionals, and remained a significant armed force in nationalist areas, they would never resume a campaign against state forces. Instead, they increasingly directed their political energies and animosity against the Provisionals. They characterised the Provisional IRA as sectarian and motivated by Catholic communalism, and argued that it was not Republican at all, but the descendant of the conservative, right-wing populist Catholic communal politicians who had been the chief opponents of radical republicanism within the nationalist community in Belfast.

The fact that the Officials ended up on the furthest margins of political life in the North and were completely overshadowed by the Provisionals should not obscure the fact that a large proportion of those at the core of the radical republican milieu prior to 1969 remained active in the Officials, and steered the development of the movement. It was in this sense a more direct descendant of the radical republican milieu of the mid 1960s than the Provisional IRA was. Renaming the party *Sinn Féin* the Workers' Party, and then the Workers' Party, the Official Republicans progressed from a policy that was hostile to both the British state and the Provisionals to a policy that identified violent Provisional republicanism as the central political problem afflicting northern society. The Workers' Party eventually muted all criticism of state security forces, endorsed the criminalisation of republican prisoners (including members of the Official IRA), and offered full support to British security forces on the grounds that 'it was only the state forces which could defeat provisionalism' (Seán Garland, quoted in Hanley and Millar 2010: 387). The paradoxical outcome was that an important core element in the radical milieu moved to a position that was ferociously critical of this mass mobilisation and almost completely alienated from the massively expanded militant milieu. The importance of this wing of the movement is reflected in the fact that it built a small but energetic and successful political party south of the Irish border. In the Republic of Ireland their electoral support completely dwarfed that of their former compatriots in the Provisionals. South of the border the Workers' Party was not an insignificant rump of the pre-1969 movement but a core element that successfully expanded. North of the border, however, the Official movement's position of increasingly uncritical support for the state saw them grow more and more isolated from the broader militant republican milieu. Frustrated with the leadership, the great majority of its militant activists in the North broke away in 1974 to form a splinter group, the INLA. When, in 1980 and 1981, the Provisional IRA and the INLA launched hunger strikes aimed at securing changes in prison conditions, many Official Republicans in the North supported the hunger strikers and significant numbers of them moved from the Officials to the Provisionals as a direct consequence (Hanley and Millar 2010). As the Official Republican leadership became increasingly distant from the militant mood in the wider republican milieu, its support in the North declined to vanishing point. Former IRA members, former internees, and key leadership figures from the mid and late 1960s – such as Tomás MacGiolla, Proinsias de Rossa, Eamon Smullen, Seán Garland, Des O'Hagan and Cathal Goulding – went on to be active and prominent within the Workers' Party. But they were now almost entirely detached from that powerful and extensive militant republican milieu in the North. This produced the paradox of a radical leadership that rejected, and was alienated from, the mass mobilisation.

Conclusion: Extending the model

Malthaner and Waldmann (2014) have recently emphasised the dynamic character of the relationship between milieu and militant groups while also touching on the connections between this relationship and changes in the wider environment:

> Radical milieus are not static but dynamic, constantly re-negotiated relational formations that are transformed over the course of violent conflicts. The

processes in which they emerge and evolve are shaped, in particular, by interactions with their wider political and societal environment, on the one side, and by relations with the violent group, on the other side.

Despite this acknowledgement of the wider context, research on milieu has tended to focus on the relationship between milieu and militant organisations. This chapter suggests that the dynamics of this relationship are shaped by the wider context in unexpected ways. A broader political crisis can abruptly expand a pre-existing radical milieu and militant organisation to the extent that the original milieu and organisation are transformed and, to a certain extent, overwhelmed. Newly mobilised activists and the people who form the newly expanded milieu bring with them motivations and demands that arise directly from the context of mass mobilisation. Their demands and preferences can create severe tensions with the existing leadership. Rather than simply reinforcing existing organisations and the existing milieu, the expanded milieu can challenge and transform them. The Irish case indicates that mass mobilisation can present an existential challenge to existing radical organisations, producing pressures to abandon core elements of their long-term programmes, pressures for escalation that spins out of the leadership's control, and the creation of a newly radicalised mass force that moves decisively beyond the influence and control of the original leadership.

Given that mass mobilisation is often crucial in providing political openings for militant organisations, and given that small radical milieus usually exist prior to mass mobilisation, the transformation of existing milieus and militant groups through mass mobilisation is arguably the most important aspect of the relationship between militants, milieu and context. We need only think of recent mass mobilisations in Libya, Egypt and Syria to appreciate just how ubiquitous this pattern is. In all of these cases transformative events and the associated mass mobilisation expanded a pre-existing radical Islamist milieu and militant organisations. In all three cases mobilisation escaped the control of pre-existing groups and threw up important new forces.

Future research might focus more sharply on the way in which mass mobilisation transforms, disrupts, and challenges the existing radical milieu and militant organisations. It would treat mass mobilisation as a site of intense struggle and tension, tracing the dynamics and outcomes of the struggles between the newly mobilised militants and the newly expanded milieu on the one hand, and the older milieu and militant organisations on the other. In this regard, both spatial and temporal aspects of mass mobilisation are crucial. Generational tensions between those who were active and sympathetic prior to mass mobilisation and those who mobilise in the context of a political crisis show the importance of temporal factors in shaping the relationship between milieu and militant organisations. Mass mobilisation also tends to intensify the territorialisation of the radical milieu, thus changing the balance between powerful local identities and the ideological positions advanced by the national leaderships of militant organisations.

References

Bishop, P. and Eamonn M. (1988) *The Provisional IRA,* London: Corgi.

Bosi, L. (2006) 'The dynamics of social movement development: Northern Ireland's civil rights movement in the 1960s', *Mobilization: An International Quarterly,* 11(1): 81–100.

— (2007) 'Social movement participation and the 'timing' of involvement: The case of the Northern Ireland civil rights movement', *Research in Social Movements, Conflicts and Change,* 27: 37–61.

— (2008) 'Explaining the emergence process of the civil rights protest in Northern Ireland (1945–1968): Insights from a relational social movement approach', *Journal of Historical Sociology,* 21(2–3): 242–71.

Bowyer Bell, J. (1972) *The Secret Army: A History of the IRA, 1915–1970,* London: Sphere Books.

Bradley, G. and Feeney, B. (2009) *Insider: Gerry Bradley's Life in the IRA,* Dublin: O'Brien Press.

Collins, E. and MacGovern, M. (1997) *Killing Rage,* London: Granta.

Coogan, T. P. (1987) *The IRA* (tenth impression), London: Fontana.

Daly, M. E. and O'Callaghan, M. (2007) *1916 in 1966: Commemorating the Easter Rising,* Dublin: Royal Irish Academy.

De Fazio, G. (2009) 'Civil rights mobilization and repression in Northern Ireland: A comparison with the US deep South', *The Sixties,* 2(2): 163–85.

Doherty, S.P. (1993) *The Volunteer: A former IRA man's true story,* London: Fount.

English, R. (2004) *Armed Struggle: The History of the IRA,* London: Pan.

Farrell, M. (1980) *Northern Ireland: The Orange State,* London: Pluto.

Hanley, B. and Millar, S. (2010) *The Lost Revolution: The Story of the Official IRA and the Workers' Party,* London: Penguin.

Malthaner, S. and Waldmann, P. (2014) 'The radical milieu: Conceptualizing the supportive social environment of terrorist groups', *Studies in Conflict & Terrorism,* 37(12): 979–98.

Maney, G. M. (2008) 'From civil war to civil rights and back again: The interrelation of rebellion and protest in Northern Ireland, 1955–1972', *Research in Social Movements, Conflicts and Change,* 27: 3–35.

— (2012) 'The paradox of reform: The civil rights movement in Northern Ireland', *Research in Social Movements, Conflicts and Change,* 34: 3–26.

Moloney, E. (2002) *A Secret History of the IRA,* London: Penguin.

O'Brien, C. C. (1972) *States of Ireland,* London: Hutchinson.

O'Callaghan, M. (2007) 'From Casement Park to Toomebridge: The commemoration of the Easter Rising in Northern Ireland in 1966', in M. O'Callaghan and M. E. Daly (eds) *1916 in 1966,* Dublin: Royal Irish Academy, pp. 86–147.

O' Callaghan, M. and Daly, M. E. (eds) (2007) *1916 in 1966,* Dublin: Royal Irish Academy.

O'Callaghan, S. (1999) *The Informer,* London: Corgi.

Ó Dochartaigh, N. (1999) 'Housing and conflict: Social change and collective action in Derry in the 1960s', in G. O'Brien (ed.) *Derry and Londonderry: History and Society,* Dublin: Geography Publications, pp. 625–46.

—   (2004) *From Civil Rights to Armalites: Derry and the Birth of the Irish Troubles,* expanded 2nd edn., Basingstoke/New York: Palgrave Macmillan.

—   (2013) 'Images from the inside: Michael Rodgers' photographs of the civil rights campaign and the birth of the troubles in Derry', *Field Day Review,* 9: 74–99.

Patterson, H. (1989) *The Politics of Illusion: A Political History of the IRA,* London: Hutchinson Radius.

Purdie, B. (1988) 'Was the civil rights movement a Republican/Communist conspiracy?', *Irish Political Studies,* 3(1): 33–41.

—   (1990) *Politics in the Streets,* Belfast: Blackstaff Press.

Sewell, W. H. (2005) *Logics of History: Social Theory and Social Transformation,* Chicago: University of Chicago Press.

Sweetman, R. (1972) *On Our Knees: Ireland 1972,* London: Pan.

Waldmann, P. (2008) 'The radical milieu: The under-investigated relationship between terrorists and sympathetic communities', *Perspectives on Terrorism,* 2(9): 25–7.

White, R. W. (2006) *Ruairí Ó Brádaigh: The Life and Politics of an Irish Revolutionary,* Bloomington: Indiana University Press.

Chapter Fifteen

From Legitimation to Rejection of Violence: The Shifting Stance of the Radical Milieu in Italy during the 1970s

Luca Falciola

Theories of the radical milieu emphasise that armed organisations depend heavily on their constituencies for moral and practical sustenance. Active supporters and sympathisers contribute to shaping identities, defining incentives, and establishing norms of expected behaviours. Research shows that the radical milieu's impact on the dynamics of violence is ambivalent (Malthaner and Waldmann 2014). On the one hand, it may contribute to processes of radicalisation and escalation of violence, but on the other, it can also generate de-radicalising and de-escalating outcomes. Specifically, studies suggest that the radical milieu usually exerts 'a moderating influence on assessments of the political consequences and moral costs of escalating conflict processes' (Neidhardt 2011: 435). In other words, the radical milieu can act as a connector between the armed groups' far-reaching strategies and people's more realistic expectations.

However, the nature and the extent of the ties between armed groups and radical milieu are still uncharted territory. Only a few empirical studies have explored such interactions in depth (Waldmann 2006). Scholarly attention has mainly focused on the processes of recruitment within contentious social networks (della Porta 1988), or on community engagement for counterterrorism (Spalek 2014). Moreover, the literature has failed to explain whether and how the radical milieu can shift its perspective from supporting violence to rejecting it, or vice versa. Yet, given the milieu's transformative power over armed fringes, the question is both empirically significant and policy-relevant.

To achieve a better understanding of the relationship between violent fringes and radical milieu, the present research investigates the following two aspects: 1) the conditions under which the radical milieu is likely to encourage violence in armed groups, and the way this support is both expressed and perceived, and 2) which factors may foster a change of orientation within the radical milieu and drive it towards a more critical attitude *vis-à-vis* violence.

This chapter analyses the case of Italian leftist armed groups of the 1970s and their supportive environment. During this period, armed vanguards perpetrated hundreds of attacks against people and property (della Porta and Rossi 1984) in the absence of explicit criticism from their milieu. However, after a few years of encouragement and silent endorsement, the radical milieu increasingly perceived violence as negative and threatening, progressively withdrawing its legitimation and support. Yet, this shift materialised too late to be directly decisive, since leftist armed groups – sustained for a long time – had already caused a heavy death toll and were fighting a self-referential war against state apparatuses.

The intensity of revolutionary violence in Italy stands out against other Western developed countries (Sánchez-Cuenca 2009). The two main leftist clandestine organisations seeking a radical political change through proletarian armed struggle were the Red Brigades and Front Line. A wide array of smaller groups, sharing the same goals, also contributed to disseminating violence across time and space. Neo-fascist groups further propelled the levels of civil strife by means of indiscriminate attacks on civilians and street fights with leftist militants. The Christian Democratic Party (DC) represented the keystone of the 'system of power' under attack, but the Italian Communist Party (PCI), which gradually extended its institutional responsibilities during the 1970s, also played a pivotal role. The cycle of contention as a whole emerged around 1968 and substantially declined after 1982.

The first part of this chapter demonstrates the extent to which the legitimation of political violence in the Italian context was widespread, enduring, and resilient. It also provides evidence that armed groups were embedded in a dense web of relations with their constituencies, which offered decisive incentives for the escalation. The research focuses on three main areas that were particularly tied to armed vanguards: the student movement, the communist workers, and the radical intellectuals.

In the second part, the chapter analyses the cognitive shift through which the radical milieu came to perceive violence as undesirable, eventually rejecting it. The research shows that such a change of perspective resulted from an incremental process entailing both emotional experiences and rational considerations. The chapter identifies four key traumatic events and four main logical arguments that elicited discussion on the meaning and effectiveness of violence. The research finally demonstrates that the timing and non-linearity of this process jeopardised the moderating capacities of the radical milieu.

The chapter offers a historical analysis of the still under-investigated Italian radical milieu. The research draws on a wide range of primary sources: radical magazines and documents (mainly from the Feltrinelli Foundation collection), Italian Communist Party archives, and militants' memoirs. The radical milieu included both the so-called Old and New Left, i.e., the political spectrum from the PCI to Autonomia Operaia, whose borders with armed groups were porous. The main arenas of leftist debates were systematically analysed, with specific regard to the period 1977–9, which represents the turning point of the evolution of the role of the radical milieu.

Studying the radical milieu

This chapter adopts Malthaner and Waldmann's (2014) definition of radical milieu as indicating the 'immediate social environment' that provides armed groups with moral and logistical support. The milieu shares 'experiences, symbols, narratives, and frameworks of interpretation' with violent fringes and their respective social networks are interlinked.

More specifically, armed groups see themselves as representing this population and fighting on its behalf. It gives 'meaning and legitimacy' to their political program and violent means. From the radical milieu violent militants derive symbolic and material resources. On the one hand, normative standards, moral sustenance, and solidarity. On the other hand, recruits, money, weapons, shelter, legal aid, and information. However, I believe, with Malthaner (2011: 39–51), that legitimacy and moral support are much more relevant to urban contemporary armed groups than is material help, 'and their withdrawal could prove even more devastating'. Indeed, in the Italian context, multiple testimonies confirm this necessity of constant approval and solidarity by the radical milieu. Although armed vanguards were theoretically supposed to 'force the situation' and introduce 'a step forward' regardless of the legitimation of the masses (Novelli and Tranfaglia 1988: 251–2), militants belonging to violent organisations were constantly monitoring the attitude and judgment of the milieu. As a result, they extracted incentives for their actions and (re)oriented their strategies and means accordingly. Hence, this chapter focuses primarily on symbolic resources, ranging from explicit support and vocal endorsement to silent complicity.

If the radical milieu influences armed fringes, the opposite is also true. The milieu is equally sensitive to this interaction and modifies both its judgment and attitude *vis-à-vis* violent groups over time. As a consequence, the research employs a diachronic and relational analysis. Although different Italian armed groups addressed slightly different social environments, and since the latter also changed over time, the research – for the sake of generalisation – glosses over these nuances. Yet, the reader should bear in mind that the radical milieu is internally differentiated and its boundaries are in constant evolution.

There is a twofold bias in historical sources describing the interaction between milieu and armed groups. Retrospectively, armed militants tend to amplify the support and solidarity they enjoy, whereas the radical milieu tends to stress its non-involvement, criticism, and isolation from and of violent groups. On one side, armed groups present themselves as peoples' avengers with a popular mandate; on the other, the radical milieu proclaims its non-involvement, picturing violent fringes as private warriors without followers. The research, in order to reduce this bias, crosschecks different sources. Moreover, it is worth noting that the immediate supportive environment usually represents only a section of the wider audiences that armed groups seek to address (Malthaner and Waldmann 2014), because revolutionary leftists often claim to fight in the name of abstract categories, such as the proletariat, or exploited people.

Finally, encouragement and legitimacy are, to a large extent, a matter of perception. We know that self-deception was widely diffused among armed militants, who were used to mistaking meaningless gestures for deliberate political solidarity. They also interpreted some grass-roots campaigns and mass protests as unequivocal requests for violent intervention (della Porta 1990a; Guicciardi 1988: 91). Although the gap between the solidarity perceived by armed militants and the solidarity expressed by the radical milieu may be considerable, the crucial point is the level of consensus that violent groups felt around them. The chapter consistently takes into consideration not only objective conditions but also subjective perceptions.

A widespread and resilient legitimation of violence

The student movement

The leftist archipelago that emerged in Italy in the wake of the social struggles of 1968 and 1969 was particularly vast. Although fragmented from both an ideological and an organisational point of view, leftist revolutionary groups were numerous, with large memberships (della Porta 1990b: 276). A myriad of collectives blossomed around universities, factories, and low-income neighbourhoods. Some of them actively supported and promoted armed struggle, others just proclaimed the necessity of a violent upheaval, while still others observed violent escalation with benevolence or indifference. Yet, their common denominator was – for about a decade and with a few exceptions – that they were not taking a clear stance against violence. Militants who engaged in armed action, if criticised, were commonly identified as 'comrades who are going wrong'. Yet, they were still comrades fighting on the same front, deserving protection as well as public support.

The literature has extensively analysed the bulk of violent theorisations elaborated by Italian leftist groups (Ventrone 2012). Encouragement, justifications, and recruitment for the benefit of armed organisations had been disclosed and started around 1969–70. Yet, for the sake of my argument, I suggest focusing on the persistent and lively presence of a recognisable movement over many years. French literature labelled the Italian 1970s 'the long May', implying a decade-long extension of the contentious politics of May 1968 (Sommier 1998: 48). More specifically, I argue that the rise of a 'second cycle of protest' (Edwards 2009) around 1976–7 is the main reason for the milieu of violent groups being particularly vast and enduring among radical students and youngsters.

In contrast to other Western countries, where political mobilisation had dried up by the first half of the 1970s, Italian social movements experienced a substantial revitalisation. This guaranteed continuity over ten years and provided a second generation of leftist militants, much more impatient and demanding than before. A new wave of protests and social struggles emerged, triggered by both the economic crisis and the Communist Party's strategy of compromise. Thousands of demonstrators invaded city centres, sabotage actions increased, 'proletarian appropriations' proliferated, firearms started circulating above ground, and violence against property and people boomed. Armed nuclei merged into pacific marches where they also found refuge, giving a vivid impression of collective violence. Revitalisation also involved ideological repertoires, which were updated by virtue of theoretical elaboration from autonomous groups, and were realigned with socio-economic evolutions (i.e. industrial restructuring and growth of the service sector). New proletarian rebels – unemployed or underemployed, often graduates – seemed to make the scene. Political cynicism and antagonism *vis-à-vis* the legal order were their signatures (Benecchi 1977: 107–11).

The journalists who went to interview the young protagonists of the movement were puzzled by their dangerous familiarity with violence. As a young woman told *Corriere della Sera* (23 April 1977), 'We are so used to Molotov cocktails, struggle with police, that we are almost indifferent in the face of death. We don't feel anything more, even though, rationally, we are against violence'. A fellow comrade added, 'If I saw a comrade taking aim and killing, I would never report him. Institutions are always the enemy. Being comrades is also a moral agreement'. The 'diffused illegality' of this period materialised in a continuum ranging from simple 'auto-reductions' of electricity bills to the shootings of policemen during demonstrations. Such a movement not only provided a large space of recruiting and support for underground organisations but also, and above all, reinforced the idea of the feasibility of revolution.

In particular, Autonomia Operaia – though strategically challenging the role of isolated vanguards – constantly promoted the construction of an 'armed movement' and never called into question the legitimacy of violence (*Rosso per il Potere Operaio*, May 1978). Indeed, during the 1970s, autonomous groups actively helped clandestine militants, for example when they escaped from prisons (Calogero, Fumian and Sartori 2010: 51). More significantly, they were able to simultaneously operate above and under ground, by virtue of a few secret armed branches that grew out of their security services (della Porta 1990b: 114–18). The Red Brigades (BR) were structured along a twofold dimension too. They had regular clandestine activists – named *regolari* – who were cut off from society, and militants still living above ground – named *irregolari* – interacting with the movement while operating illegally within the organisation (Clementi 2007: 101). This 'double level of militancy' is a peculiar feature of the Italian context and suggests that the boundaries between violent groups and their radical milieu, under various circumstances, faded away.

In addition, Front Line – the most relevant armed organisation after the BR – was born in the wake of 1976–7, with the aim to keep overt and clandestine militancy entangled. Front Line member Marco Fagiano significantly recalls, 'I had the feeling that everything was about to collapse: weapons on the streets were like the flagpoles of previous periods, and guerrilla attacks that started from demonstrations were a daily practice'. In a similar vein, Susanna Ronconi, another Front Line militant, remembers the way the group *Senza tregua* – which would later merge with Front Line – was easily recruited into the movement during the second half of 1970s, and enjoyed the 'immediate readiness to combat' (Novelli and Tranfaglia 1988: 294, 235). Both Enrico Baglioni and Diego Forastieri Molinari, who also joined Front Line, stressed the symbolic value of this 'climate of civil war' – 'the impression of being on the eve of a pre-insurrectional situation' – and the ensuing discussions about the urgency of taking up arms (Guicciardi 1988: 117–27). Indeed, the movement greeted Front Line's inaugural attack with unequivocal approval: on

April 1976, six hours after the killing of right-wing representative Enrico Pedenovi in Milan, 5,000 young leftists marched near the place of the murder, yelling, 'ten, a hundred, a thousand Pedenovis' (Bollati 2001: 23, 74). Enrico Galmozzi, one of the killers, confirms they perceived a mass legitimacy, 'something like a political demand to intervene at that level' (Guicciardi 1988: 58–60).

Thanks to this revitalisation of the radical milieu, the BR also regained momentum after the arrests of the previous years and consolidated their new strategy, implying direct attacks against state representatives. Their first intentional victim was indeed public prosecutor Francesco Coco, killed on June 1976. As Moretti (1994: 101–13) recalls, '[i]n all the 1976–77 public demonstrations, "Coco, Coco, Coco, it is still too little" was among the most chanted slogans: in the famous assortment of the movement that action had been approved.' Analogously, the BR militant Prospero Gallinari interpreted the contentious level of the social struggles in 1977 and the marches singing the praises of the BR as 'an explicit validation' of their strategy:

> I feel pride and enthusiasm in my chest. I feel that this testimony of shameless sympathy demonstrated by a legal movement is the best confirmation that the practice of the organization is deep rooted in the social contradictions and tensions of the country. (Gallinari 2006: 150–6)

Within the movement of 1977, BR – although ideologically quite distant from the student milieu – recruited a new generation and enjoyed solidarity and shelter (Faranda's testimony in *Commissione stragi* 1998). Ultimately, from the BR's point of view, the mass diffusion of highly violent repertoires displayed that a 'creeping civil war' was already underway and that the BR only needed to develop it (Brigate Rosse 1978: 96).

The communist workers, the PCI, and the trade unions

Italy was, during the 1970s, characterised by a significant degree of militant workers' sympathy towards armed fringes. Historical evidence clearly outlines an area of appreciation of leftist violence within large factories, especially in the industrial regions in the North.

The BR and – before this – its embryonic organisations *Collettivo politico metropolitano* and *Sinistra proletaria* grew out of Milanese factories, such as Magneti-Marelli, Falck, Breda, Sit-Siemens, Alfa, and Pirelli. Factory brigades never had more than ten members per plant, but exerted a much larger influence (*Senza padroni: Giornale dell'Assemblea Autonoma dell'Alfa Romeo* 1975). Alberto Franceschini, a BR leader, remembers going to the Pirelli factory gates to speak with workers, and eating at the Siemens canteen along with the workers. He also recalls that workers took advantage of the first BR attacks. Indeed, these actions threatened factory bosses, who consequently limited their demands. Similarly, Roberto Ognibene stresses the general reticence, and Lauro even claims that the BR had to filter and restrain the overabundant 'requests for war' coming from the social base (Bocca 1985: 57–60). According to testimonies, the BR could rely on 100 active supporters within the Sit-Siemens factory in Milan, twenty-seven of whom were later arrested for participation in armed struggle (Moretti 1994: 21). Up until 1974, the BR were also able to combine armed propaganda with influence over labour negotiations, by means of two members within the Sit-Siemens factory council (Galli 1991). In 1977, 400 Magneti-Marelli workers signed a solidarity plea for seven armed militants who had been arrested near Verbania, Piedmont, while doing military training (Cavallini 1978: 201–2).

In the area of Turin, the BR enjoyed some degree of consensus and support, chiefly at the Fiat, Lancia, and Pininfarina factories. Communist workers at Fiat Mirafiori admit – albeit reluctantly – that there was the 'hope' among them that 'some clamorous action could hasten the solution of dramatic problems' (Cavallini 1978: 58). More blatantly, Moretti (1994: 49–54) wrote that, in the early 1970s, in Milan and Turin they 'seem to have a boundless horizon, [they] feel not only sympathy but also willingness'. The industrial cluster of Genoa replicated this situation, especially at Ansaldo meccanico, Italsider, and Italcantieri.

In the eyes of the BR, workers not only refused to denounce people who were discovered to sustain or participate in sabotages and attacks, but also 'betrayed a sort of satisfaction towards those who put into practice announcements that, up until that point, had been only shown off' (Guagliardo's testimony, in Bianconi 2011: 206). According to the BR leader Renato Curcio (1993: 80) in February 1973, when they released their first kidnap victim – half-naked and in chains – close to the Fiat factory gates, dozens of workers saw him without providing first aid. The BR immediately inferred workers' tolerance, if not complicity, in revolutionary violence. Similarly, the next kidnappings – Amerio and Macchiarini – were followed by such approval by workers that the BR interpreted it as 'excitement' and 'growth of political space' in factories. For the first time, workers started to spontaneously seek them out (Franceschini's and Besuschio's testimonies in Zavoli 1995: 105–8). In a similar vein, the lack of participation in the strike against the BR's kidnapping of judge Mario Sossi, in May 1974, was seen as the workers' endorsement of the action. The BR proudly exhibited the Ansaldo autonomous workers' leaflet declaring their opposition to the strike: 'Let the bosses express this kind of solidarity act, we don't have anything in common with them.' (Soccorso Rosso 1976: 219–20)

As violent groups progressed in their escalation, targeting people and resorting to assassinations, violent fringes gradually lost support among workers. However, the persistent lack of solidarity with the victims of terrorism, and the absence of a clear condemnation of the language of arms nurtured violent groups' illusion of enjoying a hidden sympathy. A couple of articles by Giampaolo Pansa provide a clear example of such circumstances. In November 1977, on the day after the BR killing of journalist Carlo Casalegno in Turin, Pansa went to interview workers at the Fiat Mirafiori factory gates. The workers did not express unanimous condemnation of the murder, gave contradictory answers, and showed a certain degree of indifference. The strike against terrorism was considered somewhat unfair, since nobody had been protesting when poor workers died. Although a former partisan, Casalegno was labelled a representative of the Turin bourgeoisie due to the fact that he wrote for the Agnelli family's newspaper. The general stance was that the establishment, with its lies and corruption, did not deserve any defence (*Corriere della Sera*, 18 and 19 November 1977). The survey, of course, was not scientifically reliable. Yet it gave quite a realistic picture, confirmed by other similar interviews and by the scarce participation in the strike (Tobagi, in *Corriere della Sera*, 19 November 1977).

Armed militants were generally persuaded that the hard-fighting minority of the workers' movement was only 'the tip of a very large iceberg' (Ronconi's testimony, in Novelli and Tranfaglia 1988: 233). In other words, they pictured the Italian Communist Party as undermined by a cleavage between the leadership, increasingly integrated within the democratic system, and the still rebellious rank and file, waiting for genuine subversion. Up until the late 1970s, when the BR and other armed groups clearly demonised the PCI, they still hoped that the 'contradiction' between leadership and base was alive and ready to explode. The BR's reasoning proceeded as follows: 'They knew us and they did not denounce us, they talked with us, we talked. They may have disagreed, they called us every name under the sun, but they were comrades, they were not the state [...]. This base could not help but influence the party leaders' (Moretti 1994: 171).

Various factors contributed to building this belief. First, a few distinguished personalities belonging to the PCI, such as former partisan Pietro Secchia and Giambattista Lazagna, were accommodating and sometimes collaborative with armed militants. They contributed to the diffusion of a nostalgic memory of partisan guerrilla and proletarian justice (*La guerriglia in Italia* 1969: 5–16). Lazagna was also twice arrested and jailed for 'subversive association' (Griner 2014: 171–2). The PCI, during the early 1970s, was well aware that a few on the leftist fringe, even within the Communist membership, were taking up arms. The party even knew the names and backgrounds of young extremists. For years, BR members could go to PCI festivals and eat with Communist activists (Franceschini, Buffa, and Giustolisi 1996: 81). In 1974, the PCI also initiated secret negotiations for bringing the BR back within the boundaries of legality. In exchange, the PCI promised preferential judicial treatment by sympathetic judges, but only a few militants accepted the deal (Fasanella and Franceschini 2004: 129). However, the official PCI strategy was to publicly deny the red matrix of violence. While hoping to reintegrate the hardliners with brokerage, the party shifted attention to the dangers of neo-fascist plots. Terrorism was pictured as a fascist provocation or a version of the so-called 'strategy of tension' (i.e., a plan to restore an authoritarian order by means of disorder). PCI executive Giuliano Ferrara explains this ambiguity:

> [...] on the one hand, we did not want to believe it and so we hid the problem behind the concept of workers' opacity, on the other hand, we were not able to recognize it and to dismiss as provocative any form of workers' autonomy outside the party and the trade union. Thus, extremist workers were provocateurs [...] and we branded them as red fascists. (Spezie 2001: 57)

Thus, the BR were always presented as 'self-styled' or 'so-called', and the PCI's official newspaper *l'Unità* used the acronym 'BR' instead of 'Red Brigades', in order to avoid association with the adjective 'red' (Fasanella and Rossa 2006: 9).

As Taviani (2003) demonstrates, this political line had to be revised once leftist armed groups raised the stakes by killing people and the Communist Party unequivocally sided with state institutions. The shift came late though: it was prepared in 1975, but materialised only around 1977–8. The party gradually acknowledged the existence of leftist terrorism as distinct from fascist terrorism. As a consequence, party media increasingly demonised violent fringes and de-solidarisation intensified.

However, internal documents show that behind the official façade, the process was far less straightforward. Up until November 1977, when murderous leftist actions were hitting the headlines, communist leaders were still concerned about 'the presence of nuclei of terrorists and groups of support in some factories and companies in Turin, Milan, Genoa, and Rome'. In a closed meeting, the communist shadow Minister of the Interior Ugo Pecchioli acknowledged that 'attacks against bosses and chief technicians come from "internal" tip-offs; there is an extension of the area of solidarity'. Pecchioli also asked party leaders for increased vigilance, because the PCI's democratic mobilisation was showing 'signs of weakness'. More explicitly, Pecchioli stigmatised 'equivocal presences and zones of tolerance' within trade unions, labelling communist trade unionists' behaviour *vis-à-vis* terrorism 'totally inadequate'. During the same meeting, the Communist Party delegate from Lombardy acknowledged that they had failed to isolate terrorism and remembered that, in some high schools, news of terrorist attacks would usually be welcomed with rounds of applause. The delegate explained that after autonomist militants killed a young policeman in Milan, trade unions were not even able to promote a petition or a strike to protest against violence (PCI Archives, 24 November 1977). In the fall of 1978, at the height of leftist violent attacks, Pecchioli privately admitted that the escalation of subversive violence had to be explained in terms of the existence of 'large backgrounds, protective buffers, made up of quite extensive areas of solidarity, cover-up, or at least indifference and disengagement among young people, underprivileged persons, the public sector, intellectuals, and also workers' fringes' (PCI Archives, September 1978).

The Communist Party's concern regarding the infiltration of violent extremists within trade unions, and the ensuing solidarity with armed groups was, to a certain extent, justified. Italian trade unions (CGIL, CISL, and UIL) were probably 'the most politicised in the world' and achieved great success during the 1970s (Accornero 1992: 193). Indeed, between 1970 and 1975, violent fringes tried to connect with factory workers' struggles and recruit among workers. Yet, trade unions were not worried about this penetration. Instead, they initially reacted with a mix of 'benevolent justification' and a 'calculated conspiracy of silence'. Later, when sabotage and attacks scared factory management, terrorist threats were sometimes employed as a negotiation tool. Trade unionists suggested during consultations that if factory management had not accepted a concession, the exasperation may have led to dangerous consequences, so it was much better to reward the trade unions' sense of responsibility (*Prospettiva sindacale*, September 1982). In November 1977, while Turin labour union leader Cesare denounced the presence of a BR organised cluster within the Fiat factory, syndicalist and sociologist Bruno Manghi admitted to the existence of a small area of sympathisers, and a much larger – and growing – 'area of indifference' in many factories in northern Italy. Manghi self-critically acknowledged the responsibility of trade unions and leftist parties, who 'discussed the forms of violence, but not violence itself. The problem is not judging whether violence pays or not, but rejecting violence' (*Corriere della Sera*, 20 November 1977).

Consistent with the PCI's change of strategy, trade unions began to actively fight against leftist political violence only after 1977–8. In the same period – although the political analysis was still biased and the presence of violent leftist clusters in factories was still denied by many local representatives – trade unions officially ended their solidarity with armed fringes (Magnanini 2006: 127–31). The leadership clearly disassociated itself, firmly condemning terrorism. By contrast – as sociologist Aris Accornero (1992: 196) pointed out – the rank and file had 'more contrasting feelings' and in some factories a 'confused *omertà*' persisted.

To conclude, few workers were deeply sympathetic to violent means, and criticisms were common. Yet, for a long time, the majority of workers did not consider leftist violent groups as dangerous enemies and did not take a stance against the barbarisation of political struggle (Galli 1991: 91).

The radical intellectuals

The situation described above was to a certain extent echoed in the ambiguous stance of many established intellectuals, who expressed sympathetic judgments *vis-à-vis* violent fringes or, at least, did not criticise them when they targeted political symbols. Their reasoning, in brief, followed this logic: we cannot, in the face of state institutions that are corrupt and that conspire with neo-fascism, criticise violent rebellion, even if we do not approve of it. This 'intellectuals' divorce from the state', as historian Ventura (1984) named it, nurtured some resonant campaigns in defence of the right to rebel and to violently attack political adversaries. Two examples are illustrative. In 1971, in the middle of a campaign led by the leftist group Lotta Continua against the police commissioner Luigi Calabresi – protagonist of a contested investigation against anarchists – more than 800 of the most prestigious figures of the Italian cultural establishment signed a plea that was published in several issues of the magazine *l'Espresso*. Calabresi was called a 'torturer commissioner', responsible for the death of one anarchist, and was harshly criticised in a sort of moral lynching.[1] A few months later, when the

---

1. Calabresi, whose innocence was later proved, was killed in 1972. According to judicial inquiries, a Lotta Continua commando conducted the action., On 18 May 1972, the magazine *Lotta Continua* praised the murder of the commissioner as 'an act in which the exploited people recognise their desire for justice'.

public prosecutor of Turin indicted the editors of the magazine *Lotta Continua* for incitement to crime, fifty renowned intellectuals and artists sent him an open letter. They endorsed some of the most radical *Lotta Continua* statements, which were contested by the jury, such as 'class struggle, let's arm the masses' or 'let's fight with arms against the state until the liberation from bosses and from exploitation' (Brambilla 2010: 142).

In the course of the 1970s, many other petitions followed – e.g., in support of the journalists of the BR's unofficial magazine *Controinformazione*, or in solidarity with German jailed militants in Stammhein – marking a period of unprecedented political engagement (*il manifesto*, 7 August 1977; 20 October 1977). In 1977, in the middle of an escalation of leftist violence, many Italian intellectuals still refused to rally around the flag and defend political institutions. Writer Leonardo Sciascia's view is emblematic: 'I don't understand what police and justice are defending [...] and I would understand even less myself acting as a caryatid to avoid this collapse or decay the responsibility of which is certainly not mine' (*Corriere della Sera*, 12 May 1977). Similarly, in March 1978, after the kidnap of Aldo Moro, while a large number of intellectuals signed a petition against terrorism and committed themselves to the safeguarding of institutions (*l'Unità*, 18 March 1978), a still significant number of intellectuals – although condemning the attack – were protesting against the emotional blackmail that imposed a choice between uncritically siding with political order and understanding the terrorists (*il manifesto*, 24 March 1978). Once again, unapologetic defence of the state was seen as extremely problematic.

Meanwhile, other intellectuals were directly engaged in helping violent extremists against 'state repression'. In the name of the right to dissent, the future Nobel laureate Dario Fo and his wife the actress Franca Rame founded the Soccorso Rosso Militante (SRM). Established in 1972 to distribute funds collected during theatre shows to leftist campaigns, the association became a structured organisation that provided material, legal, and moral aid to militants while they were fugitives, on trial, or arrested. The SRM monitored conditions of detention, helped prisoners' families in need, offered free legal support by distinguished lawyers, and orchestrated propaganda actions asserting the innocence of those indicted. The organisation issued communiqués, documents, interviews, and publications rejecting all charges and presenting counter-investigations. In some cases, the protection of civil rights was motivated by genuine reasons; in others it was clearly spurious.

For example, in 1972, after a juvenile brawl, anarchist Giovanni Marini fatally stabbed Carlo Falvella, an innocent right-wing militant. The SRM promptly took on the defence of Marini, 'guilty of surviving a fascist aggression', mobilised many intellectuals, and sponsored three pamphlets claiming his innocence (see, for instance, Soccorso Rosso Militante 1974). Umberto Terracini – communist heavyweight, republican founding father, and member of Parliament – led the pool of defence lawyers. Marini was proven guilty and was sentenced to nine years, but served only four, and during his detention he received Italy's most prestigious poetry award (Telese 2006: 53–4). The SRM also contributed to the large campaign for the innocence of the three leftist militants who, in April 1973, set fire to the apartment of right-wing militant Mario Mattei, causing the death of two of his sons. Leftist supporters – notorious politician Riccardo Lombardi and prominent intellectual Alberto Moravia among them – portrayed the so-called 'arson of Primavalle', later recognised as a deliberate anti-fascist attack by a leftist commando, as a fascist private feud, born within the local section of the Italian Social Movement (MSI) (Collettivo di Potere Operaio 1974). The three leftists were acquitted and immediately escaped abroad. Years later they were condemned in absentia and never paid for their militant action.

Similarly, during the trial for the Primavalle attack in February 1975, leftist militants killed a Greek right-wing militant, Mikis Mantakas. Two were indicted. There followed another mobilisation in defence of their innocence. Once again, the SRM, as well as prominent intellectuals such as Natalia Ginzburg, sided with the two indicted, fabricated the case of an unjust accusation, and maintained the thesis of another fascist feud. Leftist magistrates were present at hearings in order to exert pressure on their colleagues and to push for an acquittal. The two leftists who were on trial left the country (Telese 2006: 257).

Campaigns for the innocence of leftist militants continued during the second half of the 1970s, when two SRM lawyers, Sergio Spazzali and Giovanni Cappelli, were also accused of actively participating in the armed organisations they were defending in court, by smuggling weapons and offering refuge to terrorists (*il manifesto*, 13 May 1977). Both of them, having been proven guilty, left the country (Griner 2014: 163–9). Eventually, the SRM published an apologetic collection of texts, issued by the BR, with the aim of offering 'militant solidarity' to their comrades, who were victims of bourgeois misinformation (Soccorso Rosso 1976). So, for many years, this critique of state apparatuses, and the missed condemnation of subversion by Italian intellectuals, were interpreted as endorsements of violent means.

The cognitive shift: from legitimation to rejection of violence

The emotional backlash

Four murderous attacks, perpetrated by leftist groups, fostered the process of revision through which the radical milieu came to perceive violence as undesirable. This section reconstructs these tipping points and emphasises three main features. First, they generated an immediate backlash and triggered a debate about the meaning and the repercussions of violent escalation. Second, three of the murders had a direct emotional impact on the radical milieu. Third, the process of reconsideration – confirming the strong resiliency of the legitimation of violence – evolved with difficulty and faced many obstacles. Indeed, while criticism of violent means developed, general support for revolutionary goals lived on for some time.

The first step coincided with the death of Roberto Crescenzio in Turin. Roberto was a twenty-two-year-old university student, working class, apolitical. On 1 October 1977, an antifascist demonstration was held in the centre of the city. Clashes with police and vandalism followed. A group of leftist militants hastily organised a raid against a bar vaguely known to be a meeting point for fascists. In that bar, sitting indoors with a friend, Crescenzio was having a drink. The commando launched a few Molotov cocktails that set fire to the bar. Crescenzio, who took refuge in the restroom, suffered severe burns and died after three days of agony. Rage and outrage pervaded the city (*la Stampa*, 4 October 1977). Communist Party representatives firmly condemned the violence and the irresponsibility of extremist groups. The PCI's youth organisation (FGCI) organised a collection of signatures against violence, denouncing the virulence of autonomist leftist groups (Sanlorenzo 1989: 124). Communist mayor Novelli affirmed before Turin City Council that 'with these individuals it is not possible to argue because, like beasts, they do not have a brain' and invited people to avoid any justification and tolerance towards them. Communist workers at Fiat felt particularly touched because, as they declared, Crescenzio 'was a poor guy with whom everyone could easily identify himself or his son' (Cavallini 1978: 71). More than 20,000 people attended Crescenzio's funeral, and factories closed down for fifteen minutes. A period of disorientation and self-analysis began within the student New Left. For the first time, an innocent bystander had died during political action, and 'shifting the blame was not valid any longer'. Lotta Continua representative Pietro Marcenaro significantly declared, '[a] movement that calls itself communist, that fights against the power to affirm the reasons of life, if it does not want to destroy itself, cannot see a young guy burnt alive and then move on as if this was something normal.' (*Lotta Continua*, 6 October 1977) Readers' letters to *Lotta Continua* confirm the emotional turmoil and the rise of crucial questions. Donatella, a militant, wrote:

I would like the comrades to discuss with me the painful problem of the balance between the response against fascism and respect for human life. Maybe the rage nullifies the value of life? I cannot accept rage without humanity. It is an awful contradiction (*Care compagne, cari compagni* 1978: 230).

However, reactions within the movement varied significantly. Some talked about a 'technical error', others asked why Crescenzio was in a fascist bar, implying the victim's guilt. Other militants reacted to the crisis of consciousness by claiming that Crescenzio was a victim of state violence, and criticised the growing moral concerns as 'petty bourgeois' (*Ombre rosse*, December 1977).

The second step was the above-mentioned BR killing of journalist Carlo Casalegno. The ensuing emotional reaction was widespread, and several leftist personalities consequently criticised the diffused sympathy and complicity with violent fringes (*il manifesto*, 20 November 1977). A group of intellectuals from Turin – Norberto Bobbio, Italo Calvino, and Primo Levi, among others – condemned 'any tolerance or indifference or ambiguity towards terrorists' (*la Repubblica*, 27–8 November 1977). Casalegno's son Andrea was a Lotta Continua member, and two of his comrades went to interview him while his father was still in intensive care. Andrea criticised the de-humanisation of revolutionary struggle as well as his own group. However, the interview with Andrea Casalegno was very cautious and Andrea still showed some respect for the BR, defined as 'neither monster nor demons' (*Lotta Continua*, 19 November 1977). Moreover, the reception of the interview both within Lotta Continua and in the leftist movement at large was often very cold (*la Repubblica*, 27–8 November 1977; *l'Espresso*, 4 December 1977). Lotta Continua representative Luciano Bosio, for example, expressed his disagreement with 'a chorus' that called into question 'the legitimacy of retaliation and the death penalty against counter-revolutionaries'. We could not endorse, Bosio wrote, 'a new humanity grounded on the values of the bourgeois family' (*Lotta Continua*, 22 November 1977; 27–8 November 1977: 10). Eventually, Andrea Casalegno had to clarify his position and justify his previous criticisms (*Lotta Continua* 27–8 November 1977: 5).

The third step coincided with the kidnapping and subsequent murder of former Italian prime minister and president of Christian Democracy, Aldo Moro, in March–May 1978. The communist reaction was quite strong and monolithic. Strikes and protests against terrorism showed mass participation. This resulted in BR's surprise at 'the degree of PCI's integration within the state'. Although they had hit the heart of the political system and were judging the hated Moro with traditional leftist arguments, the communist base was showing little or no sympathy (Moretti 1994: 172). Many radical intellectuals were clearer than ever before in their condemnation of violence (*il manifesto* 28 March 1978). By restoring the death penalty, wrote Sciascia, the BR not only 'lost the revolutionary legitimacy or the legality they crazily pretend to represent, but they made more difficult and painful the protection of liberty for those who defend it for everybody' (*la Repubblica*, 19 April 1978). However, in this case, too, it is hard to trace a clear-cut reaction from the radical milieu. If the left as a whole firmly condemned the BR attack, and Lotta Continua expressed 'revulsion against the action and the practice of the BR' (*Lotta Continua*, 17 March 1978), a few young radicals and working class people were reportedly quite passive and indifferent. In some cases, solidarity was expressed exclusively with the five bodyguards killed during the abduction, while Moro's destiny was considered unimportant (*Lotta Continua*, 17 March 1978). In some others, the usual code of silence was respected. After the killing of Moro, during a large student assembly at the University of Rome, a BR member took the floor in order to explain why they killed the hostage. Everybody knew his identity, but nobody reported him to police (Gallinari 2006: 208). Leftist Catholics were particularly touched by the event and revised their previous endorsements of revolutionary violence. Yet they still attributed the main responsibility for the murder to the DC and the political institutions (Panvini 2014: 372–3). Autonomia Operaia, while criticising the BR's estrangement from the movement, explicitly censured the 'metaphysic condemnation of violence' rising within leftist constituencies as a result of the emotional shock (*Rosso per il Potere Operaio*, April 1978). Autonomist militant Franco Piperno portrayed the revival of 'the sacredness of life' as 'naïve generosity'. According to him, it was still 'scandalously possible that the death of a man translat[ed] into freedom and life for others' (*pre–print*, December 1978).

The fourth and more decisive step was the killing of Guido Rossa, on January 1979. Rossa was a thirty-four-year-old metalworker at Italsider in Conigliano, near Genoa. Delegate at the factory council on behalf of the Communist trade union, he had been a PCI member since the age of twenty-four. On October 1978 he reported a fellow comrade to the police for distributing BR propaganda leaflets within the factory. A few other persons had taken notice of the same BR supporter, but it was Rossa alone that signed the report and his name also appeared in local newspapers. For the first time, a worker had dared to expose a terrorist follower within a factory. Although Rossa remained quite isolated among trade unionists and workers, both the opacity and the fear that assured protection of the BR and their supporters were about to dissolve (*Corriere della Sera*, 19 November 1977). As a result, the BR decided on an exemplary punishment against the 'spy and traitor' Rossa and sent a commando to shoot at him. The action resulted in the death of the target. According to the BR's logic, the communist base would now finally take a stand and side with their revolutionary project. By contrast, not only civil society, but also the entire left reacted against this extremist violence more strongly than ever before. The murder of a worker, it goes without saying, deeply touched communist sensibilities. 250,000 people joined the funeral, where workers raised their fists and chanted slogans such as 'BR go away/we already have bosses against us' or 'BR/SS' (Fasanella and Rossa 2006: 50). Trade union leader Luciano Lama self-critically admitted that they should have been 'one sole collective witness against the enemy of democracy' much earlier (Bianconi 2011: 94). BR leader Enrico Fenzi confirmed that the attack 'locked out any possible dialogue with workers in Genoa' (Zavoli 1995: 220). Lotta Continua leader Luigi Manconi said that 'never before has the logic that underlies the BR's choice of target and his "annihilation" been so private and corporative; never before has one of their actions appeared so clearly a sectarian revenge.' He added that workers' solidarity with Rossa simply 'ridiculed' BR's statements (Manconi 1979: 7–19). Grief and solidarity surfaced all around the country, especially in Turin, where communist representative Dino Sanlorenzo organised a mass inquiry on terrorism. Almost all families living in the city received a survey through which they were given the opportunity to anonymously report events that could help police identify people involved in political violence. Useful reports were few, but answers were numerous and people's courage gradually re-emerged (Sanlorenzo 1989: 175–97).

The rational arguments

During the period 1977–9, several rational arguments against violence emerged within the radical milieu, furthering the cognitive shift towards revulsion against violence. They were correlated with different ideological conceptions and linked to different group or individual experiences. Yet, at least four common lines of reasoning emerge across various sources, and illustrate the foundations of a change that went beyond the instinctual and emotional aversion to violence.

First, constituencies started affirming that 'wrong means distort our ends and ourselves'. Luciana Castellina, an influential journalist with *il manifesto*, wrote on November 1977 that it was important to pay attention to 'the actions that result in the negation of the contents, values, and deep reasons of the communist struggle'. Castellina significantly recalled what Horst Mahler – German lawyer and founder of the Red Army Faction – had recently told her: 'We started with the critique of My Lay and now we glorify the much worse action of Mogadishu', in which more than eighty peoples' lives were endangered (*il manifesto*, 20 November 1977). In the same vein, Gad Lerner and Andrea Marcenaro, two prominent journalists with *Lotta Continua*, wrote in 1978, '[w]e are not pacifist […] but we are not ready to exercise forms of violence that – because they do not emancipate anything – end up coercing and transforming ourselves.' Lerner and Marcenaro emphasised that '[w]e cannot avoid being interested in the life or the death of "every person in general". If we do not want even the worst Nazis to be tortured in jail, we cannot say that there are some deaths "we do not care about"' (*Lotta Continua*, 3 December 1977). Luigi Ferrajoli, a radical jurist sympathetic to the extreme fringes, added that '[m]eans, always and irremediably, jeopardise the end. […] Ends have to be immediately identifiable within means' (Ferrajoli 1979).

Second, in this period, positions asserting that violence against human beings was ideologically extraneous to the New Left background found a growing audience. For example, leftist intellectual Federico Stame claimed that the general cause of the violent escalation had to be found in the hegemony of the 'Jacobin and Bolshevik conception of political action'. 'Who exterminated millions of kulaks on behalf of the reason of state and party? […] Those who practice terrorism and violence are the last sons of Bolshevism.' Stame also rediscovered the value of democracy and the importance of fighting for it. 'Democracy', he wrote, 'is not, as Mao stated, a means, but an end' (*il manifesto*, 19 January 1978). During the kidnapping of Moro, an important clarification came also from Alberto Moravia, who unmistakably stated that he found the BR's principles and values repugnant, and reaffirmed his faith in the republic born out of the resistance movement: 'Obviously, such a conception of human rights excludes at first glance the disdain for human life, no matter whose life, and the use of man by man, conceived as an instrument rather than an end' (*la Repubblica*, 19 April 1978). Other voices portrayed political violence as intrinsically 'fascist'. As leading feminist Lidia Menapace wrote in 1978, 'violence, individual, physical, that enjoys and justifies the exemplary act as an end in itself, is always fascism, that is the oppressive side of the bourgeois power that goes deep inside every one of us' (*Sulla violenza* 1978: XV–XXI). Goffredo Fofi, writer and activist, proposed going back to the once popular concept of 'revolutionary humanism', an idea that implied 'a human visage in a society of wolves […] the discovery and claim of *tenderness*, as Guevara said, also during the harshest moments of the struggle'. Ultimately, it was crucial to oppose 'a diversity' against 'the inhumanity of the system' (*Lotta Continua*, 18 January 1978). During 1978, many Lotta Continua militants echoed the same concept to one degree or another. This urge to avoid mirroring of enemy values and tactics clearly emerges from the minutes of their assemblies. As someone self-critically complained, '[w]e are not even able to be more fair than bourgeois justice' (*Sulla violenza*, 1978: 138–52).

Third, the radical milieu stressed that the language of arms ultimately proved the weakness of insurgents' persuasion and the fragility of their arguments. In this regard, it is interesting to note the debate within the Feminist Collective of Trastevere (Rome). Their reasoning ran like this: 'It seems to us that sometimes the choice to eliminate, to kill the enemy, is the result of impotence.' Sentencing 'the monster' of death – they argued – 'is a way to exorcise his existence'. Killing, they thought, showed a lack of belief in the possibility of transformation both of oneself and of others, and thus that the struggle was completely useless (*Lotta Continua*, 26 January 1978). In a similar vein, the anti-militarist current of the autonomist movement censured the growth of a violence that 'converted the masses into spectators [...], that accumulates terror and gives up the revolutionary project in order to replace it with a simple clash' (*A/traverso*, January 1978).

Eventually, constituencies began to criticise violence as counterproductive and negative for the development of social struggle. Following the murder of Casalegno, *il manifesto* raged against terrorism by affirming that it was the strongest deterrent against the protest movement, guilty of portraying communist values with 'the aberrant look of cruelty and disdain of reason' (*il manifesto*, 17 November 1977). During the same period, this leftist newspaper also protested against autonomist violence, defined as the product of both 'political and intellectual barbarisation' and being 'oblivious to the lessons of history' (*il manifesto*, 17 May 1977, 28 August 1977). Within workers' assemblies, the BR were consistently and increasingly pictured as 'a bourgeois-intellectual élite', fighting over the heads of the working class, completely detached from real peoples' problems (Marchetti, Mobiglia, and Rolli 1979: 103). Autonomist militants from Bologna clearly stated that '[w]e have to keep this well in mind: today, whoever practices the armed struggle against police and state apparatuses risks fighting a battle which is as costly as it is backward.' The enemy was able not only to militarily defeat the movement, but also to subjugate it for a long period (*A/traverso*, May 1977). According to their view, shooting at journalists' legs or attacking 'the heart of the state' were pointless actions. Political power was elsewhere, spread across an invisible web, and controlled by the concentration of knowledge. Only 'intelligent sabotage' could defeat it (*A/traverso*, January 1978). Even the militants of *Rosso* – the mainstream current of Autonomia Operaia – criticised the BR because they helped political authorities 'to incarcerate dozens of comrades'. Indeed, in 1978, right after the kidnapping of Moro, a widespread anti-terrorist campaign targeted sympathisers and supporters. Criminalisation grew, together with the risks of being charged with complicity in terrorism. 'At this point' – *Rosso* (April 1978) reads – 'we cannot help but create a political vacuum around the BR'. Leftist writer and poet Roberto Roversi synthesised this argument when he wrote, 'the blood of common people, no matter how it is shed, always serves the prince.' From this point of view, violence was 'not so much horrible' as representing an obstacle in the process of emancipation (*il manifesto*, 5 February 1978). According to Stame, from the perspective of state powers, 'if the terrorist was not here, it would be useful to invent him' (Stame 1979: 25).

Conclusion

Historical events show that Italy was not on the verge of a civil war and that students, workers, and intellectuals were not ready to sustain a fully-fledged armed struggle, let alone embrace weapons. It was a large-scale misunderstanding. Yet, paradoxically, the illusion that subjectively pervaded armed militants was objectively grounded. The radical milieu contributed significantly to shaping the image of a highly contentious society.

As this chapter demonstrates, three main cumulative conditions weakened the radical milieu's moderating influence by delaying criticism and de-solidarisation. First, the leftist student movement was vast and enduring. During the watershed of 1976–7 in particular, the movement was able to (re)mobilise people, to renew its repertoires, and to radicalise further. Longevity and renovation over time were crucial factors. Second, radical workers, the Communist Party rank and file, and leftist trade unions gave the impression of the presence of a large sympathetic social base. Overall, with the exception of some small minorities, they did not publicly approve violent actions, but silently endorsed them. Nonetheless, armed groups predicted that, in the near future, communist workers would be ready to come out into the open. In this regard, the belief of potential within the revolutionary class par excellence was key. Third, radical intellectuals were seen as prominent spokesmen of citizens' distrust of political institutions. Even though only a tiny minority of intellectuals actively supported armed fringes, the majority expressed harsh criticisms against official politics and were consistent in not taking a clear stance against violent solutions. The broad diffusion of injustice frames, coupled with intellectuals' lack of confidence in political élites, was fundamental.

Nonetheless, the mechanisms of violence legitimation were at some point halted and reversed. The radical milieu began to question the meaning and the effectiveness of violence. Eventually, violent means were openly rejected. A combination of strictly interrelated emotional shocks and rational considerations unhinged the mechanisms of legitimation and the milieu began to play a normative role.

Four traumatic events fostered a process of reconsideration of violent repertoires. Three events, namely the killings of Crescenzio, Casalegno, and Rossa, directly affected the radical milieu. The first victim was a young proletarian above any suspicion; the second was an intellectual, former partisan, and father of a leftist militant; the third was a communist worker and syndicalist. As a matter of fact, sympathisers and supporters had to themselves experience the grief and the disorientation generated by political murders. The killing of Moro, by contrast, showcased the breakdown of an over-ambitious revolutionary strategy that failed to trigger any mass upheaval. The process of reconsideration of violence was also favoured by the creation of spaces for debate, which were accessible to and recognised by armed militants. In particular, both the magazine *Lotta Continua* and the newspaper *il manifesto* – previously sympathetic to highly contentious struggles – made room for self-critical analysis and severe comments.

As the research demonstrates, the legitimation of violence was extremely resilient. Hence, traumatic events alone do not explain the reversal of the mechanisms. A rational reconsideration was also decisive. Thus, four main arguments against the use of violence began to circulate within the radical milieu. First, violent means were irremediably endangering emancipatory ends. Second, the values of democracy and the lesson of antifascist resistance were irreconcilable with the blind cult of violence. Humanity had to be rediscovered as a revolutionary value, since it was necessary to be different from the brutality of the enemy. Third, armed struggle was a declaration of political weakness. Fourth, the military confrontation was counterproductive: violence was silencing the authentic grievances of the masses, shrinking mobilisation, and discrediting communist ideals. Armed struggle was also strategically backward. Armed assault against political power, given these conditions, was simply hopeless. Although ideology still permeated the formulation of the four arguments, their common denominator was mostly utilitarian. As expected, pragmatism and realism gradually re-emerged from the radical milieu.

Criticism and de-solidarisation finally rose to surface, yet too late to be as decisive as in some other cases, where violence-prone groups are still defining their strategies and are more receptive. Action militarisation, ideological encapsulation, and cognitive closure were already at play (della Porta 2013: 30–1). A bloody private war against the state – also implying a great deal of energy spent on the liberation of political prisoners and on revenge on traitors – substituted the initial revolutionary project. Therefore, the normative power of the radical milieu not only emerged after many victims and strategic failures, but it also saw its impact reduced due to the time delay.

References

(1978) *Care compagne, cari compagni: Lettere a Lotta Continua*, Roma: Cooperativa giornalisti Lotta Continua.

(1969) *La guerriglia in Italia: Documenti della resistenza militare italiana*, Milano: Feltrinelli.

(1978) *Sulla violenza. Politica e terrorismo: Un dibattito nella sinistra*, Roma: Savelli

Accornero, A. (1992) *La parabola del sindacato. Ascesa e declino di una cultura*, Bologna: il Mulino.

Benecchi, D. (ed.) (1977) *I non garantiti: Il movimento del '77 nelle università*, Roma: Savelli.

Bianconi, G. (2011) *Il brigatista e l'operaio: L'omicidio di Guido Rossa. Storia di vittime e colpevoli*, Torino: Einaudi.

Bocca, G. (1985) *Noi terroristi: Dodici anni di lotta armata ricostruiti e discussi con i protagonisti*, Milano: Garzanti.

Bollati, B. (2001) *Il delitto Pedenovi*, Milano: Lasergrafica Polver.

Brambilla, M. (2010) *L'Eskimo in redazione*, Milano: Ares.

Brigate Rosse (1978) 'Risoluzione della Direzione Strategica, febbraio 1978', in *Progetto memoria* (1996), *Le parole scritte*, Roma: Sensibili alle foglie.

Calogero, P., Fumian, C. and Sartori, M. (2010) *Terrore rosso: Dall'autonomia al partito armato*, Roma-Bari: Laterza.

Cavallini, M. (1978) *Il terrorismo in fabbrica*, Roma: Editori Riuniti.

Clementi, M. (2007) *Storia delle Brigate Rosse*, Roma: Odradek.

Collettivo di Potere Operaio (1974) *Primavalle incendio a porte chiuse*, Roma: Samonà e Savelli.

Curcio, R. (1993) *A viso aperto*, Milano: Mondadori.

della Porta, D. (1988) 'Recruitment process in clandestine political organizations: Italian left-wing terrorism', in B. Klandersmans, H. Kriesi and S. Tarrow (eds) *International Social Movement Research* vol. 1, Greenwich: JAI Press, pp. 155–69.

—   (1990a) 'Gli incentivi alla militanza nelle organizzazioni clandestine di sinistra', in R. Catanzaro (ed.) *Ideologie, movimenti, terrorismi*, Bologna: il Mulino, pp. 85–111.

—   (1990b) *Il terrorismo di sinistra*, Bologna: il Mulino.

—   (2013) *Clandestine Political Violence*, New York: Cambridge University Press.

della Porta, D. and Rossi, M. (1984) *Cifre crudeli: Bilancio dei terrorismi italiani*, Bologna: Istituto Carlo Cattaneo.

Edwards, P. (2009) *'More Work! Less Pay!' Rebellion and Repression in Italy, 1972–7*, Manchester: Manchester University Press.

Fasanella, G. and Franceschini, A. (2004) *Che cosa sono le BR: Le radici, la nascita, la storia, il presente*, Milano: BUR.

Fasanella, G. and Rossa, S. (2006) *Guido Rossa, mio padre*, Milano: BUR.

Ferrajoli, L. (1979) 'Critica della violenza come critica della politica', in L. Manconi (ed.) *La violenza e la politica*, Roma: Savelli, pp. 39–69.

Franceschini, A., Buffa, P. V. and Giustolisi, F. (1996) *Mara Renato e io: Storia dei fondatori delle BR*, Milano: Mondadori.

Galli, G. (1991) 'La presenza del "partito armato"', in A. Benuzzi (ed.) *Italtel: Le relazioni industriali dal '69 agli anni '80*, Milano: Franco Angeli, pp. 75–101.

Gallinari, P. (2006) *Un contadino nella metropoli: Ricordi di un militante delle Brigate Rosse*, Milano: Bompiani.

Griner, M. (2014) *La zona grigia*, Milano: Chiarelettere.

Guicciardi, L. (1988) *Il tempo del furore: Il fallimento della lotta armata raccontato dai protagonisti*, Milano: Rusconi.

Magnanini, C. (2006) *Autunno caldo e "anni di piombo": Il sindacato milanese dinanzi alla crisi economica e istituzionale*, Milano: Franco Angeli.

Malthaner, S. (2011) *Mobilizing the Faithful: Militant Islamist Groups and their Constituencies*, Frankfurt/New York: Campus Verlag.

Malthaner, S. and Waldmann, P. (2014) 'The radical milieu: Conceptualizing the supportive social environment of terrorist groups', *Studies in Conflict & Terrorism*, 37(12): 979–98.

Manconi, L. (ed.) (1979) *La violenza e la politica*, Roma: Savelli.

Marchetti, M., Mobiglia, S. and Rolli, A. (1979) 'Le Brigate Rosse e la fabbrica: Una discussione operaia', in L. Manconi (ed.) *La violenza e la politica*, Roma: Savelli, pp. 97–119.

Moretti, M. (1994) *Brigate rosse: Una storia italiana. Intervista di Carla Mosca e Rossana Rossanda*, Milano: Anabasi.

Neidhardt, F. (2011) 'Terrorism: Conditions and limits of control', in W. Heitmeyer, H-G. Haupt, S. Malthaner and A. Kirschner (eds), *Control of Violence: Historical and International Perspectives on Violence in Modern Societies*, London: Springer, pp. 431–44.

Novelli, D. and Tranfaglia, N. (1988) *Vite sospese: Le generazioni del terrorismo*, Milano: Garzanti.

Panvini, G. (2014) *Cattolici e violenza politica: L'altro album di famiglia del terrorismo italiano*, Venezia: Marsiglio.

Porzio, D. (ed.) (1977) *Coraggio e viltà degli intellettuali*, Milano: Mondadori.

Sánchez-Cuenca, I. (2009) 'Revolutionary dreams and terrorist violence in the developed world: Explaining country variation', *Journal of Peace Research*, 46(5): 687–706.

Sanlorenzo, D. (1989) *Gli anni spietati: I comunisti nella lotta contro il terrorismo. Torino 1972–1982*, Roma: Edizioni Associate.

Soccorso Rosso (1976), *Brigate Rosse: Che cosa hanno fatto, che cosa hanno detto, che cosa se ne è detto*, Milano: Feltrinelli.

Soccorso Rosso Militante (ed.) (1974) *Il caso Marini: Fuori Marini dentro i fascisti*, Verona: Bertani.

Sommier, I. (1998) *La violence politique et son deuil: L'après '68 en France et en Italie*, Rennes: Presses Universitaires de Rennes.

Spalek, B. (2014) 'Community engagement for counterterrorism in Britain: An exploration of the role of "connectors" in countering takfiri jihadist terrorism', *Studies in Conflict & Terrorism*, 37(10): 825–41.
Spezie, A. (ed.) (2001) *30 anni di BR*, Roma: Elleu.
Stame, F. (1979) 'Terrorismo e crisi dello Stato', in L. Manconi (ed.) *La violenza e la politica*, Roma: Savelli, pp. 21–32.
Taviani, E. (2003) 'PCI, estremismo di sinistra e terrorismo', in G. De Rosa and G. Monina (eds) *L'Italia repubblicana nella crisi degli anni Settanta: Sistema politico e istitutzioni*, Soveria Mannelli: Rubettino, pp. 235–75.
Telese, L. (2006) *Cuori neri*, Milano: Sperling & Kupfer.
Ventrone, A. (2012) *"Vogliamo tutto": Perché due generazioni hanno creduto nella rivoluzione 1960–1988*, Roma-Bari: Laterza.
Ventura, A. (1984) 'La responsabilità degli intellettuali e le radici culturali del terrorismo di sinistra', in C. Ceolin (ed.) *Università, cultura, terrorismo*, Milano: Franco Angeli, pp. 93–115.
Waldmann, P. (2006) 'The radical community: A comparative analysis of the social background of ETA, IRA, and Hezbollah', in J. Victoroff (ed.) *Tangled Roots: Social and Psychological Factors in the Genesis of Terrorism*, Amsterdam: IOS Press, pp. 133–45.
Zavoli, S. (1995) *La notte della Repubblica*, Milano: Mondadori.

Unpublished sources, periodicals, and newspaper articles

A/traverso (May 1977) 'Con tutta la nostra intelligenza. Ancora per una strategia del desiderio'.
— (January 1978) 'Proposta all'area dei fogli trasversali'.
— (January 1978) 'Sabotaggio e conoscenza pratica'.
Bosio, L. (22 November 1977) '"Quell'intervista non la dovevate fare"', *Lotta Continua*.
— (27–8 November 1977) 'L'attivo dei compagni di Torino', *Lotta Continua*.
Casalegno, A. (27–8 November 1977) 'Sono stato frainteso', *Lotta Continua*.
Cases, C. (24 March 1978) 'Contro il ricatto', *il manifesto*.
Castellina, L. (20 November 1977) 'Dopo le ideologie, un po' di verità', *il manifesto*.
Commissione Stragi (11 February 1998) http://www.parlamento.it/parlam/bicam/terror/stenografici/steno31.htm (accessed August 2014).
— *Verbale riunione problemi ordine pubblico con organizzazioni di Torino, Milano, Genova, Roma, Napoli, Reggio Calabria, alla luce dei recenti avvenimenti (24 novembre 1977)*, in Archives of the PCI (serie 4, sottoserie 6, UA 20).
— *Note per un aggiornamento sul fenomeno del terrorismo e della violenza (settembre 1978)*, in Archives of the PCI (serie 4, sottoserie 6, UA 19).
Feltrin, P. (1975) 'Achtung, banditi!' *Senza padroni. Giornale dell'Assemblea Autonoma dell'Alfa Romeo*: 8.

— (April 1978) 'Sia ben chiaro, non hanno nulla a che fare con l'Autonomia', *Rosso per il Potere Operaio*: 2.

— (April 1978) 'La crisi, la guerra civile, il movimento', *Rosso per il Potere Operaio*: 9.

— (May 1978) 'Linea di massa: dal partito di Mirafiori al contropotere del partito dell'autonomia. L'autonomia organizzata di fronte al "dopo-Moro"', *Rosso per il Potere Operaio*: 2.

— (September 1982) 'Sindacato e terrorismo', *Prospettiva sindacale*: 165–94.

Fofi, G. (18 January 1978) 'I giovani, la crisi e "l'umanesimo rivouzionario"', *Lotta Continua*.

Lerner, G. and Marcenaro, A. (19 November 1977) 'A colloquio col compagno Andrea Casalegno dopo l'attentato a suo padre', *Lotta Continua*.

— (3 December 1977) 'Il baratro che ci separa dai compagni delle "brigate rosse"', *Lotta Continua*.

Maiolo, T. (13 May 1977) 'Arrestati gli avvocati Spazzali e Cappelli...', *il manifesto*.

Marcenaro, P. (6 October 1977) 'Una morte a 22 anni dimostra che nulla è scontato', *Lotta Continua*.

Mieli, P. (4 December 1977) 'E se sparano a tuo padre?', *l'Espresso*.

— (18 March 1978) 'Da Milano appello di intellettuali contro l'eversione', *l'Unità*.

Moravia, A. (19 April 1978) 'Le loro azioni ci fanno orrore', *la Repubblica*.

Pansa, G. (18 November 1977) 'Interroghiamo gli operai ai cancelli di Mirafiori,' *la Repubblica*.

— (19 November 1977) 'Il palazzo corrotto aiuta i terroristi', *la Repubblica*.

Passalacqua, G. (27–8 November 1977) 'Lotta Continua "processa" le BR', *la Repubblica*.

— (19 April 1978) 'Sciascia: è la fine delle BR', *la Repubblica*.

Piperno, F. (December 1978) 'Dal terrorismo alla guerriglia', *pre-print: l'autonomia possibile*: 14–21.

Reale, R. (18 May 1972) 'La posizione di Lotta Continua', *Lotta Continua*.

— (4 October 1977) 'Morto il giovane bruciato dalle Molotov', *la Stampa*.

Rossana, R. (17 May 1977) 'Liberarsi dagli autonomi', *il manifesto*.

— (7 August 1977) 'Peggiorano le condizioni dei redattori di "Controinformazione"...', *il manifesto*.

— (28 August 1977) 'Sparare a sinistra', *il manifesto*.

— (20 October 1977) 'Le prime adesioni all'appello del "manifesto"', *il manifesto*.

— (17 November 1977) 'Quattro colpi di pistola al vicedirettore della "Stampa", Casalegno. È in fin di vita. Le BR rivendicano', *il manifesto*.

Roversi, R. (5 February 1978) 'Violenza e morale', *il manifesto*.

Sciascia, L. (12 May 1977) 'Non voglio aiutarli in alcun modo', *Corriere della Sera*.

Senese, S. (28 March 1978) 'Qual è lo stato che voglio difendere', *il manifesto*.

Stame, F. (19 January 1978) 'La democrazia non è un mezzo, è un fine', *il manifesto*.

Tobagi, W. (19 November 1977) 'Fra gli operai di Torino dopo l'appello comunista a denunciare i violenti', *Corriere della Sera*.

— (20 November 1977) 'Il terrorista in fabbrica c'è, ma si è fatto cauto', *Corriere della Sera*.

Un gruppo di compagne del Collettivo femminista di Trastevere (December 1977) 'A Torino dopo l'Angelo Azzurro', *Ombre Rosse*.

— (26 January 1978) 'Voliamo troppo in alto?', *Lotta Continua*.

— (17 March 1978) '40mila in p. Duomo: estraneità, fischi, discorsi di repertorio', *Lotta Continua*.

— (17 March 1978) 'Fabbriche bloccate 25000 a p.zza S. Carlo', *Lotta Continua*.

— (17 March 1978) 'Rapito Moro: è il gioco più pesante e sporco che sia mai stato provato sulla testa dei proletari italiani', *Lotta Continua*.

Chapter Sixteen

Dynamics of Radicalisation in the Relationship between Militant Islamist Groups and their Constituencies: The Case of al-Jamaa al-Islamiyya in Egypt, 1986–1998

Stefan Malthaner

Khaled al-Berry was a teenager of barely 15 years old when he joined al-Jamaa al-Islamiyya, a militant Islamist group, in the Upper Egyptian city of Assiut in 1987, some years before the area became the site of a violent insurgency that would ultimately claim more than 1,500 lives. He became part of a group of young activists around a local mosque, and, having shown devotion and intelligence, was put in charge of activities at his secondary school and later at his university. Mobilising students around al-Jamaa's call for a return to Islam and an Islamic society soon brought him into conflict with the school administration and later the police (al-Berry 2002: 58–61). *Al-Berry was dispelled from school and arrested, experienced maltreatment at the hands of the police, and, in the following months, witnessed an escalation of confrontations between his fellow activists and the security forces. Yet, his story, which reflects the rise of al-Jamaa in a neighbourhood of Assiut, also points to another form of conflict and radicalisation which involved violent incidents well before the start of clashes with the police. Cultivating a feeling of moral superiority and following the theological concept of "Commanding the good and prohibiting the evil", al-Berry and his friends sought to enforce their vision of an Islamic moral order in the neighbourhood and school, for example by reprimanding and threatening female students for not dressing "properly" or by harassing Christians. In fact, the first acts of violence he became involved in included beating up a boy who allegedly was homosexual and violently "punishing" a man for allegedly having insulted Islam.* (al-Berry 2002: 29–32, 55, 56, 114–16)

In recent years, the growing influence of theoretical approaches adopted from social movement studies in research on political violence has contributed to a greater emphasis on social contextualisation and a shift towards a processual perspective on radicalisation and the emergence of violence.[1] In particular, increasing attention has been paid to the *relational* quality of violent processes, that is, to interactions between various actors participant in a conflict, the mutual relations, reactions, and adaptations of which shape the escalation and development of political violence. Among the studied and identified relationships and 'arenas' of interaction (Alimi, Bosi and Demetriou 2012) are, for example, interactions between movements and counter-movements and competition between different movements and movement-organisations (*see* Alimi 2011; Alimi *et al.* 2012; della Porta 2013, 2014). The cardinal relational dynamic contributing to processes of radicalisation, however, are interactions between social movements and government authorities, that is, escalating dynamics of repression and resistance and the effects of different levels and forms of repression on mobilisation and modes of protest.[2] Whereas political opportunity models tended to view the state's 'repressive capacity' as a rather static factor determining the costs of protest (for a review, *see* Meyer 2004), it increasingly became clear that state responses influence strategic decisions by movement actors (and vice versa), and repertoires of action are shaped in mutual adaptation (McAdam 1982). Particularly since the mid-1990s a growing number of studies have examined the way in which police responses affect the development of social movements, including their radicalisation and the emergence of violent groups (della Porta 1995a, 1995b; Merkl 1995),[3] which then expanded into a distinct line of research on styles and effects of protest policing (*see* della Porta and Reiter 1998) and state repression (*see* Davenport 2000; Davenport, Johnston and Mueller 2005). Whereas most of these works focused on protest movements and militant groups in Western democracies, several studies have begun to examine the specific conditions of state repression in authoritarian regimes, and have applied social movement theory to the study of militant Islamist movements (Boudreau 2004; Wiktorowicz 2004; Hafez 2004a, 2004b).

Yet, as the story of Khaled al-Berry makes clear, the relational dynamics of political violence also involve another type of interaction. Beyond intra-movement relations, and dynamics of escalation between police and protestors,

---

1. See *inter alia* Alimi (2011); Alimi, Bosi, and Demetriou (2012, 2015); Bosi (2012); Bosi, Demetriou, and Malthaner (2014); della Porta (1995, 2008, 2013); Gunning (2009). See also special issues in *Qualitative Sociology* (vol. 31, 2008), and *Mobilization* (12(2), 2007; 17(1), 2012).

2. See in particular della Porta (1995a, 1995b, 2008, 2013) as well as Alimi, Bosi and Demetriou (2012, 2015). On escalating dynamics of repression and radicalisation see also Merkl (1995) and the earlier works of Baeyer-Katte *et al.* (1982) and Neidhardt (1981, 1989) on the protest movement and terrorist violence in Germany, these being among the first to adopt an explicitly interactional perspective. On the effects of repression and protest policing, see della Porta and Reiter (1998), Davenport (2000), and Davenport, Johnston and Mueller (2005).

3. See also the earlier works of Baeyer-Katte *et al.* (1982) and Neidhardt (1981, 1989) on the protest movement and terrorist violence in Germany. They were among the first to adopt an explicitly interactional perspective on the relation between protest movements and the state/police, but had – possibly because they were published in German – limited influence on the international discussion in the field.

militant movements and armed groups also interact with their social environment at the local level, as well as those parts of the population that are here called their 'constituencies'. This paper argues that, to expand our understanding of the processes of radicalisation, we must take into account this particular relationship and the dynamics of radicalisation it entails, as well as the way it is intertwined with the effects of repression and violent interactions between armed groups and government authorities.

In the literature on political violence and civil wars, the relationship between insurgent groups and the general population has mainly been analysed with respect to the question of what factors make certain parts of a population 'prone' to support armed groups and how insurgents and their opponents gain control over and generate compliance within certain populations, as well as with respect to the causes of one-sided violence against civilians. In other words, rather than as a subject in relational dynamics, 'the local population' has mainly been analysed as an object of mobilisation and control, and as a target of violence.[4] Earlier exceptions include Migdal (1974), who examines support as the result of exchange relationships between insurgents and local populations. More recently, Stathis Kalyvas' 'control–compliance' model – which emphasises the role of territorial control in generating collaboration with the local population, as well as the effects of contested control on patterns of selective and indiscriminate violence – has become the most prominent perspective in the study of relations between armed groups and their social environment (*see* Kalyvas 2006, 2012). While drawing on his work in examining the effects of repression on the relationship between armed groups and their constituencies (*see* below), the approach adopted here seeks to complement and go beyond this 'control–compliance' perspective by taking a closer look at interactions within local social environments as a distinct relational 'arena', identifying the relational dynamics they entail, as well as the mechanisms through which they are interlinked with wider violent processes. Of particular relevance are interactions with those parts of the population addressed by the militant groups as their constituencies, that is, with whom the militants identify, for whom they claim to fight, and from whom they expect – and to a certain extent receive – support (*see* Malthaner 2011a, 2011b). Militant groups respond to reactions from this social environment with shifts in their attitudes as well as changing patterns of behaviour, which, in turn, reshape their relationship with the local population. As is obvious from the emphasis on local settings as contexts for social relationships, this relational dynamic is to a significant degree spatially shaped. Although not at the centre of this analysis, the space dimension and the role of territories (*see* Bosi *et al.,* in this volume) are fundamental to the processes as they unfold: The way armed groups enter into relationships with certain local

---

4. For examples from the field of research on civil wars and guerilla groups, see Wolf (1969), Scott (1976), Paige (1975), and Wickham-Crowley (1992). Another line of research analyses the militants' relations with broader audiences in terms of framing and frame-alignment processes (see *inter alia* Hafez 2004a/2004b; on framing and frame alignment, see Snow/Rochford/Worden/ Benford 1986, and Benford/Snow 2000).

populations is a result of spatial shifts from open mobilisation to peripheral areas – and later to semi-clandestine/clandestine forms of operation – as well as a result of their aim to control these spaces and transform them in a particular manner. Controlling populations, here, means at the same time controlling socio-spatial settings, and the erosion of social relationships is often followed by spatial displacement.

Drawing on an analysis of interaction patterns and processes of violent escalation in the case of the militant Islamist group[5] al-Jamaa al-Islamiyya between 1986 and 1998, this chapter seeks to demonstrate, first, that the group's radicalisation involved – and was reinforced by – several characteristic patterns of aggressive interaction between the militants and their constituencies. Second, it traces the ways in which these interactions were intertwined with the effects of state repression and interactions between al-Jamaa and the police, forming, as I argue, a triangular relationship in which each relation affected the others and combined, creating a causal dynamic that shaped the trajectory of the violent conflict.

The case study is thus based on several sets of sources. First, it draws on a series of interviews with (former) al-Jamaa al-Islamiyya members, residents of neighbourhoods and towns known as al-Jamaa 'strongholds', as well as local journalists, human-rights activists, and other observers. These were carried out during several periods of field-research in Cairo and Upper Egypt between December 2003 and March 2005, and in England in April 2005 and in June/July 2005. Second, it analyses autobiographical accounts by former militants, such as the story of Khaled al-Berry (al-Berry 2002). Finally, it draws on a number of anthropological studies of specific neighbourhoods and villages during and after the violent insurgency. [6]

Al-Jamaa al-Islamiyya and its social environment

As Roel Meijer (2009b: 190) points out, al-Jamaa al-Islamiyya is an exceptionally interesting case; moreover, it is so in particular with respect to the question examined here. It illustrates the development of an Islamist movement that was initially closely embedded in its social environment, but then underwent a process of gradual radicalisation that affected – and involved – the very social ties that the group had built with parts of the population.

The Islamist current in Egypt has its origin in the Muslim Brotherhood, founded by Hassan al-Banna in 1928, which during the 1930s and 1940s developed into a mass movement with over a million members (Lia 1998).

---

5. Islamism is here understood in accordance with Hafez's (2004a: 4–5) definition: 'By Islamist I mean individuals, groups, organizations, and parties that see in Islam a guiding political doctrine that justifies and motivates collective action on behalf of that doctrine.'

6. See for example Haenni (2005) on a neighbourhood in the northeastern suburbs of Cairo, Gaffney (1997) on al-Minya, or Toth (2003) on an Upper Egyptian village. For details on field research in Egypt see Malthaner (2011b). To protect informants, no names are given in references to interviews and the place and date of interviews are identified only in very general terms.

Under Gamal Abd al-Nasser, who took over power in the Free Officers coup d'état in 1952, the Brotherhood was severely suppressed and disappeared from the political landscape, but the Islamist current gradually re-emerged after the Six Day War of 1967. Al-Jamaa al-Islamiyya developed at the radical fringe of a broader, non-militant, Islamist student movement, which began to spread at many Egyptian universities in the early 1970s, and which had, by the late 1970s, gained considerable strength in numbers and in political influence. Nasser's successor, President Anwar al-Sadat, had initially facilitated Islamist activity after he took power in 1970, because he considered the Islamists to be a counterweight to the leftist and Nasserist current. However, facing increasingly open opposition over decisions such as the Egyptian peace treaty with Israel, and offering refuge to the Shah after the Islamic Revolution in Iran in 1979, the government began to restrain the movement, and a cycle of protests and arrests began (Kepel 1985; Ramadan 1993). As a result of increasing confrontations with the government, open activities of the Islamist student movement in Cairo and Alexandria gradually ceased, and numerous student leaders from these cities joined the Muslim Brotherhood and focused on non-militant political work. By contrast, parts of the movement in Upper Egypt radicalised. A core of activists at the universities of Assiut and al-Minya formed a militant organisation and began to cooperate with a terrorist group from Cairo called al-Jihad, culminating in the assassination of President Sadat in October 1981. The assassination provoked a major crackdown and a wave of arrests, which eliminated any open presence of the militant Islamist movement until the mid-1980s. After a number of middle-ranking leaders were released from prison in 1984, al-Jamaa al-Islamiyya reorganised at the University of Assiut, but they also began to build a presence around neighbourhood mosques in Upper Egypt towns as well as in poorer neighbourhoods in the suburbs of Cairo. Establishing a following among university students and gradually winning support around neighbourhood mosques and among local residents, the group's members and supporters probably counted in the thousands in the late 1980s.[7]

In contrast to smaller militant groups such as al-Jihad, which operated clandestinely and in relative social isolation, al-Jamaa al-Islamiyya was a movement closely embedded in its social environment. As one leader from Assiut emphasised, the group's project was, from the beginning, one of *al-dawa* – calling people to Islam – and grass-roots mobilisation:

> The Dr. al-Zawahiri group [al-Jihad], they [were] believing in secret underground work. But al-Jamaa believed in the public work. In the universities, in the towns, in the streets. [...] The public revolution. How can we move the public![8]

---

7. In elections for student councils – which give a rough indication of the influence of al-Jamaa al-Islamiyya on campuses – the group won a majority of seats in 1985 and 1986 (interview with al-Jamaa student leader in Assiut, England, March 2006. See also Springborn 1989:226–7; Fariborz 1999: 149). Al-Jamaa's weekly religious lecture was allegedly attended by between 1,000 and 2,000 students, and a demonstration in protest of the killing of a student in May 1986 drew an estimated 15,000 people (Fariborz 1999: 150).

8. Interview with former al-Jamaa leader, London, July 2005.

In other words, al-Jamaa's relationship with its social environment was characterised by the group's approach of open and direct engagement with the population, including activities of 'ideological outreach' (Wickham 2002: 119) as well as social welfare services and other forms of involvement with local communities. At the University of Assiut, for example, al-Jamaa al-Islamiyya invited students to lessons on Islam, held speeches in the auditorium, and gave sermons at the university mosque, which they skilfully combined with offering help to poor students and providing services such as free lessons, cheap textbooks, separate bus transportation for women, and organising summer camps for students.[9] In neighbourhoods such as Ayn Shams and Imbaba in the suburbs of Cairo – which had been largely neglected by the Egyptian government – the Islamists not only preached and formed study groups at local mosques, but they also collected money to support needy families; offered basic medical care; gave out free meals on the Feast of Sacrifice; moved against criminal gangs; patrolled the areas at night; organised market activities, and mediated in family-conflicts.[10] In sum, al-Jamaa al-Islamiyya formed relationships with various parts of its social environment, which entailed different kinds of support and approval. Its young followers around university groups and local al-Jamaa sheikhs were directly involved with the group and identified with its political and cultural programme. They adopted a distinct attire and lifestyle, forming the core of an Islamist subculture that conveyed a strong sense of belonging and identity, held together by close personal bonds. Relations with local residents rested, to some degree, on sympathy for al-Jamaa's political and cultural message, too. People shared the group's disdain for the government's corruption and arbitrary police harassment, and many respected their emphasis on Islamic values. But approval among the local population was also based upon al-Jamaa's social welfare services and on the fact that the group provided some sort of order to the neighbourhoods. In turn, al-Jamaa received donations from merchants, as, for example, in Imbaba (Haenni 2005: 33–5, 105, 115–18), which enabled them to expand their welfare activities.

Confrontations between al-Jamaa and the police began in the late 1980s. They started at the local level, for example at the University of Assiut, where confrontations developed out of clashes between al-Jamaa and other students, forcing university authorities, and finally the police, to intervene. Similarly, in neighbourhoods such as Ayn Shams, conflicts with neighbourhood residents and local policemen triggered a major police operation in 1987. The police intervened in Imbaba in 1992 after the Islamists had begun to openly challenge the government's authority, publicly announcing the birth of the 'Islamic Republic of Imbaba' at a makeshift press conference in July 1991.[11] These local confrontations gradually escalated into a violent conflict at national

---

9. Interview with al-Jamaa student-leader from Assiut, England, March 2006.

10. Interviews with residents of Ayn Shams, Cairo, December 2004, March 2005; on Imbaba, see Haenni (2005: 40–2, 73–8), and *Al-Ahram*, weekly ed., 17–23 December 1992.

11. AP, 19 July 1992.

level. After one militant leader was killed, al-Jamaa retaliated by assassinating politicians, marking the beginning of a gradually escalating violent insurgency that included attacks against policemen, Christians, and foreign tourists, mainly in Upper Egypt, lasting until 1998 and costing about one and a half thousand lives (Hafez 2004a: 34).

Interactions between militant groups and their constituencies: Dynamics of radicalisation and violent escalation

'Radicalisation' is here understood to denote a shift in the perspectives and attitudes of political actors, as well as changes in repertoires of action towards – as Charles Tilly and Sidney Tarrow called it – increasing 'assertiveness' (Tilly and Tarrow 2006: 217), that is, towards uncompromising attitudes and towards an increasing acceptance and adoption of confrontational and violent means.[12] As Sedgwick notes, radicalisation is not an unproblematic concept, because it is used with very different meanings, and because it focuses analytical attention on the 'radical' actor:

> The concept of radicalization emphasizes the individual and, to some extent, the ideology and the group, and significantly de-emphasizes the wider circumstances [...]. (Sedgwick 2010: 480–1)

In other words, radicalisation is often understood as something that 'happens with' a somehow 'deviant' actor, rather than something that emerges from interactions between the various actors involved in a conflict. However, this decontextualisation is misleading, not only because radicalisation is often the result of interactions between militant groups and their adversaries (*see* della Porta 1995a, 2013), but also because – as this paper seeks to show – radicalisation entails the transformation of relationships between militants and their social environment: it involves changes in the militants' attitudes towards, and the forms of their engagement with, a population, and is accompanied and reinforced by dynamics of interaction between the militant groups and their social environment.

In the case of al-Jamaa al-Islamiyya, two main development patterns can be identified which entailed a mutually reinforcing dynamic of increasing resentment, hostility, and violence. The first regards the Islamists' agenda of fighting 'moral corruption' and imposing an Islamic moral order in neighbourhoods and towns under their (partial) control, which gradually evolved into a campaign of violently enforcing norms of moral conduct that undermined local support. The second pattern was triggered when confrontations between al-Jamaa and the police escalated, and during the later development of the violent insurgency. Here, the

---

12. On the concept of radicalisation see also McCauley and Moskalenko (2008), and Sedgwick (2010).

militants reacted with violence to signs of weakening support and collaboration with the police, triggering a dynamic that resulted in the gradual isolation of the militants as well as in a loss of constraints on violent practices.

a) Commanding right and forbidding evil: The radicalisation of the fight against moral corruption

Al-Jamaa al-Islamiyya's relationship with the Muslim population entailed a particular ambivalence. On the one hand, the group closely identified with the population and cultivated a self-image of being a 'popular movement' with strong local support.[13] On the other hand, following the Islamist thinker Sayyid Qutb, the group saw society as being in a state of '*jahiliyya*', that is, in a state of ignorance similar to the times before the Prophet Mohammad (Qutb 1981: 15, 152), and emphasised the need for true believers to separate from all infidels and from society's corrupting influences (al-Berry 2002: 88–9). This perspective entailed what Patrick Haenni called a 'polemic' attitude towards their constituencies (Haenni 2005: 145, 146, 192–4): an attitude that not only entailed the belief in moral and spiritual superiority but also challenged people's customs and traditions, and established social hierarchies. In addition to calling people to Islam (*al-dawa*), the group also saw itself from the very beginning as on a mission of 'commanding what is right and forbidding what is wrong' (*al-amr bi-l-ma'ruf wa-l-nahi 'an al-munkar*), a concept also known as *hisba*, which, in its traditional meaning, is bound to the authority of a legitimate ruler, but was transformed by al-Jamaa into an activist 'programme of changing evil by force' (Meijer 2009b: 194). In relation to their social environment, this meant that on university campuses and in neighbourhoods, al-Jamaa attempted to enforce (their vision of) Islamic norms of moral conduct on the Muslim population, initially mainly by 'advising' and reprimanding people (Gaffney 1997: 278; al-Berry 2002: 52–6; Meijer 2009b: 191–5). At the University of Assiut in the mid-1980s, for example, al-Jamaa sought to 'Islamicise' campus life by establishing separate areas for male and female students in auditoriums and cafeterias, protesting against music performances/recitals, film screenings, or mixed holiday trips, as well as by approaching students having conversations with students of the opposite sex, or female students who were not dressed 'properly'. As one former al-Jamaa leader from Assiut admitted, these interventions could turn into harassment and intimidation when students refused to obey,[14] and on a number of occasions al-Jamaa members violently attacked music groups, or subjected alleged 'transgressors' to punishment beatings (al-Berry 2002: 113–17; Gaffney 1997: 278; Ramadan 1993: 162, 163). In some instances, these encounters

---

13. This self-image was apparently upheld even against contradicting evidence. In 1997, when the insurgency in Upper Egypt was clearly weakened, one of the group's leaders abroad still claimed: 'The Gama'a Islamiyya is spread throughout the Egyptian principalities, [...] and receives great support from the people. [...] Many are continuing to join the Gama'a.' Interview published in *Nida'ul Islam* (April/May 1997).

14. Interview with former al-Jamaa leader, England, June 2007.

became increasingly hostile, such as one incident in which al-Jamaa members reprimanded a student for talking to a girl (who turned out to be his fiancée). After the young man refused to accept their demands and got angry, the situation escalated into a fight that ended up involving dozens of students.[15]

Expanding their activities beyond the university, in the mid-1980s al-Jamaa began 'fighting corruption' in the city of Assiut, too, harassing couples holding hands or otherwise behaving 'improperly'; beating up alleged homosexuals; publicly flogging drunks; enforcing a ban on alcohol by threatening merchants and stopping trucks carrying cases of beer, and burning down video-shops.[16] These acts seem to have become increasingly violent and, in some instances, women were reportedly attacked with acid for not wearing the veil.[17] As Osama Hafez – one of the group's original leaders – explained during the leadership's later 'revisions' of the group's faults and mistakes, these 'violations' severely undermined their support among the population of Assiut:

> [These acts had] a negative effect on the population and produced aversion against the Islamic groups and the call to Islam. This is what happened in Assiut and it is the reason that people in Egypt regarded all men wearing beards with hostility and mistrust. It affected the stability of the city [of Assiut] and hurt the call to Islam.[18]

Equally prominent were al-Jamaa's efforts to 'prohibit the evil' in Imbaba, a Cairo suburb where, in the absence of government authorities, the group had gained a considerable degree of control over certain neighbourhoods in the late 1980s. There, al-Jamaa interrupted wedding celebrations playing music or having dancers, reprimanded women for 'un-Islamic' attire, banned smoking the waterpipe (hookah or shisha) and playing cards in tea shops, and even burned down shops selling 'improper' videos or alcohol (Haenni 2005: 103–5). These incidents, however, provoked increasing resentment among the population, as one resident explained:

> Basically I agree with them [al-Jamaa al-Islamiyya], but I refuse some of their ways of behaviour. [...] The *shisha* [waterpipe], for example, they say that it is *haram* [forbidden], but I say that it is *makruh* [not recommended, but allowed]; they condemn wedding ceremonies with dance and music [...] and that is indispensable for us.[19]

---

15. Interview with former al-Jamaa member, England, June 2007.
16. Interview with Assiut resident, Assiut, April 2004; al-Berry 2002: 55; Rubin 1990: 73; Ramadan 1993: 162, 163.
17. Interview with Assiut resident, April 2004.
18. Quoted by Mukrim M. Ahmad, in *Al-Mussawar*, no. 4055, 28 June 2002: 8–10.
19. Quoted in Haenni 2005: 104, author's translation.

Al-Jamaa, in turn, seemed to react to the growing resentment with an upsurge in coercive and violent acts against 'corruption', attacking video stores and shops run by Christians, which led to a further withdrawal of support. As Haenni argues in his analysis of developments in Imbaba, this process also affected support among merchants at the local market, who had provided the militants with the financial means to run their welfare services, leading to a decrease in donations. Lacking funds, the group then began to extort money not only from Christians, but also from Muslim shop owners, which, in turn, led to further deterioration of the relationship between al-Jamaa and the local population (Haenni 2005: 33–8, 103–5, 115–18).

In sum, al-Jamaa al-Islamiyya's efforts to 'prohibit the evil' and impose norms of moral conduct on the population seemed to trigger sequences of interaction in which the people's refusal to meet with the Islamists' 'advice' and the rejection of al-Jamaa's agenda of cultural transformation resulted in increasingly aggressive and ultimately violent acts on the part of the militants, which, in turn, further undermined sympathies for the group. While rigid and forceful in their emphasis on Islamic law from the very beginning, the group became increasingly aggressive and violent in their dealing with the population as a result of a process that was driven, if not caused, by a dynamic of interaction that reinforced the radicalisation of al-Jamaa's attitude and repertoires of action in relation to their social environment. Thereby, as is discernible also in al-Berry's account, enforcing an Islamist moral order was closely intertwined with gaining control over a university or neighbourhood. Thus, rejecting the militants' claim to moral authority meant challenging their power. So, their aggressive response to resistance seemed to originate from the urge to uphold sacred commands as well as from the need to assert the group's authority.

b) Violence, withdrawal of support, and the struggle for control during the violent insurgency

When confrontations between al-Jamaa al-Islamiyya and the police escalated into a violent insurgency, a second pattern of radicalisation became discernible. Relations between the militants and the local population became entwined in a dynamic of violence, which affected social ties, and was, at the same time, reinforced by the gradual withdrawal of support, local resistance, and – ultimately – the isolation of the militant groups.

Developments differed between Upper Egypt and Cairo suburbs. In Ayn Shams, clashes with security forces began as early as 1988, after an attempt by the police to arrest alleged al-Jamaa members at the local mosque turned into a standoff. During the ensuing riots, not only many young sympathisers but also many ordinary residents sided with the militants, including, according to one witness, elderly women throwing stones from balconies.[20] Yet this support

---

proved relatively short-lived. When the clashes started, numerous alleged Islamist militants were arrested and Ayn Shams was put under a curfew, which also closed down the open market. While people were furious about the arbitrary arrests, the suffering of many families, and the disruption of social life in the neighbourhood, they nevertheless seemed disinclined to bear the risk of being arrested or suffer other reprisals for their involvement with the Islamists. Many young followers changed their white *galabiyyas* – long traditional garments that became a symbol for the Islamists – for a pair of trousers and shaved their beards to avoid persecution. After the curfew was imposed, the area calmed down and any open presence of the Islamists vanished, with al-Jamaa al-Islamiyya forced to operate underground; but even its clandestine presence in the neighbourhood seemed weak.[21]

A similar process took place in Imbaba, which, after the militants' bold announcement of the 'Islamic Republic of Imbaba', became the site of a large police operation in December 1992, in which 14,000 policemen were deployed to cordon off the area and arrest the alleged militants. However, at this time, relations between al-Jamaa and the local population in Imbaba seemed to have already become tense after the militants' 'fight against corruption' had turned into a campaign of coercion, and even if many people were reluctant to cooperate with the police, the security forces were met with very little resistance and there were no reports of residents openly siding with al-Jamaa. In the face of the escalating violence, people turned away from the group, and Imbaba, too, became calm relatively quickly.[22] In both cases, the militants' growing social isolation at the local level led to their withdrawal from these neighbourhoods and contributed to a shift in the repertoires of action towards a terrorist campaign at the national level. As a direct reaction to the incidents in Ayn Shams, al-Jamaa carried out a series of bombings, targeting politicians, including an attack on the Minister of the Interior, Zaki Badri, in December 1989. The group from Imbaba apparently split after the events in 1992, with some members leaving the group, while other parts radicalised. A faction of al-Jamaa-members from Imbaba was allegedly responsible for a series of bomb attacks on cafés in the central squares of Cairo in 1993 (Haenni 2005: 118–22, 125–8), while other militants left the neighbourhood for training camps in Afghanistan, and, after their return, took part in the violent campaign in other parts of the country. In other words, during the escalating confrontations, al-Jamaa al-Islamiyya's supportive milieu in these neighbourhoods fragmented as a result of police pressure, and residents as well as young sympathisers withdrew from involvement with the group. The gradual isolation, then, forced the militants to go underground or to leave the areas, and, at the same time, reinforced a process or radicalisation that entailed a shift in their violent repertoires of action from local efforts to create Islamised spaces towards a terrorist campaign at the 'national level', that is, against the government, as well as towards indiscriminate bombings against the civilian population.

---

21. Personal interviews with residents of Ayn Shams, Cairo, December 2004; March 2005.
22. Personal interview with local journalist, Cairo, February 2004; Haenni 2005:125–8; see also *Al-Ahram* (weekly ed.), 10–16 December 1992, 17–23 December 1992.

In Upper Egypt, al-Jamaa al-Islamiyya's position had been even stronger than in Cairo. The group had built a large following both among students and among local residents in many towns and villages, and it controlled numerous mosques and neighbourhoods (Hafez 2004a: 84). In some instances, sympathisers and followers withdrew quickly from involvement with al-Jamaa when problems with the police began, as, for example, al-Berry reports from his secondary school in Assiut, where '[w]e lost the terrain we had conquered even quicker than we had won it' (al-Berry 2002: 64). But, by and large, support among the population and in particular its core following seemed more resilient. Well into the violent insurgency, protest marches by al-Jamaa-sympathisers drew thousands of people.[23] In Upper Egypt, too, a process of isolation and radicalisation took place, which began in a similar pattern of support eroding under the pressure of violent confrontations, but which was then exacerbated by a dynamic evolving from al-Jamaas' increasingly violent struggle to regain control over the population.

In Upper Egypt, the strain of the violent insurgency (and counter-insurgency) on the civilian population was enormous. Villages were put under curfew, thousands of young men were arrested, and the local economy was brought to a standstill (Roussillon 1994: 237–9; HWR report 1993). At the beginning, however, repressive police measures increased resentment among the population, and continuing support for the Islamists seemed to prevent any collaboration with the security forces.[24] This seemed to change around late 1993, after the police had begun to show some restraint in the area of Assiut, but also after relations between al-Jamaa and the population had become increasingly tense as a result of more and more coercive and violent acts of 'prohibiting the evil', involving, as mentioned above, not only severe beatings but also acid attacks and other atrocities. In addition, in the second half of the year 1993, al-Jamaa not only escalated its attacks against policemen, but also planted a number of bombs in cafés and other public places in the city, targeting the civilian population.[25] Weakening support, then, seemed to be accompanied by a slowly growing willingness to collaborate with the police, to which the militants reacted with a campaign of threats and assassinations of alleged informers, thus further undermining support relationships with the local communities. In Assiut – and particularly in Mallawi, which became the centre of violent attacks from 1994 onward – al-Jamaa targeted a growing number of Muslim villagers whom they accused of having betrayed militants to the police.[26]

---

23. See AFP, 31 May 1993; Toth 2003: 559, 561; Roussillion 1994: 246, 247.

24. As indicated by a report of Interior Minister Abdel Halim Moussa on a violent attack: 'As a result of the sway exercised by the extremists over the village, none of the villagers came forward to testify. Although the incident took place in broad daylight, police have yet to find a single witness.' Cited in *Al-Ahram* (weekly ed.), 7–13 May 1992.

25. Report by the Egyptian Organization of Human Rights (EOHR), excerpts published in *Al-Ahram* (weekly ed.), 22 January – 2 February 1994.

26. Cases reported by newspapers and human rights organisations increased from three in 1993 to thirty-eight in 1995. See also Khaled Dawoud's account of the situation in Mallawi, AP, 18 October 1994.

Over time, the categories of people targeted as 'collaborators' broadened, and included not only individuals giving information to the police, but any form of involvement with the authorities: village guards, sheikhs at local mosques who accepted government control, or tractor drivers who helped clear sugar-cane fields (used by the militants as hideouts).[27] Moreover, these attacks became more and more brutal and turned into a campaign of deliberate atrocities to frighten the population into refraining from collaborating with the police. In several incidents reported between 1995 and 1997, militants killed and beheaded alleged informers in front of village communities, which were forced to watch.[28] In some instances, attacks against village guards, farmers, or local policemen then triggered another pattern of interaction that drew violence into the relation between al-Jamaa al-Islamiyya and local communities, namely revenge cycles in which family members attacked the families of Islamist militants, and vice versa. In November 1994, for example, al-Jamaa killed a guard at a mosque in a village near Mallawi. Shortly after, family members of the victim took revenge on the father of one of the attackers, to which the militants responded by killing two members of this family and, some weeks later, attacked the mosque, killing nine people including another two members of the family.[29]

In sum, in the case of al-Jamaa al-Islamiyya, the dynamics of interaction between the militants and parts of their social environment contributed to a process of radicalisation that entailed increasingly aggressive forms of action and, ultimately, the use of extreme forms of violence. In their efforts to 'prohibit the evil', the militants responded to signs of resistance by shifting from a strategy of ideological outreach to imposing a moral order by force. During the violent insurgency, the militants reacted to signs of faltering support by assassinating alleged informers, which escalated into a campaign of terrorist violence against local communities. Both dynamics were, in a way, self-reinforcing. Increasing violence against the population further undermined support and increased the militants' social isolation. As the account of al-Berry indicates, this process was accompanied by a shift in perspective towards this population, which, by the late 1980s, began to include notions of legitimising a violent struggle not only against the 'infidel' ruler, but also against the Muslim community. He cites an internal document, entitled 'The fight against the community which refuses to accept God's Law', which states that:

This is about fighting and attacking the entire community that rejects the application of [even only] a single one of God's laws. This is an obligation. This fight is an even greater source of virtue than the fight against the unbelievers.[30]

---

27. See reports in AFP, 27 February 1996; *Al-Ahram*, 14 April 1994.
28. AFP, 14 September 1995; DPA, 3 August 1995, 25 October 1996. In that phase of the conflict, killing collaborators had become, as one human rights activist from Mallawi put it, the militants' main form of violence in the area (cited in DPA, 25 October 1996).
29. See AFP, 8 December 1994; AFP, 3 June 1995; AP, 5 June 1995.
30. Cited in al-Berry (2002: 43–4), translation by the author.

Completing the triangle: The relationship between militant groups and their constituencies and processes of violent repression

The purpose of this chapter is to draw attention to interactions between militant groups and their constituencies as a particular 'arena' of relational dynamics that has so far not received sufficient attention in the study of processes of political violence. It argues that particular patterns of interaction between militant groups and their local, partially supportive, social environment can contribute to processes of radicalisation and violent escalation. Yet these dynamics do not unfold in isolation, independent from other relational 'arenas' (to use the terminology of Alimi *et al.* 2012). On the contrary, interactions between militant groups and their social environment are closely intertwined with interactions between the militants and the police, and patterns of state control and repression. This forms a triangular relational dynamic in which the actors' strategies and relations are shaped by – and, in turn, influence – interactions between the other sides.

The following sections briefly illustrate this triangular pattern of relational dynamics between al-Jamaa al-Islamiyya, their constituencies in neighbourhoods and towns, and the police. I will focus, here, on four specific patterns of interrelation that shaped the process of escalation by inducing or contributing to important shifts in the form and scale of violent interactions: (1) the way in which local relations triggered police intervention; (2) scale-shifts in repressive strategies induced by the police's perception of support relationships; (3) the transformation of support relationships during the escalation of the violent conflict; and (4) the weakening of the insurgents' military capabilities and the radicalisation of violent practices.

Local relationships as triggers for police intervention

A first way in which relations between the militant group and its local social environment became intertwined with processes of repression was by triggering police intervention at universities and in certain neighbourhoods. This process evolved along two main steps. First, al-Jamaa came to be perceived as a threat by the authorities because of their local support and influence, which represented a challenge to the state's authority and legitimacy. As one leader of al-Jamaa explained, the fact that al-Jamaa offered basic medical services, organised the market, and mediated in conflicts in the neighbourhood of Ayn Shams, demonstrated, in a way that was visible to all, that the state was unable or unwilling to do so – a challenge that the state could not and would not tolerate:

> The government was angry. Why? [...] Because if you succeed, it means the government is bad. [...] This is the real reason for what happened in Ayn Shams. [...] Why they said they [al-Jamaa al-Islamiyya] are building a state inside the state.[31]

---

31. Interview with former al-Jamaa leader, England, March 2006.

In a second step, police intervention was then typically triggered by events that publicly demonstrated the militants' increasing boldness as local 'rulers', or events that emerged from the escalation of local conflicts resulting from attempts to impose an Islamic moral order. In Ayn Shams, for example, headlines were made when members of al-Jamaa publicly flogged a man as a punishment for alleged adultery, forcing the authorities to react.[32] Similarly, at the University of Assiut, complaints about harassment by al-Jamaa members triggered police intervention on the campus. And the major police operation in Imbaba in December 1992 followed a press conference a few months before, in which al-Jamaa leaders had announced the Islamic Republic of Imbaba.[33] In other words, the challenge – perceived and actual – of al-Jamaa to the state's authority was to a considerable extent based upon support-relations established in local settings, and, in some cases, interactions with local residents triggered police intervention, initiating a chain of events that led to an escalating violent insurgency.

Scale-shifts in repressive strategies induced by the police's perception of support relationships

In the following process of escalating repression, the forms of violent police strategies seemed to change in reaction to what was perceived as support from parts of the local population for al-Jamaa, shifting from arresting individual militants to police operations against local mosques, to measures that aimed at controlling entire communities or neighbourhoods. In Ayn Shams in 1987, for example, police first intervened in the neighbourhood to arrest suspected militant leaders. After the neighbourhood's Adam Mosque became notorious as an alleged stronghold of the group, larger police forces were deployed in search-and-arrest operations around the mosque after Friday prayers. When these operations turned into street battles in which local residents were observed to side with the militants, and police found people unwilling to collaborate, another scale shift took place, with the police's repressive strategy now aimed at controlling the entire neighbourhood by imposing a curfew and indiscriminately arresting large numbers of young people.[34]

---

32. Interviews with residents of Ayn Shams, December 2004; see also the report by Nabil Omar, *Ruz al-Yussif*, Cairo, 19 December 1988.

33. See AP, July 19 1992; UPI, 19 December 1992.

34. Interviews with residents of Ayn Shams, December 2004. On developments in Ayn Shams see also *Al-Wafd*, Cairo, 14 August 1988; *Ruz al-Yussif*, Cairo, 19 December 1988; *New York Times*, 11 December 1988. In Imbaba, where the police intervention took place five years later, in 1992, the expectation of similar problems led the authorities to adopt a more indiscriminate strategy from the very beginning, which focused on controlling the local population as much as on arresting suspected militants, in an operation that involved around 14,000 troops and sealed off a considerable part of the city for months.

The transformation of support relationships during the escalation of the violent conflict

A third pattern in the triangular pattern of relational dynamics described above was the way in which escalating repression transformed relationships between the militant Islamists and their (supportive) social environment in local settings. In some cases, arbitrary arrests and police violence initially seemed to increase sympathy with the Islamists among young followers and local residents. But the security forces' ability to (re)assert control over local spaces necessarily resulted in a fundamental change in the conditions of support relationships. Where police intervened with overwhelming force, imposed curfews, and arrested all young men with beards and *galabiyyas*, al-Jamaa al-Islamiyya was no longer able to openly engage with their social environment by preaching or providing social services, and the group was forced underground. Thereafter, pressure from the police upon the militant group resulted in increased aggression towards the local population, as one resident of Imbaba explained: 'The Islamists were a [mere] nuisance, until clashes with the police began. Then they hit anyone who got in the way.'[35] At later stages of the conflict, during the violent insurgent campaign in Upper Egypt, pressure by the police forced the militants underground and created a need for secrecy and control of information, as well as prevention of the local population collaborating with the police. This triggered the dynamic of eroding support and coercion between the militants and their social environment described above. This triangular dynamic coalesced into a process in which the militant group grew increasingly isolated and in which the causal impact of either relational mechanism became closely intertwined, with violent confrontations, degrading insurgent strength, and erosion of support relationships and local control mutually reinforced each other. This process is, obviously, to some extent driven by the dynamic described by Kalyvas in his 'control–compliance' model and his theory of the logic of selective and indiscriminate violence in civil wars (*see* Kalyvas 2006: 146–208; 2012), whereby territorial control by superior military forces exacerbated the need to control information while reducing the armed group's ability to obtain it voluntarily or via selective coercion, thus triggering an escalating dynamic of violence and decreasing control. Yet, as this study seeks to demonstrate, this process is closely intertwined with parallel relational dynamics that cannot be captured by the control–compliance model alone.

The weakening of the insurgents' military capabilities and the radicalisation of violent practices

Finally, the erosion of support among the local population and their increasing isolation affected the militants' capacity to withstand police pressure and avoid persecution, but it also entailed a radicalisation of violent practices. In the areas of Assiut and Mallawi the police seemed able to push the militants out of these areas

---

35. Resident of Imbaba, quoted in *Al-Ahram* (weekly ed.), 17–23 December 1992.

also as a result of their loss of support in local communities. After a relatively short period of time militant activities decreased and shifted to other areas.[36] Moreover, from 1996 onward, reports of militants hiding in sugar-cane fields or dry irrigation tunnels became more frequent, indicating that they were unable to find shelter in village communities. Social isolation thus contributed to the gradual defeat of the militants in their conflict with the police. This was, however, also accompanied by a loss of constraints on violent practices. From 1996 onward, the number of massacres of Christian or Muslim civilians and of foreign tourists increased, culminating in the attack at Luxor, in which fifty-eight tourists and four Egyptian guards were killed.[37] From the relational perspective proposed here, this development can be interpreted as resulting – in part – from a loss of constraints on violent practices as a result of the erosions of support relationships and the mechanisms of social control they entail. The militants' social isolation not only undermines normative orientation towards a population, but it also entails an exacerbation of hostility in relation to their enemy as well as in relation to their constituencies.

Conclusions

Building on an understanding of political violence and radicalisation as processes driven by relational dynamics, this paper argues that to expand our understanding of violent processes, we have to take into account interactions between armed groups and their social environment, and particularly their supportive social environment. Referring to the case of al-Jamaa al-Islamiyya it shows that within this relationship, patterns of interaction can emerge that entail causal dynamics contributing to the escalation of violent conflicts and the radicalisation of militant groups. In the case of al-Jamaa al-Islamiyya two mechanisms seemed particularly powerful. First, a dynamic of aggressive interactions triggered by the militants' attempts to transform the Muslim community's social and cultural order – to 'Islamise' the local society – which initiated a cycle of rejection and radicalisation that gradually undermined local support. Second, the escalating violent insurgency and the shift towards more clandestine forms of organisation and operation triggered a dynamic of weakening social control, attempts to enforce compliance through coercion, and the gradual social isolation and radicalisation of the militant group. The paper further argues that these interactions between the armed groups and their social environment are thus not isolated from other relational mechanisms, but closely intertwined with patterns of interactions with state security forces, either as triggers or in the form of mutually reinforcing dynamics of escalation. Relations

---

36. Around mid-1994, the number of attacks in the area of Assiut decreased rapidly, but increased in the al-Minya region, only to decrease again after about two years. See analysis of event-data on the conflict in Upper Egypt in Malthaner 2011b: 170–2.

37. On the Luxor massacre, see 'Louxor: Synthése de l'attentat du 17 novembre 1997' (Swiss Federal Police, March 2000).

between militants, police, and local social environments thus form a triangular relational pattern in which dynamics of interactions on all three sides mutually influence and shape each other.

The purpose of this paper is to draw attention to the relationship between armed groups and their local social – particularly their supportive – environment as a distinct and important 'arena' for interactions and relational dynamics. It has to be emphasised that this arena is not equally present and relevant in all processes of political violence. In fact, the reason that it has not been the subject of closer examination in, for example, della Porta's comparative analysis of clandestine political violence is that she focuses on groups that operate underground and have only limited contact with their social environment beyond fellow activists in the broader social movement from which they emerge (*see* della Porta 2013). She analyses processes of isolation and encapsulation of small militant groups in relation to broader movements – to some extent resembling those described here – which are driven, first of all, by organisational dynamics and the transformation of protest movements during phases of violent escalation. Yet, the point made here is that we need to recognise that far from all militant groups correspond to this type of largely or fully clandestine groups described by della Porta. Many groups operate in a semi-clandestine or partly open manner and engage directly with their constituencies and their social environment on the local level, either as a result of their agenda of creating a particular social and cultural order, or as part of a strategy to control certain spaces and strongholds (*see* Bosi and Malthaner, forthcoming). In these cases, it is crucial to recognise the role of dynamics of interaction within this emerging relational arena at the local level, which, as this chapter seeks to show, may not only contribute to dynamics of escalation and radicalisation but also crucially interferes with mechanisms of repression and resistance. The difference between the processes described here and trajectories of isolation and encapsulation in the case of fully clandestine groups becomes clear when we look at the accompanying dynamics of violence. In the case of clandestine groups this is mainly a process of withdrawal that can reinforce radicalisation through the increasing lack of social 'grounding', and the loss of a sense of reality among members of the isolated group. In the case of al-Jamaa al-Islamiyya, social isolation was paradoxically driven by the need to control their social environment during the violent insurgency, and the group's eroding capability to do so, which resulted in the escalation of coercive violence in relation to the population they initially sought to mobilise, culminating in a campaign to terrorise this population into compliance in an attempt to compensate for the loss of support. In other words, social isolation, in this case, is accompanied by a process of violent radicalisation in direct interaction with the militants' social environment.

References

al-Berry, K. (2002) *La terre est plus belle que le paradis*, Paris: JC Lattès.

Alimi, E. (2011) 'Relational dynamics in factional adoption of terrorist tactics: A comparative perspective', *Theory and Society,* 40(1): 95–119.

Alimi, E., Bosi, L. and Demetriou, C. (2012)'Relational dynamics and processes of radicalization: A comparative framework', *Mobilization,* 17(1): 7–26.

—   (2015) *The Dynamics of Radicalization: A Relational and Comparative Perspective*, Oxford: Oxford University Press.

Baeyer-Katte, W. V., Claessens, D., Feger, H. and Neidhardt F. (1982) *Analysen zum Terrorismus 3: Gruppenprozesse*, Opladen: Westdeutscher Verlag.

Benford, R. and Snow, D. (2000) 'Framing processes and social movements: An overview and assessment', *Annual Review of Sociology*, 26: 611–39.

Bosi, L. (2012) 'Explaining pathways to armed activism in the Provisional IRA, 1969–1972', *Social Science History*, 36(3): 347–90.

—   (2013) 'Safe territories and political violence: The persistence and disengagement of violent political organizations', *Nationalism and Ethnic Politics,* 19(1): 80–101.

Bosi, L., Demetriou, C. and Malthaner, S. (eds) (2014) *Dynamics of Political Violence: A Process-Oriented Perspective on Radicalization and the Escalation of Political Conflict,* Farnham/London: Ashgate.

Bosi, L. and Malthaner, S. (forthcoming) 'Political violence', in D. della Porta and M. Diani (eds) *Oxford Handbook of Social Movements*, Oxford: Oxford University Press.

Boudreau, V. (2004) *Resisting Dictatorship: Repression and Protest in Southeast Asia*, Cambridge: Cambridge University Press.

Crenshaw, M. (1995) 'Thoughts on relating terrorism to historical contexts', in M. Crenshaw (ed.) *Terrorism in Context*, Pennsylvania: The Pennsylvania State University Press, pp. 3–24.

Davenport, C. (ed.) (2000) *Paths to State Repression*, Lanham: Roman and Littlefield.

—   (2005) 'Repression and mobilization: Insights from political science and sociology', in C. Davenport, H. Johnston and C. Mueller (eds) *Repression and Mobilization*, Minneapolis, University of Minnesota Press, pp. vii–xli.

Davenport, C., Johnston, H. and Mueller, C. (eds) (2005) *Repression and Mobilization*, Minneapolis: University of Minnesota Press.

della Porta, D. (1995a) *Social Movements, Political Violence, and the State: A Comparative Analysis of Italy and Germany*, Cambridge: Cambridge University Press.

—   (1995b) 'Left-wing terrorism in Italy', in M. Crenshaw (ed.) *Terrorism in Context*, Pennsylvania: The Pennsylvania State University Press, pp. 105–9.

—   (2008) 'Research on social movements and political violence', *Qualitative Sociology*, 31: 221–30.

—   (2009) 'Social movement studies and political violence', Lecture at the Centre for Studies in Islamism and Radicalization, Department of Political Science, Aarhus University, Denmark, 29 May 2009.

—   (2013) *Clandestine Political Violence*; Cambridge: Cambridge University Press.

—   (2014) 'Competitive escalation during protest cycles: Comparing left-wing and religious conflicts', in L. Bosi, C. Demetriou, and S. Malthaner (eds) *Dynamics of Political Violence: A process-oriented perspective on radicalization and the escalation of political conflict*, Farnham/London: Ashgate,pp. 93–114.

della Porta, D. and Reiter, H. (eds) (1998) *Policing Protest: The Control of Mass Demonstrations in Western Democracies*, Minneapolis: University of Minnesota Press.

Fandy, M. (1994) 'Egypt's Islamic Group: Regional revenge?', *Middle East Journal*, 48(4): 607–25.

Fariborz, A. (1999) *Die ägyptische Studentenbewegung: Ursachen, Auswirkungen und Perspektiven des sozialen Protests*, Hamburg: Lit Verlag.

Gaffney, P. D. (1997) 'Fundamentalist preaching and Islamic militancy in Upper Egypt', in R. S. Appleby (ed.) *Spokesmen for the Despised: Fundamentalist Leaders of the Middle East*, Chicago/London: The University of Chicago Press, pp. 257–93.

Gunning, J. (2007) 'A case for critical terrorism studies', *Government and Opposition*, 42(3): 363–93.

—   (2008) *Hamas in Politics: Democracy, Religion, Violence*, London: Columbia University Press.

—   (2009) 'Social movement theory and the study of terrorism', in R. Jackson M. B. Smyth and J. Gunning (eds) *Critical Terrorism Studies: A New Research Agenda*, London: Routledge, pp. 156–77.

Hafez, M. (2004a) *Why Muslims Rebel: Repression and Resistance in the Islamic World*, Boulder and London: Lynne Rienner Publishers.

—   (2004b) 'From marginalization to massacres: A political process explanation of GIA violence in Algeria', in Q. Wiktorowicz (ed.) *Islamic Activism: A Social Movement Theory Approach*, Bloomington and Indianapolis: Indiana University Press, pp. 37–60.

Hafez, M. and Wiktorowicz, Q. (2004) 'Violence as contention in the Egyptian Islamic movement', in Q. Wiktorowicz (ed.) *Islamic Activism: A Social Movement Theory Approach*, Bloomington and Indianapolis: Indiana University Press, pp. 61–88.

Haenni, P. (2005) *L'ordre des caïds: Conjurer la dissidence urbaine au Caire*, Paris: Karthala.

Kalyvas, S. N. (2006) *The Logic of Violence in Civil War*, Cambridge: Cambridge University Press.

—   (2012) 'Micro-level studies of violence in civil war: Refining and extending the control–collaboration model', *Terrorism and Political Violence*, 24(4): 658–68.

Kepel, G. (1985) *The Prophet and the Pharaoh*, Berkeley: University of California Press.

Lia, B. (1998) *The Society of the Muslim Brothers in Egypt: The Rise of an Islamic Mass Movement*, Reading: Ithaca Press.

Malthaner, S. (2011a) 'Fighting for the community of believers: Dynamics of control in the relationship between militant Islamist movements and their constituencies', in Heitmeyer *et al.* (eds) *Control of Violence: Historical and International Perspectives on Violence in Modern Societies,* New York: Springer, pp. 445–66.

— (2011b) *Mobilizing the Faithful: The Relationship Between Militant Islamist Groups and their Constituencies*, Frankfurt and New York: Campus.

McAdam D. (1982) *Political Process and the Development of Black Insurgency 1930–1970*, Chicago: University of Chicago Press.

— (1983) 'Tactical innovation and the pace of insurgency', *American Sociological Review*, 48(6): 735–54.

McAdam, D., Tarrow S. and Tilly C. (2001) *Dynamics of Contention*, Cambridge: Cambridge University Press.

McCauley, C. and Moskalenko, S. (2008) 'Mechanisms of political radicalization: Pathways toward terrorism', *Terrorism and Political Violence*, 20(3): 415–33.

Meijer, R. (2009a) 'Introduction', in R. Meijer (ed.) *Global Salafism: Islam's New Religious Movement,* London: Hurst & Company, pp. 1–32.

— (2009b) 'Commanding right and forbidding wrong as a principle of social action: The case of the Egyptian al-Jama'a al-Islamiyya', in R. Meijer (ed.) *Global Salafism: Islam's New Religious Movement,* London: Hurst & Company, pp. 189–220.

Merkl, P. (1995) 'West German left-wing terrorism', in M. Crenshaw (ed.) *Terrorism in Context*, Pennsylvania: The Pennsylvania State University Press, pp. 160–210.

Meyer, D. S. (2004) 'Protest and political opportunity', *Annual Review of Sociology*, 30: 125–45.

Meyer, D. S. and Staggenborg, S. (1996) 'Movements, countermovements, and the structure of political opportunity', AJS, 101(6): 1628–60.

Migdal, J. S. (1974) *Peasants, Politics, and Revolution: Pressures Toward Political and Social Change in the Third World*, Princeton: Princeton University Press.

Neidhardt, F. (1981) 'Über Zufall, Eigendynamik und Institutionalisierbarkeit absurder Prozesse: Notizen am Beispiel einer terroristischen Gruppe', in H. V. Alemann and H. P. Thurn (eds) *Soziologie in weltbürgerlicher Absicht. Festschrift für René König*, Opladen: Westdeutscher Verlag.

— (1989) 'Gewalt und Gegengewalt: Steigt die Bereitschaft zu Gewalteskalation mit zunehmender staatlicher Kontrolle und Repression?', in W. Heitmeyer *et al.* (eds) *Jugend – Staat – Gewalt: Politische Sozialisation von Jugendlichen, Jugendpolitik und politische Bildung,,*Weinheim/München: Juventa, pp. 233–43.

Paige, J. M. (1975) *Agrarian Revolution: Social movements and export agriculture in the underdeveloped world*, New York: The Free Press.

Qutb, S. (1981) *Milestones*, Delhi: Markazi Maktaba Islami.

Ramadan, A. A. (1993) 'Fundamentalist influence in Egypt: The strategies of the Muslim Brotherhood and the takfir groups', in M. E. Marty and R. S. Appleby (eds), *Fundamentalisms and the State: Remaking Politics, Economies, and Militance*, Chicago: The University of Chicago Press, pp. 152–83.

Rousillon, A. (1994) 'Changer la société par le jihad: 'Sédition confessionnelle', attentats contre les touristes et violence qualifiée d'islamique en Égypte', in R. Bocco and M. R. Djalili (eds) *Moyen-Orient: migrations, démocratisation, mediations*, Paris: Presses Universitaires de France, pp. 237–66.

Rubin, B. (1990) *Islamic Fundamentalism in Egyptian Politics*, London: Macmillan.

Rucht, D. (2004) 'Movement allies, adversaries, and third parties', in D. A. Snow, S. A. Soule and H. P. Kriesi (eds) *The Blackwell Companion to Social Movements*, London: Blackwell Publishing, pp. 197–216.

Scott, J. C. (1976) *The Moral Economy of the Peasant*, New Haven: Yale University Press.

Sedgwick, M. (2010) 'The concept of radicalization as a source of confusion', *Terrorism and Political Violence*, 22(4): 479–94.

Snow, D., Rochford, B. E., Worden, S. K., Benford, R. D. (1986) 'Frame alignment processes, micromobilization, and movement participation', *American Sociological Review*, 51: 464–81.

Springborn, R. (1989) *Mubaraks Egypt: Fragmentation of the Political Order*, Boulder and London: Westview Press.

Tarrow, S. (1998) *Power in Movement: Social Movements and Contentious Politics*, Cambridge: Cambridge University Press.

Tilly, C. (1978) *From Mobilization to Revolution*, Reading, Mass: Addison-Wesley.

Tilly, C. and Tarrow, S. (2006) *Contentious Politics*, Boulder: Paradigm Publishers.

Toth, J. (2003) 'Islamism in southern Egypt: A case study of a radical religious movement', *International Journal of Middle East Studies*, 35(4): 547–72.

Wickham, C. R. (2002) *Mobilizing Islam: Religion, Activism, and Political Change in Egypt*, New York: Columbia University Press.

Wickham-Crowley, T. P. (1992) *Guerrillas and Revolution in Latin America: A Comparative Study of Insurgents and Regimes since 1956*, Princeton: Princeton University Press.

Wiktorowicz, Q. (2004) 'Islamic activism and social movement theory', in Q. Wiktorowicz (ed.) *Islamic Activism: A Social Movement Theory Approach*, Bloomington and Indianapolis: Indiana University Press, pp. 1–33.

Wolf, E. R. (1969) *Peasant Wars of the Twentieth Century*, New York: Harper & Row Publishers.

Appendices – Data and Sources

Chapter Six

Interview with student activist, Turin, 7 June 2013.

Chapter Nine

Interview A, Turkey, December 2012.
Interview C, Turkey, December 2012.
Interview D, Turkey, December 2012.
Interview E, Turkey, December 2012.
Interview F, Turkey, December 2012.
Interview G, Turkey, December 2012.
Interview H, Belgium, December 2012.
Interview K, France, December 2012.
Interview L, August 2013.

Chapter 10

Interview with senior ex-combatant, Abidjan, 19 October 2012.
Interview with regular ex-combatant, Abidjan, 22 October 2012.
Interview with civilian, Abidjan, 23 October 2012.
Interview with civilian A, Abidjan, 29 October 2012.
Interview with civilian B, Abidjan, 29 October 2012.
Interview with civilian, Abidjan, 30 October 2012.

Chapter Thirteen

Interview with Amir al-Jaysh, A. (a leader of the jihad groups in the 1970s), 2012.
Interview with Faraj, A. (a leader of the jihad groups in the 1970s), 2012.
Interview with Farghali, M. (a former member of the IG), 2014.
Interview with Fathi, M. (member of the IG), 2012.
Interview with Habib, K. (a leader of the jihad groups in the 1970s), 2012.
Interview with Hafez, O. (second-in-command of the IG), 2013.
Interview with Hamad A. (mufti of the IG), 2013.
Interview with Ibrahim, N. (former second-in-command of the IG), 2013.
Interview with Jahin, S. (a leader of the JG in prison), 2012.
Interview with Na'im, N. (a leader of the JG in the 1990s), 2014.
Interview with Qassem, O. (a leader of the JG in prison), 2012.
Interview with Salem, M. (a leader of the JG in the 1990s), 2013.
Interview with Taha, R. (leader of the IG abroad in the 1990s), 2013.

Index

Numbers in italics refer to materials in Figures and Tables

Lightning Source UK Ltd.
Milton Keynes UK
UKOW06f2305071016

284759UK00001B/39/P

9 781785 522376